BE STRONG DEVOTIONAL

EVERYDAY READING TO STRENGTHEN YOU

MARTIN OSSEI

LIFE AND SUCCESS PUBLISHING
www.abookinsideyou.com

Copyright © 2014 Martin Ossei

All rights reserved. No part of this publication may be produced, distributed, or transmitted in any form or by any means, including photocopying, recording, or other electronic or mechanical methods, without the prior written permision of the publisher, except in the case of brief quotations embodied in critical reviews and certain other noncommercial uses permitted by copyright law.

For permission requests, write to the publisher, addressed "Attention: Permissions Coordinator" at the email address below:

Life and Success Media Ltd

e-mail: info@lifeandsuccessmedia.com

www.lifeandsuccessmedia.com

Unless otherwise stated, all scripture quotations are taken from the Holy Bible, New King James Version. Quotations marked NKJV are taken from the HOLY BIBLE, NEW KING JAMES VERSION. Copyright © 1973, 1978, 1984 by International Bible Society. Used by permission of Hodder and Stoughton Ltd, a member of the Hodder Headline Plc Group. All rights reserved. "NKJV" is a registered trademark of International Bible Society. UK trademark number 1448790.

Quotations marked KJV are from the Holy Bible,

King James Version.

ISBN Number: 978-1-63752-459-6

Cover Design: Allan Sealy

Table of Contents

INTRODUCTION	4
THE GOOD NEWS	5
JANUARY	7
FEBRUARY	39
MARCH	69
APRIL	101
MAY	133
JUNE	165
JULY	197
AUGUST	229
SEPTEMBER	261
OCTOBER	293
NOVEMBER	325
DECEMBER	357

INTRODUCTION

This book in your hand is going to help you live a victorious kingdom life. Jesus Christ has paid a heavy price for your salvation. Embrace this salvation and enjoy the heavenly life God has planned for you. We are blessed in this generation to have the Bible. There is nothing more powerful than the Word of God. God created everything we see by His word and He has given us this ability to create with his word. Let us endeavour to eat, sleep and embrace God's Word.

Be Strong Devotional has been designed to help you have a word in your spirit each day. The word in your spirit is life in your spirit. There is inspired scripture for each day of the year, a short commentary and a simple prayer. This is for your meditation. Others have used it as a family devotional bringing the family together for a time of prayer and discussion. It can also be used for small group discussion. The year is divided into six bi-monthly parts with each part focussed on a foundational subject in our Christian walk.

The 6 subjects covered are: The Blood and the Cross, The Holy Spirit, God's Promises, Love, Victory in Jesus Christ, Thanksgiving, Praise and Harvest.

These 6 titles were originally published in six separate booklets. After several praise reports and feedback, I was persuaded to put all in one volume. This is what you have in your hands. Enjoy good fellowship with the Father, Son and Holy Spirit.

The Good News

John 3:16

For God so loved the world that he gave his one and only Son, that whoever believes in him shall not perish but have eternal life.

In a world where we are bombarded with so much bad news, people tend to be suspicious of good news. Thus the expression "Too good to be true." The account of Jesus Christ and His already accomplished mission on earth is GOOD NEWS and TRUE. Jesus came in the flesh as man to pay for the sins of all men by dying on the Cross at Calvary. Sin is what separates us from God our creator. Man has been separated from God from the time the first man, Adam, disobeyed God. Jesus through his obedience even to death paid the price for the disobedience of Adam. God's promise to us is that if we would believe in the finished work of Jesus and receive the salvation He offers, we will be reconciled to God. We become part of God's family and heirs of everything that is God's. Jesus rose from the dead and is now Master of all creation. If you believe this, pray the prayer below and enjoy eternal life.

PRAYER:

Father, I thank you for your love and your redemption plan. Dear Jesus I believe that you have paid the price for my sins through your death on the Cross. I identify with your death and resurrection. I throw all my sins in your Blood. I receive my salvation and rulership with you today. Amen

Be Strong Devotional

January
The Cross and the Blood

The foundation of our Christian walk is the Cross of Jesus Christ. Jesus Christ shed His blood on the cross of Calvary to reconcile a separated world to God. What an awesome truth of God everyone has to know and be intimately acquainted with.

Make the Cross and the Blood the foundation of everything you do and you are on solid ground. My prayer for you is that you would have an intimate knowledge of the power of the Cross and Blood of Jesus Christ

1st January
THE CROSS OF JESUS IS OUR STARTING POINT

Colossians 1: 19-23

"For it pleased the Father that in Him all the fullness should dwell, and by Him to reconcile all things to Himself, by Him, whether things on earth or things in heaven, having made peace through the blood of His cross.

And you, who once were alienated and enemies in your mind by wicked works, yet now He has reconciled in the body of His flesh through death, to present you holy, and blameless, and above reproach in His sight— if indeed you continue in the faith, grounded and steadfast, and are not moved away from the hope of the gospel which you heard, which was preached to every creature under heaven, of which I, Paul, became a minister."

Praise God we have made it to the beginning of another year. The Cross of Jesus Christ should be the starting point of anything we do. This is because by Jesus' death on the Cross and His resurrection, He has given us a new lease of life. We who were once completely cut off from God are now reconciled to God through Jesus death on the Cross.

Please do not take this price lightly. Jesus has paid this price to bring the light of God into our darkness; the knowledge of God for our ignorance and the peace of God for our confusion. Remember the sacrifice on the Cross as your starting point every day of this year. This will surely release a new boldness and faith in your life. Expect to see great changes in your life this year as you hold on to the Cross of your salvation. God's grace has saved us from the wickedness of the world by reconciling us to Himself.

PRAYER

Dear Father, I thank you for the Cross of Jesus Christ. Your love for me has redeemed me from the wickedness of sin. Help me to be conscious of the great price you paid for my deliverance. Please order my steps today.

Further reading: Isaiah 53

2nd January
IT IS FINISHED

John 12:24-33

> "Most assuredly, I say to you, unless a grain of wheat falls into the ground and dies, it remains alone; but if it dies, it produces much grain. He who loves his life will lose it, and he who hates his life in this world will keep it for eternal life. If anyone serves Me, let him follow Me; and where I am, there My servant will be also. If anyone serves Me, him My Father will honour. "Now My soul is troubled, and what shall I say? 'Father, save Me from this hour'? But for this purpose I came to this hour. Father, glorify Your name." Then a voice came from heaven, saying, "I have both glorified it and will glorify it again." Therefore the people who stood by and heard it said that it had thundered. Others said, "An angel has spoken to Him."
>
> Jesus answered and said, "This voice did not come because of Me, but for your sake. Now is the judgment of this world; now the ruler of this world will be cast out. And I, if I am lifted up from the earth, will draw all peoples to Myself." This He said, signifying by what death He would die."

Our Saviour Jesus Christ came to this world for a purpose: To pay the price of sin by dying on the Cross and saving us from the penalty of sin. What is the penalty of sin? The bible tells us that because of sin we have fallen short of the glory of God. The glory of God is all that God is: His majesty, strength, wisdom and beauty. Jesus became a seed that was to produce many sons and daughters of glory. When Jesus hung on the Cross and shouted "It is finished", he meant the battle is now won and the children of glory must arise. You are a child of glory. Arise today and display the majesty, strength and wisdom of God.

PRAYER
Thank you Father for the Cross. I am a child of glory and the world will see your glory through me today.

Further reading: John 12

3rd January
THE POWER OF THE CRUCIFIED CHRIST

1 Corinthians 2:1-8

> "And I, brethren, when I came to you, did not come with excellence of speech or of wisdom declaring to you the testimony of God. For I determined not to know anything among you except Jesus Christ and Him crucified. I was with you in weakness, in fear, and in much trembling. And my speech and my preaching were not with persuasive words of human wisdom, but in demonstration of the Spirit and of power, that your faith should not be in the wisdom of men but in the power of God. However, we speak wisdom among those who are mature, yet not the wisdom of this age, nor of the rulers of this age, who are coming to nothing. But we speak the wisdom of God in a mystery, the hidden wisdom which God ordained before the ages for our glory, which none of the rulers of this age knew; for had they known, they would not have crucified the Lord of glory."

What challenging encouragement by Paul. He does not need excellence of speech, persuasive words or human wisdom to convince the world of the power of God. All he needed to demonstrate the power of God was to tell people about the death of Jesus Christ on the Cross of Calvary. In the Cross is the wisdom and power of God. Think of the day in history when Jesus shouted "It is finished" and gave up His life. This moment changed the destiny of the world. Because of this one act, a hopeless world has received the hope of salvation. It is impossible to imagine the extent of the spiritual explosion that took place. However we do know that this spiritual explosion produced physical earthquakes and even dead people were raised on the day. This performance from heaven was just so that you and I would have a new life. Walk in newness of life today.

PRAYER
Thank you Jesus, that by the Cross I am a new creation and there is no condemnation.

Further reading: Matthew 27

4th January
THE CURSE IS DESTROYED

Galatians 3:10-13

"For as many as are of the works of the law are under the curse; for it is written, "Cursed is everyone who does not continue in all things which are written in the book of the law, to do them." But that no one is justified by the law in the sight of God is evident, for "the just shall live by faith." Yet the law is not of faith, but "the man who does them shall live by them."

Christ has redeemed us from the curse of the law, having become a curse for us (for it is written, "Cursed is everyone who hangs on a tree"), that the blessing of Abraham might come upon the Gentiles in Christ Jesus, that we might receive the promise of the Spirit through faith."

Many have approached me concerned about a curse that hanged over their lives because of their heritage. My answer has always been the scripture above. Though the above scripture specifically refers to the curse that hanged over the Jews because they could not obey all of the law, the death of Jesus on the Cross was a curse that destroyed all curses. Make this good news yours today. No curse hangs over your life. Jesus nailed every curse on the Cross. Satan is an opponent who fights dirty. He knows you are under no curse but takes advantage of your ignorance and bullies you with fear. Let Satan know that you know your new status in Christ by quoting the above scripture to him every time he tries to make you afraid. You are free from every curse. Keep the word of God in your mouth and stay in fellowship with other believers. Keep your body healthy with physical exercises and good eating habits. Expect a long, strong, healthy and happy life free of any curse.

PRAYER

Dear Jesus, thank you that your death on the Cross has brought me a strong, healthy and happy life.

Suggested reading: Numbers 21:1-9; John 3:14-21

5th January
FOLLOW JESUS WITH YOUR OWN CROSS

Matthew 16:24-27

> "Then Jesus said to His disciples, "If anyone desires to come after Me, let him deny himself, and take up his cross, and follow Me. For whoever desires to save his life will lose it, but whoever loses his life for My sake will find it. For what profit is it to a man if he gains the whole world, and loses his own soul? Or what will a man give in exchange for his soul? For the Son of Man will come in the glory of His Father with His angels, and then He will reward each according to his works."

When Jesus encourages us to take up our cross and follow Him, He is asking us to sacrifice our own life so we can take up His better life. Without Jesus, our lives are controlled by the thoughts of our mind and the desires of our flesh. Our minds are usually influenced by our learning and environment. Our physical bodies seem to have cravings of its own. It tends to develop appetites that are ungodly and self-destructive. Jesus is asking us to nail these fleshly lusts to the Cross and take up an appetite for more of Him. Our greed, immorality and pride must be defeated every day. Our excessive desire for entertainment, food (gluttony) and talking (garrulity) must all be nailed to the Cross daily. We must renew our minds with the word of God and walk in the companionship of the Holy Spirit daily. The Holy Spirit is with you to help as you embark on this warfare of the Spirit against the flesh.

PRAYER

Thank you Holy Spirit that you are with me today to reveal to me every part of me that needs to be crucified. I pick up my cross today and will pick it up everyday to follow in the footsteps of my big brother Jesus Christ.

Further reading: Mark 10

6th January
EXPERIENCE GOD'S BEST THROUGH HUMILITY

Philippians 2: 5-11

> "Let this mind be in you which was also in Christ Jesus, who, being in the form of God, did not consider it robbery to be equal with God, but made Himself of no reputation, taking the form of a bondservant, and coming in the likeness of men. And being found in appearance as a man, He humbled Himself and became obedient to the point of death, even the death of the cross. Therefore God also has highly exalted Him and given Him the name which is above every name, that at the name of Jesus every knee should bow, of those in heaven, and of those on earth, and of those under the earth, and that every tongue should confess that Jesus Christ is Lord, to the glory of God the Father."

The aim of the Cross was not to elevate Jesus. It was a humiliating sacrifice for the benefit of the world so that the world would be reconciled to God. Jesus thought about us and humbled himself for our sake so we could also taste of the joy of being with God. He was elevated because he paid this price of humility. Humble yourself under God today. Present yourself as a vessel for God to use to meet other people's needs and you will receive elevation like Jesus did.

PRAYER
Thank you Father for the example of Jesus Christ. I humble myself under your hand today. Use me for your glory.

Suggested reading: Phillipians 2

7th January
THE CROSS IS THE GAME CHANGER

2 Corinthians 5: 17-21

> *"Therefore, if anyone is in Christ, he is a new creation; old things have passed away; behold, all things have become new. Now all things are of God, who has reconciled us to Himself through Jesus Christ, and has given us the ministry of reconciliation, that is, that God was in Christ reconciling the world to Himself, not imputing their trespasses to them, and has committed to us the word of reconciliation.*
>
> *Now then, we are ambassadors for Christ, as though God were pleading through us: we implore you on Christ's behalf, be reconciled to God. For He made Him who knew no sin to be sin for us, that we might become the righteousness of God in Him."*

Our struggles end at the Cross of Jesus Christ. This is like a father returning home to find the house thrashed by the children. The children are all filthy and confused. Big brother Jesus steps up and accepts responsibility and takes the punishment for all of us. Through this act of selflessness by brig brother Jesus, father forgives, restores the house, cleans us children up. He promises to forgive us every time we come to him in repentance because of the one sacrifice of big brother. The benefit of the Cross is much greater than what I have just described. The Cross has made you a new creation. Enjoy your new life now. It is fully paid for.

PRAYER

Thank you Father for this new life. You have given me hope where there was no hope. I will confidently walk in my new status.

Further reading: 2 Corinthians 5

8th January
OUR DEBT IS PAID IN FULL

Hebrews 7: 23-28

> "Also there were many priests, because they were prevented by death from continuing. But He, because He continues forever, has an unchangeable priesthood. Therefore He is also able to save to the uttermost those who come to God through Him, since He always lives to make intercession for them. For such a High Priest was fitting for us, who is holy, harmless, undefiled, separate from sinners, and has become higher than the heavens; who does not need daily, as those high priests, to offer up sacrifices, first for His own sins and then for the people's, for this He did once for all when He offered up Himself. For the law appoints as high priests men who have weakness, but the word of the oath, which came after the law, appoints the Son who has been perfected forever."

In the Old Testament, the priests presided over the sacrifice of animals for the forgiveness of their sins. Yet because this did not meet the requirement of God, they kept sacrificing again and again. When Jesus hung on the Cross, He was the high priest and at the same time the sacrificial lamb. This sacrifice satisfied God for eternity. The debt of the sins of mankind was fully paid. There was no need for any further sacrifice for sin. The bible tells us that the wages of sin is death but the gift of God is eternal life through Christ Jesus (Romans 6:23). Because Jesus has fully paid for our sins, we should no longer suffer the consequence of sin: Death, sickness and lack. There is the story of a man who purchased a ticket on a boat from England to America. For the entire journey, he stayed in his cabin never once reporting for dinner in the ships because he could not afford it. What he did not know was that the cost of his meals was included in the price of the ticket. Enjoy the full freedom purchased by the Cross.

PRAYER

Thank you Jesus for the full payment for my redemption. I will walk fully in it from today.

Further reading: Hebrews 2

9th January
REAL LOVE

John 15: 11-17

> "These things I have spoken to you, that My joy may remain in you, and that your joy may be full. This is My commandment, that you love one another as I have loved you. Greater love has no one than this, than to lay down one's life for his friends. You are My friends if you do whatever I command you. No longer do I call you servants, for a servant does not know what his master is doing; but I have called you friends, for all things that I heard from My Father I have made known to you. You did not choose Me, but I chose you and appointed you that you should go and bear fruit, and that your fruit should remain, that whatever you ask the Father in My name He may give you. These things I command you, that you love one another."

Our greatest possession is our life. Without life everything is useless. We can give our kingdoms and physical possessions away and be called generous but giving of your life is the ultimate expression of love. Jesus gave His life for us. I call this real life. What is the ultimate gift you can give to Jesus to express your true love? It is your life. What is the best expression of your love to others? The giving of your life. Jesus advises us to love others as we love ourselves. Pause and think about this. There is much gain in living this kind of life: You will be full of joy, a friend of Jesus, bear much fruit and whatever you ask God, He will do for you. Amazing grace. Rejoice today as you walk in real love.

PRAYER

Thank you Jesus for your love. Help me Holy Spirit to show this real love to others.

Further reading: John 15

10th January
AMAZING LOVE

Isaiah 53: 7-10

"He was oppressed and He was afflicted. Yet He opened not His mouth; He was led as a lamb to the slaughter, And as a sheep before its shearers is silent, So He opened not His mouth. He was taken from prison and from judgment, And who will declare His generation? For He was cut off from the land of the living; For the transgressions of My people He was stricken. And they made His grave with the wicked—But with the rich at His death, Because He had done no violence, Nor was any deceit in His mouth. Yet it pleased the Lord to bruise Him; He has put Him to grief. When You make His soul an offering for sin, He shall see His seed, He shall prolong His days, And the pleasure of the Lord shall prosper in His hand."

This passage expresses the amazing love of the Father and the Son. The Father had a desire to be fulfilled, the pleasure of His heart. The Son is the instrument He uses. Though it was a painful experience, the Son did not open His mouth till the task was completed. The pleasure of the Father's heart was to reconcile the world to Himself. This remains the Father's desire today. Our captain, Jesus, has destroyed the power of Satan. Jesus wants us to partake in this victory by letting the world know that Satan is defeated and bring everyone back to the Father. The Father has a pleasure and you have been chosen as the son to fulfill this pleasure. Let us be silent and steadfast enduring the pain of the task and bring the world back to our Father. Our reward is to sit with Jesus in a high place in His kingdom.

PRAYER

Thank you Father for choosing me for this honourable task. Strengthen me with boldness, patience and endurance for this assignment.

Further reading: Songs of Solomon 2

11th January
ALONE WITH GOD

Scripture reading: Isaiah 53: 3-5

"He is despised and rejected by men, A Man of sorrows and acquainted with grief. And we hid, as it were, our faces from Him; He was despised, and we did not esteem Him. Surely He has borne our griefs And carried our sorrows; Yet we esteemed Him stricken, Smitten by God, and afflicted. But He was wounded for our transgressions, He was bruised for our iniquities; The chastisement for our peace was upon Him, And by His stripes we are healed."

Our walk with God can feel lonely but is never lonely. God is more than enough. He desires our complete attention. We must separate our hearts and minds for His instructions at all times. Remember the desire of God's heart is to bless the world. Only He can give the truth, the direction and the platform for this blessing to take place. He has sent us to change the world with His love. We take our instructions for this task directly from the Holy Spirit. We would face some rejection as the world loves its own and hate change. Take heart, the battle is already won and the kingdoms of this world will become the kingdom of the Father and the Son. Jesus was despised and crucified. He was the stone that the builders rejected that has become the important corner stone. You may be facing rejection now but rejoice for in the eyes of God, you are an important stone on which He is building his kingdom. Endeavour to hear the voice and direction of God and do not seek to be part of the crowd. God has sent you to bring the world to Him, not to follow the world to hell. The Holy Spirit is forever with you as your faithful companion.

PRAYER

Thank you Father, that you have promised never to leave me nor forsake me. I am yours even when I am rejected. Holy Spirit I know you are with me to comfort me when I am lonely.

Further reading: Psalm 23

12th January
BE HEALED IN JESUS NAME

1 Peter 2: 21-25

For to this you were called, because Christ also suffered for us, leaving us an example, that you should follow His steps: "Who committed no sin, Nor was deceit found in His mouth"; who, when He was reviled, did not revile in return; when He suffered, He did not threaten, but committed Himself to Him who judges righteously; who Himself bore our sins in His own body on the tree, that we, having died to sins, might live for righteousness—by whose stripes you were healed. For you were like sheep going astray, but have now returned to the Shepherd and Overseer of your souls.

Peter is reminding us that Jesus through His obedience took the punishment for our healing. One of the most devastating things we have been exposed to by our separation from God, is sickness and disease. Our ignorance exposed us to all sorts of attack of infirmity. The purpose of the Cross of Jesus Christ was to restore us into fellowship with our father God. This restoration includes being healed in our bodies. The glory of God burns away all sickness. Sin and sickness cannot stand before God. If you have received the price paid on the Cross then you stand before God. Sin therefore has no right to be there with you. In the Name of Jesus, I command every disease to disappear from your body. You can do it yourself. Command every sickness and pain in your body to disappear in the Name of Jesus and it would obey. Sickness is a thief trying to steal your joy. Do not tolerate it. Use all proper means to deal with it. Your best weapon is the word of God in your mouth

PRAYER
Thank you Jesus that by your stripes, I am completely healed.

Further reading: Psalm 103

13th January
DEATH IS CONQUERED FOREVER

John 11: 25-27

> *"Jesus said to her, "I am the resurrection and the life. He who believes in Me, though he may die, he shall live. And whoever lives and believes in Me shall never die. Do you believe this?" She said to Him, "Yes, Lord, I believe that You are the Christ, the Son of God, who is to come into the world."*

Jesus did not remain dead after His crucifixion on the Cross. He resurrected from the dead on the third day. By His resurrection, He showed that He had conquered death. Death had no power over Him. Death has no power over some one born of God. Death came into the world as a result of sin. God specifically told the first man, Adam that if he sinned, he would die. The wages of sin is death. However it was impossible for death to forever have a hold on the world God Himself had created. It was only a matter of time for God to show who was boss. Our Father God is the master planner. Jesus Christ came to deliver the final blow to death. His resurrection astounded all the agents of death, both demons and men. This one act has put them on the defensive ever since. Eternal life has come. If you have accepted Jesus' sacrifice on the cross, you have eternal life and will never die. This means you will not be separated from God again. Except you choose to separate yourself. You may put this earthly body away but you will go on living with Jesus for eternity. Rejoice, this is amazing. Amazing love, how can it be that my God should die for me.

PRAYER

Thank you Father for this amazing love that has taken away my hopelessness and replaced it with everlasting life. Holy Spirit, please continually remind of this reality.

Further reading: John 11

14th January
SATAN IS DEFEATED

Hebrews 2: 14-18

"Inasmuch then as the children have partaken of flesh and blood, He Himself likewise shared in the same, that through death He might destroy him who had the power of death, that is, the devil, and release those who through fear of death were all their lifetime subject to bondage. For indeed He does not give aid to angels, but He does give aid to the seed of Abraham. Therefore, in all things He had to be made like His brethren, that He might be a merciful and faithful High Priest in things pertaining to God, to make propitiation for the sins of the people. For in that He Himself has suffered, being tempted, He is able to aid those who are tempted."

Jesus became a man like us so He could openly defeat Satan and remove the fear that we have had of Satan. Everyone, both supporters and enemies saw this battle and the result. His enemies tried to lie about it but were in no doubt about who the winner was. We know Jesus is the winner because He has revealed it to us through the Holy Spirit. He is very much alive in our hearts and is true to His promise of being with us wherever we go. Every time Satan sees you, he sees Jesus and is terrified. He may make some defensive roars but cannot bite. He is defeated. We know it and he knows it. Never let him frighten you with his roars. Let Him know who you are and the fact that you come in the Name of Jesus. Cast out devils and take dominion wherever you are. Satan has been tormenting the world for far too long. The world is waiting for you to demonstrate to them the defeat of Satan and to impart unto them the power of the Holy Spirit to defeat the enemy.

PRAYER
In the name of Jesus, I cast out Satan and his devils from my family, my community and my friends.

Further reading: Hebrews 12

15th January
REMEMBER THE CROSS

1 Corinthians 11:23-26

> "For I received from the Lord that which I also delivered to you: that the Lord Jesus on the same night in which He was betrayed took bread; and when He had given thanks, He broke it and said, "Take, eat; this is My body which is broken for you; do this in remembrance of Me." In the same manner He also took the cup after supper, saying, "This cup is the new covenant in My blood. This do, as often as you drink it, in remembrance of Me." For as often as you eat this bread and drink this cup, you proclaim the Lord's death till He comes."

Jesus Himself told the disciples when He broke bread and shared wine with them, to continually do this in remembrance of Him. Paul explains in the above scripture that each time we did this, we proclaimed the Lord's death till He comes again. Why do we need to remember the Lords death? The Cross is the substance and proof of our covenant with God. Christ body, represented by the bread and His blood represented by the wine are the emblems of the covenant. This command of Jesus should not be taken lightly. As often as we can, let us remind ourselves of the death of Jesus Christ by enacting the Lord's supper. We can do this on our own, with our family, friends or in church. You can do this as often as you can. Do not let it become a mere ritual but a meaningful act of remembrance of a powerful covenant. This can be as refreshing as cool water in a dry desert and remind you of your victory in Christ. Walk in victory.

PRAYER

Dear Jesus, as I take part in the Lord's supper, I thank you for your love which was displayed on the Cross. I remember the death that gave me this victory in which I stand.

Further reading: Luke 22: 7-37

16th January
THE BLOOD OF JESUS SPEAKS

Hebrews 12: 22-24

"But you have come to Mount Zion and to the city of the living God, the heavenly Jerusalem, to an innumerable company of angels, to the general assembly and church of the firstborn who are registered in heaven, to God the Judge of all, to the spirits of just men made perfect, to Jesus the Mediator of the new covenant, and to the blood of sprinkling that speaks better things than that of Abel."

Scripture is telling us today that through the acceptance of Jesus Christ in our lives, we have come to a good place. We have come to the city of God; the company of angels; the church of the firstborn Jesus and a covenant of forgiveness. The sprinkling of blood is an act of covenant that brings two people as equal partners in a joint venture. The sprinkling of the Blood of Jesus on us makes us equal partners with Jesus in the kingdom of God. This scripture compares the Blood of Jesus with the blood of Abel. Abel was the son of the first man Adam. He was killed by his brother Cain out of envy. Scripture tells us that his blood cried out for revenge to God. The Blood of Jesus on the other hand, which was voluntarily poured out for all, cries out 'Mercy'. Let all come to Jesus and obtain mercy in their time of need. The blood of Jesus speaks mercy over you today. When the Father sees you, He sees mercy. When the enemy sees you, he runs because he is scared of the Blood of Jesus. It reminds him of the humiliating defeat he suffered at the Cross of Calvary. Walk with confidence under the covering of the Blood of Jesus. You are covered.

PRAYER

Dear Father, I thank you for the Blood of Jesus which loudly speaks mercy over me.

Further reading: Genesis 4

17th January
BLOOD IS LIFE

Leviticus 17: 10-11

> "And whatever man of the house of Israel, or of the strangers who dwell among you, who eats any blood, I will set My face against that person who eats blood, and will cut him off from among his people. For the life of the flesh is in the blood, and I have given it to you upon the altar to make atonement for your souls; for it is the blood that makes atonement for the soul."

God is very serious about blood. He is very clear that blood must not be eaten as the life of the person or animal is in the blood. Blood should therefore be used for sacrifice. God has given us our lives to be used as a sacrifice unto him. The Blood of Jesus was poured out as a sacrifice to the Father for us. The Blood of Jesus is the life of Jesus. When we come under the power of His blood, we have come under the power of His life. Before the death of Jesus Christ on the Cross of Calvary, God told the Israelites to approach Him with the sacrifice of animals. He was teaching them about sacrifice and blood. He was preparing them for the ultimate sacrifice of the Blood of Jesus. The blood of animals could not pay the price for man's sins. It required the life of a sinless man to pay that price. Only Jesus qualified. Today, by the grace of God Jesus has paid that price and this payment stands eternally. We do not need any more sacrifice for sin. Jesus has paid with His life for our lives. All we need to do is to give our lives wholly to him and we shall live with Him in his power. Jesus' blood has given us sweet salvation.

PRAYER

Thank you Jesus for pouring out your life for me. I also give my life completely over to you.

Further reading: Romans 12

18th January
YOU ARE CLEAN

1 John 1: 5-10

"This is the message which we have heard from Him and declare to you, that God is light and in Him is no darkness at all. If we say that we have fellowship with Him, and walk in darkness, we lie and do not practice the truth. But if we walk in the light as He is in the light, we have fellowship with one another, and the blood of Jesus Christ His Son cleanses us from all sin.

If we say that we have no sin, we deceive ourselves, and the truth is not in us. If we confess our sins, He is faithful and just to forgive us our sins and to cleanse us from all unrighteousness. If we say that we have not sinned, we make Him a liar, and His word is not in us."

The Blood of Jesus cleanses us from all sin. God's requirement is met. Let us once again enjoy sweet fellowship with our Father God through the Blood of Jesus Christ. Many of us have constantly been plagued with a guilty conscience. Our lives have always been on the defensive trying to explain ourselves. Satan whispers in our ears all the time trying to make us feel we are not capable. Sometimes he makes us feel that we are not worthy of God's love. He can make us feel so dirty about the wrong things we have done in the past. We tend to run away from our Father, God, who is ready with open arms to receive us. God is light and all about Him is love. If it was left to us, yes we were very dirty but the Blood of Jesus has cleansed us from all dirt. The Blood of Jesus washes our heart, conscience and every part of our being and makes us perfectly clean. Walk in that reality today.

PRAYER
Thank you Father that, through the Blood of Jesus, I am clean, perfectly clean.

Further reading: 1 John 5

19th January
YOU HAVE BEEN DECLARED INNOCENT

Romans 5: 6-9

"For when we were still without strength, in due time Christ died for the ungodly. For scarcely for a righteous man will one die; yet perhaps for a good man someone would even dare to die. But God demonstrates His own love toward us, in that while we were still sinners, Christ died for us. Much more then, having now been justified by His blood, we shall be saved from wrath through Him."

We have been justified by the Blood of Jesus. This simply means that we have been put before the Supreme Court of heaven and declared innocent. Jesus Christ has already paid for all our sins. He suffered the death penalty for every sin we have committed or are going to commit. Righteousness is an old English word for justified which also means innocent. God sees you as innocent if only you will accept the price paid by Jesus Christ on the Cross of Calvary. This is the good news we carry. The Blood of Jesus is always before the Father to remind Him of the sentence fully served by Jesus Christ. Satan likes to whisper guilty in our ears but we have a plea - the Blood of Jesus. When you plead the Blood of Jesus, Satan has no legs to stand on. The obedience of Jesus Christ has earned Him all authority in Heaven and earth. In fact, Jesus has been appointed the supreme judge. Even before His death and resurrection, Jesus knew His destiny and expressed it well in John 5:22 "For the Father judges no one, but has committed all judgment to the Son." Our deliverer is also our judge. We are indeed more than conquerors. Make your accusers know this and walk in the innocence freely given to you.

PRAYER

Thank you Jesus for your blood that has set me free. I accept this forgiveness and honour your blood.

Further reading: Romans 5

20th January
YOU ARE SEPARATED TO HOLINESS

Romans 6: 20-23

"For when you were slaves of sin, you were free in regard to righteousness. What fruit did you have then in the things of which you are now ashamed? For the end of those things is death. But now having been set free from sin, and having become slaves of God, you have your fruit to holiness, and the end, everlasting life. For the wages of sin is death, but the gift of God is eternal life in Christ Jesus our Lord."

Water may wash dirt of your skin but the Blood of Jesus does a lot more than that. Blood represents life. When you are washed in the Blood of Jesus, you are literally putting on the life of Christ. When John baptised in the Jordan river and many rushed to him, he told them about Jesus. He said to them that he was baptising with water but Jesus shall baptise them with the Holy Spirit and fire. What John told them was that his baptism represented admission of guilt and a turning away from the past. The baptism of Jesus Christ on the other hand was a clothing of the life of God; a new and pure life separated to God. That is a life of holiness. Holiness simply means separated to God. Commit to live a life of holiness from today. The Blood of Jesus has not cleaned you up for you to return as a pig to mud or as a dog to his vomit. You are a new creation created in Christ Jesus. Every child must be trained by the parents so they would not depart from this training when they grow up. Our Father, God, has given us the Holy Spirit as our teacher. Let us be obedient to Him. Stay away from filth and remain washed by the Blood of Jesus. Keep your mouth clean.

PRAYER

Father I am yours. Thank you for washing me clean with the blood of Jesus. I promise to walk in obedience.

Further reading: 1 Peter 1

21st January
YOU ARE IN COVENANT WITH JESUS

Romans 8:1-5

> "There is therefore now no condemnation to those who are in Christ Jesus, who do not walk according to the flesh, but according to the Spirit. For the law of the Spirit of life in Christ Jesus has made me free from the law of sin and death. For what the law could not do in that it was weak through the flesh, God did by sending His own Son in the likeness of sinful flesh, on account of sin: He condemned sin in the flesh, that the righteous requirement of the law might be fulfilled in us who do not walk according to the flesh but according to the Spirit."

A covenant is a binding agreement between two parties. A blood covenant means when one party breaks it, they must die. We have a blood covenant with Jesus. In this covenant, Jesus has committed to share His life with us if we would share our lives with Him. He has sworn to this by His own blood. It is impossible for Him to break his covenant because He has already died for it. His promises can be trusted because He has signed to it with His own blood. It is now our duty to fulfil our part of this great covenant by giving our whole life to Jesus and His cause. The cause of Jesus is to bring back the whole world to its original creator, God. The world could be a hard place but there is deliverance in the name of Jesus. There is a covenant waiting for us to put our signature to. Surrender your life completely to Jesus today.

PRAYER

Dear Jesus, thank you for the price you paid to enable me share in your inheritance. I fully surrender my life today. Let's walk together as covenant partners.

Further reading: Romans 8

22nd January
SIGNED IN BLOOD

Hebrews 10:26-29

"For if we sin wilfully after we have received the knowledge of the truth, there no longer remains a sacrifice for sins, but a certain fearful expectation of judgment, and fiery indignation which will devour the adversaries. Anyone who has rejected Moses' law dies without mercy on the testimony of two or three witnesses. Of how much worse punishment, do you suppose, will he be thought worthy who has trampled the Son of God underfoot, counted the blood of the covenant by which he was sanctified a common thing, and insulted the Spirit of grace?"

Blood covenant is a serious undertaking. It is life for life. Jesus has already committed by giving out His life. He literally poured out His blood on Calvary. This is grace. Grace is undeserved love. He did not have to do this for you and me. He could have left us to walk in our ignorance and the consequence of ignorance. If He had behaved like the majority of people, He would simply have minded his own business. Imagine how many needy people you have passed in the past week without giving a hand because you were busy minding your own business. Our business was Jesus' business. He has committed Himself to a serious covenant of rescuing us back to our Father. Let us not take this lightly. A heavy price had to be paid. Let us honour this covenant so He can equip you to help rescue the perishing. You are a serious part of God's plan to save the world. Your payment is to be a partaker of all the goodness of the kingdom of God. Arise and shine. Get up now and enjoy this wonderful grace.

PRAYER

I love you Father God. I respond to the amazing love of Jesus on the Cross of Calvary. I am serious and commit to share in this ministry of love. Help me Holy Spirit where I may fall short.

Further reading: Hebrews 10

23rd January
BE BOLD IN YOUR FRIENDSHIP WITH GOD

Hebrews 10: 19-25

> "Therefore, brethren, having boldness to enter the Holiest by the blood of Jesus, by a new and living way which He consecrated for us, through the veil, that is, His flesh, and having a High Priest over the house of God, let us draw near with a true heart in full assurance of faith, having our hearts sprinkled from an evil conscience and our bodies washed with pure water. Let us hold fast the confession of our hope without wavering, for He who promised is faithful. And let us consider one another in order to stir up love and good works, not forsaking the assembling of ourselves together, as is the manner of some, but exhorting one another, and so much the more as you see the Day approaching."

God made a covenant with Israel in the desert on their way from Egypt to Israel. You will find this in the book of Exodus in the Old Testament of the Bible. He gave rules and regulations to Israel which if they obeyed, they could enjoy His blessing. What the people of Israel could not do was to approach God for themselves. God chose a special high priest who could approach Him on their behalf once a year. The mercy seat of God was separated from the people by a heavy curtain. It is not so today for you and me. When Jesus died on the Cross of Calvary, this thick veil of separation was torn into two. The abode of God was made open to everyone who would approach Him through the Blood of Jesus. It is the Blood of Jesus that cleans us up and makes us worthy to approach God. Rise up and boldly approach your Father's throne and obtain mercy. He is lovingly waiting.

PRAYER
Thank you Father that I am not an orphan. You have rescued me by your grace. I am determined to abide in your love and house forever.

Further reading: Hebrews 9

24th January
SIT ON GOD'S LAP. YOU ARE QUALIFIED.

Ephesians 2:1-7

> "And you He made alive, who were dead in trespasses and sins, in which you once walked according to the course of this world, according to the prince of the power of the air, the spirit who now works in the sons of disobedience, among whom also we all once conducted ourselves in the lusts of our flesh, fulfilling the desires of the flesh and of the mind, and were by nature children of wrath, just as the others.
>
> But God, who is rich in mercy, because of His great love with which He loved us, even when we were dead in trespasses, made us alive together with Christ (by grace you have been saved), and raised us up together, and made us sit together in the heavenly places in Christ Jesus, that in the ages to come He might show the exceeding riches of His grace in His kindness toward us in Christ Jesus."

We thank God that it is not our sense of goodness that makes us able to approach God. Many will tell you that they are good and God knows that. The bible says that all people have sinned and fallen short of the glory of God. In other words, if God should appear without mitigation, we will all run for cover as Adam and Eve did in the garden of Eden. Of course, God does not want us to run away from Him. He is a Father and it breaks his heart when His children run away from Him. This why the price of the Blood of Jesus had to be paid to pave the way for us to have confidence towards our Father. The price has been paid and every barrier removed. Let us therefore confidently enjoy our status as children of God.

PRAYER
Thank you Father for your overwhelming love. Help me to love you just as you love me.

Further reading: Ephesians 2

25th January
YOU WERE DEAD. YOU ARE NOW ALIVE

Hebrews 13: 20-21

> *"Now may the God of peace who brought up our Lord Jesus from the dead, that great Shepherd of the sheep, through the blood of the everlasting covenant, make you complete in every good work to do His will, working in you what is well pleasing in His sight, through Jesus Christ, to whom be glory forever and ever. Amen."*

The powerful God who is able to raise the dead is in an everlasting covenant with you and I. He has made sure of this through the Blood of Jesus Christ which is forever speaking for us. If anyone is in Christ Jesus, he is a new creation. Old things are gone and new things have come. You and I by coming into this covenant relationship with God have not just become better people. We have become new people. We are born again. We have access to this wonderful life through the unmerited favour of God. He has reconciled us to Himself at a very costly price. The price was the life of His beloved Son, Jesus Christ. Only Jesus could pay that price because He was sinless and Divine law required a sinless sacrifice. God will not break His own law. If He did, He will be breaking Himself as he is one with His word. The Word of God cannot be changed because it is truth. Batter and molest it us much as you want. It cannot be destroyed. Jesus is coming back in triumph to take over and rule his possession of a new Heaven and Earth. We shall rule with Him because through His blood we have been made His brethren and co-heirs with Him. Sin had cut us away from God but the Blood of Jesus has cleaned away our sins and made us right with God. Separation from God is death. Union with God is life. You are alive.

PRAYER
Thank you Father that I am alive today. Let me give life wherever I go.

Further reading: Hebrews 13

26th January
YOU ARE FULLY PROTECTED

Exodus 12: 21-23

> "Then Moses called for all the elders of Israel and said to them, "Pick out and take lambs for yourselves according to your families, and kill the Passover lamb. And you shall take a bunch of hyssop, dip it in the blood that is in the basin, and strike the lintel and the two doorposts with the blood that is in the basin. And none of you shall go out of the door of his house until morning. For the Lord will pass through to strike the Egyptians; and when He sees the blood on the lintel and on the two doorposts, the Lord will pass over the door and not allow the destroyer to come into your houses to strike you."

When God gave this instruction to Israel through Moses, God was teaching Israel about the importance of the blood in protecting us from destruction. This was the blood of a mere lamb but it had the power to protect any household under that covering from the angel of destruction. God asked Israel to remember this day of the Passover when He brought Israel out of bondage on the back of His greatest Miracle in Egypt. What a night that would have been. All the people of Egypt including the king had lost their first born both of people and animals. Yet the Israelites have had a feast, loaded with treasure and were starting out on a journey to the Promised Land. The blood on the doorpost of the Israelites made the difference. The blood on the doorpost was the sign of the covenant that God had with Israel through their ancestor Abraham. We have a better covenant with God through the Blood of Jesus. We have become part of the family of God. If the blood of a lamb could bring such protection to Israel, imagine what the Blood of Jesus has brought to us. You are fully protected.

PRAYER
Thank you Jesus. Because of your Blood, I have no fear.

Further reading: Exodus 12

27th January
GET A LIFE

John 6: 53-58

> "Then Jesus said to them, "Most assuredly, I say to you, unless you eat the flesh of the Son of Man and drink His blood, you have no life in you. Whoever eats My flesh and drinks My blood has eternal life, and I will raise him up at the last day. For My flesh is food indeed, and My blood is drink indeed. He who eats My flesh and drinks My blood abides in Me, and I in him. As the living Father sent Me, and I live because of the Father, so he who feeds on Me will live because of Me. This is the bread which came down from heaven—not as your fathers ate the manna, and are dead. He who eats this bread will live forever."

Many of the people who heard Jesus make this statement found it strange because they took it literally. They asked themselves how this man could give them his flesh to eat and his blood to drink. The bible says some of Jesus' disciples left Him because they found Him strange. He was not talking about His physical flesh. There would not be enough to go round. Those of us living today would have missed out on this life because we did not see Jesus in the flesh. Flesh and blood represents the total person. When you eat the flesh and blood of Jesus, you are receiving the total person of Jesus Christ in you. When we take the Lord's supper, we are demonstrating the receiving of the full life of Jesus Christ in us. Jesus is the Bread of life. Jesus is the Word of God. Fill your heart with the Word of God. Do this by meditating on His Word and keeping His Word in your mouth. The bible says you will make your way prosperous when you do this.

PRAYER

Thank you Jesus for your flesh broken for me and your blood poured out for me. I have life because of this

Further reading: John 6

28th January
BLOOD OF JESUS ON MY HEAD

Matthew 27: 23-25

> *"Then the governor said, "Why, what evil has He done?" But they cried out all the more, saying, "Let Him be crucified!" When Pilate saw that he could not prevail at all, but rather that a tumult was rising, he took water and washed his hands before the multitude, saying, "I am innocent of the blood of this just Person. You see to it." And all the people answered and said, "His blood be on us and on our children."*

When the crowd responded that they were ready for the blood of Jesus to be on their heads, their anger had blinded them. The consequence of shedding innocent blood was life for life. Pilate the governor at the time knew Jesus was innocent and the people wanted him dead out of envy. He therefore washed his hands and claimed innocence in the killing of Jesus. He had the power to free Jesus and did not use it so Pilate was not innocent. He was as guilty as the people shouting 'crucify him'. History has it that the Romans later killed so many of the Jews on wooden crosses that there was a shortage of crosses. All those who were killed died out of ignorance. The Blood of Jesus cries 'Mercy' and not 'Vengeance'. If only they had recognised the power of the Blood of Jesus and repented, they would not have suffered the consequence of innocent blood. Israel still suffers this consequence. The wise ones like Paul repented and received the forgiveness and cleansing in the Blood of Jesus. Receive your forgiveness and cleansing today by allowing the Blood of Jesus to bathe you and make you whiter than snow.

PRAYER

I thank you Father for the Blood of Jesus. May the Blood of Jesus that cries 'Mercy' be on my head today.

Further reading: Matthew 27

29th January
BE HOLY

1 Corinthians 6: 9-11

"Do you not know that the unrighteous will not inherit the kingdom of God? Do not be deceived. Neither fornicators, nor idolaters, nor adulterers, nor homosexuals, nor sodomites, nor thieves, nor covetous, nor drunkards, nor revilers, nor extortioners will inherit the kingdom of God. And such were some of you. But you were washed, but you were sanctified, but you were justified in the name of the Lord Jesus and by the Spirit of our God."

Many are quick to confess that they are not holy. It is unfortunate for us to see ourselves as unholy because holiness pleases God. Holiness is simply separating yourself to God. This means you walk in obedience to God. The things that are ugly to God are ugly to us and the things that are beautiful to God are beautiful to us. Before the death of Jesus Christ on the Cross of Calvary, we had no power over sin. We were slaves to sin because we were filthy and cut away from God. Thank God for the Blood of Jesus which redeemed us, cleaned us up and justified us to be re-united with God as part of His family. Today, as part of the household of God, we have been given the identity of our heritage which is the Holy Spirit of God. Sin no longer has power over us. We have power to overcome sin. God's power in us can make us say 'No' to greed, lust and pride. The source of sin is Satan. He deceives and manipulates us to commit sin. Jesus has overcome Satan on the Cross of Calvary. The only place we can share in this victory over Satan is in Jesus and Jesus in us. To walk in this shared victory, we have to live a life of holiness separated to Him.

PRAYER
Father, I want to walk with you all the days of my life. Holy Spirit help me not to be distracted in anyway. I will be obedient to you in all things.

Further reading: 1 Corinthians chapter 6

30th January
YOUR LIFE IS VALUABLE

Revelation 5: 9-12

"And they sang a new song, saying: "You are worthy to take the scroll,

And to open its seals; For You were slain, And have redeemed us to God by Your blood Out of every tribe and tongue and people and nation. And have made us kings and priests to our God; And we shall reign on the earth." Then I looked, and I heard the voice of many angels around the throne, the living creatures, and the elders; and the number of them was ten thousand times ten thousand, and thousands of thousands, saying with a loud voice: "Worthy is the Lamb who was slain To receive power and riches and wisdom,

And strength and honour and glory and blessing!"

To be redeemed is to be bought back. You redeem your pawned items from the pawn shop. You buy them back. The Blood of Jesus bought us back from slavery. It is impossible to put a value on the Blood of Jesus. What is the value of the life of Jesus? If you can put a value on the life of Jesus then you could put a value on your life. He who is from everlasting and by whom all creation came to be is beyond value. He gave up this life for you and me to be reconciled with our Father. That is how much God values you. Men may put a price tag on us but in the eyes of God we are priceless. This also tells us that God loves us more than any man can love us. Men may belittle you but God sees you as a king and priest. Rise up and be the king and priest God has called you to be.

PRAYER

Father, I thank you for the value you put on me. Holy Spirit please open my eyes to see how God sees me and help me to ignore what men think of me.

Further reading: Revelation 5

31st January
SIGNED, SEALED, DELIVERED.

Ephesians 1: 7-12

> "In Him we have redemption through His blood, the forgiveness of sins, according to the riches of His grace which He made to abound toward us in all wisdom and prudence, having made known to us the mystery of His will, according to His good pleasure which He purposed in Himself, that in the dispensation of the fullness of the times He might gather together in one all things in Christ, both which are in heaven and which are on earth—in Him. In Him also we have obtained an inheritance, being predestined according to the purpose of Him who works all things according to the counsel of His will, that we who first trusted in Christ should be to the praise of His glory."

God had a plan for the salvation of man. Through Adam's disobedience, the world is scattered. Adam by giving his authority to Satan had brought in disorder, division and confusion. Satan is the author of confusion. Wherever you see chaos, know that Satan reigns. God is a God of order and in Him truth and strength prevail. God's purpose after the fall was to gather all things back into order. Sickness is disorder. A body in order is healthy. Lack creates confusion. Anger and hatred are products of disorder. The mission of Jesus was to gather all things in God's anointing and by so doing create order. Where Jesus is in charge there is order. Our only access to God's anointing is through the Blood of Jesus. The place of anointing is the place of heavenly inheritance. Jesus did it all. He died for us, rose again by defeating death and He anoints with the Holy Spirit to enable us walk victoriously as He does. As He is, so are we in this world. God's plan for us is signed sealed and delivered in Jesus Christ. He closely monitors our every move from his position at the right hand of the Father.

PRAYER

Thank you Jesus that you have completed all the work and invited me to share in the reward.

Further reading: Ephesians 1

Be Strong Devotional

February

1st February
THE JOY OF SALVATION

Psalm 51: 10-12

*"Create in me a clean heart, O God,
And renew a steadfast spirit within me.
Do not cast me away from Your presence,
And do not take Your Holy Spirit from me.
Restore to me the joy of Your salvation,
And uphold me by Your generous Spirit."*

Salvation is to be rescued from a bad situation. Salvation comes with great joy. Many story lines in movies are on the theme of salvation because when people are delivered from peril it brings joy to the heart. The mission of Jesus Christ on the earth was to bring salvation to all men. He brought us salvation from ignorance and sin. The world without the light of Jesus Christ is in darkness. The knowledge the world prides itself in is far short of what we could know. The prophet Isaiah prophesying about the coming of Jesus Christ put it this way: "The people who walked in darkness have seen a great light" (Isaiah 9:2). We are blessed to live in a time like this. Through the death and resurrection of Jesus Christ, salvation has come to the whole world. The choice is yours. Will you choose salvation or continue to walk in the bondage of sin and death. Trust the saving arm of God in every situation. Fear not. Don't be anxious about anything. Satan. who kept us in bondage has been defeated and we have been set free. Rejoice in your salvation today. God can never let you down if only you believe in the finished work of the Cross of Jesus Christ. This is another day the Lord has made. Rejoice and be glad in it.

PRAYER
Dear Jesus thank you for the mighty deliverance you have brought to me by your death and resurrection. I will walk in the joy of this deliverance all the days of my life.

Further reading: Isaiah 9

2nd February
SALVATION IS ONLY IN JESUS CHRIST

Acts 4: 8-12

> "Then Peter, filled with the Holy Spirit, said to them, "Rulers of the people and elders of Israel: If we this day are judged for a good deed done to a helpless man, by what means he has been made well, let it be known to you all, and to all the people of Israel, that by the name of Jesus Christ of Nazareth, whom you crucified, whom God raised from the dead, by Him this man stands here before you whole. This is the 'stone which was rejected by you builders, which has become the chief cornerstone.' Nor is there salvation in any other, for there is no other name under heaven given among men by which we must be saved."

Salvation is only in one person, Jesus Christ. Only He has paid the price for this through his death on the Cross. Jesus had one purpose for his time on earth, to pay the price for sin and save that which was lost. The lost included you and me. We were lost because we had been separated from the one who made us, God. We had fallen under the power of the world which is under the influence of Satan. We walked in darkness without knowledge. Jesus, though sinless, came to pay the price for our sins. The price of sin is death. Jesus therefore went to the Cross to die for our sins. Through this death, salvation has come to all who will call on the name of Jesus. He has already paid the price. Call on Him and be saved. In every situation where you need salvation, you can count on the Name of Jesus.

PRAYER

Thank you Jesus that you have become my salvation. You are my light, my healing, my strength, my provision and my protection. No one and nothing can save me except you.

Further reading: Acts 4

3rd February
NO SITUATION TOO HARD FOR GOD

Luke 19: 1-10

> *"Then Jesus entered and passed through Jericho. Now behold, there was a man named Zacchaeus who was a chief tax collector, and he was rich. And he sought to see who Jesus was, but could not because of the crowd, for he was of short stature. So he ran ahead and climbed up into a sycamore tree to see Him, for He was going to pass that way. And when Jesus came to the place, He looked up and saw him, and said to him, "Zacchaeus, make haste and come down, for today I must stay at your house." So he made haste and came down, and received Him joyfully. But when they saw it, they all complained, saying, "He has gone to be a guest with a man who is a sinner."*

Then Zacchaeus stood and said to the Lord, "Look, Lord, I give half of my goods to the poor; and if I have taken anything from anyone by false accusation, I restore fourfold."

And Jesus said to him, "Today salvation has come to this house, because he also is a son of Abraham; for the Son of Man has come to seek and to save that which was lost."

People had written Zacchaeus off for being too cruel to benefit from the mercy of God. Yet when Zacchaeus acknowledged Jesus Christ and turned to Him, he received salvation for himself and his house. Jesus paid the full price for all sin and the consequence of sin. No sin or sickness is too bad for redemption. Acknowledge your sinfulness and confess the Lordship of Jesus Christ over your life. Claim your complete deliverance today. Believe in your heart that Jesus has paid the price for your sins and is risen. Confess with your mouth that He is Lord and be saved now.

PRAYER

Thank you Jesus that through your total death, you have given me total salvation. I receive my total salvation now.

Further reading: Hebrews 8

4th February
SAVED FROM DESTRUCTION

Exodus 12: 12-13

> "For I will pass through the land of Egypt on that night, and will strike all the firstborn in the land of Egypt, both man and beast; and against all the gods of Egypt I will execute judgment: I am the Lord. Now the blood shall be a sign for you on the houses where you are. And when I see the blood, I will pass over you; and the plague shall not be on you to destroy you when I strike the land of Egypt."

When God asked the people of Israel to put blood on their door post, it was to show that they were people of covenant. You may be weak but no one will dare attack you if they know you are in covenant with a strong man. To be in covenant with God is to have the might of God behind you. Covenant is a marriage where you share in all things. All that you have belongs to the other party and all that the other party has belongs to you. When you are in covenant with God, He takes on your sins, sickness and weakness and gives you His righteousness, health and strength. This is what Jesus did on the Cross. Jesus tells us in John 10:10 that He brings us life. It is the enemy who brings destruction. Yet the enemy cannot touch you when it sees the blood of Jesus over you. When you are saved you are covered with the blood of Jesus. Confess the Blood of Jesus over your life at every opportunity. This will strengthen your faith and bring to your mind the salvation in which you walk. No messenger of destruction will be able to touch you because of the Blood.

PRAYER

Thank you Jesus for saving me from the destructive force of the enemy. I honour the covenant I have with you. I promise to walk in faithful partnership with you.

Further reading: Exodus 12

5th February
SAVED FROM GENERATIONAL CURSE

Exodus 34: 5-7

> "Now the Lord descended in the cloud and stood with him there, and proclaimed the name of the Lord. And the Lord passed before him and proclaimed, "The Lord, the Lord God, merciful and gracious, longsuffering, and abounding in goodness and truth, keeping mercy for thousands, forgiving iniquity and transgression and sin, by no means clearing the guilty, visiting the iniquity of the fathers upon the children and the children's children to the third and the fourth generation."

Without salvation curses are passed on from one generation to another. Mankind inherited the sin of Adam. It was for this reason that Jesus came to pay the price for sin to deliver us from this horrible curse of sin. Salvation is a cut off point for all curses. Scripture tells us that the righteous shall live by faith. It is not enough to say you are saved. You have to believe in your total salvation and restoration. You cannot believe what you do not know so we have to know the word of God. The bible tells us that faith comes by hearing the Word of God. God's love overrides the anger of sin. This is why He sent His best, Jesus Christ to come and pay for our sins and bring deliverance and reconciliation. Every generational curse is broken. You now live in generational blessing. You are born again into the family of God. Your old identity is gone. You now live under the blessing. Enjoy it. As part of the household of God, your prescription for a life free of oppression is to renew your mind with the Word of God. Do not pay any attention to thoughts that magnify the devil. He is defeated and his position is under your feet. Jesus did it but you are enjoying it because you are in covenant with Jesus.

PRAYER

Thank you Jesus for making me more than a conqueror. I am free from every generational curse. I walk in generational blessing because I am in the family of God.

Further reading: Deuteronomy 28: 1-14

6th February
GOD'S SALVATION IS SETTLED FOREVER

Isaiah 51:6

"Lift up your eyes to the heavens, And look on the earth beneath. For the heavens will vanish away like smoke, The earth will grow old like a garment, And those who dwell in it will die in like manner; But My salvation will be forever, And My righteousness will not be abolished."
Hebrews 9: 11-12

"But Christ came as High Priest of the good things to come, with the greater and more perfect tabernacle not made with hands, that is, not of this creation. Not with the blood of goats and calves, but with His own blood He entered the Most Holy Place once for all, having obtained eternal redemption."

God is so thorough in what He does that you cannot reverse it. Forever His word is settled in heaven. He has forever established salvation for us. The price Jesus paid cannot be reversed. When we look at the heavens and the earth they seem quite solid and immovable. God's word established them. Yet He says in another place that His salvation is more solid than the heavens and the earth. His salvation is signed with the pure Blood of Jesus Christ and remains forever. There is only one Jesus Christ and He could not be crucified again. He conquered death through his death and resurrection. Death is scared of Jesus Christ and will run far from Him. You can count on His eternal redemption. If you will continually abide in Him, you are eternally safe. He can never be defeated. He has defeated defeat and led captivity captive. My prayer for you today is for you to abide in Jesus Christ forever. The name of the Lord is a strong tower. The righteous run into it and they are safe.

PRAYER

Thank you Jesus for providing a solidly safe place for me to abide. Holy Spirit help me to never stray but stay in the house of the Lord forever.

Further reading: Hebrews 9

7th February
YOU ARE SAVED FROM SIN

Romans 6: 16-19

"Do you not know that to whom you present yourselves slaves to obey, you are that one's slaves whom you obey, whether of sin leading to death, or of obedience leading to righteousness? But God be thanked that though you were slaves of sin, yet you obeyed from the heart that form of doctrine to which you were delivered. And having been set free from sin, you became slaves of righteousness. I speak in human terms because of the weakness of your flesh. For just as you presented your members as slaves of uncleanness, and of lawlessness leading to more lawlessness, so now present your members as slaves of righteousness for holiness."

Before Jesus came to deal with sin on the Cross of Calvary, every one was under the control of sin. We did not have the power to resist sin. In the Old Testament God gave the people of Israel the commandments to show them what it took to become right with God. Scripture tells us that it was impossible for the people of Israel to obey the law. Sin was stronger than they were. They were therefore consistently bullied by sin. Satan kept us in fear as we walked in spiritual darkness. Jesus appeared on the scene, defeated Satan for us and broke the power of sin over us. The bully has been defeated. We are free to walk sin free before God. We have been set free from the power of sin. If you allow sin to have you then you are allowing a weakling to have you. The power of sin and death over you has been destroyed. Rejoice and live righteously. It is easier to live righteously in the kingdom of God than to live in sin.

PRAYER

Father, I thank you for the love that brought Jesus Christ to rescue me from the prison of sin. I am free and command sin to run far from me. I walk perfectly before my father in love.

Further reading: Hebrews 2

8th February
GOD HAS HEALED YOU

Psalm 103: 1-5

"Bless the Lord, O my soul; And all that is within me, bless His holy name! Bless the Lord, O my soul, And forget not all His benefits: Who forgives all your iniquities, Who heals all your diseases, Who redeems your life from destruction, Who crowns you with loving kindness and tender mercies, Who satisfies your mouth with good things, So that your youth is renewed like the eagle's."

We must confidently receive the benefits that come with walking with God. He did not save us from misery for nothing. He saved us into something beneficial. Some of the good things that salvation brings to us are listed above. These free benefits are part of God's nature and we will be denying him if we refuse to receive these gifts. A gift fulfils its purpose when the one for whom it is intended receives it. The first thing it mentions is God has forgiven us our sins. There is no sin He has not forgiven if you have come to Him with it in genuine repentance. Remember He has healed all your diseases. He says 'all' which includes those the doctors have said cannot be cured. God cannot lie. Receive this today. There are many Christians who confidently declare their salvation but find it difficult to declare their deliverance from sickness and disease. Healing from sickness and disease is part of salvation. Jesus destroyed the power of the tormentor on the Cross of Calvary. This means that we are delivered from every torment. Sickness and disease is a torment. Refuse to accept any torment. A great price has been paid for your freedom. Make a decision today not to live by what you feel or see but by what the word of God says. God's word is more real than what we see or feel.

PRAYER

Perfect Father, thank you that you have given me your perfection by making me part of your family. I declare that I am completely healed in every part of my body. I am strong.

Suggested reading: Psalm 103

9th February
CALL AND BE SAVED

Judges 3: 7-10

> "So the children of Israel did evil in the sight of the Lord. They forgot the Lord their God, and served the Baals and Asherahs. Therefore the anger of the Lord was hot against Israel, and He sold them into the hand of Cushan-Rishathaim king of Mesopotamia; and the children of Israel served Cushan-Rishathaim eight years. When the children of Israel cried out to the Lord, the Lord raised up a deliverer for the children of Israel, who delivered them: Othniel the son of Kenaz, Caleb's younger brother. The Spirit of the Lord came upon him, and he judged Israel. He went out to war, and the Lord delivered Cushan-Rishathaim king of Mesopotamia into his hand; and his hand prevailed over Cushan-Rishathaim."

The salvation of God is only a call away. Romans 10:13 tells us that whoever calls on the Name of the Lord shall be saved. The above scripture tells us that sin brings defeat. Anytime we sin we expose ourselves to the destructive powers of our enemy the devil. Yet we see that as soon as Israel called on the Lord, God sent a deliverer. You should not waste another minute under the burden of defeat. Call on the Name of Jesus now and receive your deliverance. Calling on the Name of Jesus means turning away from sin to Jesus. Sin opens the door to all sorts of attacks from the enemy. Jesus promises that He will not drive away anyone who comes to Him. God promises that as we draw near to Him, He will draw near to us. He promises that if we call, He will answer. If you need salvation now from anything you are facing, call now and receive your salvation. He has committed Himself to our salvation. Let's shame the devil who thinks we are ignorant by receiving and walking in our salvation.

PRAYER

Dear Jesus, I lay my burden at your feet today. Save me now.

Further reading: **Romans 10**

10th February
GOD WILL RESTORE WHAT YOU HAVE LOST

Amos 9: 13-15

"Behold, the days are coming," says the Lord, "When the ploughman shall overtake the reaper, And the treader of grapes him who sows seed; The mountains shall drip with sweet wine, And all the hills shall flow with it. I will bring back the captives of My people Israel;

They shall build the waste cities and inhabit them; They shall plant vineyards and drink wine from them; They shall also make gardens and eat fruit from them. I will plant them in their land, And no longer shall they be pulled up From the land I have given them," Says the Lord your God."

God does not just heal, He makes whole. If you are a leper, Jesus does not just heal and leave you with stumps where there should have been fingers or toes. That would not be complete work. He makes you whole by making your fingers or toes grow out. In the same way, God does not intend to bring you out of prison and make you wander without a home and a job. That would be incomplete work. He perfects everything he does. You must therefore expect more than just deliverance. You must also expect restoration. We are saved from sin and darkness and we are born again into a new life as children of God. You are not just delivered from Egypt into the wilderness. God has prepared a Promise Land for you. The law required a thief to restore seven fold. It will therefore not be greedy to expect a sevenfold return on anything the enemy has stolen. The above scripture tells us that when God begins to roll in His restoration it is going to be a very quick harvest that will baffle us. God's glory and abundance is beyond our imagination. Let us trust God as God. He is big and powerful.

PRAYER

Thank you Father for your restoration of all that the enemy has stolen from me. Thank you for your abundance in my life.

Further reading: Joel 2

11th February
YOU ARE COMPLETELY SAVED

Hebrews 7: 23-28

"Also there were many priests, because they were prevented by death from continuing. But He, because He continues forever, has an unchangeable priesthood. Therefore He is also able to save to the uttermost those who come to God through Him, since He always lives to make intercession for them.

For such a High Priest was fitting for us, who is holy, harmless, undefiled, separate from sinners, and has become higher than the heavens; who does not need daily, as those high priests, to offer up sacrifices, first for His own sins and then for the people's, for this He did once for all when He offered up Himself. For the law appoints as high priests men who have weakness, but the word of the oath, which came after the law, appoints the Son who has been perfected forever."

If you have come to God through Jesus Christ then be assured that you are absolutely secure. There is nothing like being partly saved where God is concerned. When you receive the salvation offered to us by God through Jesus Christ, you are completely and utterly saved to the uttermost. I deliberately repeated those words to show how thorough salvation through Jesus Christ is. Remember that ninety-nine percent free is not free. Jesus came to set the captives free. Free is hundred percent. Rejoice in your complete salvation. One of the strategies of Satan is to whisper 'incomplete' in our ears. If he cannot get us to completely deny the work on the cross, he makes us think that Jesus did not do it all. Complete faith in the totality of the finished work of Jesus Christ sets you free and pleases God. Today, know that the thorough work of the Blood of Jesus Christ has set you free from sin and its effect, sickness, lack and pain in all its forms.

PRAYER
Thank you Father that you are God almighty and your mighty hand has completely saved me. I receive my complete salvation.

Further reading: Hebrews 7

12th February
YOU ARE A SON OF GOD AND AN HEIR

Galatians 4: 3-7

"Even so we, when we were children, were in bondage under the elements of the world. But when the fullness of the time had come, God sent forth His Son, born of a woman, born under the law, to redeem those who were under the law, that we might receive the adoption as sons.

And because you are sons, God has sent forth the Spirit of His Son into your hearts, crying out, "Abba, Father!" Therefore you are no longer a slave but a son, and if a son, then an heir of God through Christ."

We have not just been saved from the darkness of this world. We have been made sons. Sons here is not just referring to those who are male but female as well. If you are a girl or woman, you also qualify as a son. In our every day language, son refers to male, but when scripture refers to sons in a context like this, it is talking about a position of authority and inheritance. God planned our adoption as sons. He thought about this, planned it and executed his plan. Your adoption as a son has taken careful planning and execution. Please don't treat what God finds so important as nothing. He had a purpose in paying this hefty price to adopt us. This is so we can become heirs of everything that is His. It is time to possess your possessions as a son of God. Someone had to die to secure you this inheritance. Take what is yours by force. There are thieves trying to steal what is yours. Do all that is in your power by the direction of the Holy Spirit to walk in the freedom for which Christ has set you free. You have been made righteous, healthy, wise, rich and peaceful.

PRAYER
Thank you Father for choosing me to be your son. I accept this great privilege and will live as your son.

Further reading: *Galatians 4*

13th February
THE GOOD WORK BEGUN IN YOU SHALL BE COMPLETED

Philippians 1: 3-6

> *"I thank my God upon every remembrance of you, always in every prayer of mine making request for you all with joy, for your fellowship in the gospel from the first day until now, being confident of this very thing, that He who has begun a good work in you will complete it until the day of Jesus Christ;" Philippians 2: 12-13*

"Therefore, my beloved, as you have always obeyed, not as in my presence only, but now much more in my absence, work out your own salvation with fear and trembling; for it is God who works in you both to will and to do for His good pleasure."

To be saved from a world of uncertainties feels good. The first day that the reality of salvation dawns on you is a feel good day. The promise above is that God will bring to a perfect conclusion what he has begun. Remember that when you are saved, you are completely saved as we discussed in previous days. Unfortunately it takes some time to walk in the total reality of this gift. This is because we need to renew our minds to this new reality in the midst of a world that is trying to challenge our salvation. We have a role to play to enable our salvation play out fully in our lives. The second scripture tells us that God Himself is moulding us and directing our steps. Our role is to completely submit to His moulding and direction. Let us with all diligence ensure that we are pliable in the hands of a mighty and loving God.

PRAYER

Father, I completely and absolutely submit to your plan for my life. If I should take a wrong step unknowingly, I give you the authority to bring me back to the right path. Thank you.

Further reading: Philippians 1

14th February
JESUS LOVES YOU MORE THAN ANYONE

John 15: 9-14

"As the Father loved Me, I also have loved you; abide in My love. If you keep My commandments, you will abide in My love, just as I have kept My Father's commandments and abide in His love.

"These things I have spoken to you, that My joy may remain in you, and that your joy may be full. This is My commandment, that you love one another as I have loved you. Greater love has no one than this, than to lay down one's life for his friends. You are My friends if you do whatever I command you."

Today is Valentines Day, a day the world has dedicated to love. It is good that the world puts a day aside to remember love. Unfortunately, the world's definition of love is different from God's definition of love. God is love and love is probably the most important word in the dictionary. Scripture tells us that perfect love drives away fear. Fear is probably the most tormenting word in the dictionary. Almost all misbehaviour by men is driven by fear. Pride is the product of fear. What the world calls love, God calls lust. Love gives. Lust wants to receive. Jesus proved His love with His sacrifice. Has anyone died for you yet to prove their love. Today, as there is a lot of love flying around, let your love be of the God kind. Let it not be the sensual kind of love but a love that is ready to sacrifice for the spiritual growth of all. Can you love your neighbour as yourself. Can you love God with everything you have. Yes you can. I want to assure you that if you can walk in this obedience, you will understand the real power of God's love. Let us share some love today of the godly kind.

PRAYER

Thank you Jesus for your love. I want to love you as you love me and love others as you love them.

Further reading: John 15

15th February
GOD IS ALWAYS RIGHT AND JUST

Psalm 119: 75,164

"I know, O Lord, that Your judgments are right, And that in faithfulness You have afflicted me." "Seven times a day I praise You, Because of Your righteous judgments." Psalm 7: 9-11

"Oh, let the wickedness of the wicked come to an end, But establish the just; For the righteous God tests the hearts and minds My defence is of God, Who saves the upright in heart. God is a just judge, And God is angry with the wicked every day."

Justice is determined by God's moral standards. God created the world and everything in it. He is the beginning of all things. Scripture tells us that He made all things and everything belongs to Him. If He started all things and all things are His then it stands to reason that He determines what is right and wrong. What He says is right is right and what He says is wrong is wrong. God is just. This sense of being right is referred to as righteousness. Only God is righteous. In scripture some people who tried to walk in obedience to God are referred to as righteous but this fell short of God's exclusive Righteousness. God's righteousness could only be given as a gift from God himself as no man could work this out. God in His mercy delivered this free gift of righteousness to the world through Jesus Christ. In Jesus Christ, sin which separated us from God's righteousness has been removed. We are justified. We can walk freely without condemnation. Hold your head up today and enjoy the free gift of righteousness.

PRAYER

Thank you Father for being a just and loving God. Thank you for making me righteous through Jesus Christ.

Further reading: Romans 3: 21-31

16th February
WE HAVE BEEN MADE RIGHT IN GOD'S EYES

1 Corinthians 1: 26-31

"For you see your calling, brethren, that not many wise according to the flesh, not many mighty, not many noble, are called. But God has chosen the foolish things of the world to put to shame the wise, and God has chosen the weak things of the world to put to shame the things which are mighty; and the base things of the world and the things which are despised God has chosen, and the things which are not, to bring to nothing the things that are, that no flesh should glory in His presence. But of Him you are in Christ Jesus, who became for us wisdom from God—and righteousness and sanctification and redemption— that, as it is written, "He who glories, let him glory in the Lord."

God's grace is made abundantly evident when we become aware of the fact that we do not deserve it. Man at his best cannot meet God's standard. Righteousness is God's character. How can we possibly have God's character if it is not offered to us as a free gift. We can try hard to copy God but it is difficult to copy something that comes from within. Righteousness is God's nature. Only He can impute it to us. Without him ascribing it to us, we do not even know what righteousness is like to enable us copy. Our attempt at righteousness is like filthy rags before God. Our only salvation is to accept the sacrifice of Jesus Christ and step into righteousness through the precious Blood that was poured out on Calvary. That is the only payment accepted before God that frees us from the bondage of sin and darkness. You always have to be conscious of the price paid for your freedom. It is the enemy's plan to keep you in bondage with lies and condemnation. Step into your freedom.

PRAYER

Thank you Jesus for my justification through your blood. I resist every condemnation and bondage.

Further reading: 1 Corinthians 1

17th February
YOU ARE JUSTIFIED IN CHRIST

Romans 8: 3-4

> "For what the law could not do in that it was weak through the flesh, God did by sending His own Son in the likeness of sinful flesh, on account of sin: He condemned sin in the flesh, that the righteous requirement of the law might be fulfilled in us who do not walk according to the flesh but according to the Spirit."

When God made a covenant with Israel in the Old Testament, He gave them the Law. It was impossible for Israel to know him through laws. You only get to really know someone through a personal relationship. Israel was so afraid of God, they didn't want to know Him personally. They gave authority to Moses to speak to God on their behalf. God spoke to Moses and gave him the right to approach Him. Yet not even Moses had a personal relationship with God. God is spirit and a different kind of being. He is God whilst Moses is man. It would therefore be difficult for Moses to know Him as He really is. The only way Moses could really have an equal relationship with God was if God became a man or if Moses became like God. This was impossible because there was a big gulf between sinful man and righteous God. This gulf was bridged by Jesus Christ. He was God who became man; paid the price of sin for man and paved the way for us to come freely to God who has now given us the status of His children. Not only had God become man through Jesus Christ but through His sacrifice, He reconciled us to God. We did not come back to God as ordinary members of His household but God receives us as His sons. We therefore are born again in the God class and inherit righteousness. Praise God.

PRAYER

Thank you Father for the love you showed by making Jesus Christ pay the price for our re-union. Thank you Jesus.

Further reading: Romans 5

18th February
PUT ON CHRIST

Ephesians 4: 17-24

> "This I say, therefore, and testify in the Lord, that you should no longer walk as the rest of the Gentiles walk, in the futility of their mind, having their understanding darkened, being alienated from the life of God, because of the ignorance that is in them, because of the blindness of their heart; who, being past feeling, have given themselves over to lewdness, to work all uncleanness with greediness.
>
> But you have not so learned Christ, if indeed you have heard Him and have been taught by Him, as the truth is in Jesus: that you put off, concerning your former conduct, the old man which grows corrupt according to the deceitful lusts, and be renewed in the spirit of your mind, and that you put on the new man which was created according to God, in true righteousness and holiness."

When you meet people, many times you are able to tell which part of the world they come from. By their skin colour or facial features one can safely guess the origin of the person. In the animal kingdom, every species of animal has its own identifying features. When we become a new creation in Christ, we also exhibit new features. This goes beyond physical appearance. In our new life, whether we are Chinese, African, Latin, Arab, Caucasian or Indian, we all put on the identity of Christ. The identity of Christ is the identity of God. We all behave like God. We possess the righteous Spirit of God and this manifests in our every day behaviour. We exhibit righteousness, peace and joy in the Holy Spirit. You should never forget that in Satan, you have an enemy who wants to steal your new righteous status from you. Don't allow him. Jesus paid a hefty price for your robe of righteousness. Keep it on.

PRAYER

Thank you Jesus for the robe of righteousness you have given to me. I resist every effort of the enemy. I will forever keep my robe on.

Further reading: Ephesians 4

19th February
ENJOY RIGHTEOUSNESS BY FAITH

Genesis 15: 1-6

"After these things the word of the Lord came to Abram in a vision, saying, "Do not be afraid, Abram. I am your shield, your exceedingly great reward." But Abram said, "Lord GOD, what will You give me, seeing I go childless, and the heir of my house is Eliezer of Damascus?" Then Abram said, "Look, You have given me no offspring; indeed one born in my house is my heir!"

And behold, the word of the Lord came to him, saying, "This one shall not be your heir, but one who will come from your own body shall be your heir." Then He brought him outside and said, "Look now toward heaven, and count the stars if you are able to number them." And He said to him, "So shall your descendants be."

And he believed in the Lord, and He accounted it to him for righteousness."

Abraham's faith made him right in God's eye. Without the sacrifice of Jesus Christ on the Cross which paved the way for man to be justified before God, it was impossible for anyone to be righteous. Righteousness is the nature of God. For you to be declared righteous is for you to have full access to God and enjoy all His goodness. Abraham lived about 2000 years before Jesus Christ paid the price for our redemption. Yet his faith was accounted to Him for righteousness. The one thing that pleases God above all is for man to believe in Him. God made man, saw man fall from grace through sin and is well aware of man's inadequacy. A loving God wants to share in all things with man. All He demands of man is faith. We show our love of God by our faith. We have to believe that God is who He says He is and rewards those who diligently seek Him.

PRAYER

Dear Father, thank you for the love that has opened all this treasure of heaven to me. I believe every promise of yours.

Further reading: Galatians 3

20th February
THE GOSPEL OF JESUS REVEALS GOD'S RIGHTEOUSNESS

Romans 1: 13-17

"Now I do not want you to be unaware, brethren, that I often planned to come to you (but was hindered until now), that I might have some fruit among you also, just as among the other Gentiles. I am a debtor both to Greeks and to barbarians, both to wise and to unwise. So, as much as is in me, I am ready to preach the gospel to you who are in Rome also.

For I am not ashamed of the gospel of Christ, for it is the power of God to salvation for everyone who believes, for the Jew first and also for the Greek. For in it the righteousness of God is revealed from faith to faith; as it is written, "The just shall live by faith."

In all things, God is right. This is because He made all things, knows the substance of all things and how best they can operate. Jesus said in John 14:6 "I am the way, the truth and the life." There is no other way outside of Jesus to God. Jesus is the only truth and without Jesus, you have no life. Jesus Christ was part of God's plan from the beginning. He who was righteous took on the sins of the world. He defeated sin and the power of sin and paved the way for all sinners to enjoy the righteousness of God. Jesus is the only way to righteousness amongst men. Anyone who would simply accept the finished work of Jesus Christ in freeing all mankind from sin and death and accept to walk with Jesus in His resurrection power is made righteous. This means he is justified to walk in the nature of God. Arise and walk like God in love, grace, mercy and power. You are justified if you have met the conditions.

PRAYER
Thank you Father for this gift of righteousness. Thank you Jesus for your death and resurrection which has made this possible.

Further reading: Romans 1

21st February
OBEDIENCE TO GOD BRINGS BLESSING

Genesis 22: 15-18

"Then the Angel of the Lord called to Abraham a second time out of heaven, and said: "By Myself I have sworn, says the Lord, because you have done this thing, and have not withheld your son, your only son— blessing I will bless you, and multiplying I will multiply your descendants as the stars of the heaven and as the sand which is on the seashore; and your descendants shall possess the gate of their enemies. In your seed all the nations of the earth shall be blessed, because you have obeyed My voice."

In an earlier reading, we saw that Abraham's faith was accounted to him as righteousness. In other words, because he believed, God has given him the privilege of standing right before God and sharing in godly privileges. The place of righteousness is the place of blessing. Blessing is favour, goodwill and good things bestowed on us by God. God has the capacity to meet every need in every life. It is not his will that any should suffer. He created man in love. It is the ignorance of man and our separation from God that brings suffering. If we are reunited with Him, there is no condemnation toward us. We are open to the wisdom and truth of God. We are members of His household and can fully partake of all that is in His house. That is definitely a place of blessing. Rejoice, your trust and obedience has put you in a place of blessing. Expect God's abundance in every area of your life. Expect healing and good health in your life. Don't accept any other report. Jesus has paid the price for peace in every area of your life. Expect God's provision financially and in every area of need. You live in a house of blessing. It will be strange not to walk in it. Walk in blessing.

PRAYER

Thank you Father that I am blessed. You have made me whole and provided every need.

Further reading: Isaiah 40

22nd February
THE RIGHTEOUS SHALL BE FRESH AND FLOURISHING

Psalm 92: 12-15

"The righteous shall flourish like a palm tree, He shall grow like a cedar in Lebanon. Those who are planted in the house of the Lord Shall flourish in the courts of our God. They shall still bear fruit in old age; They shall be fresh and flourishing, To declare that the Lord is upright; He is my rock, and there is no unrighteousness in Him."

This psalm is a heartfelt thanksgiving song to a good God who takes good care of His own. The palm tree is known for its usefulness. Its branches could be used for construction, its fruit is edible, oil and wine can be extracted from it and many other uses. The palm tree stands solid and immovable. This is how the righteous is described. Are you righteous? Have you accepted the sacrifice of Jesus Christ on the Cross of Calvary as well as His resurrection from the dead? Have you made Jesus the Lord of your life? Then you are righteous. You have every right to partake in every possession that belongs to your father, God. Many have developed a captivity mind set. A tamed domesticated lion still finds it difficult to exercise its rights as king of the jungle when released into the wild. Many righteous have this mindset and makes it difficult for them to walk in the blessings of righteousness. God has spoken freshness over you. He says your portion is to be flourishing. You will not wither and you will be strong. He has spoken over you that you will look better in your old age and your strength will be renewed. Receive God's truth and prosper rather than follow your mindset from experiences and misinformation from your past. Scripture encourages us to renew our mind to the word of God. When you read God's word, accept it as truth. There is no other truth.

PRAYER

Thank you Father for your love. I am fresh, strong and flourishing in Jesus name.

Further reading: Psalm 92

23rd February
SIN HAS NO POWER OVER YOU

Romans 6: 10-14

"For the death that He died, He died to sin once for all; but the life that He lives, He lives to God. Likewise you also, reckon yourselves to be dead indeed to sin, but alive to God in Christ Jesus our Lord.

Therefore do not let sin reign in your mortal body, that you should obey it in its lusts. And do not present your members as instruments of unrighteousness to sin, but present yourselves to God as being alive from the dead, and your members as instruments of righteousness to God. For sin shall not have dominion over you, for you are not under law but under grace."

It is really difficult to fight sin when you don't have the ammunition to. The author of sin is Satan. He suggests things to our minds and manipulates our flesh to get us to sin. The wages of sin is death. Satan is spirit and it is impossible to defeat him in the flesh. Thank God for Jesus who through His death on the Cross of Calvary defeated Satan in the spirit and exposed him as a defeated foe. Scripture says Jesus made a public spectacle of Satan. The author of sin is defeated and he no longer has any power over you and me. As we walk in Christ, Satan and his cohorts as scared of us. When they see us, they see Jesus and this reminds them of their defeat. We should not allow them to trick us into sin. They have no power over us and sin has no power over us. When we fall for their deceit, we have brought ourselves under their power and disaster waits. Let us rather submit to the author and finisher of our faith who is Jesus Christ and walk in righteousness rather than sin.

PRAYER

Thank you Father, that sin has no dominion over me. I walk in righteousness. I am clean. No sin can contaminate me.

Further reading: Romans 6

24th February
BE A SLAVE TO RIGHTEOUSNESS

Romans 6: 16-18

> *"Do you not know that to whom you present yourselves slaves to obey, you are that one's slaves whom you obey, whether of sin leading to death, or of obedience leading to righteousness? But God be thanked that though you were slaves of sin, yet you obeyed from the heart that form of doctrine to which you were delivered. And having been set free from sin, you became slaves of righteousness."*

Because God created every person in His own image, He had to give each one of us our free will. If He imposed His will on us, we would be like robots. He would not like anyone to impose his will on Him, likewise He would not impose His on anyone. For us to walk in God's will therefore, we would have to make that choice. We would have to submit our will to His will. Satan, on the other hand, puts pressure on us. He seeks to compel us to do his will. Satan does all in his power to forcibly steer us in the path of sin. The choice is still on every individual to say 'yes' to God or Satan. If you say 'yes' to sin, you are a slave of sin. If you say 'yes' to righteousness, you are a slave to righteousness. You cannot sit on the fence. If you do not say 'yes' to righteousness, sin will put so much pressure on you that you may fall to it. James 4:7 says, "Submit to God, resist the devil and he will flee from you." The word submit shows that you have to make the choice to come under God. The word resist implies that satan is using force and needs resistance. Please don't leave it to chance. Be a slave to righteousness and resist sin. The place of righteousness is a place of blessing.

PRAYER

Thank you Father for your grace that has made me righteous. I choose today to be a slave of righteousness rather than a slave of sin.

Further reading: Psalm 1

25th February
YOU ARE AN AMBASSADOR OF RIGHTEOUSNESS

2 Corinthians 5: 17-21

> *"Therefore, if anyone is in Christ, he is a new creation; old things have passed away; behold, all things have become new. Now all things are of God, who has reconciled us to Himself through Jesus Christ, and has given us the ministry of reconciliation, that is, that God was in Christ reconciling the world to Himself, not imputing their trespasses to them, and has committed to us the word of reconciliation. Now then, we are ambassadors for Christ, as though God were pleading through us: we implore you on Christ's behalf, be reconciled to God. For He made Him who knew no sin to be sin for us, that we might become the righteousness of God in Him."*

If you have voluntarily given your life to Jesus Christ and received Him in your heart then you are truly born again. Your life is completely new. Your old life is gone. It is a death and resurrection experience. You died to a life of sin and you are resurrected to a life of righteousness. This is the greatest miracle that could happen to any person. Everyone needs to experience this new life. It is God's will that everyone should have this experience. In an instant you are changed from being a sinner who is far away from God to being a saint who lives in the house of God as a family member. All it takes for this miraculous change to take place is to believe in your heart that Jesus Christ has served the sentence for all your sins and to declare with your mouth that Jesus is the Lord of your life. Your mouth is the spokesperson of your heart. Your resurrection life, which is glorious, will be a sign to the world of the truth of Jesus Christ. God glorifies you to be His ambassador.

PRAYER

Thank you for this robe of righteousness that makes me your ambassador. I will be a good ambassador and represent you faithfully.

Further reading: 2 Corinthians 5

26th February
BE A RIGHTEOUS JUDGE

1 Kings 3: 9-13

"Therefore give to Your servant an understanding heart to judge Your people, that I may discern between good and evil. For who is able to judge this great people of Yours?"

The speech pleased the Lord, that Solomon had asked this thing. Then God said to him: "Because you have asked this thing, and have not asked long life for yourself, nor have asked riches for yourself, nor have asked the life of your enemies, but have asked for yourself understanding to discern justice, behold, I have done according to your words; see, I have given you a wise and understanding heart, so that there has not been anyone like you before you, nor shall any like you arise after you. And I have also given you what you have not asked: both riches and honour, so that there shall not be anyone like you among the kings all your days."

Most people in their lives will be faced with the challenge of making judgement between two people. This could be your children, work colleagues or sometimes between total strangers. Those of us in Christ carry a glory that we may not be aware of but people honour. If you live a life as a true ambassador of Christ, many will approach you expecting you to give them a just solution. As a representative of God you have to give righteous judgement. Many are influenced by their relationships and prejudiced minds to make twisted judgements. God abhors unrighteous judgement. Repent of any wrong judgements you have made in the past and commit yourself to righteous impartial judgement from today. In the scripture above, God was pleased with Solomon and rewarded him because he acknowledged God's love for justice and sought his help in administering justice. God is a righteous judge and we must be just and impartial in every judgement we make. When we please God, he greatly rewards us.

PRAYER

Thank you Father for being just. Help me to be righteous in every judgement I make.

Further reading: John 8

27th February
LOVE FROM A PURE HEART

1 Timothy 1: 3-7

> "As I urged you when I went into Macedonia—remain in Ephesus that you may charge some that they teach no other doctrine, nor give heed to fables and endless genealogies, which cause disputes rather than godly edification which is in faith. Now the purpose of the commandment is love from a pure heart, from a good conscience, and from sincere faith, from which some, having strayed, have turned aside to idle talk, desiring to be teachers of the law, understanding neither what they say nor the things which they affirm."

God is very concerned about the state of your heart because your heart determines who you are. Life can flow out of your heart or death can flow out. Proverbs 4: 23 tells us to keep our hearts with all diligence as issues of life flow from it. Jesus told his listeners who were questioning him about external rituals that these rituals were not as important as the heart. In Matthew 15:19 He says, "For out of the heart proceed evil thoughts, murders, adulteries, fornications, thefts, false witness, blasphemies." The heart is the core of our being. Righteousness within produces righteousness without. When Jesus comes to live in you, He has brought righteousness within. Ensure that He has a place to lay His head in your heart. You are bound to produce righteousness without. Love from a pure heart and a good conscience is where God intends for everyone to be. That is where we ought to be. We should allow nothing to affect this purity. The product of walking in this righteousness is true and sincere faith. Sin defiles your conscience and blocks you from walking in true love. Make a decision today to forgive everyone. Ask the Holy Spirit to help you. Call on the Blood of Jesus to cleanse you and enjoy walking in the peace and righteousness of God.

PRAYER

Thank you Father, the Blood of Jesus has cleansed me from all unrighteousness. I walk in the confidence of your word.

Further reading: 1 Timothy 1 & 2

28th February
YOU ARE IN THE SPIRIT

Romans 8: 1-9

"There is therefore now no condemnation to those who are in Christ Jesus, who do not walk according to the flesh, but according to the Spirit. For the law of the Spirit of life in Christ Jesus has made me free from the law of sin and death. For what the law could not do in that it was weak through the flesh, God did by sending His own Son in the likeness of sinful flesh, on account of sin: He condemned sin in the flesh, that the righteous requirement of the law might be fulfilled in us who do not walk according to the flesh but according to the Spirit. For those who live according to the flesh set their minds on the things of the flesh, but those who live according to the Spirit, the things of the Spirit. For to be carnally minded is death, but to be spiritually minded is life and peace. Because the carnal mind is enmity against God; for it is not subject to the law of God, nor indeed can be. So then, those who are in the flesh cannot please God. But you are not in the flesh but in the Spirit, if indeed the Spirit of God dwells in you. Now if anyone does not have the Spirit of Christ, he is not His."

You have the Spirit of God in you so you are in the spirit. This means that you are walking in God's righteousness. Though sin in your flesh may try hard to control you, the Spirit of God in you is much greater than the sin that dwells in your flesh. The scripture later tells us that the power of the Spirit of God in you will drive out the sin in your flesh. Seek to be led by the spirit of God and sin will flee from you. End this month and begin next month on a high note of righteousness.

PRAYER
Thank you Jesus for setting me free from slavery to sin and my flesh. The life I live now, I live in the spirit trusting in God my father. I expect your goodness in the month of March.

Further reading: Romans 8

29th February
WITH JESUS YOU ARE RIGHT

Romans 8:1-2

> *"There is therefore now no condemnation to those who are in Christ Jesus, who do not walk according to the flesh, but according to the Spirit. For the law of the Spirit of life in Christ Jesus has made me free from the law of sin and death."*

29th of February occurs every 4 years and is commonly referred to as a leap day. Our common calendar has 365 days in a year. This is supposed to reflect the time the earth circles around the sun. The actual time it takes for the earth to circle around the sun is 365 days and nearly 6 hours. It is therefore necessary for an extra day to be inserted every four years to make up for the shortfall. In fact the actual calculation is more complicated than what I have simplified above. Man in his search for truth has complicated God's simplicity. This is why the Grace of God gave us the Cross. Through the Cross, Truth that seemed so far away has been brought close. The righteousness of God has been made available to us. Righteousness is old English for 'rightness'. God is right because He started all things. His promise is that when you respond to his invitation and receive Him into your heart, He will also receive you into Himself and you can therefore share in His rightness. As long as you don't allow your flesh to dictate to you but you allow His Spirit to be your guide, you are right and clean. Satan constantly tries to whisper words of condemnation and discouragement to us. Encourage yourself with God's word above that the life of Jesus has set us free from every condemnation. You are right because Jesus is right. You live in Him and He lives in you. Put your head to rest and enjoy living a free life under the law of the Spirit of life in Christ Jesus. Enjoy your leap day. You are in covenant with Jesus and He cannot let you down.

PRAYER

Amazing love, how can it be that you my God should die for me? Your grace has taken on my sin and given me Your righteousness. I am very grateful. Holy Spirit, help me never to stray from this love.

Further reading: Romans 8

March
The Holy Spirit

The Holy Spirit is the third person of the Trinity. He is God. He is a gift of God to each one of us who would receive Him. He is in us to transform us from the inside to be like God. He comes upon us to give us power to operate like God. He comes with us to guide protect and comfort us in our time of need. The Holy Spirit is a close friend. Acknowledge His presence by faith and don't go far away from Him. My prayer is that you would be well acquainted with the Holy Spirit and His presence will transform your life.

1st March
THE PROMISE

Acts 1:4-8

> "And being assembled together with them, He commanded them not to depart from Jerusalem, but to wait for the Promise of the Father, "which," He said, "you have heard from Me ⁵for John truly baptized with water, but you shall be baptized with the Holy Spirit not many days from now." ⁶Therefore, when they had come together, they asked Him, saying, "Lord, will You at this time restore the kingdom to Israel?" ⁷And He said to them, "It is not for you to know times or seasons which the Father has put in His own authority. ⁸But you shall receive power when the Holy Spirit has come upon you; and you shall be witnesses to Me in Jerusalem, and in all Judea and Samaria, and to the end of the earth."

God promised the world a Saviour. God fulfilled His promise by giving us Jesus Christ who through His death on the Cross and His resurrection brought salvation to the world. Many rejected Him because He did not come the way they expected. Jesus is the only Saviour of the world. Jesus whilst on earth also promised to send the Holy Spirit who would empower us to become and behave as sons of God. On the day of Pentecost, this promise was fulfilled. God, the Holy Spirit came to abide with and empower us forever. If you have received the Saviour, receive the Holy Spirit as well. The way you receive the Saviour is to invite Him into your life. The way you receive the Holy Spirit is to invite Him in. He has promised to answer us when we call on Him. God is true to His word and will perform what He has promised. Enjoy the friendship of the Holy Spirit today.

PRAYER

Thank you Father for our Saviour Jesus Christ. I receive every benefit of my salvation today. Thank you Jesus for the Holy Spirit. Holy Spirit, I welcome you in my life. Empower and guide me in all I do. Amen

Further reading: John chapter 14

2nd March
GOD WITH US

Genesis 1:1-3

¹In the beginning God created the heavens and the earth. ²The earth was without form, and void; and darkness was on the face of the deep. And the Spirit of God was hovering over the face of the waters. ³Then God said, "Let there be light"; and there was light.

And the angel answered and said to her, "The Holy Spirit will come upon you, and the power of the Highest will overshadow you; therefore, also, that Holy One who is to be born will be called the Son of God.
Luke 1:35

The first scripture above describes the scene at the beginning of creation. After stating that God created the heavens and the earth, the bible mentions the presence of the Spirit of God hovering over the face of the waters and then God speaks. The Spirit of God is not different from God and the Word of God is not different from God. This is the first appearance of what Christians call the 'Trinity' – 3 persons in one God. Jesus Christ, the Son of God is referred to as the 'Word of God' in John Chapter 1. The Spirit of God in the Old Testament is referred to as the Holy Spirit in the new. God's Word and His Spirit are God. In the second reading, a similar scenario occurs. This concerns Jesus Christ, the mediator of the new covenant. Jesus Christ, the Word of God and second person of the trinity was going to be made flesh (John 1:14). The process involved the Holy Spirit, the Spirit of God overshadowing Mary. The baby will be called the Son of God. Another name will be Emmanuel, God with us. The Trinity is present here too. The Holy Spirit is God with us. God lives in you if the Holy Spirit is in you. Rejoice, God has given you a gift that cannot be surpassed.

PRAYER
Thank you God for being in me and with me. Please never leave me. Holy Spirit, help me never to stray from your presence.

Further reading: Luke 1:26-45

3rd March
WITH GOD NOTHING IS IMPOSSIBLE

Luke 1:30-37

> *Then the angel said to her, "Do not be afraid, Mary, for you have found favor with God. ³¹And behold, you will conceive in your womb and bring forth a Son, and shall call His name Jesus. ³²He will be great, and will be called the Son of the Highest; and the Lord God will give Him the throne of His father David. ³³And He will reign over the house of Jacob forever, and of His kingdom there will be no end." ³⁴Then Mary said to the angel, "How can this be, since I do not know a man?" ³⁵And the angel answered and said to her, "The Holy Spirit will come upon you, and the power of the Highest will overshadow you; therefore, also, that Holy One who is to be born will be called the Son of God. ³⁶Now indeed, Elizabeth your relative has also conceived a son in her old age; and this is now the sixth month for her who was called barren. ³⁷For with God nothing will be impossible."*

The bible says no one has seen the Father at any time. The Son of God, Jesus, His Word has declared Him. People have seen His Word made flesh in the person of Jesus Christ. We have known Him and His Power through the agency of the Holy Spirit. With God nothing is impossible. As humans, there are many things that seem impossible with us, not with God. He is able to make both a virgin and an old barren woman conceive by the power of the Holy Spirit. Invite God into your impossible situation and receive your miracle today. Don't put much faith in what limited man says. Put your faith in what God says. He whose ability and understanding is far beyond what we can imagine has a solution for us. The bible says the wisest man is foolish before God and the strongest man is weak before God. Don't be bullied by human knowledge.

PRAYER
Almighty God, I surrender my thoughts my will, my strength and my life to you today. Take charge. I will be obedient.

Further reading: John 11:1-44

4th March
THIS POWER IS FREE FOR YOU AND YOUR CHILDREN

Acts 2:36-39

> ^{36}"Therefore let all the house of Israel know assuredly that God has made this Jesus, whom you crucified, both Lord and Christ."
>
> ^{37}Now when they heard this, they were cut to the heart, and said to Peter and the rest of the apostles, "Men and brethren, what shall we do?"
>
> ^{38}Then Peter said to them, "Repent, and let every one of you be baptized in the name of Jesus Christ for the remission of sins; and you shall receive the gift of the Holy Spirit. ^{39}For the promise is to you and to your children, and to all who are afar off, as many as the Lord our God will call."

Peter's response to the question of his listeners would have been an exciting moment for those who believed. Many had travelled to Jerusalem to celebrate the feast of Pentecost. They were there to perform a religious duty. This time God burst through with the outpouring of the Holy Spirit. They were witnesses and they were being told that they could receive the Holy Spirit in their lives if they would repent and be baptized. The account tells us that 3000 of them took this offer and received the totality of God in their lives. Friend, this free offer stands as fresh today as it was on the day of Pentecost. Those of us who already have the Holy Spirit, let us not ignore Him. I acknowledge Him when I wake up first thing in the morning. I speak to Him throughout the day. He is my trusted companion in all I do. If you haven't received the Holy Spirit, invite Him in today and He will come. He is on assignment to restore you to what God purposed you to be.

PRAYER
Thank you Jesus for the Holy Spirit. Holy Spirit, I honour you above all. You are my best friend. Help me to love you more.

Further reading: Acts chapter 2

5th March
RECEIVE AND WALK IN GOD'S TOTAL GIFT

Acts 8:14-17

Now when the apostles who were at Jerusalem heard that Samaria had received the word of God, they sent Peter and John to them, [15]who, when they had come down, prayed for them that they might receive the Holy Spirit. [16]For as yet He had fallen upon none of them. They had only been baptized in the name of the Lord Jesus. [17]Then they laid hands on them, and they received the Holy Spirit.

The above scripture shows that you can receive the good news of the salvation of Jesus Christ and still not walk in the power of the Holy Spirit. Philip had preached the gospel of Jesus Christ in Samaria. Many people had repented on hearing the message of the Cross. The people had received part of the gift of heaven, salvation from sin and the consequence of sin but they had not received the gift of the Holy Spirit. They could not receive the Holy Spirit because Philip probably did not speak about the Holy Spirit. Today there are many churches that do not highlight the gift of the Holy Spirit. You cannot receive a gift you do not know about. If you have received salvation through Jesus Christ then make your redemption complete by receiving the Holy Spirit. Ask God to baptize you with Holy Spirit today. If you ask in Faith, God will baptize you. He will give you a sure sign that will convince you that He has come. Don't settle for part. Many so called Christians walk in weakness and defeat because of ignorance. You are not one of those. Go for all that Heaven has to offer. I declare that you will walk in the power of the Holy Spirit to the praise and glory of our Father in heaven.

PRAYER

Baptize me afresh today Holy Spirit. I need you today in everything I do. I need you in my mind, my mouth, my strength and everything I do.

Further reading: Acts chapter 8

6th March
NOT BY YOUR STRENGTH BUT BY GOD'S SPIRIT

Zechariah 4:5-9

> [5]Then the angel who talked with me answered and said to me, "Do you not know what these are?" And I said, "No, my lord." [6]So he answered and said to me: "This is the word of the Lord to Zerubbabel: 'Not by might nor by power, but by My Spirit,' Says the Lord of hosts. [7]'Who are you, O great mountain? Before Zerubbabel you shall become a plain! And he shall bring forth the capstone With shouts of "Grace, grace to it!"'" [8]Moreover the word of the Lord came to me, saying: [9] "The hands of Zerubbabel Have laid the foundation of this temple; His hands shall also finish it. Then you will know That the Lord of hosts has sent Me to you.

Zerubbabel had the unenviable task of rebuilding God's temple in Jerusalem. Solomon built the original temple. Solomon was a king, with lots of slaves, friends, great authority and limitless resources yet it was a challenging task. Zerubbabel with a group of exiles and limited resources was therefore greatly challenged to undertake this task. Yet he had been chosen by God. God assures him that he was not chosen to do this in his own human strength but by the Spirit of God. God never leaves us alone. You may be facing an assignment today that seems overwhelming. Know that when God says His Spirit is with you, He is not just there as a spectator. He is there ready to guide you, give you wisdom and ability to accomplish it. What seems like a mountain will become a plain. I command every mountain in your life, family, health, business to become a plain, in the name of Jesus. I decree that what God has purposed for your life shall come to pass. I silence the mouth of the enemy. 'Be still and know that I am God', says the Lord. Have a blessed day with the companionship of the Holy Spirit.

PRAYER

Thank you Father that you have given me the assurance that you are with me. Holy Spirit, I go out confidently today knowing you are in me and by my side.

Further reading: Zechariah chapter 4

7th March
GOD WITH YOU EVERYWHERE

Psalm 139:7-14

> "Where can I go from Your Spirit? Or where can I flee from Your presence? If I ascend into heaven, You are there; If I make my bed in hell, behold, You are there. If I take the wings of the morning, And dwell in the uttermost parts of the sea, Even there Your hand shall lead me, And Your right hand shall hold me. If I say, "Surely the darkness shall fall on me," Even the night shall be light about me; Indeed, the darkness shall not hide from You, But the night shines as the day; The darkness and the light are both alike to You. For You formed my inward parts; You covered me in my mother's womb. I will praise You, for I am fearfully and wonderfully made; Marvelous are Your works, And that my soul knows very well."

The one thing that made King David outstanding among his contemporaries was that he knew about God and did not ignore Him. He acknowledged God and gave Him the honour due Him. God therefore honoured Him with wisdom, strength and a deeper revelation of Himself. Many of the psalms in the Bible were written by King David. In these psalms, we do not only find many prophecies about Jesus Christ, we also get insight into the activities of the Holy Spirit of God. The above psalm tells us something about the Holy Spirit. We cannot hide from Him. Wherever we go, He is there. I don't know your plan for today, but I want to assure you that whatever you plan to do today and wherever you go, the Holy Spirit will be there with you. He is with you even when you sleep. Even when you are having a horrible dream, fear not. He is there with you.

PRAYER

Thank you Holy Spirit for being there with me wherever I go. Forgive me for ignoring you. Please help me to forever be conscious of your presence. Thank you for loving me.

Further reading: Psalm 139

8th March
GOD WITH YOU FOREVER

John 14:15-18

> *"If you love Me, keep My commandments. ¹⁶And I will pray the Father, and He will give you another Helper, that He may abide with you forever— ¹⁷the Spirit of truth, whom the world cannot receive, because it neither sees Him nor knows Him; but you know Him, for He dwells with you and will be in you. ¹⁸I will not leave you orphans; I will come to you."*

The Holy Spirit has come to stay forever. This is the promise Jesus gives to his disciples. We know Jesus will not make a promise He would not keep. Where would the Holy Spirit live forever? With you. The moment you receive the Holy Spirit, know that He has come to stay forever. He is with you now. It is good to know that you have God in you now. If he is in you then he will correct everything that is wrong in you. This means that He will straighten out your thinking for you to think right. He will also heal your body. You don't expect the Holy Spirit to live in the same place as cancer. Whatever disease you have been diagnosed with, know that the Holy Spirit in you is a sign that you will be healed. Light must dispel darkness. There is a fight for your mind and body between light and darkness. The Holy Spirit represents light. Side with the Holy Spirit by believing in His power and let Him defeat those wrong things in you. The Holy Spirit brings 'ease'. Darkness brings 'dis-ease'. Fight for your ease today. You are better off confessing the Holy Spirit in you than the disease in you. The Holy Spirit is in you forever so expect a strong healthy life forever.

PRAYER

Thank you Holy Spirit for this assurance that you are with me forever. Your faithfulness assures me that no weapon against me will prosper. With your help, I will also walk in faithfulness to you.

Further reading: John chapter 14

9th March
YOUR BODY IS THE TEMPLE OF GOD

1 Corinthians 6:18-20

> *"Flee sexual immorality. Every sin that a man does is outside the body, but he who commits sexual immorality sins against his own body. [19]Or do you not know that your body is the temple of the Holy Spirit who is in you, whom you have from God, and you are not your own? [20]For you were bought at a price; therefore glorify God in your body and in your spirit, which are God's."*

One day when someone approached Jesus and said he would follow him wherever he went, Jesus answered with the statement that the Son of man has nowhere to lay His head (Matthew 8:20). The context indicates that Jesus Christ was not advertising His homelessness. With all the miracles He performed including taking money out of the mouth of a fish, Jesus could have afforded the most expensive homes and hotels. He was talking about the heart. God is too big to be contained in any building. The earth is His footstool and heaven is His throne. The only thing that is big enough to contain God is our heart. What a privilege. The whole world cannot contain God but He has made it possible for our hearts to contain Him. He calls our body His temple. He calls it his temple because He is God. The house of God is a temple. A temple is holy. If we agree that our body is His temple then we have to respect and honour our bodies as His temple. When Jesus physically walked the earth some 2000 years ago, He physically drove out those who defiled the Temple in Jerusalem by turning it into a market place (Matthew 21:12). Disrespecting our bodies hurts God. Let us enjoy the benefits of being the temple of God but also remember to be clean. We would do it to a special guest. The Holy Spirit is more than a special guest.

PRAYER

Holy Spirit, you are welcome in my heart as my very special guest. I will keep my body clean in honour of your presence. Help me.

Further reading: 1 Corinthians chapter 6

10th March
THE HOLY SPIRIT OUR HELPER

John 14:26-28

But the Helper, the Holy Spirit, whom the Father will send in My name, He will teach you all things, and bring to your remembrance all things that I said to you. ²⁷Peace I leave with you, My peace I give to you; not as the world gives do I give to you. Let not your heart be troubled, neither let it be afraid. ²⁸You have heard Me say to you, 'I am going away and coming back to you.' If you loved Me, you would rejoice because I said, 'I am going to the Father,' for My Father is greater than I.

"But when the Helper comes, whom I shall send to you from the Father, the Spirit of truth who proceeds from the Father, He will testify of Me. ²⁷And you also will bear witness, because you have been with Me from the beginning. John 15:26-27

There is no person on this earth who has never needed help to understand or undertake a task. This includes you and me. God is very aware of this. Our ignorance is the source of our woes. If we understood where we came from, the world around us and how to do the things we have to do, life would be much easier. God understands all these. He created all things and has authority over all things. We need help and God has sent us a helper in the person of the Holy Spirit. The Holy Spirit is God and knows all things and has all strength. We cannot have a better helper. Acknowledge Him today and make Him your first point of call in your time of need. He is lovingly asking you what He can do to help. Use Him. It is His pleasure to help. That is His job.

PRAYER

Father, I thank you that you have provided all answers to make my life whole. I receive you Holy Spirit as my helper in everything I do.

Further reading: John 16:16-33

11th March
FEAR NOT, GOD IS YOUR TEACHER

Luke 12:8-12

> *"Also I say to you, whoever confesses Me before men, him the Son of Man also will confess before the angels of God. ⁹But he who denies Me before men will be denied before the angels of God. ¹⁰"And anyone who speaks a word against the Son of Man, it will be forgiven him; but to him who blasphemes against the Holy Spirit, it will not be forgiven. ¹¹"Now when they bring you to the synagogues and magistrates and authorities, do not worry about how or what you should answer, or what you should say. ¹²For the Holy Spirit will teach you in that very hour what you ought to say."*

When God first created Adam, the bible says He used to spend time with Adam in fellowship. I can just imagine Adam's excitement as God taught and explained his surrounding to him. All who do not know must seek to know. Jesus came to this earth to reveal God to us. We now know the loving heart of God and His desire for everyone to become part of His family. If only the world knew, everyone would respond and enjoy the status of a prince. That is why those of us who know should make others know as well. It is not easy to change overnight from a pauper to a prince. That is why the Holy Spirit has been assigned as our teacher to teach us what to do and say in all circumstances. God knows we need help to understand His words and ways. The Holy Spirit is your teacher. He is a gentle teacher. Listen and obey His instruction today as you enjoy perfect knowledge. We all admire good teachers who have impacted our lives and given us good direction. The Holy Spirit beats them all. He is in you and with you today. Listen to Him. Don't allow the noise of the world to block His voice out.

PRAYER

Thank you, my dear teacher Holy Spirit. Please order my steps today in everything I do.

Further reading: Luke 12:1-40

12th March
THE HOLY SPIRIT SPEAKS FOR JESUS CHRIST

John 16:12-15

"I still have many things to say to you, but you cannot bear them now. ^{13}However, when He, the Spirit of truth, has come, He will guide you into all truth; for He will not speak on His own authority, but whatever He hears He will speak; and He will tell you things to come. ^{14}He will glorify Me, for He will take of what is Mine and declare it to you. ^{15}All things that the Father has are Mine. Therefore I said that He will take of Mine and declare it to you."

The Holy Spirit is our present help in our time of need. He lets us know exactly what Jesus would have done if He was physically with us today. Jesus Christ taught and did a lot when He physically walked the earth some 2000 years ago. Yet He could not have given direction and answers to everything that was going to happen through the ages. God has given us a solid foundation in the bible. We should not receive instructions that are not founded on the Bible. Yet our everyday encounters demand relevant peculiar answers which the ever present Holy Spirit is there to give to us. He will never depart from the foundation of the Bible. If you would allow Him, The Holy Spirit will give you relevant answers that will baffle you. For instance, Jesus could not have taught about computers in His time because man had not discovered computers. The Holy Spirit, however knows more about computers than anyone as computers had been in the mind of God from the beginning. There is nothing that He does not know. He is the Spirit of Christ who is the Lord of all things in Heaven and earth. He reveals the heart and knowledge of God. When the Holy Spirit speaks, Jesus has spoken. When Jesus speaks, the Father has spoken. Walk in their full authority today.

PRAYER
Thank you Jesus that you promised never to leave us and you have fulfilled your promise through the Holy Spirit. Thank you Holy Spirit, my faithful friend.

Further reading: **John chapter 14**

13th March
YOU CAN KNOW WHAT GOD KNOWS

1 Corinthians 2:9-12

> *But as it is written: "Eye has not seen, nor ear heard, Nor have entered into the heart of man the things which God has prepared for those who love Him." [10]But God has revealed them to us through His Spirit. For the Spirit searches all things, yes, the deep things of God. [11]For what man knows the things of a man except the spirit of the man which is in him? Even so no one knows the things of God except the Spirit of God. [12]Now we have received, not the spirit of the world, but the Spirit who is from God, that we might know the things that have been freely given to us by God.*

We are not only born again by the Spirit of God. The continued presence of the Holy Spirit with us means we have the complete wisdom of God available to us. Isaiah 11 verse 2 gives the Holy Spirit seven names: The Spirit of the Lord; the Spirit of wisdom; the Spirit of understanding; the Spirit of counsel; the Spirit of might; the Spirit of knowledge and the Spirit of the fear of the Lord. Please take time to meditate on each of these names. Names in scripture usually refer to what you do. When you open your heart to receive the Holy Spirit, you have given accommodation to the wisdom and understanding of God as well as all the other attributes mentioned above. There are times that we naturally walk in the wisdom of God as He lives in us. Other times, wisdom does not come easily. We don't seem to have ready answers. These are the times that we need to separate ourselves to seek His wisdom. God has an answer to every situation and His answers are good. It is up to us to seek those answers. The answer is close and in your heart. Find times to separate your heart to God today.

PRAYER

Thank you Father for your love for me and your desire for me to walk in truth. Help me to hear your voice always.

Further reading: 1 Corinthians chapter 2

14th March
PLEASE DON'T GRIEVE THE HOLY SPIRIT

Isaiah 63:10-14

But they rebelled and grieved His Holy Spirit; So He turned Himself against them as an enemy, And He fought against them. Then he remembered the days of old, Moses and his people, saying: "Where is He who brought them up out of the sea With the shepherd of His flock? Where is He who put His Holy Spirit within them, Who led them by the right hand of Moses, With His glorious arm, Dividing the water before them To make for Himself an everlasting name, Who led them through the deep, As a horse in the wilderness, That they might not stumble?" As a beast goes down into the valley, And the Spirit of the Lord causes him to rest, So You lead Your people, To make Yourself a glorious name.

The purpose of the Holy Spirit is to make God available and as close to us as the air we breath. God by the Holy Spirit brings to us everything He has to enable us enjoy life as little gods. Just as humans give birth to humans, dogs give birth to dogs, God also gives birth to gods. Statements like these frighten the fearful. They see them as arrogant statements trying to make oneself equal with God. The truth is the opposite. It is not man desiring to be like God but it is God who has offered His godliness to us by making us His children. Being like God is not just having the great power of God but also having His love and His sacrificial humility. It grieves God when this great offer of love to us is treated with disrespect. In the above scripture the people of Israel sing about the goodness of God. They also recall the time when they rejected the Holy Spirit of God and made God their enemy. Friend, you don't want God to be your enemy. Honour His Holy Spirit and enjoy His goodness.

PRAYER

Thank you Holy Spirit. Your love for me and the gifts you bring to me are beyond my understanding. Please help me never to grieve you.

Further reading: Isaiah chapter 63

15th March
HONOUR THE HOLY SPIRIT WITH YOUR WORDS

Matthew 12:31-33

> "Therefore I say to you, every sin and blasphemy will be forgiven men, but the blasphemy against the Spirit will not be forgiven men. ^{32}Anyone who speaks a word against the Son of Man, it will be forgiven him; but whoever speaks against the Holy Spirit, it will not be forgiven him, either in this age or in the age to come. ^{33}"Either make the tree good and its fruit good, or else make the tree bad and its fruit bad; for a tree is known by its fruit."

Blasphemy is speaking evil of God. When Jesus walked the earth, the people saw Him as a man. Jesus was telling the people that if they insulted Him as a man they could be forgiven. What would be unforgivable is if they spoke evil about God. God has made an awesome sacrifice to enable us enjoy His goodness which includes healing and provision. What prompted this comment was that Jesus by the power of the Holy Spirit had delivered a blind and dumb man from evil spirits. The Pharisees knew this was the work of the Holy Spirit but out of envy said it was the work of the devil. Jesus made it clear to them that a devil cannot cast out a devil. Only God's power can cast out devils. It is the practice in certain parts of the world like Africa and South America where you see idol worshippers and fetish priests pretend to cast out devils from witches. This is a deception. A house divided against itself cannot stand. There is nothing like good idolatry and bad idolatry. white or black witchcraft. They are both evil. The Holy Spirit is God. God is good. Keep His praise in your mouth under all circumstances. Don't blaspheme the Holy Spirit. Every good thing is of God. Today lift the Name of Jesus wherever you go.

PRAYER

Thank you Jesus for your death and resurrection that has made it possible for me to share in the power of Heaven. I will be forever grateful.

Further reading: Matthew 12:1-37

16th March
FATHER, SON, HOLY SPIRIT AND YOU

Matthew 28:16-20

Then the eleven disciples went away into Galilee, to the mountain which Jesus had appointed for them. ¹⁷When they saw Him, they worshiped Him; but some doubted. ¹⁸And Jesus came and spoke to them, saying, "All authority has been given to Me in heaven and on earth. ¹⁹Go therefore and make disciples of all the nations, baptizing them in the name of the Father and of the Son and of the Holy Spirit, ²⁰teaching them to observe all things that I have commanded you; and lo, I am with you always, even to the end of the age." Amen.

Jesus paid the price for our sins with His sacrificial death on the Cross and his resurrection. In the above scripture, He announces to the disciples that all authority both in heaven and earth are in His hands. By saying this, He meant that everything must submit to His name. He had the power to do and undo according to the good pleasure of His will. With this authority, Jesus orders His disciples to go and make disciples of all nations. In His name the disciples possessed the same authority as Jesus. We are all His disciples sent out in His name to make disciples of all nations. His complete authority resides in His name. He is not just our commander, He is our big brother. By His intervention and through the Holy Spirit we have all become children of God. We therefore walk in the total power of God. Do not think of yourself any less. When Jesus commands us to baptize the people in the name of the Father, Son and Holy Spirit, He was showing us that these three were equal and the same. By adding you and I to this, He has promoted us to a position of immense authority. See yourself as God sees you today. You are in full partnership with the Father, Son and Holy Spirit.

PRAYER

Thank you Father for counting me worthy of this partnership and making me part of your family. I will tell the world about you and bring others into our family.

Further reading: Matthew chapter 28

17th March
YOU HAVE AN ADVOCATE

John 16:5-7

"But now I go away to Him who sent Me, and none of you asks Me, 'Where are You going?' ⁶But because I have said these things to you, sorrow has filled your heart. ⁷Nevertheless I tell you the truth. It is to your advantage that I go away; for if I do not go away, the Helper will not come to you; but if I depart, I will send Him to you.

When Jesus walked the earth, he was great help to His disciples. If you are walking with a man of wisdom like Jesus Christ, that would be most comforting. He was a healer and miracle worker as well. When Jesus told them about His departure back to His father in heaven, the disciples were disappointed. Their helper, protector and provider was about to leave them. Jesus however assured them that it was to their advantage that He went away because he would send them the Holy Spirit who would be able to help them in ways He Jesus in the flesh could not. The Greek word translated 'Helper' in the scripture above could also mean intercessor, consoler, comforter and advocate. An advocate is one who speaks for you and defends you publicly. What Jesus could not do in His flesh was to be a comforter to everybody in the world at the same time. The Holy Spirit can do that. The flesh of Jesus was a limitation. Friend, the Holy Spirit can help everyone in everyway in the whole wide world at the same time and still have limitless reserve energy. This is He who is your friend and mine. You have an advocate. Many people think they would be better off if they could see Jesus in the flesh. Jesus says, His Spirit, the Holy Spirit will be more beneficial to you than you meeting Him in the flesh. Welcome your heavenly helper and friend today.

PRAYER
Thank you Holy Spirit. Help and speak for me every step of the way today.

Further reading: John chapter 16

18th March
CONVICTION IS GOOD, CONDEMNATION IS BAD

John 16:7-11

⁷Nevertheless I tell you the truth. It is to your advantage that I go away; for if I do not go away, the Helper will not come to you; but if I depart, I will send Him to you. ⁸And when He has come, He will convict the world of sin, and of righteousness, and of judgment: ⁹of sin, because they do not believe in Me; ¹⁰of righteousness, because I go to My Father and you see Me no more; ¹¹of judgment, because the ruler of this world is judged.

God does not condemn us. In other words, He does not pronounce a guilty verdict over us. Instead His Spirit convicts us. This means that the Holy Spirit makes us aware of our sins. His purpose for doing this is to enable us change course for the right direction. God does not want anyone to suffer the consequence of sin which is death. His desire is for us to come to the place of repentance. This means that He wants us to turn from our sins to Him so we will be forgiven, cleansed and enjoy His righteousness. One of the major assignments of the Holy Spirit is to convict the world of sin. Where the Holy Spirit is, sinful people must become aware of their sins. In other words, if you have the Holy Spirit in you, sinful people must be convicted around you. When Jesus told His disciples that the power of the Holy Spirit will make them witnesses, He also meant that their presence will bring repentance. Not only does the Holy Spirit convict of sin, He also convinces you of righteousness. It is only the Holy Spirit who can give you the assurance that you are standing right with God. We will talk more about this another day. Why don't you respond to the conviction of the Holy Spirit and turn around and be healed.

PRAYER
Thank you Father for giving us the Holy Spirit to convict us. I promise to respond to your conviction with repentance.

***Further reading:** Acts chapter 1*

19th March
YOU ARE AS RIGHTEOUS AS GOD IS

2 Corinthians 5:16-21

> *Therefore, from now on, we regard no one according to the flesh. Even though we have known Christ according to the flesh, yet now we know Him thus no longer. ¹⁷Therefore, if anyone is in Christ, he is a new creation; old things have passed away; behold, all things have become new. ¹⁸Now all things are of God, who has reconciled us to Himself through Jesus Christ, and has given us the ministry of reconciliation, ¹⁹that is, that God was in Christ reconciling the world to Himself, not imputing their trespasses to them, and has committed to us the word of reconciliation. ²⁰Now then, we are ambassadors for Christ, as though God were pleading through us: we implore you on Christ's behalf, be reconciled to God. ²¹For He made Him who knew no sin to be sin for us, that we might become the righteousness of God in Him.*

Our former life and its condemnation makes it difficult for many Christians to accept their new position of righteousness in Christ Jesus. The truth is that by the act of death and resurrection of Jesus Christ, a way into righteousness has been opened to everyone. The purpose of Jesus on the Cross was to pay the price for our sins which always brings condemnation. The Blood of Jesus is a powerful spiritual detergent that has cleansed us completely. If you receive this sacrifice for forgiveness today, you are like you never sinned. You are as clean as God. You live in Jesus Christ and can approach the Father at any time. The one person who makes this truth a reality is the Holy Spirit. John 16:8 says the Holy Spirit convicts us of sin, righteousness and judgment. This means that the Holy Spirit makes you realize the real state you are in as far as righteousness is concerned. He convinces you that you are righteous if you really are. Walk in righteous confidence today.

PRAYER
Thank you Jesus that through your sacrifice I am righteous. Thank you Holy Spirit for your conviction. I will walk in confidence of my righteousness today.

Further reading: 2 Corinthians chapter 5

20th March
YOU HAVE BEEN JUDGED AND FOUND CLEAN

John 5:24-30

"Most assuredly, I say to you, he who hears My word and believes in Him who sent Me has everlasting life, and shall not come into judgment, but has passed from death into life. ²⁵Most assuredly, I say to you, the hour is coming, and now is, when the dead will hear the voice of the Son of God; and those who hear will live. ²⁶For as the Father has life in Himself, so He has granted the Son to have life in Himself, ²⁷and has given Him authority to execute judgment also, because He is the Son of Man. ²⁸Do not marvel at this; for the hour is coming in which all who are in the graves will hear His voice ²⁹and come forth—those who have done good, to the resurrection of life, and those who have done evil, to the resurrection of condemnation. ³⁰I can of Myself do nothing. As I hear, I judge; and My judgment is righteous, because I do not seek My own will but the will of the Father who sent Me.

Jesus is the righteous judge. Satan is the accuser of the brethren. Jesus is the deliverer. Satan is the condemner. If judgment is in the hands of our brother Jesus then we are on good ground. Jesus is our brother because we have believed that He has paid the price for all our offences. As a righteous judge, Jesus could not simply declare judgment in our favour if the penalty for sin was not paid. The judge did not want to condemn anyone so he stepped down from His judgment seat and served the sentence of the world's sins by dying on the Cross. By doing so he shut the accuser's mouth forever. If the sentence has been served and we have received our freedom then every accusation is a deception to put us in self condemnation. The Holy Spirit convinces us of our new status but also makes us aware of judgment every time we go back to sin.

PRAYER

Thank you Holy Spirit for convicting me of sin, righteousness and judgment. I will respond to your prompting in everything I do.

Further reading: John chapter 5

21st March
YOU HAVE SKILL FOR YOUR ASSIGNMENT

Exodus 31:1-5

Then the Lord spoke to Moses, saying: ²"See, I have called by name Bezalel the son of Uri, the son of Hur, of the tribe of Judah. ³And I have filled him with the Spirit of God, in wisdom, in understanding, in knowledge, and in all manner of workmanship, ⁴to design artistic works, to work in gold, in silver, in bronze, ⁵in cutting jewels for setting, in carving wood, and to work in all manner of workmanship.

There is nothing that beats doing what God has called you to do. You enjoy what you do because you have the skill and you see positive fruit. God will not send you to do something without equipping you. Only cruel taskmasters will send you to do things without the necessary equipment. When God asked Moses to build Him a tabernacle, He gave him an elaborate plan of intricate designs. He even specified the exact materials to use which were not everyday material. He demanded this from a people on a journey in the middle of a desert. The tabernacle was built to full specifications because He had skilled men in place and had entrusted all the material needed to people who would make it available when needed. God will never ask you for something you don't have because he is the source of all things. In the Old Testament where the Holy Spirit had not been given to all who would receive Him, God called special people like Bezalel and gave them skill by the power of the Holy Spirit. Today, Jesus has made the power of the Holy Spirit available to anyone who will ask in faith. If you have believed and received the sacrifice of Jesus on the Cross then the baptism of the Holy Spirit is your right. When the Holy Spirit comes to make His home with you, you are fully equipped for any godly assignment.

PRAYER

Thank you Holy Spirit that it is not by my might nor by my ability but by you. Direct my steps and stay with me as I undertake my assignment.

Further reading: Exodus chapter 31

22nd March
THE HOLY SPIRIT GIVES EXTRAORDINARY STRENGTH

Judges 14:5-6

So Samson went down to Timnah with his father and mother, and came to the vineyards of Timnah. Now to his surprise, a young lion came roaring against him. ⁶And the Spirit of the Lord came mightily upon him, and he tore the lion apart as one would have torn apart a young goat, though he had nothing in his hand. But he did not tell his father or his mother what he had done.

When God needs a fighter, He gives fighting skills. When God needs a worshipper, He gives worshipping skills. When He needs a builder, He gives building skills. He needed a strong man to fight for Israel against the Philistines and He endowed Samson with so much strength that he killed a lion with his bare hands. Some one may just need strength to get out of bed or out of a wheel chair. In the name of Jesus, I command strength into you now to rise up. Whatever strength you need today, the Holy Spirit has more than enough for you to perform any task He has assigned to you. If God has sent you, He will provide. It is important that whatever assignment you intend to undertake you pass it by God and ensure that it is His will. If it is His will, be rest assured that what you need to accomplish it will be provided. He is God. I have met many Christians who are undertaking an assignment for God but become anxious along the way doubting God's provision or wisdom. This anxiety is a carry over from our past life when we did not have God. Now we have God and the Holy Spirit is our helper. Let us not be anxious about God's provision ever. If He has assigned you, He will equip.

PRAYER

Thank you faithful Father. Send me and I will go. Thank you Holy Spirit that you are always around to strengthen and equip me.

Further reading: Judges chapter 14

23rd March
PROMOTION BY THE WISDOM OF GOD

Genesis 41:37-41

> So the advice was good in the eyes of Pharaoh and in the eyes of all his servants. ^{38}And Pharaoh said to his servants, "Can we find such a one as this, a man in whom is the Spirit of God?" ^{39}Then Pharaoh said to Joseph, "Inasmuch as God has shown you all this, there is no one as discerning and wise as you. ^{40}You shall be over my house, and all my people shall be ruled according to your word; only in regard to the throne will I be greater than you." ^{41}And Pharaoh said to Joseph, "See, I have set you over all the land of Egypt."

The wisdom that the spirit of God gives can take you from being a prisoner to becoming the top man in the palace of the king. This is what happened to Joseph. He was a prisoner who was respected even in prison because of his relationship with almighty God. There came a time when the king of the powerful nation of Egypt was at his wits end. He needed some answers desperately that no one could provide except God. There are many questions that only God can answer. God had his man who was Joseph. Joseph was in prison but it didn't matter because only he could deliver this wisdom to the king. He received his promotion. With the Holy Spirit in you, you are open to God's wisdom. This wisdom from God is going to bring you promotion. There are questions that only God can answer and you are God's man. God set up the situation for Joseph so God's name will be glorified. When He is glorified, the messenger who brought God receives promotion. God is going to set up a situation for you to display his glory because you have the Holy Spirit. Your audience will not only marvel at the greatness of God but they will also be grateful to you for bringing God to them.

PRAYER
Thank you father for marking me for promotion with your Holy Spirit. There is no limit to the plans you have for me and I am grateful.

Further reading: Genesis chapter 41

24th March
OBEDIENCE TO GOD'S SPIRIT BRINGS GREATNESS

2 Samuel 23: 1-4

Now these are the last words of David. Thus says David the son of Jesse; Thus says the man raised up on high, The anointed of the God of Jacob, And the sweet psalmist of Israel: "The Spirit of the Lord spoke by me, And His word was on my tongue. The God of Israel said, The Rock of Israel spoke to me: 'He who rules over men must be just, Ruling in the fear of God. And he shall be like the light of the morning when the sun rises, A morning without clouds Like the tender grass springing out of the earth, By clear shining after rain.'

David, undoubtedly the greatest king Israel had, gives the secret to his greatness at the end of his life. His secret was hearing the voice of God's Spirit and being obedient to it. The Bible is filled with accounts of people who did exploits in obedience to the Spirit of God. The books in the bible were written by the direction of the Holy Spirit for teaching, rebuking, correcting and training in righteousness. That is why the bible is the most powerful book in the world. The words in it are God breathed. He who inspired these writings lives in us now. He can give us all the wisdom we need for greatness if we are ready to listen and obey Him. To listen, you have to recognize his continuous presence in you and with you. You also have to separate yourself to Him to hear from Him. In a very noisy world, it is important that we are able to separate our spirits in order to hear the Holy Spirit. Paul prays for the Ephesian church in Ephesians 1:18 as I pray for you today: "That the eye of your understanding be enlightened to know the hope and glorious inheritance to which He has called the saints". Walk in obedience.

PRAYER

Holy Spirit, order my steps and I will obey. I acknowledge your presence with me all the time. Help me never to be distracted.

Further reading: 2 Samuel 23: 1-7

25th March
THE HOLY SPIRIT GIVES POWER TO PROPHESY

Micah 3: 7-8

So the seers shall be ashamed, And the diviners abashed; Indeed they shall all cover their lips; For there is no answer from God." But truly I am full of power by the Spirit of the Lord, And of justice and might, To declare to Jacob his transgression And to Israel his sin.

To prophesy is to speak for God. To speak for God is an honourable office. If the Holy Spirit lives in you and you listen to Him then you can be a speaker for God. One of the reasons why God has given us His Spirit to live in us is so that we could speak for Him. This is His world that through ignorance is being manipulated by deceitful beings. What does a good and loving God do in the circumstance? He creates the opportunity for those who are willing to become part of His family. He gives power through the baptism of the Holy Spirit for His family to reveal the truth about Him to an ignorant world. Micah, in the above scripture is claiming the credentials to speak God's heart to the people of Israel. What are His credentials? He is full of power by the Spirit of God. In the Old Testament, God anointed special individuals for special assignment. In the new covenant. He has poured out His Spirit on all flesh. If you will receive Him, you can be filled with the Holy Spirit like Micah and have the credentials to speak for God. God wants to use you to correct many wrong things around you. Be determined to hear the voice of the Spirit and God will use you to correct many wrongs. You are an agent of God to bring deliverance to a world in captivity and oppression. There are many deceivers in the world today. If you don't allow the Holy Spirit to release the truth through you then deception will lead people into destruction and hell.

PRAYER

Father, use me to speak for you. Anoint my lips. I will not be afraid of their faces but tell the world what you have sent me to tell them.

Further reading: Micah chapter 3

26th March
YOU ARE EMPOWERED FOR MINISTRY

Matthew 3: 13-17

Then Jesus came from Galilee to John at the Jordan to be baptized by him. ¹⁴And John tried to prevent Him, saying, "I need to be baptized by You, and are You coming to me?" ¹⁵But Jesus answered and said to him, "Permit it to be so now, for thus it is fitting for us to fulfill all righteousness." Then he allowed Him. ¹⁶When He had been baptized, Jesus came up immediately from the water; and behold, the heavens were opened to Him, and He saw the Spirit of God descending like a dove and alighting upon Him. ¹⁷And suddenly a voice came from heaven, saying, "This is My beloved Son, in whom I am well pleased."

Jesus' public ministry began at age 30. We qualify it as 'public' because as his conception was by the Holy Spirit, every action of His from the day of His birth could be considered ministry. The word ministry simply means service. At age 30 when His public ministry begins, Jesus does three things: 1. He turns towards the man of God at the time, John. This was the closest Jesus could come to repentance. Remember He could not repent because He never sinned. 2. He was baptized by John and 3. The Holy Spirit descended on Him for ministry. These were the 3 steps Peter gave to the people in Acts 3:38 when they asked him what to do after the preaching of the gospel. Everyone needs to go through these steps. Believe in your heart and confess with your mouth the Lord Jesus Christ which represents your repentance; be baptized in water; and be baptized in the Holy Spirit. The Holy Spirit is for ministry. If you are baptized in the Holy Spirit then you qualify as a minister. If ministry is service then you need something to serve. The Holy Spirit comes with enough goodies to serve the people with: the gospel, healing, deliverance and restoration.

PRAYER
Thank you Holy Spirit for ordaining me to serve in your name. You have equipped me with something to serve with. Use me. I am available.

Further reading: Matthew chapter 3

27th March
YOU HAVE THE POWER TO REPRESENT JESUS CHRIST

Acts 1:4-8

> ^{4}And being assembled together with them, He commanded them not to depart from Jerusalem, but to wait for the Promise of the Father, "which," He said, "you have heard from Me; ^{5}for John truly baptized with water, but you shall be baptized with the Holy Spirit not many days from now." ^{6}Therefore, when they had come together, they asked Him, saying, "Lord, will You at this time restore the kingdom to Israel?" ^{7}And He said to them, "It is not for you to know times or seasons which the Father has put in His own authority. ^{8}But you shall receive power when the Holy Spirit has come upon you; and you shall be witnesses to Me in Jerusalem, and in all Judea and Samaria, and to the end of the earth."

Jesus had promised the disciples that they were going to do greater works than they had seen Him do in their midst. How were they going to do this? They were going to do this by the same power by which He had worked the miracles, the Holy Spirit. Jesus mission was to reveal the Father to the world and pay the price for the world to be reconciled to the Father. Our work is to reveal Jesus to the world and pay the price of bringing the world into Jesus Christ. The price Jesus paid was the penalty of death on the cross for our sins. The price we pay is to submit our will to the will of Jesus Christ and face the persecution we are bound to face in the preaching of the gospel. Both Jesus, while He walked in the flesh, and us, the church, need the Holy Spirit. When we have the Holy Spirit we have God. It therefore becomes easy for us to represent Him. Our mere presence becomes a witness. You have the power. Use it.

PRAYER

Thank you Jesus for the baptism of the Holy Spirit that has made us your natural representatives. It is an honour to represent you.

Further reading: Acts chapter 1

28th March
WE MUST DIE TO LIVE

John 12:23-26

But Jesus answered them, saying, "The hour has come that the Son of Man should be glorified. ²⁴Most assuredly, I say to you, unless a grain of wheat falls into the ground and dies, it remains alone; but if it dies, it produces much grain. ²⁵He who loves his life will lose it, and he who hates his life in this world will keep it for eternal life. ²⁶If anyone serves Me, let him follow Me; and where I am, there My servant will be also. If anyone serves Me, him My Father will honour.

Dying to live sounds strange to a world obsessed with life. People would rather live to live but God in His wisdom has created the law of seedtime and harvest. One grain falls in the ground, dies and by its death produces much harvest. Jesus Christ as an only son has produced many sons for God through His death. Such dying ends up in resurrection with great authority. If those who killed Jesus knew this principle of God, they would not have plotted and killed Jesus. Jesus came for the purpose of dying to produce many sons. The enemies of Jesus played perfectly into God's plan. In our walk with God we could face persecutors who scheme to bring us down. Psalm 2 says God sits in Heaven and laughs at them. They think they are pushing you to your grave but unknowingly, they are pushing you to your resurrection. The scripture above was the response Jesus gave when His disciples informed Him that the Greeks also wanted to see Him. He knew that in His flesh, He could not reach the whole world but by His death, He could produce many brethren who could reach the world. You and I are products of this seed. We are now born again by the Spirit of God. Let us do it as Jesus did it.

PRAYER
Dear Jesus, thank you for the seed you sowed on Calvary that has made a hopeless person like me have hope. I can call Almighty God my father. Help me Holy Spirit to walk in this authority.

Further reading: John 12

29th March
YOU HAVE POWER TO ENDURE

Psalm 23: 1-4

The Lord is my shepherd; I shall not want. He makes me to lie down in green pastures; He leads me beside the still waters. He restores my soul; He leads me in the paths of righteousness For His name's sake. Yea, though I walk through the valley of the shadow of death, I will fear no evil; For You are with me; Your rod and Your staff, they comfort me.

Jesus is the good shepherd. The good shepherd takes care of his sheep. The sheep are very important to the shepherd so he protects them. The shepherd is responsible for the survival and growth of the sheep. The sheep have no care in the world as long as they have a good shepherd. Their enemies have to contend with the shepherd not them. That is why David says he will not be afraid though he walks in the shadow death. He is not afraid because he knows God, his shepherd is with him and comforts him. Jesus has given us the Holy Spirit to be our guide just as shepherds guide their sheep. The Holy Spirit is not just our guide and protector but He has also come to live in us. He gives us strength to endure. Before the Holy Spirit came to live inside of me, I used to be afraid of little things. Since He came, fear has been replaced with faith. The things that used to scare me, scare me no more. He strengthens me with endurance. With him in you, be assured that nothing can overcome you. As He reveals the Lordship and authority of Jesus to us, we receive the assurance in our spirits that Jesus Christ is Lord of all and the race is already won. This gives us the energy to press on to the finish enduring the challenges. I assure you today that you will not fail. The enemy has been taken care of and will not prevail.

PRAYER

Thank you Holy Spirit that your presence with me gives me strength to endure. I promise to be bold and patient in all I do.

Further reading: Psalm 23

30th March
PRESS ON TO VICTORY

Hebrews 12:1-2

> *Therefore we also, since we are surrounded by so great a cloud of witnesses, let us lay aside every weight, and the sin which so easily ensnares us, and let us run with endurance the race that is set before us, ²looking unto Jesus, the author and finisher of our faith, who for the joy that was set before Him endured the cross, despising the shame, and has sat down at the right hand of the throne of God.*

Jesus' motivation for endurance was the joy that was set ahead of Him. The scripture above is encouraging us to be like Jesus who did not look at the prevailing circumstance but was encouraged by what lay ahead. What lies ahead for us is a more glorious life and eternity with God. 2 Corinthians 4:17 encourages that our present challenges are nothing compared to the glory that is being worked in us. Paul says "when I am weak then I am strong". Let us not ignore the presence of the Holy Spirit with us who will not allow us to be tempted beyond our ability to bear it. He guides and protects. Jesus as Lord of all is watching over us to ensure that we do not fall. You are safe to press on. Press through the resistance to your destiny. Challenges could bring discouragement and a desire to give up. Don't give up. When you give up on a profitable venture, you lose out. Your enemy rejoices. Let us persevere in faith and not allow the death of Jesus on the Cross to be in vain. By His death and resurrection, He conquered death and made a prisoner of the things that get us into bondage. We are therefore free. Though we are completely free, our minds have to receive this reality. As we press through in the face of challenges, the reality of our new freedom comes out. Our faith increases and enables us to walk in greater authority.

PRAYER

Thank you Jesus for the gift of the Holy Spirit. Holy Spirit, strengthen me to endure and press on to my destiny.

Further reading: Hebrews chapter 12

31st March
STRENGTHEN YOUR INNER MAN

2 Corinthians 4:15-18

> *For all things are for your sakes, that grace, having spread through the many, may cause thanksgiving to abound to the glory of God. [16]Therefore we do not lose heart. Even though our outward man is perishing, yet the inward man is being renewed day by day. [17]For our light affliction, which is but for a moment, is working for us a far more exceeding and eternal weight of glory, [18]while we do not look at the things which are seen, but at the things which are not seen. For the things which are seen are temporary, but the things which are not seen are eternal.*

The Bible tells us that whatever we see comes from the unseen. As good as science is, it can only work with physical things. There is therefore a limit to science. Although scientists have attempted to trace all things to one material thing, they get stuck about how this one material thing came about. They can only speculate beyond the first point. God, the creator of all things has no beginning and no end. That gives us a certainty on creation that no scientist can have. How can we be so certain about God being true? We know God is true because the Holy Spirit who is God lives in us and has revealed this truth to us. I once did not believe until God revealed Himself to me through someone speaking to me about the good news of Jesus Christ. That is why we should not condemn those who are ignorant but rather give them the good news of the Cross of Jesus Christ. When I received the salvation of Jesus Christ, the Holy Spirit opened my eyes to the reality of spiritual life, the inner man. When your spiritual life is strong, you are strong. Develop your inner man by building up your spiritual life.

PRAYER
Dear father thank you for inviting me to partake in your kind of life. Thank you Jesus for making this possible by your death on the Cross. Holy Spirit help me strengthen my inner man in order to walk in newness of life.

Further reading: 2 Corinthians chapter 4

April

1st April
BE LED BY THE SPIRIT OF GOD

Numbers 9:17-23

> *Whenever the cloud was taken up from above the tabernacle, after that the children of Israel would journey; and in the place where the cloud settled, there the children of Israel would pitch their tents. ¹⁸At the command of the Lord the children of Israel would journey, and at the command of the Lord they would camp; as long as the cloud stayed above the tabernacle they remained encamped. ¹⁹Even when the cloud continued long, many days above the tabernacle, the children of Israel kept the charge of the Lord and did not journey. ²⁰So it was, when the cloud was above the tabernacle a few days: according to the command of the Lord they would remain encamped, and according to the command of the Lord they would journey. ²¹So it was, when the cloud remained only from evening until morning: when the cloud was taken up in the morning, then they would journey; whether by day or by night, whenever the cloud was taken up, they would journey. ²²Whether it was two days, a month, or a year that the cloud remained above the tabernacle, the children of Israel would remain encamped and not journey; but when it was taken up, they would journey. ²³At the command of the Lord they remained encamped, and at the command of the Lord they journeyed; they kept the charge of the Lord, at the command of the Lord by the hand of Moses.*

The people of Israel were wise to allow the Spirit of God to lead them. They would not move till the cloud moved. Where God is taking you, you have never been. It makes sense to wait for his direction. God's ways and thoughts are far better than man's thoughts. The purpose for God giving us His Holy Spirit is to lead us unto all truth. Let us not ignore the Holy Spirit. What is the purpose of doing your own thing when the master of all knowledge and wisdom is right there with you? Consult Him.

PRAYER

Thank you Holy Spirit for being with me. I don't want to go anywhere without you.

Further reading: Numbers chapter 9

2nd April
THE CHURCH WAS BORN BY THE HOLY SPIRIT

Acts 2:1-3

> When the Day of Pentecost had fully come, they were all with one accord in one place. ²And suddenly there came a sound from heaven, as of a rushing mighty wind, and it filled the whole house where they were sitting. ³Then there appeared to them divided tongues, as of fire, and one sat upon each of them. ⁴And they were all filled with the Holy Spirit and began to speak with other tongues, as the Spirit gave them utterance.

The church of Jesus Christ must be nothing less than the Holy Spirit in action. In reality, no gathering of the saints should pass without the power of God being displayed. Where two or three are gathered together in the name of Jesus, the Holy Spirit is there. Where the Holy Spirit is there is a display of God's power. Every time you attend church service or a prayer meeting, expect the supernatural because a gathering of the saints is a platform for the display of God's power. The disciples of Jesus were just expectant followers till the Holy Spirit came on the day of Pentecost. From that day, the Church was born with power from on high. A mild bunch of followers became bold preachers of the gospel of Jesus Christ. From that day, the Holy Spirit came to stay. His home was our hearts. When two or more spirit filled believers come together there must be a strong show of the presence of the Holy Spirit. When we fail to recognize the personality of the Holy Spirit, we will reduce our relationship with Him to lifeless rituals. When we do this, our church services could be boring and we will not experience the power of God to heal and deliver. From today don't have another dry church service. Invite the Holy Spirit and expect a mighty move of God.

PRAYER
Lord Jesus, you build your church and the gates of hell shall not prevail against it. I pray that in my own church and other churches, your power will manifest strongly every time there is a meeting of the saints.

Further reading: Acts chapter 2

3rd April
GOD'S WORD IN YOUR MOUTH IS POWERFUL

Mark 11:22-26

> So Jesus answered and said to them, "Have faith in God. ^{23}For assuredly, I say to you, whoever says to this mountain, 'Be removed and be cast into the sea,' and does not doubt in his heart, but believes that those things he says will be done, he will have whatever he says. ^{24}Therefore I say to you, whatever things you ask when you pray, believe that you receive them, and you will have them. ^{25}"And whenever you stand praying, if you have anything against anyone, forgive him, that your Father in heaven may also forgive you your trespasses. ^{26}But if you do not forgive, neither will your Father in heaven forgive your trespasses."

If you believe in your heart, you can command a mountain to move and it will. What do you believe in your heart? Do you believe in the Lordship of Jesus Christ and His ability to do all things? The only way you can have this sort of faith is if the word of God dwells solidly in your heart. How does the word of God dwell solidly in your heart? When the Holy Spirit establishes it there. It is the spirit of the word that gives life. Without the Holy Spirit, the words of the Bible are mere words. With the Holy Spirit, these same words give life and can even raise the dead. Paul says the letter kills but the spirit gives life (2 Corinthians 3:6). If the Spirit of God dwells in you, He confirms the word of God you hear. This establishes faith in you. When you have faith, you are like a loaded gun. You are established in righteousness. When you speak with faith, it is like pressing the trigger. The bullet of God's word goes forth to perform what you have sent it to do. God's word in your mouth is powerful if you will solidify it with faith in your heart.

PRAYER

I command every mountain that stands in the way of God's peace in my life to be removed today. I send the word of God to go forth and heal all my family in the Name of Jesus.

Further reading: Mark chapter 11

4th April
THE WORD OF GOD CAN RAISE THE DEAD

John 5:24-29

> "Most assuredly, I say to you, he who hears My word and believes in Him who sent Me has everlasting life, and shall not come into judgment, but has passed from death into life. ²⁵Most assuredly, I say to you, the hour is coming, and now is, when the dead will hear the voice of the Son of God; and those who hear will live. ²⁶For as the Father has life in Himself, so He has granted the Son to have life in Himself, ²⁷and has given Him authority to execute judgment also, because He is the Son of Man. ²⁸Do not marvel at this; for the hour is coming in which all who are in the graves will hear His voice ²⁹and come forth—those who have done good, to the resurrection of life, and those who have done evil, to the resurrection of condemnation.

When God created the Heavens and the earth, He spoke things into being. When He spoke, there was power in His word to create what He had spoken. The power in His word was the Holy Spirit. Jesus in the above scripture says the dead will hear His voice and be resurrected. It is the Holy Spirit who does the work even as Jesus speaks. We know the Holy Spirit raises the dead. Romans 8:11 tells us that it was the Holy Spirit who raised Jesus from the dead and continues to remind us that this same Holy Spirit dwells in us. If the Holy Spirit who raised Jesus from the dead dwells in you then He is definitely taking care of every part of your body that is dead. This is an assurance that sickness has no place in your body. If the Holy Spirit dwells in you, He is already working on your sickness. Why don't you quicken this process by using the trigger of your mouth. Command that part of your body that is sick to obey the word of God.

PRAYER

In the Name of Jesus I command every infirmity and deadness in me to be restored and made whole.

Further reading: **John chapter 5**

5th April
YOU ARE FREE FROM THE LAW OF SIN AND DEATH

Romans 8:1-4

> There is therefore now no condemnation to those who are in Christ Jesus, who do not walk according to the flesh, but according to the Spirit. ²For the law of the Spirit of life in Christ Jesus has made me free from the law of sin and death. ³For what the law could not do in that it was weak through the flesh, God did by sending His own Son in the likeness of sinful flesh, on account of sin: He condemned sin in the flesh, ⁴that the righteous requirement of the law might be fulfilled in us who do not walk according to the flesh but according to the Spirit.

God's law was good. Everything that comes from God is good. Yet every time the people of Israel saw the commandments of God, they saw sin and death. This was because they could not obey those laws. If only they could obey those laws, it would be their passports to a rewarding partnership with God. Yet what was good became a rope of condemnation around their necks. Jesus came on the scene, destroyed the power of sin and death and opened the way for life in Him. If we have received Him and walk in His righteousness, His total obedience to God has been imputed to us. This means that we did not do the obedience. Jesus did the obedience on our behalf. We can therefore enjoy the results. We are free from the law of sin and death because Jesus has borne that responsibility. Even at the times when we disobey, we can turn around in repentance and ask for forgiveness. We are now sons of God and the Spirit of God in us confirms this. Sin and death have no power over us. Don't allow sin and death to bully you any longer. You are free so live like a free man.

PRAYER

Thank you Jesus for my redemption. I am free from the law of sin and death. I am now part of God's family. I am a free person living in God's household.

Further reading: Romans 7:9 – 8:4

6th April
YOU ARE OF THE SPIRIT

Romans 8:5-11

For those who live according to the flesh set their minds on the things of the flesh, but those who live according to the Spirit, the things of the Spirit. ⁶For to be carnally minded is death, but to be spiritually minded is life and peace. ⁷Because the carnal mind is enmity against God; for it is not subject to the law of God, nor indeed can be. ⁸So then, those who are in the flesh cannot please God.

⁹But you are not in the flesh but in the Spirit, if indeed the Spirit of God dwells in you. Now if anyone does not have the Spirit of Christ, he is not His. ¹⁰And if Christ is in you, the body is dead because of sin, but the Spirit is life because of righteousness. ¹¹But if the Spirit of Him who raised Jesus from the dead dwells in you, He who raised Christ from the dead will also give life to your mortal bodies through His Spirit who dwells in you.

There are two ways to live your life. You can live in the flesh or in the Spirit. Those who do not have the Spirit of God have no choice but to live in the flesh. For those of us who have believed and received the price paid by Jesus Christ, we have a choice. We can choose to live in the flesh or the Spirit. Those who live in the flesh mind the things of the flesh. The things of the flesh are the things that the flesh craves like all lusts, revelry, sexual immorality, entertainment and the like. Those who are of the Spirit mind the things of the Spirit like fellowship with God through the Holy Spirit. The scripture warns that running after the cravings of the flesh leads to death whilst seeking more of God will give you life. The flesh compels us so we must resist it. You are of the Spirit so mind the things of the Spirit.

PRAYER
Thank you father. I am of the Spirit and will not allow my flesh to push me. I seek after the things of the Spirit.

Further reading: Romans 8:5-39

7th April
CHECK YOUR FRUIT

Galatians 5:16-23

I say then: Walk in the Spirit, and you shall not fulfill the lust of the flesh. ¹⁷For the flesh lusts against the Spirit, and the Spirit against the flesh; and these are contrary to one another, so that you do not do the things that you wish. ¹⁸But if you are led by the Spirit, you are not under the law. ¹⁹Now the works of the flesh are evident, which are: adultery, fornication, uncleanness, lewdness, ²⁰idolatry, sorcery, hatred, contentions, jealousies, outbursts of wrath, selfish ambitions, dissensions, heresies, ²¹envy, murders, drunkenness, revelries, and the like; of which I tell you beforehand, just as I also told you in time past, that those who practice such things will not inherit the kingdom of God. ²²But the fruit of the Spirit is love, joy, peace, longsuffering, kindness, goodness, faithfulness, ²³gentleness, self-control. Against such there is no law.

What you have in you is what will come out. Without the Holy Spirit, your flesh would drive you to some of the fleshly works that are described above. These works always lead to death. This means that if you are led to pursue idolatry, hatred, sexual immorality or any of the fleshly works listed above, you are opening yourself to physical and emotional diseases which will steal life from you. If you, on the other hand, allow the Holy Spirit to be the centre of your life, you will produce the acceptable spiritual fruits described above. You will be of great value to people wherever you are. The world is waiting for loving, peaceful, joyful and gentle people. The fruits of the Spirit described above make up the character of the Holy Spirit so if He is in you, kindness, gentleness, self control and the others will be your nature. You can check who rules your life by the fruit you produce. If you see the works of the flesh, then it is time to turn around and build your inner man through fellowship with the Holy Spirit by spending time in prayer and study of the word.

PRAYER

Holy Spirit you are the centre of my life. I desire that the people around may enjoy your fruits in me.

Further reading: Galatians 5

8th April
WALK IN LOVE

Ephesians 5:1-10

Therefore be imitators of God as dear children. ²And walk in love, as Christ also has loved us and given Himself for us, an offering and a sacrifice to God for a sweet-smelling aroma. ³But fornication and all uncleanness or covetousness, let it not even be named among you, as is fitting for saints; ⁴neither filthiness, nor foolish talking, nor coarse jesting, which are not fitting, but rather giving of thanks. ⁵For this you know, that no fornicator, unclean person, nor covetous man, who is an idolater, has any inheritance in the kingdom of Christ and God. ⁶Let no one deceive you with empty words, for because of these things the wrath of God comes upon the sons of disobedience. ⁷Therefore do not be partakers with them. ⁸For you were once darkness, but now you are light in the Lord. Walk as children of light ⁹(for the fruit of the Spirit is in all goodness, righteousness, and truth), ¹⁰finding out what is acceptable to the Lord.

'Walking in love' is the one instruction you would receive from God if He had to summarize all His commandments into one phrase. When His disciples asked Him what was the greatest commandment, Jesus simply told them to love God with all they have and to love other people as they loved themselves. He explains that all the commandments hinge on this. The nature of God is love. When the Holy Spirit comes to live in us, love has come to live in us. Love therefore comes out of us. The Holy Spirit is too big to stay dormant in us. He overflows us like a cup that runs over. Let us not put covering on the love overflow from the Holy Spirit with our unbelief and negative attitudes. Let us be determined to walk in love. Scripture tells us that he who walks in love knows God. Check your love walk today and make the necessary adjustments. Forgive and show mercy. That is the nature of God.

PRAYER

Dear Holy Spirit, because of your presence in me, I will walk in love in everything I do. May people around me benefit from your goodness through me.

Further reading: Ephesians chapter 5

9th April
REJOICE ALWAYS

1 Thessalonians 5:16-24

Rejoice always, [17]pray without ceasing, [18]in everything give thanks; for this is the will of God in Christ Jesus for you. [19]Do not quench the Spirit. [20]Do not despise prophecies. [21]Test all things; hold fast what is good. [22]Abstain from every form of evil. [23]Now may the God of peace Himself sanctify you completely; and may your whole spirit, soul, and body be preserved blameless at the coming of our Lord Jesus Christ. [24]He who calls you is faithful, who also will do it.

Joy is one of the fruits of the Spirit. This shows that God is a joyful person and therefore desires for us to manifest the fruit of joy. Scripture tells us that the joy of the Lord is our strength. If we desire to walk in strength always then we must rejoice always. The more of the Holy Spirit we have, the greater the joy that flows out of us. God does not come in degrees so what I mean by more of the Holy Spirit is allowing Him to reign in our lives. God lives in us and we must give Him the attention. We could be so distracted with other things that the Holy Spirit in us could be ignored. If we do this, we will not benefit from His mighty power. If we ignore the Holy Spirit, our flesh dictates to us and steals our joy. When our joy is stolen, we are rendered weak. A person with the Holy Spirit is most powerful. Do not allow any distractions to steal this precious gift of God. Acknowledge the presence of the Holy Spirit wherever you go and let the joy of the Lord strengthen you through every situation. I pray that great shall be your peace and laughter. Joy is deeper than happiness although happiness is part of Joy. Joy is deep and comes from the Holy Spirit. The happiness that does not come from the Holy Spirit is dependent on circumstances and changes as circumstances change. Stay with the joy of the Lord. He is faithful and everlasting.

PRAYER

Thank you Holy Spirit for everlasting joy.

Further reading: 1 Thessalonians chapter 5

10th April
PATIENCE IS A VIRTUE

James 1:2-8

> ²*My brethren, count it all joy when you fall into various trials,* ³*knowing that the testing of your faith produces patience.* ⁴*But let patience have its perfect work, that you may be perfect and complete, lacking nothing.* ⁵*If any of you lacks wisdom, let him ask of God, who gives to all liberally and without reproach, and it will be given to him.* ⁶*But let him ask in faith, with no doubting, for he who doubts is like a wave of the sea driven and tossed by the wind.* ⁷*For let not that man suppose that he will receive anything from the Lord;* ⁸*he is a double-minded man, unstable in all his ways.*

The scripture above tells us that God has a purpose in the challenges and delays we face. He is working out patience in us which will turn out for our good. Patience is one of the fruits of the spirit. This shows that God is patient. If you are a witness of God, then you have to manifest patience. Jesus says in Acts 1:8 that the Holy Spirit brings us power to be His witnesses. This means that with the Holy Spirit in us, when people see us, it would be like they have seen Jesus. Jesus also makes it clear that when you see Him, you have seen God. Let us therefore walk in patience to manifest the patience of God. Patience is a product of love. Perfect patience makes you perfect and complete. In your time of waiting, God has promised that He will give you wisdom if you ask for it. Every time I have gone to God to find out the reason for a delay, He has revealed to me. This wisdom from God always brings greater strength to endure. Ask Him for wisdom and He will keep nothing away from you. He will positively protect and encouraged you towards the destiny of total peace he has planned for you.

PRAYER

Thank you Holy Spirit for this gift of patience you have deposited in my life. I am grateful that you are with me as I move towards the destiny you have planned for me.

Further reading: James chapter 1

11th April
BE GENTLE. GOD IS GENTLE.

Matthew 11:25-30

> At that time Jesus answered and said, "I thank You, Father, Lord of heaven and earth, that You have hidden these things from the wise and prudent and have revealed them to babes. [26]Even so, Father, for so it seemed good in Your sight. [27]All things have been delivered to Me by My Father, and no one knows the Son except the Father. Nor does anyone know the Father except the Son, and the one to whom the Son wills to reveal Him. [28]Come to Me, all you who labor and are heavy laden, and I will give you rest. [29]Take My yoke upon you and learn from Me, for I am gentle and lowly in heart, and you will find rest for your souls. [30]For My yoke is easy and My burden is light."

How do people see you? Are you a gentle man or woman? If you are gentle then you are showing a character trait of God. Jesus says we should learn from His gentle and humble ways. Proverbs 24:15 says "By patience and self control a ruler is persuaded and a gentle tongue breaks a bone". Gentleness is powerful. Every character trait of God is very powerful. In a world where anger and greed make us bark at each other, a gentle spirit is a welcome presence. Jesus warns us that with His gentle Spirit, we go as lambs among wolves but He also encourages us that we should not be afraid because He is master of the world. What a suffering person needs is a gentle word. It is Satan who accuses, condemns and is angry. Father God is gentle, calling His children back home. You are a new creation created in Christ Jesus to do good works. You are gentle by nature. Do not allow any other strange behaviour to use your body as a platform to launch attacks on others. You are of the spirit as the Holy Spirit dwells in you.

PRAYER

Thank you Father for giving your gentle Spirit freely to me. My desire is that when people see me, they will see you. Help me Holy Spirit.

Further reading: Matthew chapter 11

12th April
DON'T BE RASH IN YOUR DECISIONS

2 Peter 1:2-8

> *Grace and peace be multiplied to you in the knowledge of God and of Jesus our Lord, ³as His divine power has given to us all things that pertain to life and godliness, through the knowledge of Him who called us by glory and virtue, ⁴by which have been given to us exceedingly great and precious promises, that through these you may be partakers of the divine nature, having escaped the corruption that is in the world through lust. ⁵But also for this very reason, giving all diligence, add to your faith virtue, to virtue knowledge, ⁶to knowledge self-control, to self-control perseverance, to perseverance godliness, ⁷to godliness brotherly kindness, and to brotherly kindness love. ⁸For if these things are yours and abound, you will be neither barren nor unfruitful in the knowledge of our Lord Jesus Christ.*

I have seen many Christians seriously embarrassed because of the lack of self-control. One of the strategies of Satan is to wind us up to the point of making you take a rash decision or make an uncontrolled statement. A Christian walking in faith and at rest in his soul is the devil's nightmare. Any time you give up the virtue of self-control, you are bound to make a wrong decision. I always caution people that if you are pushed, don't do it. Anytime you are pushed to do something, you lose control. The Spirit of God is gentle and will not push you. You make the right decisions when you are sober. Do not be in a rush till you know the mind of Christ which only the Holy Spirit can gently reveal to you. If the Holy Spirit is in you then you have the ability to control your emotions and words. Don't allow Satan to push you. Satan's strategy is to bring you to a place where he can condemn you. You are of the household of God so enter His rest and control your words and action.

PRAYER

I thank you father that I am sober and in control of my words and actions. I will not be driven by any one to say the wrong words or take the wrong actions.

Further reading: 2 Peter chapter 1

13th April
PEACE THAT DEFIES ALL UNDERSTANDING

John 14:25-31

"These things I have spoken to you while being present with you. ²⁶But the Helper, the Holy Spirit, whom the Father will send in My name, He will teach you all things, and bring to your remembrance all things that I said to you. ²⁷Peace I leave with you, My peace I give to you; not as the world gives do I give to you. Let not your heart be troubled, neither let it be afraid. ²⁸You have heard Me say to you, 'I am going away and coming back to you.' If you loved Me, you would rejoice because I said, 'I am going to the Father,' for My Father is greater than I. ²⁹"And now I have told you before it comes, that when it does come to pass, you may believe. ³⁰I will no longer talk much with you, for the ruler of this world is coming, and he has nothing in Me. ³¹But that the world may know that I love the Father, and as the Father gave Me commandment, so I do. Arise, let us go from here.

Jesus is called the Prince of peace. When the angels announced the birth of Jesus to shepherds in Bethlehem, they declared that peace had come on earth and He has brought good will to all men. There is no real peace without Jesus Christ. The world cannot even imagine the peace that God brings. What the world calls peace is just a little respite in a chaotic world. The world without Jesus Christ is upside down, inside out and there is no way it can know any peace. Jesus came to bring the world to order and thereby establish peace. The peace that Jesus brings to the world is through the Holy Spirit. One of the fruits of the Holy Spirit is peace. When the Holy Spirit comes to live inside you, you don't only experience inner peace, you bring peace wherever you go. Experience real peace today in Jesus name.

PRAYER

Lord Jesus, by your grace I am walking in peace I cannot possibly explain. May this fragrance of peace be with me wherever I go.

Further reading: John chapter 14

14th April
CAN YOU SEE JESUS?

John 16:16-22

A little while, and you will not see Me; and again a little while, and you will see Me, because I go to the Father." [17]Then some of His disciples said among themselves, "What is this that He says to us, 'A little while, and you will not see Me; and again a little while, and you will see Me'; and, 'because I go to the Father'?" [18]They said therefore, "What is this that He says, 'A little while'? We do not know what He is saying."

[19]Now Jesus knew that they desired to ask Him, and He said to them, "Are you inquiring among yourselves about what I said, 'A little while, and you will not see Me; and again a little while, and you will see Me'? [20]Most assuredly, I say to you that you will weep and lament, but the world will rejoice; and you will be sorrowful, but your sorrow will be turned into joy. [21]A woman, when she is in labor, has sorrow because her hour has come; but as soon as she has given birth to the child, she no longer remembers the anguish, for joy that a human being has been born into the world. [22]Therefore you now have sorrow; but I will see you again and your heart will rejoice, and your joy no one will take from you.

When I tell unbelievers I walk and talk with Jesus, they stare at me with suspicion. I am not surprised at this as Jesus himself said we believers would see Him but the world would not. The world can only see Jesus through us. By the Holy Spirit baptism we are witnesses. You and I living today did not see Jesus in the flesh because we live out of time. We only know Jesus through the Holy Spirit. When Jesus said his disciples would see him, He did not mean in the flesh. He would no longer live in the flesh after His death and resurrection. One of the names of the Holy Spirit is the Spirit of Christ.

PRAYER

Thank you Holy Spirit for revealing Jesus Christ to me. You have opened my eyes to see and live with Jesus Christ.

Further reading: John chapter 16

15th April
HOLD ON TO THE HOLY SPIRIT

Psalm 51:7-12

Purge me with hyssop, and I shall be clean; Wash me, and I shall be whiter than snow. Make me hear joy and gladness, That the bones You have broken may rejoice. Hide Your face from my sins, And blot out all my iniquities. Create in me a clean heart, O God, And renew a steadfast spirit within me. Do not cast me away from Your presence, And do not take Your Holy Spirit from me. Restore to me the joy of Your salvation, And uphold me by Your generous Spirit.

David in this Psalm pleads with God not to take His Holy Spirit away from Him. In our day, the Holy Spirit has come to stay. God has not given His Holy Spirit to us for a moment. Jesus promised that the Holy Spirit will be with us forever. God will not take His Spirit from us. Rather, we could turn our back on the Holy Spirit David was anointed by the Holy Spirit to perform his assigned role as a king. He did not have a right to the Holy Spirit. He did not have a father and son relationship with God. God could therefore take His Spirit away from Him. He could therefore pray this kind of prayer. Those of us who have become the children of God through the Cross of Jesus Christ, however, have a right to the Holy Spirit. He is family and cannot walk out on us. We could walk out on Him though. Please don't. Like David, recognize the importance of the companionship of the Holy Spirit and endeavour to hold on to Him. Spend time in fellowship with Him. Build your spiritual man by praying in other tongues. If you don't pray in this essential heavenly language, then desire it. God will give it to you. It is a great help in prayer. The Bible says when you pray in the Spirit, you speak mysteries to God. Don't discount any gift from God. Desire it.

PRAYER

Thank you Holy Spirit for your faithfulness. Help me to be faithful to our relationship.

Further reading: Psalm 51

16th April
POWERFUL GIFTS FROM THE HOLY SPIRIT

1 Corinthians 12:1-11

Now concerning spiritual gifts, brethren, I do not want you to be ignorant: ²You know that you were Gentiles, carried away to these dumb idols, however you were led. ³Therefore I make known to you that no one speaking by the Spirit of God calls Jesus accursed, and no one can say that Jesus is Lord except by the Holy Spirit. ⁴There are diversities of gifts, but the same Spirit. ⁵There are differences of ministries, but the same Lord. ⁶And there are diversities of activities, but it is the same God who works all in all. ⁷But the manifestation of the Spirit is given to each one for the profit of all: ⁸for to one is given the word of wisdom through the Spirit, to another the word of knowledge through the same Spirit, ⁹to another faith by the same Spirit, to another gifts of healings by the same Spirit, ¹⁰to another the working of miracles, to another prophecy, to another discerning of spirits, to another different kinds of tongues, to another the interpretation of tongues. ¹¹But one and the same Spirit works all these things, distributing to each one individually as He wills.

When the Holy Spirit comes into our lives, He brings gifts that we should not be ignorant of. Whilst many acknowledge the power of the Holy Spirit, they ignore the gifts He brings. The scripture above tells us that these gifts are given to each one of us for the benefit of all. Scripture tells us that all creation earnestly waits for the manifestation of the sons of God. What are they waiting to receive from the sons of God? They are waiting to receive the power of God manifesting through His gifts. You are a candidate for producing signs and wonders. Do not be ignorant of it or ignore it. It is not just for your benefit but for the benefit of all. God willing, we shall explore some of these gifts in the coming days.

PRAYER

Thank you Father for these spiritual gifts. I am ready to be used by you to bring salvation and healing to a needy world.

Further reading: 1 Corinthians chapter 12

17th April
HEALING IS A GIFT OF THE HOLY SPIRIT

Matthew 12:15-23

⁵But when Jesus knew it, He withdrew from there. And great multitudes followed Him, and He healed them all. ¹⁶Yet He warned them not to make Him known, ¹⁷that it might be fulfilled which was spoken by Isaiah the prophet, saying: "Behold! My Servant whom I have chosen, My Beloved in whom My soul is well pleased! I will put My Spirit upon Him, And He will declare justice to the Gentiles. He will not quarrel nor cry out, Nor will anyone hear His voice in the streets. A bruised reed He will not break, And smoking flax He will not quench, Till He sends forth justice to victory; And in His name Gentiles will trust." ²²Then one was brought to Him who was demon-possessed, blind and mute; and He healed him, so that the blind and mute man both spoke and saw. ²³And all the multitudes were amazed and said, "Could this be the Son of David?"

When sick people came to Jesus, He healed them. God can always prove He is a good God by mending what is broken, spiritual or physical. If God could not heal the sick, that would make Him less than God. Jesus operated by the power of the same Holy Spirit we have. As He walked the earth as man, he would have been powerless without the Holy Spirit. Every action He took was a manifestation of the Holy Spirit. When He healed, it was by the power of the Holy Spirit. When we walk in the power of the same Holy Spirit, the gift of healings is available to us. We have the ability to bring healing to the sick just as Jesus did. Go and heal the sick in the Name of Jesus. When you command sickness to go in the Name of Jesus, the Holy Spirit will get into action and drive sickness out. The Name of God is glorified when people get healed in His name.

PRAYER

Thank you Father for the gifts of the Holy Spirit. I desire to walk in the gift of healing wherever I go. I will bring glory to your name.

Further reading: Matthew 12

18th April
EXPECT THE MIRACULOUS

Acts 9:36-43

At Joppa there was a certain disciple named Tabitha, which is translated Dorcas. This woman was full of good works and charitable deeds which she did. ³⁷But it happened in those days that she became sick and died. When they had washed her, they laid her in an upper room. ³⁸And since Lydda was near Joppa, and the disciples had heard that Peter was there, they sent two men to him, imploring him not to delay in coming to them. ³⁹Then Peter arose and went with them. When he had come, they brought him to the upper room. And all the widows stood by him weeping, showing the tunics and garments which Dorcas had made while she was with them. ⁴⁰But Peter put them all out, and knelt down and prayed. And turning to the body he said, "Tabitha, arise." And she opened her eyes, and when she saw Peter she sat up. ⁴¹Then he gave her his hand and lifted her up; and when he had called the saints and widows, he presented her alive. ⁴²And it became known throughout all Joppa, and many believed on the Lord. ⁴³So it was that he stayed many days in Joppa with Simon, a tanner.

Jesus went to the cross and grave to bring hope to mankind. Jesus did not remain in the grave but rose to enable us all share in the resurrection power of God. Peter displayed this power in Joppa at a funeral. He commanded the dead body to live and the dead came alive. The disciples who sent for Him also had equal access to the Holy Spirit. The difference here was that they did not exercise their faith. Friend, the same Spirit that raised Jesus from the dead dwells in you. Believe in His power and exercise your faith by commanding good situations in the Name of Jesus. Your faith will grow as you operate the Word of God and see its results. Expect miracles from the Holy Spirit.

PRAYER

Precious Holy Spirit, I thank you that you have made available the gift of working miracles to me. I look forward to seeing miracles wherever I go to the praise of your glory.

Further reading: Acts chapter 9

19th April
FAITH THAT RAISES THE DEAD

John 11:1-11

> Now a certain man was sick, Lazarus of Bethany, the town of Mary and her sister Martha. ²It was that Mary who anointed the Lord with fragrant oil and wiped His feet with her hair, whose brother Lazarus was sick. ³Therefore the sisters sent to Him, saying, "Lord, behold, he whom You love is sick."⁴When Jesus heard that, He said, "This sickness is not unto death, but for the glory of God, that the Son of God may be glorified through it."⁵Now Jesus loved Martha and her sister and Lazarus. ⁶So, when He heard that he was sick, He stayed two more days in the place where He was. ⁷Then after this He said to the disciples, "Let us go to Judea again."
>
> ⁸The disciples said to Him, "Rabbi, lately the Jews sought to stone You, and are You going there again?" ⁹Jesus answered, "Are there not twelve hours in the day? If anyone walks in the day, he does not stumble, because he sees the light of this world. ¹⁰But if one walks in the night, he stumbles, because the light is not in him." ¹¹These things He said, and after that He said to them, "Our friend Lazarus sleeps, but I go that I may wake him up."

Every believer must walk by faith because you cannot walk with Jesus if you don't believe in the price He paid on the Cross for our freedom. 1 Corinthians 12:9 however talks about a special gift of faith available to us from the Holy Spirit. There are circumstances where you need more as Jesus faced when He knew His friend Lazarus was dead. The Holy Spirit in special circumstances gives you a special gift of faith. Jesus Christ was going to raise Lazarus from the dead, which He did a few days later. This special faith helped remove the fear of his disciples. May the Lord give you special faith that will take away the fear of the people around you. Raising the dead combined the gifts of faith, miracle and healing.

PRAYER

Thank you Holy Spirit for faith to raise the dead.

Further reading: John chapter 11

Be Strong Devotional

20th April
SPECIAL KNOWLEDGE

John 4:13-19

> [13] Jesus answered and said to her, "Whoever drinks of this water will thirst again, [14] but whoever drinks of the water that I shall give him will never thirst. But the water that I shall give him will become in him a fountain of water springing up into everlasting life." [15] The woman said to Him, "Sir, give me this water, that I may not thirst, nor come here to draw." [16] Jesus said to her, "Go, call your husband, and come here." [17] The woman answered and said, "I have no husband." Jesus said to her, "You have well said, 'I have no husband,' [18] for you have had five husbands, and the one whom you now have is not your husband; in that you spoke truly." [19] The woman said to Him, "Sir, I perceive that You are a prophet.

Jesus has paid the full price for our peace. By Jesus dying and rising, He has destroyed the power of death that kept us in bondage and fear. Because He is risen, we are now able to boldly become part of God's family and share in God's knowledge. We have the Holy Spirit. The Holy Spirit's gifts are to introduce God to a situation. When God comes in, He brings the supernatural to repair a broken situation. When you walk in the power of the Holy Spirit, you will make statements that will sometimes invite comments of 'How did you know?' You may not have known but God knows everything. God is in the business of saving the world and will use every weapon He has to bring this to come to pass. May the Lord use you as a vessel of His word of knowledge to build His kingdom. Expect God to speak His mysteries through you today. This is not magic so don't try to conjure it up. Walk in love, integrity and obedience and you will be surprised by how God will use you as a vessel of His supernatural power. You are in a powerful covenant.

PRAYER

Thank you father for choosing, calling, justifying and glorifying me to stand in covenant with you. Help me Holy Spirit in my time of weakness that I may not be offensive to my God.

Further reading: John chapter 4

21st April
GOD'S WISDOM TO DIRECT YOUR FUTURE

Acts 10:17-23

> [17]Now while Peter wondered within himself what this vision which he had seen meant, behold, the men who had been sent from Cornelius had made inquiry for Simon's house, and stood before the gate. [18]And they called and asked whether Simon, whose surname was Peter, was lodging there. [19]While Peter thought about the vision, the Spirit said to him, "Behold, three men are seeking you. [20]Arise therefore, go down and go with them, doubting nothing; for I have sent them." [21]Then Peter went down to the men who had been sent to him from Cornelius, and said, "Yes, I am he whom you seek. For what reason have you come?" [22]And they said, "Cornelius the centurion, a just man, one who fears God and has a good reputation among all the nation of the Jews, was divinely instructed by a holy angel to summon you to his house, and to hear words from you." [23]Then he invited them in and lodged them. On the next day Peter went away with them, and some brethren from Joppa accompanied him.

God knows the end from the beginning and is ready to reveal the future to whom He can trust. There is no point in God keeping something a secret from you if He needs your help to get it established. He trusted Peter and needed him to bring salvation to Cornelius and his household He had sent an angel to tell Cornelius to look for a man called Peter. God loved the generosity of Cornelius and needed someone to bring the gospel of Jesus Christ to him. God loves generous people but good deeds alone will not take you to heaven. You need to respond to the invitation of Jesus Christ. The world needs the gospel. You are God's agent. If God can trust you, He will give you word of wisdom as He gave Peter. You will know what is going to happen before it does and the Holy Spirit will also tell you what to do.

PRAYER
Holy Spirit, help me to trust you more. Please help me to walk in step with you, not ahead of you or behind you.

Further reading: Acts chapter 10

22nd April
ABILITY TO SEPARATE GOOD SPIRIT FROM BAD SPIRIT

Acts 16:16-18

[16] Now it happened, as we went to prayer, that a certain slave girl possessed with a spirit of divination met us, who brought her masters much profit by fortune-telling. [17] This girl followed Paul and us, and cried out, saying, "These men are the servants of the Most High God, who proclaim to us the way of salvation." [18] And this she did for many days. But Paul, greatly annoyed, turned and said to the spirit, "I command you in the name of Jesus Christ to come out of her." And he came out that very hour.

Scripture encourages us to test all spirits. There are good and bad spirits. Whilst the Holy Spirit is genuine and truthful, the spirit of Satan is deceitful and cunning. We are told in the Bible to watch and pray so we are not deceived. Prayer helps us discern right from wrong. Prayer makes us sharp in the spirit and we can easily identify what is wrong. Satan can be so deceptive sometimes appearing as an angel of light. The Holy Spirit equips us with the gift of discerning of spirits to help us foil his schemes. In the above scripture Satan used the slave girl to continually be proclaiming that Paul and his team are servants of God and proclaiming the truth. On the surface she seemed to be confirming the truth of what Paul was doing but Paul saw through the deception. Satan has nothing good to say about God. Watch out for people who are trying to cash in on your popularity by pretending to be on your side. May the Lord give you the gift of the discerning of spirits that will enable you to identify what is genuine from what is fake; what is from God and what is from Satan.

PRAYER

Dear father, I have made my choice for you and refuse to be deceived. Holy Spirit, I count on you to help me discern what is godly and what is evil.

Further reading: Acts chapter 16

23rd April
SPEAK FOR GOD

Revelation 1:1-3

> ¹*The Revelation of Jesus Christ, which God gave Him to show His servants—things which must shortly take place. And He sent and signified it by His angel to His servant John, ²who bore witness to the word of God, and to the testimony of Jesus Christ, to all things that he saw. ³Blessed is he who reads and those who hear the words of this prophecy, and keep those things which are written in it; for the time is near.*

Prophecy means to speak for God. God gives you a revelation or instruction and you act as His spokesman to release it to the people. The first 3 verses of the book of revelation quoted above summarizes the work of prophesy. Jesus tells us that the books of the Bible are about Him. Jesus is the beginning and the end. Paul says in Jesus all things consist. All revelation and all prophecy are aimed at establishing His kingdom. John receives this prophecy and makes it known. When you receive God's word and obey it you will be blessed. It is God's desire to bless the whole world. He needs someone who will speak for Him. In Isaiah 6:8, the Lord asked "whom shall I send?" and Isaiah responded to God that he was ready to be sent. If you are ready to be sent, God is looking for a spokesman. He is waiting to give you the gift of prophecy through the Holy Spirit to enable you reveal His heart and direction to His church. For you to enjoy this anointing, you need to commit yourself to an intimate relationship with the Father. If you want to hear the heart of God, you must be close to Him. The Bible describes John as the disciple whose head was on the chest of Jesus when they sat in fellowship. No wonder the awesome prophecy of the book of revelation was given to him. Commit yourself to prayer and an intimate walk of obedience with Jesus Christ today. You will receive secrets from heaven to pass on.

PRAYER

Send me Lord. I am ready to speak for you. Holy Spirit, help me develop an intimate relationship with you.

Further reading: Revelation chapter 1

24th April
ABILITY TO SPEAK IN HEAVENLY AND EARTHLY LANGUAGES

Acts 2:1-4

> *¹When the Day of Pentecost had fully come, they were all with one accord in one place. ²And suddenly there came a sound from heaven, as of a rushing mighty wind, and it filled the whole house where they were sitting. ³Then there appeared to them divided tongues, as of fire, and one sat upon each of them. ⁴And they were all filled with the Holy Spirit and began to speak with other tongues, as the Spirit gave them utterance.*

What a wonderful sign God gave to the Jewish believers who were gathered in prayer on the day of Pentecost. When you begin to speak in a language you have not learnt, it is a sure sign of identity change. Scripture tells us that the mouth speaks out of the abundance of the heart. This is God's language and He can use it for whatever the desire of His heart is. On the day of Pentecost, it was not only a sign to the disciples, God used it as a sign to the people who were gathered there from different nations. The Bible tells us that the different people from the different nations who had gathered in Jerusalem heard them speak in their own languages. This was a miracle of God using the gift of tongues. The Bible tells us in 1 Corinthians 14:2 that there are times that we use this heavenly language to speak mysteries in the spirit to God. There are other times when this language of God is used for prophecy in which case we need an interpretation for people to understand. People have debated at length about this gift. Like Paul, my exhortation to you today is to desire spiritual gifts. Desire to speak in other tongues. Paul says, praying in the spirit builds us up spiritually. Please stop debating and start receiving this precious gift.

PRAYER

I am blessed to speak in the language of God. Father use your words in my mouth to do what pleases you.

Further reading: Acts chapter 2

25th April
YOU CAN UNDERSTAND SPIRITUAL LANGUAGE

Acts 2:5-12

> [5]*And there were dwelling in Jerusalem Jews, devout men, from every nation under heaven.* [6]*And when this sound occurred, the multitude came together, and were confused, because everyone heard them speak in his own language.* [7]*Then they were all amazed and marveled, saying to one another, "Look, are not all these who speak Galileans?* [8]*And how is it that we hear, each in our own language in which we were born?* [9]*Parthians and Medes and Elamites, those dwelling in Mesopotamia, Judea and Cappadocia, Pontus and Asia,* [10]*Phrygia and Pamphylia, Egypt and the parts of Libya adjoining Cyrene, visitors from Rome, both Jews and proselytes,* [11]*Cretans and Arabs—we hear them speaking in our own tongues the wonderful works of God."* [12]*So they were all amazed and perplexed, saying to one another, "Whatever could this mean?"*

Yesterday we spoke about how God's language is used for God's purpose. When the disciples spoke, it was a sign to them because they were speaking a language that was foreign to them and it was not by choice. Heaven had invaded the privacy of their vocal chords. The second amazing thing is what is described above. People from different nations could hear them in their own languages. I do not believe the disciples were speaking in their individual languages. That would have created confusion. I believe a miracle happened between the utterance of God's language and the ears of the listeners. The Holy Spirit brought an interpretation to their ears. The Holy Spirit has a gift called 'interpretation of tongues', which interprets the language of God to a language understood by the listener. You are called by God to stand between Him and the world. That is what Jesus did for all of us. By the baptism of the Holy Spirit, we are not only part of the family of God, we are commissioned to stand in the gap with Jesus Christ. Desire to supernaturally interpret the language of God for the benefit of the world.

PRAYER

Thank you Father that you have not just put your language in my mouth but you have also given me the ability to interpret. Help me to stand in the gap for the world.

Further reading: 1 Corinthians chapter 14

26th April
EVERYONE HAS A GIFT

Romans 12:1-8

¹I beseech you therefore, brethren, by the mercies of God, that you present your bodies a living sacrifice, holy, acceptable to God, which is your reasonable service. ²And do not be conformed to this world, but be transformed by the renewing of your mind, that you may prove what is that good and acceptable and perfect will of God. ³For I say, through the grace given to me, to everyone who is among you, not to think of himself more highly than he ought to think, but to think soberly, as God has dealt to each one a measure of faith. ⁴For as we have many members in one body, but all the members do not have the same function, ⁵so we, being many, are one body in Christ, and individually members of one another. ⁶Having then gifts differing according to the grace that is given to us, let us use them: if prophecy, let us prophesy in proportion to our faith; ⁷or ministry, let us use it in our ministering; he who teaches, in teaching; ⁸he who exhorts, in exhortation; he who gives, with liberality; he who leads, with diligence; he who shows mercy, with cheerfulness.

God has given everyone a gift that lives with you. I call them gift in residence because we tend to move naturally in these gifts. It comes so naturally that people may think you were born with it. The Holy Spirit may endow you with a leadership ability, a teacher's ability, a desire to serve, encourage or be generous. It could be a feeling of mercy. Every Christian must walk in a measure of all these gifts. Yet when we talk of a special gift of the Holy Spirit, we are talking about an operation in that gift that is above normal. Identify your gift and be grateful to God for it. Don't compare yourself to others or condemn others for not being as generous as you or operate in leadership like you. Their gift may be different from yours.

PRAYER

Thank you Father for my special gift. Holy Spirit help me to excel in this gift you have given to me and help me to use it for the benefit of your kingdom.

Further reading: Romans chapter 12

27th April
YOU ARE A LEADER

Matthew 28:16-20

> *Then the eleven disciples went away into Galilee, to the mountain which Jesus had appointed for them. ¹⁷When they saw Him, they worshiped Him; but some doubted. ¹⁸And Jesus came and spoke to them, saying, "All authority has been given to Me in heaven and on earth. ¹⁹Go therefore and make disciples of all the nations, baptizing them in the name of the Father and of the Son and of the Holy Spirit, ²⁰teaching them to observe all things that I have commanded you; and lo, I am with you always, even to the end of the age." Amen.*

The Holy Spirit brings knowledge and authority. These are two words associated with leadership. When Jesus told the disciples that all authority has been given to Him in heaven and earth, He was telling them that He was leader in heaven and earth. He therefore sent them in that authority to lead the world back to God. This sending includes you and me. He did not send us without authority. He told His disciples in Acts chapter 1 to wait for the Holy Spirit who will give them the power of leadership to lead the world to Him. With the Holy Spirit in your life, you are a leader. What else will you do with the Holy Spirit except to demonstrate the love and power of God to the world. Scripture tells us that the world is waiting for the sons of God. You are a child of God appointed to demonstrate the power of the Holy Spirit to the world. The world is waiting for your leadership. You may be thinking I do not qualify. Your leadership is not by your own ability or appointment. Your knowledge and authority is from the Holy Spirit. If you don't provide godly leadership in your family, who should. If godly people like you do not take up their responsibility, other people controlled by ungodly forces will seek to lead. Rise up and be the leader.

PRAYER

Thank you Holy Spirit that by your presence in me, you have made me a leader. I will take up my calling and lead the world to you.

Further reading: Matthew chapter 28

28th April
YOU ARE SALT AND LIGHT

Matthew 5:13-16

> "You are the salt of the earth; but if the salt loses its flavour, how shall it be seasoned? It is then good for nothing but to be thrown out and trampled underfoot by men.
>
> [14]"You are the light of the world. A city that is set on a hill cannot be hidden. [15]Nor do they light a lamp and put it under a basket, but on a lampstand, and it gives light to all who are in the house. [16]Let your light so shine before men, that they may see your good works and glorify your Father in heaven.

The only thing that can dispel darkness is light. It is only the light of God that can get rid of the darkness in this world. This is why God has made us light. Jesus says in John 8:12 that He is the light of the world and anyone who follows Him shall not walk in darkness but have the light of life. The only way we could lighten up the world as Jesus did is to have the same spirit Jesus had, the Holy Spirit. Because you have the Holy Spirit, the light of God shines through you. Everyone who has the Spirit of God gives off God's glory. When people see you, they see God in you. The less of your flesh they see, the more of God they see in you and therefore the brighter the light that dispels darkness. Our responsibility is to live more for God and less for ourselves. Paul says in Galatians 2:20 that he is crucified with Christ so he no longer lives for himself but Christ lives through Him. If we can offer ourselves for Christ to use us as vessels, God will be so pleased with us and our reward shall be great. Salt is a flavor and a preservative. God has chosen you to be salt and light in this world.

PRAYER
Thank you Father for choosing me and giving me the quality to be salt and light in the world. Holy Spirit help my light to shine and be a sweetener wherever I am.

Further reading: Matthew chapter 5

29th April
THE POWER TO CREATE

Psalm 104:24-32

O Lord, how manifold are Your works! In wisdom You have made them all. The earth is full of Your possessions—This great and wide sea, In which are innumerable teeming things, Living things both small and great.

There the ships sail about; There is that Leviathan Which You have made to play there. These all wait for You, That You may give them their food in due season. What You give them they gather in; You open Your hand, they are filled with good. You hide Your face, they are troubled; You take away their breath, they die and return to their dust. You send forth Your Spirit, they are created; And You renew the face of the earth. May the glory of the Lord endure forever; May the Lord rejoice in His works. He looks on the earth, and it trembles; He touches the hills, and they smoke.

God is powerful. He creates great things out of nothing. This is good news. It means that He can meet every need of ours even if it means having to create it out of nothing. We can trust in His love. God's Word is as powerful as Himself because He creates everything through His Word. God's Spirit is as powerful as Himself. We read from the scripture above that He sends forth His Spirit and things are created. We are born again by the Spirit of God. The Spirit of God lives in us and we have this creative force in us which we can release by our words. Because the Spirit of God lives in us, our words become as powerful as God's words. They are powered by His Spirit in us. We therefore create with our words. Watch therefore the words that come out of your mouth. If God's Spirit is in you then you must create good things with your words. Let your words bless and not curse. Only Satan creates monsters with his words. Don't be an agent of Satan.

PRAYER

Thank you Father for the power to create. I will create good situations with my words.

Further reading: Psalm 104

30th April
YOU ARE A NEW CREATION

2 Corinthians 5:16-21

Therefore, from now on, we regard no one according to the flesh. Even though we have known Christ according to the flesh, yet now we know Him thus no longer. ¹⁷Therefore, if anyone is in Christ, he is a new creation; old things have passed away; behold, all things have become new. ¹⁸Now all things are of God, who has reconciled us to Himself through Jesus Christ, and has given us the ministry of reconciliation, ¹⁹that is, that God was in Christ reconciling the world to Himself, not imputing their trespasses to them, and has committed to us the word of reconciliation. ²⁰Now then, we are ambassadors for Christ, as though God were pleading through us: we implore you on Christ's behalf, be reconciled to God. ²¹For He made Him who knew no sin to be sin for us, that we might become the righteousness of God in Him.

A good way to end this spring month is to remind ourselves of our new status in Christ. Spring marks the season of new life. In God's calendar, He invited all Israel to celebrate the feast of Passover and first fruits with Him in spring. You are born again into the family of God. You are no longer the old you subject to the influence of the world. You operate by the power of the Holy Spirit not by the manipulation of sin. We are a new creation. We are not under sin so we are under no condemnation. By the grace of God we are righteous. Instead of condemnation, we have an inheritance. Instead of Satan forcing us into sin, we have the Holy Spirit gently guiding us unto liberating truth. We have even been entrusted with the job of reconciling the world to God by the power of the Holy Spirit. This is an outstanding promotion. Let us not take this gift lightly. Let us be thankful to God for this and let us pursue this assignment with faithfulness. The Holy Spirit is with you forever.

PRAYER

Thank you Father for your love that has brought me into your family and the assignment you have entrusted to me. I promise to be a faithful witness to you big brother Jesus.

Further reading: 2 Corinthians 5

May
God's Promises

The Bible is a book of promises by God. God's covenant with us is that He makes a promise and we accept the promise. Ephesians 2:11-13 tells us that we were strangers to God's covenant of promise. He had a covenant of promise with Israel. The rest of the world were called gentiles. Through Jesus Christ we have all now become partakers of the covenant of promises. Know the promises of God and accept them as yours. My prayer is that you will know that God's promises are for you and that you will receive and walk in them.

1st May
GOD'S WORD IS SETTLED

Psalm 119:89-96

Forever, O Lord, Your word is settled in heaven. Your faithfulness endures to all generations; You established the earth, and it abides. They continue this day according to Your ordinances, For all are Your servants. Unless Your law had been my delight, I would then have perished in my affliction. I will never forget Your precepts, For by them You have given me life. I am Yours, save me; For I have sought Your precepts. The wicked wait for me to destroy me, But I will consider Your testimonies. I have seen the consummation of all perfection, But Your commandment is exceedingly broad.

God cannot lie because He is truth. He is the source of all truth. Truth simply agrees with what is real or exists. For instance I can tell you there is a tree in my garden and it will be truth because there really is a tree in my garden. However it is not an everlasting truth. I could remove the tree tomorrow and what is true today would not be true tomorrow. God however is the creator of all things. When he speaks, it is absolute truth because he is telling you about something He has made himself. God does not tell stories. He tells you what is. We know Him by his word. Christianity is the only way of life that has the Word of God instead of a bunch of stories and rules. His word reveals who God is. He cannot change who he is so you can count on his word as truth and settled. Every promise God gives to us is not to give us false hope. He means it and has the ability to bring it to pass. He has promised to be a good Father to us if we are ready to be his sons. Take him at his word today and begin to enjoy the benefits of being a son of God. If God has promised, believe it. He is faithful and true.

PRAYER

Father, I thank you that your word concerning me is settled in heaven. Help me Holy Spirit to receive every promise as truth and walk in your plan for my life.

Further reading: Numbers 23:16-26

2nd May
GOD'S DESIRE WILL BE ACCOMPLISHED

Isaiah 55:8-11

> "For My thoughts are not your thoughts, Nor are your ways My ways," says the Lord. "For as the heavens are higher than the earth, So are My ways higher than your ways, And My thoughts than your thoughts "For as the rain comes down, and the snow from heaven, And do not return there, But water the earth, And make it bring forth and bud, That it may give seed to the sower And bread to the eater, So shall My word be that goes forth from My mouth; It shall not return to Me void, But it shall accomplish what I please, And it shall prosper in the thing for which I sent it.

God started all things. He created the heavens and the earth. He also created you and me. Our parents gave birth to us but we came from some place to be in our father's seed and mother's womb. Psalm 139 tells us that God made us. Even before our substance was formed, he knew us. He had a good plan for us. God did not make us to struggle in life. We struggle out of ignorance or disobedience. Our ignorance of the existence and loving goodness of God makes us want to help ourselves. We cannot help ourselves if we do not know our maker's plan for our lives. The life of Jesus on this earth was to cure this ignorance. He showed us the way to our creator. His death and resurrection removed the dividing wall between us and our creator. His sending of the Holy Spirit opened us up to the knowledge of the plan of God. No one needs to be ignorant any longer. Let us shout this salvation on the mountain tops, in the highways and byways to everyone walking in ignorance and bring them to the light. As we know the truth, let us walk in obedience to God's plan for His desire shall surely come to pass. Walking in disobedience is walking in darkness.

PRAYER

Thank you father for your good plans which shall come to pass in my life. I trust your promises and hold on to your light. I know victory is mine.

Further reading: Psalm 139

3rd May
ALL GOD'S PROMISES ARE YES IN JESUS CHRIST

2 Corinthians 1:18-22

> *But as God is faithful, our word to you was not Yes and No. [19]For the Son of God, Jesus Christ, who was preached among you by us—by me, Silvanus, and Timothy—was not Yes and No, but in Him was Yes. [20]For all the promises of God in Him are Yes, and in Him Amen, to the glory of God through us. [21]Now He who establishes us with you in Christ and has anointed us is God, [22]who also has sealed us and given us the Spirit in our hearts as a guarantee.*

It is impossible for God to make a promise he can't fulfil. God does not get involved in idle talk. When the word comes out of his mouth, he means it. He sends the word forth with a purpose. God's words are like loaded bombs which cannot fail. The death of Jesus Christ was a blood oath to tell the world that he would perform his promise. If we would receive these promises in our hearts, they would explode in our hearts and bring fulfilment. For us not to receive God's promise as truth is to make God less than God. It is also unbelief in the finished work of the cross. The bible tells us that without faith, we cannot please God. God's promises are yes and amen in Jesus Christ. When God tells you He has healed all your diseases, that is truth. Shout 'yes' in your spirit. Do not listen to any other voices. Don't receive any other voice. It could be the voice of so called knowledgeable men or the voice of pain. God's voice must be respected above these other voices. If He has said it, it is truth. Keep it in your mouth and keep saying it in agreement to his word. The light of God's word in your mouth will overcome every darkness.. You will rise up from defeat and live victoriously with God. Rise up today and enjoy everlasting life with your father.

PRAYER

Thank you Father that you have blessed me with amazing promises. Thank you that your love and integrity cannot make you lie. You are a holy God and I love you.

Further reading: 2 Corinthians 1

4th May
YOU CAN TRUST THE BIBLE

2 Timothy 3:12-17

Yes, and all who desire to live godly in Christ Jesus will suffer persecution. ¹³But evil men and impostors will grow worse and worse, deceiving and being deceived. ¹⁴But you must continue in the things which you have learned and been assured of, knowing from whom you have learned them, ¹⁵and that from childhood you have known the Holy Scriptures, which are able to make you wise for salvation through faith which is in Christ Jesus. ¹⁶All Scripture is given by inspiration of God, and is profitable for doctrine, for reproof, for correction, for instruction in righteousness, ¹⁷that the man of God may be complete, thoroughly equipped for every good work.

The Israelites were very good at keeping records. They had special secretaries who recorded history as it happened. Details of history and ancestry were passed on from generation to generation. Accuracy was very important to these scribes. These were a people who were in covenant with God. Their encounters with God were meticulously recorded. When Moses received the law on Mount Sinai, God himself wrote down the commandments on a tablet of stone. When God gave an instruction it had to be written down for the benefit of all through the ages. God asked the Israelites to write the law on their doorpost, put it on their foreheads and their wrists. Today we are so grateful that we have a collection of writing inspired by God which we call the bible. The availability of the bible is an indication of God's love to our generation. Not only is the Holy Spirit ever present with us, the Holy Spirit has put in our hands God's word to teach, reprove, correct and instruct us in righteousness. This is the work of the Holy Spirit through yielded men. A lot of the work the Holy Spirit does on this earth is through men. If you will make yourself available, God will speak through you and your word will be trusted. The bible can be trusted.

PRAYER

Father, I thank you for the bible. You have demonstrated your love for the world through the many promises in the Bible. I believe your word is truth.

Further reading: 2 Timothy chapter 3

5th May
THOUGHTS OF PEACE

Jeremiah 29:10-14

> *For thus says the Lord: After seventy years are completed at Babylon, I will visit you and perform My good word toward you, and cause you to return to this place. [11]For I know the thoughts that I think toward you, says the Lord, thoughts of peace and not of evil, to give you a future and a hope. [12]Then you will call upon Me and go and pray to Me, and I will listen to you. [13]And you will seek Me and find Me, when you search for Me with all your heart. [14]I will be found by you, says the Lord, and I will bring you back from your captivity; I will gather you from all the nations and from all the places where I have driven you, says the Lord, and I will bring you to the place from which I cause you to be carried away captive.*

God is a good God. He loves people. We are all made in the image of God. He reminds us in the above scripture that His thoughts towards Israel was peace. This means that he did not want Israel to be in want in any area of their lives. His dealings with Israel was to show us the heart of God. Today if we have received the sacrifice of Jesus Christ on the cross and made him the Lord of our lives, we stand in a better covenant than what Israel had with God. We are now part of the family of God. God is now obliged to ensure our peace and prosperity. Unless we forcibly detach ourselves from Jesus, we must expect a good future. We have stepped into the kingdom of God where peace is the currency. I plead with you to stay in Jesus and enjoy this peace which defies all understanding. Don't try to understand it. Just enjoy it. Believe and enjoy every promise in his word.

PRAYER

What a mighty God you are. Thank you for your thoughts towards me; thoughts of peace to give me a future and a hope. I embrace my good future with hope. I love you too.

Further reading: Jeremiah chapter 29

6th May
LAY YOUR BURDEN DOWN

Matthew 11:27-30

All things have been delivered to Me by My Father, and no one knows the Son except the Father. Nor does anyone know the Father except the Son, and the one to whom the Son wills to reveal Him. ^{28}Come to Me, all you who labor and are heavy laden, and I will give you rest. ^{29}Take My yoke upon you and learn from Me, for I am gentle and lowly in heart, and you will find rest for your souls. ^{30}For My yoke is easy and My burden is light."

Every person carries a burden. Life is a burden with its many unanswered questions. How did man come to be? Why me? How do I meet all my physical, health, emotional and financial needs? These are just a few of the questions that burden us. The bible says that without Jesus we are all groping in darkness. Thank God for Jesus, the light of the world who through His intervention on the cross has brought us face to face with God. What was hidden has now been revealed. In Jesus, all things consist. Jesus has come to free us. Come and lay down the burden you have carried. He has come to give us rest. He has defeated death and by so doing destroyed the greatest of all burdens - sin. The wages of sin is death. He took our sins on the cross, paid the penalty for sin by dying; and defeated death by rising from the dead. If you have received Jesus as your Lord and become part of the family of God, you do not need to carry the burden of sin, sickness and lack any longer. Receive your peace now. The punishment for your peace was laid on Him. He has paid the price for your peace so you can share in His total peace today. Jesus wants to walk with you so take His yoke and learn from him as you walk with him daily. No more burdens for you. Put them all on his altar today.

PRAYER

Jesus, I lay my burdens on your altar today. Thank you for the price you paid for my peace. I receive your freedom and rest in my life today.

Further reading: Matthew chapter 11

7th May
GOD'S LOVE IS GUARANTEED

Romans 8:35-39

Who shall separate us from the love of Christ? Shall tribulation, or distress, or persecution, or famine, or nakedness, or peril, or sword? 36As it is written: "For Your sake we are killed all day long; We are accounted as sheep for the slaughter." 37Yet in all these things we are more than conquerors through Him who loved us. 38For I am persuaded that neither death nor life, nor angels nor principalities nor powers, nor things present nor things to come, 39nor height nor depth, nor any other created thing, shall be able to separate us from the love of God which is in Christ Jesus our Lord.

We can count on the love of God. God is love. Although our God is more powerful than any other being, there are times that we see other entities display some power. The one thing that clearly distinguishes our God from others is His love. He created a beautiful world out of love. If the world looks ugly now, it is because it has been corrupted through ignorance and separation from God. Beneath all the ugliness and corruption is a beautiful creation. The corruption we see is temporary. It shall be removed and we will see the real world as God intended it to be. We will see the love of God clearly as the corruptible is swallowed up by the incorruptible. Love started everything and love will finish it. God's love is incorruptible and guaranteed. He cannot deny or change himself. That is who he is. If you are with God, expect love. All the promises he makes to man are founded in love. He promises healing to the sick; deliverance to the bound; provision to the poor and freedom to those in captivity. If you are in a bad situation, he promises deliverance into a good situation. I don't know what you are going through today but you can count on the love of a Father from God.

PRAYER

Thank you father for love that is guaranteed. Holy Spirit help me never to depart from this love but abide in the house of God forever.

Further reading: Romans chapter 8

8th May
EVERLASTING LIFE

John 3:14-17

> *And as Moses lifted up the serpent in the wilderness, even so must the Son of Man be lifted up, [15]that whoever believes in Him should not perish but have eternal life. [16]For God so loved the world that He gave His only begotten Son, that whoever believes in Him should not perish but have everlasting life. [17]For God did not send His Son into the world to condemn the world, but that the world through Him might be saved.*

The promise of everlasting life is the king of all promises. God has promised us everlasting life if we would believe in Jesus Christ. Everlasting life simply means a life that will never end. When the bible talks about everlasting life, it is not just talking about a life that will go on forever, but is also talking about a good quality life. Life in this context in the bible means living like God. Many find it difficult to receive this promise as we are surrounded by decay and death. Friend, this is a clear promise of God so receive it today. Because you have believed in Jesus Christ and received Him as the master of your life, God has changed your quality of life. You are now living in the kingdom of God with a godly quality of life. You can also expect a life with God forever. The boundary of death is removed forever. You may put this flesh you carry around with you away but be assured that as God has promised, your life will continue into eternity. Rejoice, you have been born again to die no more. Fear not. Your old fearful life is gone. You are now living by faith in the word of God. You have faith in you to believe every promise of God. Keep the faith alive by continually reminding yourself of this promise. Speak it aloud so you can hear it and even unseen spirits around you can hear it.

PRAYER

Thank you my father for giving me everlasting life. I am no longer afraid of death because you have overcome death for me. I will reign with you in your kingdom Lord Jesus.

Further reading: John chapter 3

9th May
HIS VOICE GIVES LIFE

John 5:24-29

> "Most assuredly, I say to you, he who hears My word and believes in Him who sent Me has everlasting life, and shall not come into judgment, but has passed from death into life. ^{25}Most assuredly, I say to you, the hour is coming, and now is, when the dead will hear the voice of the Son of God; and those who hear will live. ^{26}For as the Father has life in Himself, so He has granted the Son to have life in Himself, ^{27}and has given Him authority to execute judgment also, because He is the Son of Man. ^{28}Do not marvel at this; for the hour is coming in which all who are in the graves will hear His voice ^{29}and come forth—those who have done good, to the resurrection of life, and those who have done evil, to the resurrection of condemnation.

Jesus speaking makes a great promise in the above scripture. He promises that anyone who would listen to his word and believe in God has already been declared innocent and will not face the judgment of death. His promise is true. Please listen and receive his word today and save yourself from the torture of judgment. The word of Jesus is life. Even the dead will be raised as they hear the voice of Jesus Christ. One of the greatest gifts we have is the bible. In it God reveals his heart to us. One of the ways in which we can hear the voice of God is to read and meditate on the word of God in the bible. Believe that whatever the bible says you are, that is who you are. You have the Spirit of God living in you. When you speak the word of God out loudly it is powered by God's Spirit in you. This gives life to the word you have spoken and makes it very powerful. Speak to dead situations and watch them come to life. The voice of God raises the dead. It is in your mouth.

PRAYER

In the name of Jesus, I speak life to every part of my body now. My body will work perfectly. I have life in my mouth and will not hesitate to use it.

Further reading: John chapter 5

10th May
LIVING IN GOD'S HOUSE FOREVER

Psalm 23

The Lord is my shepherd; I shall not want. He makes me to lie down in green pastures; He leads me beside the still waters. He restores my soul; He leads me in the paths of righteousness For His name's sake. Yea, though I walk through the valley of the shadow of death, I will fear no evil; For You are with me Your rod and Your staff, they comfort me. You prepare a table before me in the presence of my enemies; You anoint my head with oil; My cup runs over. Surely goodness and mercy shall follow me All the days of my life; And I will dwell in the house of the Lord Forever.

It is a wonderful privilege to have Jesus as our shepherd. For us to abandon such a great and loving shepherd will be folly. There was a time when I did not know Jesus. I had no one to lead, guide and protect me. I was led by the ignorance of the world. I followed what was fashionable in the world. My gods were the intellectuals and the so called great of the world. I thank God for coming into my hopeless darkness and rescuing me into his marvelous light. I now have a good shepherd in Jesus Christ and I intend to live with him forever. I will live in God's house forever. If Jesus is not your shepherd yet, then make him your shepherd today. He makes a big difference. He actually brings life to your life. Receiving Jesus is like a long awaited homecoming. You don't come to go. You come to stay. You are in God's house if you have received Jesus. You have access to everything that is in God's house: Protection, provision, healing and deliverance. Wherever you go and whatever you do today, remember He is with you because you are in him. What a glorious truth that you need to make real to your soul.

PRAYER

Father, I promise not to step out of your house. I will live in your house forever; that I may take hold of that for which you took hold of me.

Slowly read Psalm 23 again making every promise yours.

11th May
YOU ARE A CITIZEN OF HEAVEN

Philippians 3:17-21

> *Brethren, join in following my example, and note those who so walk, as you have us for a pattern. [18]For many walk, of whom I have told you often, and now tell you even weeping, that they are the enemies of the cross of Christ: [19]whose end is destruction, whose god is their belly, and whose glory is in their shame—who set their mind on earthly things. [20]For our citizenship is in heaven, from which we also eagerly wait for the Saviour, the Lord Jesus Christ, [21]who will transform our lowly body that it may be conformed to His glorious body, according to the working by which He is able even to subdue all things to Himself.*

When you live in a place for a while, the way and character of the place will begin to rub off on you. When you become a citizen of heaven, heaven must rub off on you. If you are a citizen of heaven, you must walk like a citizen of heaven. You must also enjoy the privileges that come with being a citizen of heaven. There are some who try to work their way into heaven. You cannot work your way into heaven by yourself. I have met people who are trying to be as good as they can be so per chance they can make it to heaven. The requirements for permanent stay in heaven are spiritual. You cannot satisfy in the physical. These requirements are fully met in the Lord Jesus Christ. All you need to do then is to receive Jesus Christ into your life and you would have fulfilled the requirements in full. This free gift of Jesus Christ and the love displayed on the cross of Calvary transforms our hearts. Friend, enjoy today every thing in heaven. It is your right as a citizen of heaven. Enjoy life to the full as part of the family of God. Walk in the glory, mercy and grace of heaven.

PRAYER

Thank you Jesus for making it possible for me to partake in the citizenship of heaven. I now understand that I am a citizen of heaven and an ambassador on earth. Help me Holy Spirit to fulfill my responsibilities and enjoy my privileges.

Further reading: Philippians chapter 3

12th May
THE RESURRECTION AND THE LIFE

John 11:21-27

Now Martha said to Jesus, "Lord, if You had been here, my brother would not have died. ²²But even now I know that whatever You ask of God, God will give You." ²³Jesus said to her, "Your brother will rise again." ²⁴Martha said to Him, "I know that he will rise again in the resurrection at the last day." ²⁵Jesus said to her, "I am the resurrection and the life. He who believes in Me, though he may die, he shall live. ²⁶And whoever lives and believes in Me shall never die. Do you believe this?" ²⁷She said to Him, "Yes, Lord, I believe that You are the Christ, the Son of God, who is to come into the world."

Martha was a religious person. She knew that God had promised the resurrection of the dead at the end of the age. She believed in this and it probably gave her hope that she was going to see her brother Lazarus again at the time of the resurrection of the dead. Jesus had better news for her. She didn't have to wait till the end of the age to see death swallowed up in victory by life. Jesus revealed to Martha that in him, Jesus Christ death is defeated. He revealed that he is the resurrection and the life. Martha received this revelation. He trusted Jesus and was ready to receive whatever he said as truth. Trust Jesus today and receive whatever he says as truth. If you will believe, you would see the power of God. Jesus immediately after this show of Martha's faith, raised Lazarus from the dead. He had been buried for four days. We can give up so easily as we consider death as final. The life of Jesus goes beyond death. A few weeks or months after raising Lazarus from the dead, Jesus himself was going to offer himself to be killed for the sins of the world and openly defeat death by rising again on the third day. You have life in Jesus.

PRAYER

Thank you Jesus. I believe that you are the resurrection and the life. In you I have life.

Further reading: John chapter 11

Be Strong Devotional

13th May
MORTALITY TO IMMORTALITY

1 Corinthians 15:50-54

Now this I say, brethren, that flesh and blood cannot inherit the kingdom of God; nor does corruption inherit incorruption. [51]Behold, I tell you a mystery: We shall not all sleep, but we shall all be changed— [52]in a moment, in the twinkling of an eye, at the last trumpet. For the trumpet will sound, and the dead will be raised incorruptible, and we shall be changed. [53]For this corruptible must put on incorruption, and this mortal must put on immortality. [54]So when this corruptible has put on incorruption, and this mortal has put on immortality, then shall be brought to pass the saying that is written: "Death is swallowed up in victory."

The above revelation assures us that the days of death as the world sees it today are numbered. Death has become a destroyer of people's hopes and joys. Death puts fear in people's hearts. Fear does not come from God. Instead faith, hope and love come from God. Death has been a strong weapon of Satan to put fear in people. The bible tells us in Hebrews 2:14 & 15 that one of the reasons why Jesus went to the cross of Calvary was to defeat death and free people from the fear of death. This assignment he accomplished with distinction by making a public spectacle of Satan and exposing him as toothless. For us who have received Jesus and therefore become one with him, we have already overcome Satan in the name of Jesus. The bible tells us that as we behold the face of Jesus as in a mirror, we are being changed from glory to glory. What this means is that as Jesus is revealed to us day by day through his word, mortality is being clothed with immortality. We are becoming more like him. Strength is replacing weakness; health is replacing sickness, beauty is replacing ashes. Keep your eyes on Jesus and let life replace death.

PRAYER

Thank you father for this hope that you have given to us. Mortality has been replaced by immortality. Death is swallowed up in victory.

Further reading: 1 Corinthians chapter 15

14th May
LIFE ABIDES IN YOU

1 John 2:24-27

Therefore let that abide in you which you heard from the beginning. If what you heard from the beginning abides in you, you also will abide in the Son and in the Father. [25]And this is the promise that He has promised us—eternal life. [26]These things I have written to you concerning those who try to deceive you. [27]But the anointing which you have received from Him abides in you, and you do not need that anyone teach you; but as the same anointing teaches you concerning all things, and is true, and is not a lie, and just as it has taught you, you will abide in Him.

The word abide simply means live. The title above could therefore read life lives in you. From the reading above, we know that when we receive Jesus Christ, life has come to live in us. It tells us that not only has life come to live in us, we also live in life. This means that God lives in us and we also live in God. We are empowered by God living in us. We are equipped with the knowledge and ability of God. Jesus said that the things that he did when he walked the earth we could even do more because he lives in us. We are also assured of our protection and his glory over us because we live in him. If anyone wants to challenge us, they must challenge him first like chicks under their mother's wings. What a place to be. If the enemy can distract you from that place of protection, he has got you. On the other hand, if the enemy can deceive you that you do not have the ability of God residing in you, he has got you. You are in a good location friend. Receive, meditate and confess this reality. Don't dwell or confess any other lie. Because of Jesus, you are blessed and no one can touch it.

PRAYER
Thank you father for the revelation that only I can give my blessing away and no one can touch it. Holy Spirit help me not to be distracted.

Further reading: 1 John chapter 2

15th May
YOUR MANSION IN HEAVEN

John 14:1-6

> "Let not your heart be troubled; you believe in God, believe also in Me. ²In My Father's house are many mansions; if it were not so, I would have told you. I go to prepare a place for you. ³And if I go and prepare a place for you, I will come again and receive you to Myself; that where I am, there you may be also. ⁴And where I go you know, and the way you know." ⁵Thomas said to Him, "Lord, we do not know where You are going, and how can we know the way?" ⁶Jesus said to him, "I am the way, the truth, and the life. No one comes to the Father except through Me.

You may not see Jesus face to face now but prepare yourself to see him face to face later. He lives in you. Be conscious of his presence with you all the time. He is not here to distract you from your assignment but to empower you for the assignment. You may be privileged to se him in a vision every now and then. Visions are given to encourage us. Visions are when our spiritual eyes are open to perceive happenings in the spirit. His encouragement is to refresh us for our assignment. Our assignment is given to us by his word. Whether we see him or not, let us receive his word and walk in obedience. The assignment of Jesus at this moment is to intercede for us and prepare our mansions. Jesus is indeed preparing a great reward for us as we complete our assignment. Our assignment is to bring the world back to God. We have been made ministers of reconciliation to reconcile the world back to God. When you finish your assignment, Jesus will gratefully welcome you into your mansion and your place will be by his side forever. Congratulations, you have life everlasting. There is space in life everlasting for the whole world. Let them know.

PRAYER

Dear Holy Spirit, help me perform my task of reconciling the world to the father. Jesus, thank you for preparing my place for me. Father I thank you for your love.

Further reading: John chapter 14

16th May
THE BREAD OF LIFE

John 6:35-40

> *And Jesus said to them, "I am the bread of life. He who comes to Me shall never hunger, and he who believes in Me shall never thirst. ^{36}But I said to you that you have seen Me and yet do not believe. ^{37}All that the Father gives Me will come to Me, and the one who comes to Me I will by no means cast out. ^{38}For I have come down from heaven, not to do My own will, but the will of Him who sent Me. ^{39}This is the will of the Father who sent Me, that of all He has given Me I should lose nothing, but should raise it up at the last day. ^{40}And this is the will of Him who sent Me, that everyone who sees the Son and believes in Him may have everlasting life; and I will raise him up at the last day."*

Bread is probably the most common food in the world. When Jesus therefore says I am the bread of life, he is saying that I am the food that will give you life. In other words, crave for me more than you crave for bread. Some people wake up in the morning and crave their morning cup of tea more than they crave for Jesus. Some people are in such a hurry to make money that they forget to pray and acknowledge the waiting love of Jesus. Some people may have such strong desires for certain things that they think their lives depend on those things. Jesus is telling us that if we desire real life then he is the person we should eat. He promises that if you eat him you would be satisfied. In John chapter 4, he makes a similar statement to a woman from Samaria. He tells her that he, Jesus, is living water and if you drink him you would never thirst. When you drink ordinary water you would thirst again. Don't forget to crave more for the word of God than food.

PRAYER

Bread of life, feed me today. I desire you more than the deer desires water. Holy Spirit, order my steps today.

Further reading: John chapter 6

17th May
TO LIVE IS CHRIST

Philippians 1:19-24

> For I know that this will turn out for my deliverance through your prayer and the supply of the Spirit of Jesus Christ, [20]according to my earnest expectation and hope that in nothing I shall be ashamed, but with all boldness, as always, so now also Christ will be magnified in my body, whether by life or by death. [21]For to me, to live is Christ, and to die is gain. [22]But if I live on in the flesh, this will mean fruit from my labor; yet what I shall choose I cannot tell. [23]For I am hard-pressed between the two, having a desire to depart and be with Christ, which is far better. [24]Nevertheless to remain in the flesh is more needful for you

The apostle Paul had such a wonderful revelation of life in Jesus Christ. He was sold out. He knew his assignment and was keen on completing his assignment. He also knew that if he should depart from this world, he was going to his reward. He confides that he did not know which to choose. He confesses that the reward looks a better prospect but there are people on the earth who could be helped with the anointing on his life. I pray that the Holy Spirit will give you a revelation of life as Paul had. He sees death as a door into eternity with Jesus Christ. That is a real exciting prospect. May we be able to say like Paul when the time comes for us to depart that we have fought a good fight, finished the course and now ready for our reward. For Paul, to live was Christ. Christ was responsible for taking care of his needs and he was responsible for taking care of the needs of Christ. Be swallowed up in Christ and let mortality be swallowed up in immortality. Enjoy life in Christ.

PRAYER

Father, I thank you for the example set by Paul our brother. Holy Spirit, help me stay the course and not be distracted. To live is Christ.

Further reading: Philippians chapter 1

18th May
HE GIVES POWER TO THE WEAK

Isaiah 40: 29-31

He gives power to the weak, And to those who have no might He increases strength. Even the youths shall faint and be weary, And the young men shall utterly fall, But those who wait on the Lord Shall renew their strength; They shall mount up with wings like eagles, They shall run and not be weary, They shall walk and not faint.

What a mighty God we serve. In God even the weak can shout for joy because they will not remain weak. Whilst in the natural, every ability can fade and even the strong can be weakened, those who put their trust in the Lord will be strong even when they are weak. We associate old age with weakness but the Lord gives an assurance that he will make us strong even in our old age. Someone once remarked that God's promises are unbelievable. They may be unbelievable if you view them with your natural mind. I can assure you that if you will trust and receive God's word as it is, these 'unbelievable' promises can come to pass in your life. God tells us in the bible that his ways are not our ways and his thoughts are not our thoughts. His thoughts are heavenly and our thoughts are earthly. He created everything. We are enjoying everything. It will take his mind to understand his ways. He has offered us his mind if we will receive Jesus into our lives. We can become one with him. He will come and live in us and we will live in him. If the almighty God himself lives in us then we can be assured of his strength in our lives. We can have a strong spirit, a strong mind and a strong body. Let the weak say I am strong. Yes you are strong in every area of your life.

PRAYER

Thank you father that by your intervention I am strong. No weapon against me shall prosper. I have strength to defeat any troop that rises against me.

Further reading: Isaiah chapter 40

19th May
TEACHING, PREACHING AND HEALING

Matthew 9:35-38

> *Then Jesus went about all the cities and villages, teaching in their synagogues, preaching the gospel of the kingdom, and healing every sickness and every disease among the people. ³⁶But when He saw the multitudes, He was moved with compassion for them, because they were weary and scattered, like sheep having no shepherd. ³⁷Then He said to His disciples, "The harvest truly is plentiful, but the laborers are few. ³⁸Therefore pray the Lord of the harvest to send out labourers into His harvest."*

Jesus did three things when he walked the earth in his flesh. He taught, preached and healed the sick. This continues to be the heart desire of Jesus. He desires that people would come to salvation through the preaching of the gospel; that people would have the understanding of his word through teaching. He also desires greatly that we would receive our deliverance from all sickness. Sickness is torture. It comes from hell and must be treated as such. Jesus healed the sick who came to him. Restoration to perfect health is part of the package of peace that Jesus has made available to us through his death on the cross. Let us not settle for anything less than total health. The Holy Spirit makes available to us every gift that Jesus had. Remember the Holy Spirit is the Spirit of the Father and the Son. With the power of the Holy Spirit in us, not only are we healed, we are also empowered to bring healing to those who need healing. We are commissioned to preach the gospel, teach the word of God and heal the sick. We are anointed just as Jesus was to undertake this assignment on his behalf. Jesus walked in divine health. We can also walk in divine health. This is God's promise to you. Receive it today. Rise up, take your mat and walk. In other words, rise up in faith out of every infirmity today. You are strong.

PRAYER

Thank you Jesus for your heart to heal. I believe that no sickness can stand before the power of your life. I receive my healing today and I will take your healing wherever I go.

Further reading: Matthew chapter 9

20th May
POWER TO HEAL THEM ALL
Luke 6:17-19

> *And He came down with them and stood on a level place with a crowd of His disciples and a great multitude of people from all Judea and Jerusalem, and from the seacoast of Tyre and Sidon, who came to hear Him and be healed of their diseases, 18as well as those who were tormented with unclean spirits. And they were healed. 19And the whole multitude sought to touch Him, for power went out from Him and healed them all.*

The people came from their cities and villages not only to listen to Jesus but also to be healed by him. The people saw him as a healer of diseases so the sick came to him in their numbers and they were not disappointed. He healed them all. They would have brought all kinds of illnesses but Jesus had enough power in him to heal everyone. The scripture says power went out of him to heal every sickness. Even those who were possessed by demons were delivered. There is no sickness that Jesus cannot heal. Some sick have accepted their condition and learnt to live with it. I encourage you to expose every infirmity in your life to the healing power of Jesus. Even when the medical experts say there is no cure, remember it is the opinion of mere men. Let God be true and every man a liar. God can heal every disease. He even raises the dead. Man's knowledge is limited. God's power is unlimited. If you call on him today, he has promised to answer you. Every father wants his children to be happy. If you were God, would you not heal your children? I can imagine the joy with which the sick people returned to their towns and villages healed. I can almost hear them talking about Jesus and praising him for their healing. We make God happy when we rise up from our infirmities and give him the glory for it. He will do it for you to the praise of his glory.

PRAYER
Father, I thank you for my complete healing. I lay down my sickness at your feet Lord Jesus.

Further reading: Luke chapter 6

21st May
HE HEALS ALL OUR DISEASES

Psalm 103:1-5

Bless the Lord, O my soul; And all that is within me, bless His holy name! Bless the Lord, O my soul, And forget not all His benefits: Who forgives all your iniquities, Who heals all your diseases, Who redeems your life from destruction, Who crowns you with loving kindness and tender mercies, Who satisfies your mouth with good things, So that your youth is renewed like the eagle's

From the above psalm we know that one of the things God does is heal diseases. The good news is that he does not heal just some diseases but all diseases. There is no disease which is excluded. This includes headaches, cancers, blood and heart diseases, hernias, blindness and deafness. In fact, everything that steals your health, small or big, he heals them all. Don't miss out on this benefit. The first benefit mentioned here is forgiveness from sin. Sin is your most deadly enemy. Sin keeps you away from God. This is why Jesus went to the cross of Calvary to pay the price for our sins so we could be reconciled to God. The next thing God does after forgiving our sins is to heal our diseases. The removal of sin makes us righteous. This means that the removal of sin gives us right standing with God and we have access into his presence. Disease cannot stand the light of his presence. This means that you must expect healing if you live in his presence. Believe his promise to heal all your diseases and don't treat this benefit of God lightly. When a gift is offered, it has to be received. Receive your healing today in the name of Jesus. Do not be like that cripple who went for prayer to cure his addiction to cigarettes but had accepted his inability to walk as something he had to live with for the rest of his life. God heals cripples too. Enjoy divine health from today with no intrusion.

PRAYER

Thank you Father for forgiving my sins and healing all my diseases. Your love for me is amazing.

Further reading: Psalm 103

22nd May
RIGHTEOUSNESS PRODUCES HEALING

Malachi 4:1-3

> "For behold, the day is coming, Burning like an oven, And all the proud, yes, all who do wickedly will be stubble. And the day which is coming shall burn them up," Says the Lord of hosts, "That will leave them neither root nor branch. But to you who fear My name The Sun of Righteousness shall arise With healing in His wings; And you shall go out And grow fat like stall-fed calves. You shall trample the wicked, For they shall be ashes under the soles of your feet On the day that I do this," Says the Lord of hosts.

God's word has always divided the world into two sets of people. Those who fear him and those who do not fear him. He warns those who do not fear him to prepare for the worst because they have rejected his protection. It is only under God's protection that we can escape the disasters of this world. On the other hand, he promises those who have received him, protection and provision from his bountiful supply. God has promised us righteousness. This means the right to approach him and enjoy the abundance of his grace. Before the death and resurrection of Jesus Christ, it was almost impossible to approach God. He gave Israel a set of laws to obey to be considered righteous. The bible says that Israel could not obey these laws because they did not have the capacity to do so. We must rejoice in our age as the death of Jesus Christ has made it much easier for us to approach God. Through his death, Jesus Christ paid for our sins and therefore removed the barrier between us and God. All we need to do is to accept what Jesus has done and walk in righteousness before God. When you walk in the light of God's righteousness, you walk in his healing. Righteousness is like a sun that brings healing. Receive your righteousness and healing today.

PRAYER

Thank you Jesus for paying the price for my righteousness. I receive my healing as I walk in righteousness.

Further reading: Malachi chapter 4

23rd May
BY HIS STRIPES WE ARE HEALED

Isaiah 53:4-5

> *Surely He has borne our griefs And carried our sorrows; Yet we esteemed Him stricken, Smitten by God, and afflicted. But He was wounded for our transgressions, He was bruised for our iniquities; The chastisement for our peace was upon Him, And by His stripes we are healed.*

Jesus has paid the price for our healing. There is no reason why we have to walk around sick. On the cross, Jesus paid the penalty for our sins and not only for our sins but also diseases. Every disease including HIV and all forms of cancer were put on Jesus Christ as he hung on the cross. He nailed them to the cross, went into the house of death and defeated the devil himself who is the source of death. The source of all sickness and death has been defeated. We should believe and receive this great salvation otherwise Satan will deceive us into walking in bondage to sin and sickness though we have been freed from them. Every beating Jesus received was for our healing. God specifically put our freedom from sickness in the above scripture to motivate us to receive our healing. The new life we receive from Jesus Christ is a righteous and healed life. We need to enforce it in our own lives as we have authority over our lives. God will not violate this authority. He has given us our free will. He has provided everything pertaining to life and godliness to us. We have to forcibly take it. We have an enemy in Satan who is trying to deceive us not to enjoy this offer from God. God will not force you to receive anything from him. He offers it and you will have to receive it. You receive salvation by turning away from your sins to Jesus and accepting the lordship of Jesus. You receive healing by affirming the lordship of Jesus and commanding every sickness to leave your body. Do that today.

PRAYER
In the name of Jesus, I declare you Lord Jesus as the Lord of my life. I command you (name your sickness), leave my body now.

Further reading: Isaiah chapter 55

24th May
HE WILL BIND YOU UP

Hosea 6:1-3

Come, and let us return to the Lord; For He has torn, but He will heal us; He has stricken, but He will bind us up. After two days He will revive us; On the third day He will raise us up, That we may live in His sight. Let us know, Let us pursue the knowledge of the Lord. His going forth is established as the morning; He will come to us like the rain, Like the latter and former rain to the earth.

Let's return to the Lord. He is the healer. Although God takes responsibility for the bad things that happen to Israel in the Old Testament, real responsibility lay with Israel itself. For instance if God says to Israel that if you abandon my ways I will make your enemies defeat you, he is not saying he is personally going to wake up your enemy to come and defeat you. When you make a choice of disobeying God, you are also opting out of his protection. Disobedience means you want to do things your own way. If you are able to do things your way then you are able to defend yourself. Without God, you are exposed to a 'survival of the fittest' world. The weak is always prey to the strong. God does not need to go and wake up your enemies. The survival of the strong depends on the tributes of the weak. Return to the Lord and he will bind your wounds up. It is rough out there. The apostle James says that we should not blame God when we fall into temptation because God cannot tempt you with evil. Although God has supreme power to influence every situation, he is limited by your choice. Make a good choice today by approaching the father for your healing. He has promised to bind up your wound and raise you up. God does not change. He is the same yesterday, today and forever. He will do what he has promised.

PRAYER

Thank you father for your promise to heal, revive, bind up and raise me. I have chosen to be with you forever. I receive my total restoration today in the name of Jesus.

Further reading: Hosea chapter 6

25th May
STRONG, FRESH AND FRUITFUL

Psalm 1:1-3

Blessed is the man who walks not in the counsel of the ungodly, Nor stands in the path of sinners, Nor sits in the seat of the scornful; But his delight is in the law of the Lord, And in His law he meditates day and night. He shall be like a tree Planted by the rivers of water, That brings forth its fruit in its season, Whose leaf also shall not wither; And whatever he does shall prosper.

The hidden desire of every heart is to be strong (fit and healthy), fresh (evergreen), and fruitful (multiply). This is the promise God gives to those who trust and delight in his word. There are other things competing for our attention. The advice of ungodly people is one of them. You cannot base your life on the limited knowledge of man. Some have studied books and are quite knowledgeable in certain areas of life. Thank God for people who have studied to help us understand the environment we live in. Yet all the education and knowledge we have is less than one percent of the knowledge available. Scientific research confirms that we use only a small percentage of the capacity of our brain. God has one hundred percent of all knowledge because he created all things. This knowledge of God is available to us through His Word revealed to us by the power of the Holy Spirit. Why should we seek advice from the ungodly who, at best, have less than one percent of knowledge when the source of all knowledge has opened to us the good treasure of his glory? Why should we enjoy the company of sinners when the blood of Jesus has opened the door of righteousness to us. Sin leads to death, righteousness to life. Why should we be friends with proud people who look down on others when the king of kings is calling us to his side. He is full of love for others and wants to serve them with strength, freshness and fruitfulness. Meditate on the word of God day night and enjoy real life.

PRAYER
Thank you father for your word and the many good promises in your word. I will meditate on your word and make my way prosperous.

Further reading: Psalm 1

26th May
FRESH AND FLOURISHING

Psalm 92:10-15

But my horn You have exalted like a wild ox; I have been anointed with fresh oil. My eye also has seen my desire on my enemies; My ears hear my desire on the wicked Who rise up against me. The righteous shall flourish like a palm tree, He shall grow like a cedar in Lebanon. Those who are planted in the house of the Lord Shall flourish in the courts of our God. They shall still bear fruit in old age; They shall be fresh and flourishing, To declare that the Lord is upright; He is my rock, and there is no unrighteousness in Him.

There is nowhere in the bible where it states that if you are faithful with the Lord, disease will attack you and you shall suffer. Rather, God's promises to those who would come to him and trust in him are wonderful and uplifting. Sometimes it sounds too good to be true. This is because he is a good God. In John 10:10, Jesus tells us that while there is a thief whose aim towards people is to steal, destroy and kill them, the purpose of Jesus is to bring abundant life. God is good and he is also almighty. This means that there is nothing he cannot do. He can create anything he wants to create. He can also raise the dead. It is this God who is promising the righteous that they will flourish like a palm tree, bear fruit in old age and they shall be fresh and flourishing in the house of God. If you have made Jesus your Lord, you qualify for all these promises. When I think of all the promises God gives to those who trust in him, I cannot help but flow in grateful praise. What have I done to deserve all these promises? His love entered my darkness, lifted me into his light, made me a prince of heaven and is showering me with such blessing. I am fresh and flourishing. He has said it so I am. My feeling has nothing to do with it.

PRAYER

Father I am so grateful. Your promises are so wonderful to me. I believe every promise and will walk in each of them.

Further reading: Psalm 92

27th May
JESUS IS WILLING TO HEAL YOU

Luke 5:12-16

> And it happened when He was in a certain city, that behold, a man who was full of leprosy saw Jesus; and he fell on his face and implored Him, saying, "Lord, if You are willing, You can make me clean." ¹³Then He put out His hand and touched him, saying, "I am willing; be cleansed." Immediately the leprosy left him. ¹⁴And He charged him to tell no one, "But go and show yourself to the priest, and make an offering for your cleansing, as a testimony to them, just as Moses commanded." ¹⁵However, the report went around concerning Him all the more; and great multitudes came together to hear, and to be healed by Him of their infirmities. ¹⁶So He Himself often withdrew into the wilderness and prayed.

This question of the leprous man to Jesus is a question that many people seeking healing have asked themselves. There are some who believe that Jesus healed people in his time but does not heal people now. Jesus is alive and has not changed. He continues to heal. He has anointed us who have come into him to bring healing to the world. There is a second group that sees God as a healer but are not sure whether he wants to heal them now. The leper above fell into the second category. He knew that if Jesus was willing, he was capable of healing him of his leprosy. Jesus' response confirmed the character and nature of God. God is willing to heal everyone. He accomplished healing for us at Calvary. 1 Peter 2:24 puts our healing in the past tense. This means that the willingness of Jesus has already been demonstrated by him taking all our sicknesses on the cross. We need to receive this promise by faith by reminding ourselves of the penalty paid. We need to keep the word of healing in our mouths. Rejoice for God is willing and capable to heal and cleanse you.

PRAYER

Thank you for your love that wants to see me well. I thank you father for your willingness to clean me up from every disease. I receive my healing today.

Further reading: Luke chapter 5

28th May
YOUR WITHERED HAND SHALL GROW OUT

Mark 3:1-5

> And He entered the synagogue again, and a man was there who had a withered hand. ²So they watched Him closely, whether He would heal him on the Sabbath, so that they might accuse Him. ³And He said to the man who had the withered hand, "Step forward." ⁴Then He said to them, "Is it lawful on the Sabbath to do good or to do evil, to save life or to kill?" But they kept silent. ⁵And when He had looked around at them with anger, being grieved by the hardness of their hearts, He said to the man, "Stretch out your hand." And he stretched it out, and his hand was restored as whole as the other.

There are certain infirmities that many accept as normal and therefore decide to live with it. A withered hand could be one such disability. Do not accept any disability as normal. Please don't walk around feeling sorry for yourself if you have any infirmity. I am not advocating that. I am encouraging you not to give up on God who is able to heal all diseases. The attitude of the Jews in the synagogue was interesting. They knew Jesus would heal the infirmity of the man if he came face to face with it. One would have thought they would be happy to have a healer in the house. Instead they were ready to reject the healer for their own entrenched errors on the doctrine of the sabbath. The Light of the world was in their midst but they chose to ignore him because his presence undermined their authority. Don't let anyone block your healing with their religion. Jesus heals all diseases. Receive your healing. If your healing is delayed, don't try to explain it away. As long as you are standing in righteousness, continue to thank God for your healing. As a father treats his son so does God treat us. He will not give us sickness to teach us a lesson. You will not do that to your child.

PRAYER
Thank you father that you want to see me well and whole. I declare with faith that every organ in my body is functioning properly.

Further reading: Mark chapter 3

29th May
DEMONS MUST OBEY

Mark 1:21-27

> Then they went into Capernaum, and immediately on the Sabbath He entered the synagogue and taught. ²²And they were astonished at His teaching, for He taught them as one having authority, and not as the scribes. ²³Now there was a man in their synagogue with an unclean spirit. And he cried out, ²⁴saying, "Let us alone! What have we to do with You, Jesus of Nazareth? Did You come to destroy us? I know who You are—the Holy One of God!" ²⁵But Jesus rebuked him, saying, "Be quiet, and come out of him!" ²⁶And when the unclean spirit had convulsed him and cried out with a loud voice, he came out of him. ²⁷Then they were all amazed, so that they questioned among themselves, saying, "What is this? What new doctrine is this? For with authority He commands even the unclean spirits, and they obey Him."

There are some who are troubled by demonic spirits deeply affecting their thoughts and emotions. This man affected by demons was probably a regular attender at the synagogue. His behavior was probably strange but no one in the synagogue could do anything about it. When Jesus turned up, he did something about it. Are you experiencing extreme emotions and thoughts you can't explain. Jesus can do something about that. Spiritual things are spiritually discerned. I have interactions with people who say they are Christians but do not believe in the existence of demons. There are many encounters in the bible with demons. These are foul spirits who try to drive you to do wrong things you would normally not do. Ignorance makes you an easy target for these demons. Every spirit filled Christian has the power to drive out demons. Jesus through the Holy Spirit has empowered us with the same power with which he performed miracles. If it is strange, speak to the demon and drive it out. If you walk separated to God and in the freshness of the word, demons will be scared to come near you.

PRAYER

Dear Jesus, thank you for seating me with you far above every principality and power. I am fully armed against any demonic power.

Further reading: Mark chapter 1

30th May
HEALING WILL FOLLOW YOU

Mark 16:14-18

Later He appeared to the eleven as they sat at the table; and He rebuked their unbelief and hardness of heart, because they did not believe those who had seen Him after He had risen. ^{15}And He said to them, "Go into all the world and preach the gospel to every creature. ^{16}He who believes and is baptized will be saved; but he who does not believe will be condemned. ^{17}And these signs will follow those who believe: In My name they will cast out demons; they will speak with new tongues; ^{18}they will take up serpents; and if they drink anything deadly, it will by no means hurt them; they will lay hands on the sick, and they will recover."

The ministry of Jesus did not end with his ascension into heaven after the resurrection. When he walked the earth mainly in the land of Israel, he was demonstrating to the people of Israel the goodness of heaven that God wanted the earth to experience. Israel was in covenant with God because of the obedience of Abraham. Jesus was therefore born a Jew in fulfillment of a promise made to Abraham. However the mission of God was to reconcile the world to Himself. Jesus could not accomplish this in the flesh. He was therefore going to recruit many brethren, impart His Spirit on them and watch them do what he demonstrated in the first place. Righteousness with God has brought us healing. We have not just been healed, we have also been empowered to bring healing to the world. The scripture above tells us that as we have received this invitation of Jesus Christ, signs and wonders will accompany our preaching of the good news. This includes healing and driving out demons. The power of heaven has been made available on earth. This power is in our hearts, mouths and hands. Walk in healing from today. Receive healing and bring healing to others who need it.

PRAYER

Thank you Jesus for this wonderful privilege of carrying your healing power. I trust your word that when I lay my hands, the sick shall be healed.

Further reading: Mark chapter 16

31st May
RISE UP AND WALK

Acts 3:1-8

Now Peter and John went up together to the temple at the hour of prayer, the ninth hour. ²And a certain man lame from his mother's womb was carried, whom they laid daily at the gate of the temple which is called Beautiful, to ask alms from those who entered the temple; ³who, seeing Peter and John about to go into the temple, asked for alms. ⁴And fixing his eyes on him, with John, Peter said, "Look at us." ⁵So he gave them his attention, expecting to receive something from them. ⁶Then Peter said, "Silver and gold I do not have, but what I do have I give you: In the name of Jesus Christ of Nazareth, rise up and walk." ⁷And he took him by the right hand and lifted him up, and immediately his feet and ankle bones received strength. ⁸So he, leaping up, stood and walked and entered the temple with them—walking, leaping, and praising God.

A lame man who had no hope received restoration by the power of the Holy Spirit. Because of his lameness, he could not work. He was reduced to begging for money so he could look after himself. Money was his God. If you could give him some money, he would worship you. Today there are many who would worship you if you could give them some money. We are in a world that worships money. Yet there is a power that surpasses money. This is the power of the Holy Spirit. For this lame man, a good day would be the day that he would make a lot of money. He would be carried home and sitting on his legs gleefully count his money. An encounter with two followers of Christ was going to change all that. Peter announces to him that they do not have the money he is asking for but they have something else. He commanded the man to rise up and walk in the name of Jesus Christ. The man did not only walk but he was leaping and praising God. This would delight God. You are also a Christian go and do likewise.

PRAYER
Thank you Jesus for this power. I am stepping out boldly in your name.

Further reading: Acts chapter 3

June

1st June
GOD HAS PREPARED A GOOD LAND FOR YOU

Deuteronomy 8:6-11

> "Therefore you shall keep the commandments of the Lord your God, to walk in His ways and to fear Him. ^{7}For the Lord your God is bringing you into a good land, a land of brooks of water, of fountains and springs, that flow out of valleys and hills; ^{8}a land of wheat and barley, of vines and fig trees and pomegranates, a land of olive oil and honey; ^{9}a land in which you will eat bread without scarcity, in which you will lack nothing; a land whose stones are iron and out of whose hills you can dig copper. ^{10}When you have eaten and are full, then you shall bless the Lord your God for the good land which He has given you. ^{11}"Beware that you do not forget the Lord your God by not keeping His commandments, His judgments, and His statutes which I command you today.

God created all things. Everything belongs to God. He gives it out as he wills. You are a child of God and an heir. You are therefore entitled to a good portion of God's creation. In the above scripture, God is reminding Israel that he is bringing them to a good land. Israel is entitled to this good land because of a promise that God had made to Abraham and his descendants. God's gift to man when he created man was the beautiful land that he had created. He had blessed man to be fruitful, multiply, occupy, subdue and have dominion over the earth. When the first man disobeyed God, thereby refusing this covenant promise, the land no longer worked for him. One of the things God said to man after the disobedience was that he would sweat to get anything beneficial from the land. God sets up and removes kings. When Jesus paid the price for reconciliation, he made it possible for us to regain a right for the land to work for us. When we receive Jesus we have become part of his family and receive a right to what is his. God has prepared a good land for you.

PRAYER

Thank you father for my good inheritance. The land will work for me.

Further reading: Deuteronomy 8

2nd June
GOD'S PROVISION GUARANTEED

Matthew 6:25-30

²⁵"Therefore I say to you, do not worry about your life, what you will eat or what you will drink; nor about your body, what you will put on. Is not life more than food and the body more than clothing? ²⁶Look at the birds of the air, for they neither sow nor reap nor gather into barns; yet your heavenly Father feeds them. Are you not of more value than they? ²⁷Which of you by worrying can add one cubit to his stature? ²⁸"So why do you worry about clothing? Consider the lilies of the field, how they grow: they neither toil nor spin; ²⁹and yet I say to you that even Solomon in all his glory was not arrayed like one of these. ³⁰Now if God so clothes the grass of the field, which today is, and tomorrow is thrown into the oven, will He not much more clothe you, O you of little faith?

God is all powerful. Through our reconciliation with him, he has become our father. The above scripture calls Him our heavenly father. The scripture makes an interesting comparison. If our heavenly father takes time to feed birds and clothe flowers that are less important than you, how is he possibly going to leave you out. He reprimands the listeners to have faith in God. You have come back home by being born again. Stop worrying about your needs because your provision is guaranteed. For many people, their mindset is locked up in the lifestyle they had before they came to know God. Before we knew God, we had to struggle for everything we needed. We were our own source. Under the curse of Eden, we had to sweat to eat. We are no longer under bondage. Jesus Christ has come to set us free and made us joint heirs with him. As all things belong to him, so has our provision been guaranteed. Fear not, you will never lack.

PRAYER

Father I thank you for the new status in which I stand. How wonderful it is to know that I am a son and heir. I will walk in obedience as a true son.

Further reading: Matthew 6

3rd June
YOU ARE MARKED FOR GOD'S BLESSING

Deuteronomy 28:1-5

> "Now it shall come to pass, if you diligently obey the voice of the Lord your God, to observe carefully all His commandments which I command you today, that the Lord your God will set you high above all nations of the earth. ²And all these blessings shall come upon you and overtake you, because you obey the voice of the Lord your God: ³"Blessed shall you be in the city, and blessed shall you be in the country. ⁴"Blessed shall be the fruit of your body, the produce of your ground and the increase of your herds, the increase of your cattle and the offspring of your flocks. ⁵"Blessed shall be your basket and your kneading bowl.

Deuteronomy chapter 28 sets out the blessings we should expect when we walk with God. It also sets out the curses that will come our way when we walk in disobedience to God. As a child of God, know that you are marked for God's blessing. It is only a wicked father who will keep good away from his children. No good father will rain curses on his child. Be confident of the fact that you have the mark of God's family. God is a good father. To know how good God is, think of the best person you can think of and multiply their goodness a billion times. In other words, you cannot measure God's goodness. The day you stepped out of your sinful nature into God's righteousness, you were marked for God's blessing: His total provision and protection. Don't be anxious another minute of your life. It is not your responsibility to work for your provision any longer. Your responsibility is to believe that Jesus has paid the price to bring you into the household of God. The fruit of this move is that you are under God's blessing. He is obligated to take care of you. Rejoice for he has promised that if you come to him no one can take you out of his hands. Please don't jump out yourself.

PRAYER
Thank you father for this total salvation which is beyond my understanding. Help me Holy Spirit to fully walk in my status.

Further reading: Deuteronomy 28:1-14

4th June
WHATEVER YOU DO SHALL PROSPER

Psalm 1:1-3

Blessed is the man Who walks not in the counsel of the ungodly, Nor stands in the path of sinners, Nor sits in the seat of the scornful; But his delight is in the law of the Lord, And in His law he meditates day and night. He shall be like a tree Planted by the rivers of water, That brings forth its fruit in its season, Whose leaf also shall not wither; And whatever he does shall prosper. The ungodly are not so, But are like the chaff which the wind drives away. Therefore the ungodly shall not stand in the judgment, Nor sinners in the congregation of the righteous. For the Lord knows the way of the righteous, But the way of the ungodly shall perish.

Your prosperity is very important to God. When you prosper, you have the peace of mind and gratitude to praise God. Your joy is the desire of your father in heaven. That is why the bible says there is fullness of joy in his presence and pleasure at his right hand. The scripture above encourages us to delight in the word of God and meditate on it day and night. The promise is that if we do this, everything we do shall prosper. We are also warned not to associate or follow the advice of sinners. God's word is truth and he does not want us to mix it with any other word. Some Christians tend to respect the words of men more than the word of God especially words from so called experts. Many people will choose to respect the word of the medical consultant even if it is contrary to the healing word of God. Many will believe the conclusions of the financial expert even when it is contrary to God's promise of provision. Friend, flee the counsel of the ungodly, the path of sinners and the seat of the scornful. Rather delight and meditate on the word of God and prosper in everything you put your hands to.

PRAYER
I thank you father that your plan for me is to prosper me. I will walk in your prosperity all the days of my life.

Further reading: Psalm 2

5th June
EXPECT MULTIPLE RETURNS

Luke 6:37-38

Judge not, and you shall not be judged. Condemn not, and you shall not be condemned. Forgive, and you will be forgiven. ³⁸Give, and it will be given to you: good measure, pressed down, shaken together, and running over will be put into your bosom. For with the same measure that you use, it will be measured back to you."

The covenant of seedtime and harvest established in Genesis 8:22 is a spiritual law that goes back to the time of the creation of man. In Genesis chapter 1, after God had made the heavens and earth, he created man in his own image. God in verse 29 of the same chapter asked man to use every seed bearing fruit and seed bearing herb for food. A seed that is planted produces much fruit. Jesus said that unless a grain of seed falls down and dies, it abides alone but when it dies it produces much fruit. A farmer sows seed to produce a harvest. The above scripture promises that whatever seed we sow will produce much fruit. God will release special rain to our seed. It is only a cursed land that does not produce a good harvest. Our land is not cursed. God through Jesus Christ has given us a good inheritance. Expect a good return for every seed you sow. The land we have inherited as children of God is better than the land Israel inherited. Let godly words and good deeds be your seed and inherit abundant blessing and fruit of righteousness. God is big and provides abundant return. Trust in his promise of good returns for your investment. Your faith is demonstrated by the seed you sow. The apostle Paul says in 2 Corinthians 9:6 that he who sows sparingly will reap sparingly and he who sows bountifully will reap bountifully. Be determined to demonstrate your faith by sowing bountifully and expect a bountiful harvest.

PRAYER

Thank you father for the promise of a good return on my harvest. Whatever you have given to me I will use it as seed for a good return. Help me Holy Spirit.

Further reading: Luke chapter 6

6th June
HUNDREDFOLD RETURN

Mark 10:28-31

Then Peter began to say to Him, "See, we have left all and followed You." ^{29}So Jesus answered and said, "Assuredly, I say to you, there is no one who has left house or brothers or sisters or father or mother or wife or children or lands, for My sake and the gospel's, ^{30}who shall not receive a hundredfold now in this time—houses and brothers and sisters and mothers and children and lands, with persecutions—and in the age to come, eternal life. ^{31}But many who are first will be last, and the last first."

When you make a decision to follow Jesus, you are bound to lose some things. You may have to let go of some friends, desires and possessions. Your walk with Jesus is like a marriage. The bible tells us concerning marriage that we leave certain things in order to cleave to our wife. When you are born again, you are born again into a new life. The new life brings you new aspirations and desires. In the above scripture, Peter reminded Jesus that they had left their businesses, property and family to follow Jesus. The response of Jesus was very encouraging. He assures Peter that there is a good return for whatever you sacrifice for the sake of following Jesus Christ. Jesus promises that you will reap a hundredfold in this life. In other words your reward is not just in heaven but here on this earth and now. God promises that you will receive a hundredfold return on your business, property and family here in this life. You cannot lose with God. He is the creator of all things and owns all things. You are in very rich company if you align with God. When you withhold your strength, time and possessions from God, you are taking life into your own hands. Make the best investment you have ever made by giving your life and all you possess to God. Expect a hundredfold return as God can never lie to you.

PRAYER

Thank you Jesus for the promise of a hundredfold return. You left everything you had and offered your life for my salvation. I offer everything I have to you in return.

Further reading: Mark chapter 10

7th June
YOU HAVE POWER TO GET WEALTH

Deuteronomy 8:11-18

"Beware that you do not forget the Lord your God by not keeping His commandments, His judgments, and His statutes which I command you today, ¹²lest—when you have eaten and are full, and have built beautiful houses and dwell in them; ¹³and when your herds and your flocks multiply, and your silver and your gold are multiplied, and all that you have is multiplied; ¹⁴when your heart is lifted up, and you forget the Lord your God who brought you out of the land of Egypt, from the house of bondage; ¹⁵who led you through that great and terrible wilderness, in which were fiery serpents and scorpions and thirsty land where there was no water; who brought water for you out of the flinty rock; ¹⁶who fed you in the wilderness with manna, which your fathers did not know, that He might humble you and that He might test you, to do you good in the end— ¹⁷then you say in your heart, 'My power and the might of my hand have gained me this wealth.' ¹⁸"And you shall remember the Lord your God, for it is He who gives you power to get wealth, that He may establish His covenant which He swore to your fathers, as it is this day.

The bible tells us that every good thing comes from God. All things belong to him. He gives it to whom he wills. Wealth that does not come from God does not last. You have to fight to protect it or fight to gain more. It is God who gives the power to get wealth as the above scripture says. God has promised to give Israel land that flows with milk and honey. Milk represents the prosperity of their business as Israel was made up of mainly animal farmers. Honey represents the natural resource of the land. God assures them that they would be wealthy but in their wealth they should not forget he is the source of their wealth. As a brother of Jesus you belong to the household of God. The wealth of God is your portion. Walk in it.

PRAYER
Thank you father that because I am family, you have given me power to get wealth.

Further reading: Deuteronomy chapter 8

8th June
WEALTH AND RICHES WILL BE IN YOUR HOUSE

Psalm 112

> *Praise the Lord! Blessed is the man who fears the Lord, Who delights greatly in His commandments. His descendants will be mighty on earth; The generation of the upright will be blessed. Wealth and riches will be in his house, And his righteousness endures forever. Unto the upright there arises light in the darkness; He is gracious, and full of compassion, and righteous. A good man deals graciously and lends; He will guide his affairs with discretion. Surely he will never be shaken; The righteous will be in everlasting remembrance. He will not be afraid of evil tidings; His heart is steadfast, trusting in the Lord. His heart is established; He will not be afraid, Until he sees his desire upon his enemies. He has dispersed abroad, He has given to the poor; His righteousness endures forever; His horn will be exalted with honor. The wicked will see it and be grieved; He will gnash his teeth and melt away; The desire of the wicked shall perish.*

The promises of God to the righteous are so good that there is the tendency to feel that he is not talking about you. We must remember that God cannot exaggerate. To describe God, multiply exaggeration by a billion times and you will still not reach who God really is. Small in God's eyes is still bigger than anything we can think of. This is why the humility with which Jesus walked amongst men and allowed himself to be crucified as a common criminal astounds us. The humility with which this great God can come and live in our little hearts overpowers our thoughts. Friend the reconciliation that Jesus' death on the cross brought makes us righteous. Righteousness means we are like God. We have been translated to the God class and that gives our hearts the capacity to receive God. The promise of God to the righteous is that wealth and riches will be in his house. God is talking about you. Receive it today.

PRAYER

Father, I confidently receive wealth and riches in my house because I live in your house. I do not expect anything less.

Further reading: Psalm 113

9th June
YOU SHALL EAT THE GOOD OF THE LAND

Isaiah 1:16-20

> *"Wash yourselves, make yourselves clean; Put away the evil of your doings from before My eyes. Cease to do evil, Learn to do good; Seek justice, Rebuke the oppressor; Defend the fatherless, Plead for the widow. "Come now, and let us reason together," Says the Lord, "Though your sins are like scarlet, They shall be as white as snow; Though they are red like crimson, They shall be as wool. If you are willing and obedient, You shall eat the good of the land; But if you refuse and rebel, You shall be devoured by the sword"; For the mouth of the Lord has spoken.*

The land produces good as well as bad. The willing and obedient shall eat the good of the land. The unwilling and disobedient shall eat of the bad of the land. If you turn your back on the Lord and his word, you will eat of the bad of the land because you are disobedient. The sinner cannot hear or understand the ways of God. If you are in sin now, God is inviting you to turn to him and abandon your sin. He has promised that if you turn to him, he will clean you up. The greatest sinner who comes to God becomes the purest saint. God himself is going to give you a righteous bath. When you receive this righteous bath, your portion becomes the good of the land not the bad. It is not God's will that any should eat of the bad of the land. People eat of the bad out of ignorance or rebellion. You are not one of those. If there is anything you don't understand, the door to God is open. He is ready to reason things out with you. God needs you. That is why he paid the hefty price of the cross. He needs to restore us to his blessing which was his purpose for creating us. We need him more than anything.

PRAYER
Father I choose you today. Cleanse me that I may eat of the good of the land.

Further reading: Isaiah chapter 1

10th June
PROSPERITY IN THE MIDST OF FAMINE

Genesis 26:1-5, 12-14

> *There was a famine in the land, besides the first famine that was in the days of Abraham. And Isaac went to Abimelech king of the Philistines, in Gerar. Then the Lord appeared to him and said: "Do not go down to Egypt; live in the land of which I shall tell you. ³Dwell in this land, and I will be with you and bless you; for to you and your descendants I give all these lands, and I will perform the oath which I swore to Abraham your father. ⁴And I will make your descendants multiply as the stars of heaven; I will give to your descendants all these lands; and in your seed all the nations of the earth shall be blessed; ⁵because Abraham obeyed My voice and kept My charge, My commandments, My statutes, and My laws." ¹²Then Isaac sowed in that land, and reaped in the same year a hundredfold; and the Lord blessed him. ¹³The man began to prosper, and continued prospering until he became very prosperous; ¹⁴for he had possessions of flocks and possessions of herds and a great number of servants. So the Philistines envied him.*

When you walk with God, prevailing economic conditions should not affect you. For a farming population, drought means the drying up of livelihood. Where there is drought, there is famine and famine produces death. God gives life not death. Isaac was in the midst of a famine. As everyone does, he was ready to migrate to Egypt where there was food. People always migrate from where there is lack to where there is abundance. Even animals do that. Animals can walk for hundreds of miles to be in a better economic environment. God tells Isaac not to go to Egypt and Isaac obeyed. I can imagine how some of his own friends and servants would tell him about how wrong his decision was. You can never be wrong with God. He obeyed and reaped a great harvest in the land of famine. He became rich in the midst of poverty. That is your portion.

PRAYER

Thank you father that you can bless me right here where I am. I will only move by your direction.

Further reading: Genesis chapter 26

11th June
JEHOVAH JIREH, THE LORD WILL PROVIDE

Genesis 22:12-28

> And He said, "Do not lay your hand on the lad, or do anything to him; for now I know that you fear God, since you have not withheld your son, your only son, from Me." ¹³Then Abraham lifted his eyes and looked, and there behind him was a ram caught in a thicket by its horns. So Abraham went and took the ram, and offered it up for a burnt offering instead of his son. ¹⁴And Abraham called the name of the place, The-Lord-Will-Provide; as it is said to this day, "In the Mount of the Lord it shall be provided." ¹⁵Then the Angel of the Lord called to Abraham a second time out of heaven, ¹⁶and said: "By Myself I have sworn, says the Lord, because you have done this thing, and have not withheld your son, your only son— ¹⁷blessing I will bless you, and multiplying I will multiply your descendants as the stars of the heaven and as the sand which is on the seashore; and your descendants shall possess the gate of their enemies. ¹⁸In your seed all the nations of the earth shall be blessed, because you have obeyed My voice."

Abraham went through a test and passed with God. God had planned before the foundation of the world to send his son Jesus Christ as a sacrifice for the sins of the world. For love to blossom to full benefit between two parties, it has to be mutual. God was ready to send his only begotten son. Would man be ready to give up his best to God as God planned to do? Abraham passed that test. Isaac was his best and the bible calls Isaac Abraham's only begotten son. He was the son of promise. When God saw what Abraham had done, he had no choice but to share what he had with Him. This was a covenant of love between God and Abraham. By his obedience, Abraham had demonstrated his love and trust of God. God provided a ram for the sacrifice and their friendship was sealed. God will provide for you as you have given your life to him.

PRAYER
Thank you father that you are Jehovah Jireh, my provider. I will not be anxious as you are with me.

Further reading: Genesis chapter 22

12th June
GOD PROMISES PROVISION

Deuteronomy 6:10-14

"So it shall be, when the Lord your God brings you into the land of which He swore to your fathers, to Abraham, Isaac, and Jacob, to give you large and beautiful cities which you did not build, [11]houses full of all good things, which you did not fill, hewn-out wells which you did not dig, vineyards and olive trees which you did not plant—when you have eaten and are full— [12]then beware, lest you forget the Lord who brought you out of the land of Egypt, from the house of bondage. [13]You shall fear the Lord your God and serve Him, and shall take oaths in His name. [14]You shall not go after other gods, the gods of the peoples who are all around you.

If you have turned to God by receiving Jesus Christ, know that you have entered God's promise of a good land. God has promised provision in this land. If you can provide everything you need and walk in total peace, you do not need God. If God is inviting you to change your location then there is a good reason for this. One of his main promises at our new location is his provision. He has promised houses filled with all good things which you did not build. He also promises wells, vineyards and olive trees. Wells represent life; wine represents happiness, and oil from the olives represents health and the anointing of God. To be fully provided with these is to enjoy life to the full as God intended it to be. God always promises those who would walk with him in obedience a share in what he has. The bible tells us that the earth is the Lord's and the fullness thereof. Everything on this earth belongs to the Lord. He has made total provision for those who would trust in him. He promises provision for you. Keep away from any other voice that will tell you that he would not provide. That would make God a bad father. God is a good father.

PRAYER

I believe in you and trust in your promises. You are a good father. You have provided for me and I am grateful.

Further reading: Deuteronomy chapter 6

Be Strong Devotional

13th June
THE LAND SHALL PRODUCE

Leviticus 26:3-6

> 'If you walk in My statutes and keep My commandments, and perform them, then I will give you rain in its season, the land shall yield its produce, and the trees of the field shall yield their fruit. Your threshing shall last till the time of vintage, and the vintage shall last till the time of sowing; you shall eat your bread to the full, and dwell in your land safely. I will give peace in the land, and you shall lie down, and none will make you afraid; I will rid the land of evil beasts, and the sword will not go through your land.

There are times that the rain may fail. People farm and they don't receive a good harvest. There may be times that the trees do not yield good fruit. God is promising us in the above scripture that if you do what pleases him, this season of small harvest will not be your portion. God says that if you walk in his statutes and obey his commandments, the land will produce a bountiful harvest for you. In the old covenant, God gave certain laws. For man to walk in covenant with God, he had to fully obey these laws. Obedience of these laws obligated God to move strongly for you. It was like a signed contract. God's word is his signature. The obedience of man is man's signature. In the new covenant, our acceptance of the finished work of Jesus Christ on the cross is our signature to the covenant. The bible tells us that if we receive Jesus Christ into our lives we become the sons of God. God cannot fail to perform his side of the contract. He is obligated to be a good father to us. Whatever we would expect of a good father, we should expect from God. He will not fail us. He has power over the rain and the land. He will order the rain and land to produce for us. No good father would allow his children to walk in suffering if he could do something about it.

PRAYER

I thank you father that your love for me would not allow my land to go barren. My land is producing for me.

Further reading: Leviticus chapter 26

14th June
A FATHER GIVES GOOD GIFTS

Matthew 7:7-11

"Ask, and it will be given to you; seek, and you will find; knock, and it will be opened to you. [8]For everyone who asks receives, and he who seeks finds, and to him who knocks it will be opened. [9]Or what man is there among you who, if his son asks for bread, will give him a stone? [10]Or if he asks for a fish, will he give him a serpent? [11]If you then, being evil, know how to give good gifts to your children, how much more will your Father who is in heaven give good things to those who ask Him!

Jesus refers to the fathers in his audience as evil. He says that even as evil fathers, they would not give their children stones instead of bread or snakes instead of fish. Even evil fathers love their children and would give them good gifts. You can therefore be assured of your good gift from God who is a good father. By this example, Jesus is trying to assure everyone of God's faithfulness and love. If you are in need, ask from God and you will receive. He encourages us to knock on God's door and expect him to open. He also promises us that when we search, we shall find because God loves us and will not keep any good thing away from us. God by making us his children brings us to a place where he has no choice but to care for us and nurture us into maturity. A father must of necessity take care of his children. Our heavenly father can never fall short of the expectation of fathers. Instead he is able to love us and perform his fatherly duties beyond our expectations. He is able to do exceedingly, abundantly above what we can think or ask. God is a father to the fatherless. Earthly fathers can disappoint us. God cannot disappoint us. Expect good things from him because he is a good father.

PRAYER

Thank you father for being a father to me. What comfort it is to me that I have a father who is not only all powerful but also cares. I promise never to leave your side.

Further reading: Matthew chapter 7

Be Strong Devotional

15th June
GOOD AND PERFECT GIFT

James 1:16-25

> Do not be deceived, my beloved brethren. ^{17}Every good gift and every perfect gift is from above, and comes down from the Father of lights, with whom there is no variation or shadow of turning. ^{18}Of His own will He brought us forth by the word of truth, that we might be a kind of first fruits of His creatures. ^{19}So then, my beloved brethren, let every man be swift to hear, slow to speak, slow to wrath; ^{20}for the wrath of man does not produce the righteousness of God. ^{21}Therefore lay aside all filthiness and overflow of wickedness, and receive with meekness the implanted word, which is able to save your souls. ^{22}But be doers of the word, and not hearers only, deceiving yourselves. ^{23}For if anyone is a hearer of the word and not a doer, he is like a man observing his natural face in a mirror; ^{24}for he observes himself, goes away, and immediately forgets what kind of man he was. ^{25}But he who looks into the perfect law of liberty and continues in it, and is not a forgetful hearer but a doer of the work, this one will be blessed in what he does.

Every good gift and every perfect gift comes from God our father. If it is not from our heavenly father then it is not good and it is not perfect. If it is from him then it is good and it is perfect. He has given us good promises in his word and we must receive these good promises and walk in them. James encourages us to listen more and speak less. Let our speech be an overflow of a righteous and faithful heart. When we hear God's word we must put it into action. There is no point hearing God's word and not believing it by putting it into action. The word of God, which is described as the perfect law of liberty, will set you free and bring you much blessing.

PRAYER

Father, I thank you that every good gift and every perfect gift comes from you. I thank you that your love for me has opened me to these good and precious gifts.

Further reading: James chapter 1

16th June
WINDOWS OF HEAVEN

Malachi 3:10-12

Bring all the tithes into the storehouse, That there may be food in My house, And try Me now in this," Says the Lord of hosts, "If I will not open for you the windows of heaven And pour out for you such blessing That there will not be room enough to receive it. "And I will rebuke the devourer for your sakes, So that he will not destroy the fruit of your ground, Nor shall the vine fail to bear fruit for you in the field," Says the Lord of hosts; And all nations will call you blessed, For you will be a delightful land," Says the Lord of hosts.

A tithe means a tenth. God had asked His covenant people to bring a tenth of everything given to them to the house of the Lord. The purpose of the tithe was to take care of the priest and workers in the temple; to cover expenditure in the temple and to have food in the house of God for the poor and needy. Although God could rain down money from heaven, he had decided in his wisdom to allow man to share in what he had. There is nothing man has that he did not receive. God therefore gives the opportunity to man through tithe and offering to acknowledge that it is God who has provided and to practice this love by his giving. When we are obedient in giving our tithes, we have locked ourselves into a covenant with God. This is exciting. God promises that if you bring your tithes to provide food in his storehouses, he would open the windows of heaven and pour out his blessing on you. God is a big God and when he blesses, he blesses big. He promises to take care of any thief stealing from you. He promises that the land will produce for you and you will be fruitful. If the windows of heaven open to you, you will not have room to contain it. Bring your tithes to God. You cannot feed God. He receives your tithe to release covenant blessings to you.

PRAYER

Thank you father for everything you have given to me. I will be obedient in my tithes and offering.

Further reading: Malachi chapter 3

17th June
GOD WILL PROTECT YOU FROM EVIL

2 Thessalonians 3:1-5

> Finally, brethren, pray for us, that the word of the Lord may run swiftly and be glorified, just as it is with you, ²and that we may be delivered from unreasonable and wicked men; for not all have faith. ³But the Lord is faithful, who will establish you and guard you from the evil one. ⁴And we have confidence in the Lord concerning you, both that you do and will do the things we command you. ⁵Now may the Lord direct your hearts into the love of God and into the patience of Christ.

As Christians, we have an assignment of releasing the living word of God into a dying world. Every good Christian must dedicate his life to this purpose. A dying world needs the word to bring it back to life. That is why the bible tells us that all creation is groaning waiting for the sons of God to show up. You and I are the sons of God. We possess the word of life. Let us not hold back but deliver this gift of God to the world. The bible also makes us aware that we have evil enemies who want the world to remain dead and ignorant. Not only do they steal, kill and destroy, they also try to prevent us from delivering this message of life. God promises to deliver us from this evil one and its plans. God has complete power over Satan and his gang of demonic forces. There is no force that does not fall under the authority of almighty God. The only thing God cannot override is our free will. He has relinquished the authority to make choices for our own lives to us. If we choose to submit our will to his, we give him room to direct our paths and order our steps. If like Adam and Eve, we choose to disobey God through the lust of our eyes, the lust of the flesh and the pride of life, then we bear the consequence of separation from God. Come under his protection today.

PRAYER
Thank you father for your promise to protect me from all evil. I will walk confidently with you.

Further reading: 2 Thessalonians chapter 3

18th June
YOU ARE SPECIAL TO GOD

1 Peter 2:6-10

Therefore it is also contained in the Scripture, "Behold, I lay in Zion A chief cornerstone, elect, precious, And he who believes on Him will by no means be put to shame." ⁷Therefore, to you who believe, He is precious; but to those who are disobedient, "The stone which the builders rejected Has become the chief cornerstone," ⁸and "A stone of stumbling And a rock of offense." They stumble, being disobedient to the word, to which they also were appointed. ⁹But you are a chosen generation, a royal priesthood, a holy nation, His own special people, that you may proclaim the praises of Him who called you out of darkness into His marvelous light; ¹⁰who once were not a people but are now the people of God, who had not obtained mercy but now have obtained mercy.

If you are like me, you have probably asked yourself: " Why me and why am I in the world at this time? Why wasn't I in the world at the time of Noah or Moses or David? Evolution cannot explain this. Only a loving God who thought about you and chose you for a time like this can explain this. The above scripture says we are a chosen generation. This means you have been chosen by God to be part of this chosen generation. We have to be grateful for the honor of being in the world at a time like this. You are special to God. He also calls you a royal priest. A priest is one who stands before God on behalf of the people. A royal priest means that you do not only have the privilege of standing before God, you also have authority to administer justice amongst men. You have been brought out of darkness into the marvelous light of God. You have obtained mercy for your sins and now you are part of the people of God. You are special so show your gratitude in praises to God.

PRAYER
Thank you father for making me so special. I will continually praise you.

Further reading: 1 Peter chapter 2

19th June
THE LORD MY REFUGE

2 Samuel 22:1-4

> *Then David spoke to the Lord the words of this song, on the day when the Lord had delivered him from the hand of all his enemies, and from the hand of Saul. ²And he said: "The Lord is my rock and my fortress and my deliverer; ³ The God of my strength, in whom I will trust; My shield and the horn of my salvation, My stronghold and my refuge; My Savior, You save me from violence. ⁴ I will call upon the Lord, who is worthy to be praised; So shall I be saved from my enemies.*

Refuge is a place of shelter from danger or trouble. King David was a man of great boldness because he depended on the strength of the Lord. He always sought the Lord in what he did. The times that he depended on his own thoughts and ability, he failed miserably. God is indeed a fortress in whom we can take refuge. When we receive Jesus as our Lord, we are born again into Christ. We become the righteousness of God in Christ. The reason why we can approach God boldly is because we are hidden in Christ. The acceptance of Christ is our acceptance. Every blessing on Christ becomes our blessing. Jesus Christ in his infinite mercy has decided to share his inheritance with everyone who would come to him in faith. When you receive him, he comes to live in you and also receives you into himself. This is why every born again believer is part of the church. The church is the body of Christ. There are different local assemblies with different assignments. You must belong to a local church. The local church which is part of the universal church which is the body of Christ is your hiding place and refuge. The enemy cannot touch you as you live in Christ. He has to go past Christ to get to you. Jesus defeated Satan the king of all evil on Calvary. His gang of devils have no choice but to run from you.

PRAYER

Thank you father for being my refuge. I will fear no foe.

Further reading: 2 Samuel 22

20th June
JESUS IS ALWAYS WITH YOU

Matthew 28:16-20

Then the eleven disciples went away into Galilee, to the mountain which Jesus had appointed for them. [17]When they saw Him, they worshiped Him; but some doubted. [18]And Jesus came and spoke to them, saying, "All authority has been given to Me in heaven and on earth. [19]Go therefore and make disciples of all the nations, baptizing them in the name of the Father and of the Son and of the Holy Spirit, [20]teaching them to observe all things that I have commanded you; and lo, I am with you always, even to the end of the age." Amen.

This conversation took place just before Jesus ascended into heaven. As he left his disciples on earth, he sent them on an assignment to go into the world and make disciples of all nations, baptizing them and teaching them to be obedient to the words of Christ. He sent them out on good authority. He announces to them that all authority in heaven and earth has been given to him. This means that there is no power that can surpass his. He has been given the power to rule in both heaven and earth. The command to go in his name would have been enough for the disciples yet he gives them a further assurance that He will be there with them forever. We tend to be anxious when we are faced with the challenges of life. We become afraid when we forget that Jesus is with us. Jesus is with us wherever we go. We need to remember this promise and acknowledge his presence. His presence assures as of our protection in him and the authority of operating in His name. Jesus did not pay the hefty price of the cross to leave us alone to the bullying of the devil. He rescued us and will protect us to the end of the age. Fear not, Jesus is with you all the way. He will give you divine wisdom when you need it. He will perform his word as you declare it.

PRAYER

Thank you my dear brother and friend for always being there by my side. Holy Spirit, help me to be conscious of the presence of Jesus Christ with me all the time.

Further reading: Matthew chapter 28

21st June
YOU ARE UNDER GOD'S WINGS

Psalm 91:1-6

> He who dwells in the secret place of the Most High Shall abide under the shadow of the Almighty. ² I will say of the Lord, "He is my refuge and my fortress; My God, in Him I will trust." ³ Surely He shall deliver you from the snare of the fowler And from the perilous pestilence. ⁴ He shall cover you with His feathers, And under His wings you shall take refuge; His truth shall be your shield and buckler. ⁵ You shall not be afraid of the terror by night, Nor of the arrow that flies by day, ⁶ Nor of the pestilence that walks in darkness, Nor of the destruction that lays waste at noonday.

Every chick feels comfortable under the wings of their mother. Mother will not allow you to touch her chicks if she is able. In the same way, God will not allow anyone to touch you if you dwell in the secret place of the most high. Your protection is guaranteed if you would walk with Jesus. Psalm 91 is a wonderful psalm of protection. God assures us that our movement is under his shadow. This means that he monitors and covers us wherever we go. He also protects us from every trap of the enemy. Jesus taught his disciples to pray to the father not to lead them into temptation. He also meant to steer them away from traps of the enemy. He will deliver you from all evil. When a soldier goes out to fight, he puts on a defensive armour.. God is our defence. As we step out to fulfil our assignment, let us be confident that God protects us. No weapon fashioned against us shall prosper. Before the enemy sets out to plan his strategy against you, God already knows. When he is forging the instruments to be used against you, God knows. He knows the antidote to every foul plan of the enemy. Don't be moved. They will be hit before they try to hit you.

PRAYER

Father I thank you for covering me with your feathers. I will rest safely under your wings. My enemies will be defeated before they get anywhere near me.

Further reading: Psalm 91

22nd June
I CALLED YOU AND WILL PROTECT YOU

Isaiah 41:9-11

You whom I have taken from the ends of the earth, And called from its farthest regions, And said to you, 'You are My servant, I have chosen you and have not cast you away: Fear not, for I am with you; Be not dismayed, for I am your God. I will strengthen you, Yes, I will help you, I will uphold you with My righteous right hand.' Behold, all those who were incensed against you Shall be ashamed and disgraced; They shall be as nothing, And those who strive with you shall perish.

The best decision we have ever made or will ever make is to say 'Yes' to Jesus. When God calls, there has to be a response for God's intention to be fulfilled. When you say 'Yes' to God, you have become his responsibility. All things originate from God. He has made his desire known to us that we would be his children and he would be a father to us. What an awesome honour to have God as our father. He has put his cards on the table. All he waits for is for someone to accept this call. This person enters a covenant that is already laid down. God cannot change his mind. Remember He created the world before making man to enjoy the world. He put man in the beautiful Garden of Eden. If man had played by the rules, man would have enjoyed the Garden of Eden wherever he went. Jesus paid the price of sin, defeating the devil before inviting man to join him in celebration of the booty. He called you and will protect you. He will also provide for you. For responding to the call of God, you are now open to receiving every blessing that is his. One of the things God hates is fathers who do not look after their children or employers who cheat their workers. God will look after you well as his son and as a worker in his vineyard.

PRAYER
I thank you my father that you are faithful to your word. As you have called me, you have made provision for my protection.

Further reading: Isaiah chapter 41

23rd June
NO WEAPON AGAINST YOU SHALL PROSPER

Isaiah 54:15-17

Indeed they shall surely assemble, but not because of Me. Whoever assembles against you shall fall for your sake. "Behold, I have created the blacksmith who blows the coals in the fire, who brings forth an instrument for his work; And I have created the spoiler to destroy. No weapon formed against you shall prosper, And every tongue which rises against you in judgment you shall condemn. This is the heritage of the servants of the Lord, And their righteousness is from Me, says the Lord.

If God is not in any project, it is bound to fail. When your enemies gather to plan against you, it is definitely not God's project. If you are in Christ, then an antichrist spirit drives them and they are destined to fail. Do not be afraid of anything that people plan against you. The assurance from your heavenly father is that they would not prosper. Right from the time man disobeyed God and cut himself off from the creator, God has sought to get for himself a people who would willingly submit to him. There are many who have pleased God and received his provision and protection. In Hebrews chapter 11, many of these friends of God who by their faith did exploits are listed. God used them to show his power. When we receive Jesus as our savior and Lord, the bible tells us that we become part of the family of God. Every protection he offered Abraham, David or Israel is ours by right. His servants, the angels, become our servants. His eyes and hands are for our protection. Before they gather against you, he already knows their thoughts. He promises that they will come to you one way, they will flee seven ways. In the bible, many of the people who conspired against God's friends end up turning on each other. That is what you should expect with those who plan and speak against you.

PRAYER

Father, some may trust in physical armor protecting them but I trust in the power of your word. Your promises are sweet to my ears and I receive them with faith.

Further reading: Isaiah 54

24th June
OUR PRESENT HELP

Psalm 46:1-5

God is our refuge and strength, A very present help in trouble. Therefore we will not fear, Even though the earth be removed, And though the mountains be carried into the midst of the sea; Though its waters roar and be troubled, Though the mountains shake with its swelling. There is a river whose streams shall make glad the city of God, The holy place of the tabernacle of the Most High. God is in the midst of her, she shall not be moved; God shall help her, just at the break of dawn.

God is our present help in our time of need. This assurance from God's word is encouraging. There are times that help seems so far away when we need it. The ambulance could be delayed or you could be in the waiting room for a long time. It is great comfort to know that man has limitations but God does not. He is our present help in our time of need. He is right there with you. If you will take your eyes off your condition and fix them on the ever present help of God, anxiety will disappear, faith will appear and you will be setting yourself up for a miracle. Our heavenly father is a God of miracles. A miracle is what God is able to do against all odds. God will prove himself. If God was ordinary and could not operate against the laws of nature, he would not be God. We serve a God to whom nothing is impossible. I don't know your need now but I can assure you that God is your present help. Don't despair. He is right here with you and his desire is for your good. Trust his word today and let his promise work in your life. There is a river whose streams make glad the city of God. He has made His Spirit available through His word, drink from it and be filled with gladness.

PRAYER

Father, I love you in return. You have made your Spirit available to me. I will drink and be glad. Thank you for being my present help in time of need.

Further reading: Psalm 46

25th June
YOUR SITUATION IS WORKING FOR GOOD

Romans 8:28-32

> And we know that all things work together for good to those who love God, to those who are the called according to His purpose. [29] For whom He foreknew, He also predestined to be conformed to the image of His Son, that He might be the firstborn among many brethren. [30] Moreover whom He predestined, these He also called; whom He called, these He also justified; and whom He justified, these He also glorified. [31] What then shall we say to these things? If God is for us, who can be against us? [32] He who did not spare His own Son, but delivered Him up for us all, how shall He not with Him also freely give us all things?

When King David said that he had never seen the righteous forsaken, he was speaking the truth. It is impossible for a loving God to leave anyone who trusts in him without help. Though sometimes we may feel abandoned, God never abandons us. The scripture above tells us that all things work together for good to those who love the Lord who are also called for his purpose. Keep this promise in your mouth and it will strengthen you when you are anxious as it has done me. God's word is truth. This makes the above promise an indispensable weapon in our fight against fear. You are called for a purpose by the God who never fails. This is the God who has promised, he is with you in every situation. He is the same God who has promised that no one can snatch you from his hands. If you don't allow your fear to make you jump out of his hands, then you are safe. What you are going through now is working out for your good. You are being moulded into the image of Jesus Christ, what a privilege. Trust in God's plan for you and his ability to carry out his plan.

PRAYER

Thank you father for the assurance that as long as I love you and remain in you, everything is working out for my good. I choose to love you and remain in you.

Further reading: Romans chapter 8

26th June
PAUPER TO PRINCE

1 Samuel 2:8-10

He raises the poor from the dust And lifts the beggar from the ash heap, To set them among princes And make them inherit the throne of glory. "For the pillars of the earth are the Lord's, And He has set the world upon them. He will guard the feet of His saints, But the wicked shall be silent in darkness. "For by strength no man shall prevail. The adversaries of the Lord shall be broken in pieces; From heaven He will thunder against them. The Lord will judge the ends of the earth. "He will give strength to His king, And exalt the horn of His anointed."

This was Hannah's song of praise to the Lord. The Lord had altered her situation. Before the Lord intervened, she was ridiculed for being barren. After the Lord intervened she was able to bear a son who would become the foremost prophet in his time. Many of the people God called and elevated to positions of authority had seen themselves as unworthy because of their background. God called Gideon 'a man of valor' when he was hiding from his enemies and made him a prince in Israel. Saul, Israel's first king, thought very little of himself before God made him king. David was taken from being a shepherd boy to becoming the great king of Israel. God's intervention takes you from being a pauper to becoming a prince. By our acceptance of Jesus' death and resurrection on our behalf, we have moved from being nobodies to becoming princes of heaven. If your present location is not that of a prince, don't worry. God will make the difference today as you receive Jesus as your Lord and accept his word as truth. There are many voices we hear in this world but only God's voice through his word is true. God wants to glorify you today so don't hesitate to call on him and make a vow to walk in obedience to him from today. Watch him transform you from a pauper to a prince.

PRAYER

I have made my decision today to abide in your house as a prince. Transform me Holy Spirit.

Further reading: 1 Samuel chapter 2

27th June
SLEEP IN SAFETY

Psalm 4:1-8

Hear me when I call, O God of my righteousness! You have relieved me in my distress; Have mercy on me, and hear my prayer. How long, O you sons of men, Will you turn my glory to shame? How long will you love worthlessness And seek falsehood? But know that the Lord has set apart for Himself him who is godly; The Lord will hear when I call to Him.

Be angry, and do not sin. Meditate within your heart on your bed, and be still. Offer the sacrifices of righteousness, And put your trust in the Lord. There are many who say, "Who will show us any good?"

Lord, lift up the light of Your countenance upon us. You have put gladness in my heart, More than in the season that their grain and wine increased. I will both lie down in peace, and sleep; For You alone, O Lord, make me dwell in safety.

Jesus is called the 'Prince of Peace'. He brings peace wherever he is. The bible says he gives his beloved sleep. When you receive Jesus you cease from your own works. You enter into a covenant with him. Jesus invites us to come and lay our burdens at his feet and take up his yoke. His yoke is easy and his burden light. A yoke is a wooden bar that joins two animals together as they jointly work, pulling the plough or some other farming implement. The two animals combine their strengths. A weak animal can always depend on the stronger partner. The pair share the glory equally. When Jesus invites us to take his yoke, he is inviting us into a partnership in which he bears the greater weight. He is inviting us into work without toil. Enter this place of rest today and sleep in safety. When you sleep, he who never sleeps keeps watch over you and be assured of your safety.

PRAYER

Dear father, I will lie down and sleep in safety as your eyes are on me. I will take on your easy yoke so we can bring in the harvest together.

Further reading: Isaiah 26

28th June
FATHER OF THE FATHERLESS

Psalm 10:14-18

But You have seen, for You observe trouble and grief, To repay it by Your hand. The helpless commits himself to You; You are the helper of the fatherless. Break the arm of the wicked and the evil man; Seek out his wickedness until You find none. The Lord is King forever and ever; The nations have perished out of His land. Lord, You have heard the desire of the humble; You will prepare their heart; You will cause Your ear to hear, To do justice to the fatherless and the oppressed, That the man of the earth may oppress no more.

It is not God's will that anyone on this earth should be fatherless. Every baby is made from the seed of a father. Although many fathers have relinquished their position of fatherhood, that was not God's original intention. A father gives you identity. A father also trains the child the way to go. When Adam and Eve lost fellowship with God, they did not know the way to go. They would have brought up their own children on ignorance. They caused the ignorance the world walks in today. God in his divine mercy restored fatherhood through the sacrifice of Jesus Christ on the cross. Anyone who would receive Jesus Christ can have a father in God. In a world where many fathers have relinquished their responsibility, God has offered himself as a father to all. No one needs to be fatherless any longer. God is a father to the fatherless. There are no bastards with God. He fearfully and wonderfully made all men in his image. However, he does not force fatherhood. You will have to freely accept him as father for him to become your father. You also have to be ready to be a son to him. Our father in heaven gives hope to the hopeless. Many fatherless don't know this and are wallowing in self pity. Let us preach the good news of a father to the fatherless in all the earth.

PRAYER

Thank you father for the hope you give to many. I am assured of your unfailing love for me and I am grateful.

Further reading: Psalm 10

29th June
COVENANT OF PEACE

Ezekiel 34:25-28

> "I will make a covenant of peace with them, and cause wild beasts to cease from the land; and they will dwell safely in the wilderness and sleep in the woods. ^{26}I will make them and the places all around My hill a blessing; and I will cause showers to come down in their season; there shall be showers of blessing. ^{27}Then the trees of the field shall yield their fruit, and the earth shall yield her increase. They shall be safe in their land; and they shall know that I am the Lord, when I have broken the bands of their yoke and delivered them from the hand of those who enslaved them. ^{28}And they shall no longer be a prey for the nations, nor shall beasts of the land devour them; but they shall dwell safely, and no one shall make them afraid.

God revealed through Ezekiel the covenant of peace that he would make with Israel. He promised to get rid of wild beasts in the land. People will sleep safely in the woods and dwell fearlessly in the wilderness. If God be for you, no one can be against you. All the wild beasts are subject to the orders of God. All the trees and mountains respond to the instructions of God. When you are in covenant with God, you are safe. This prophecy looks forward to the covenant that was going to be settled by the Prince of Peace on Calvary. When you enter the kingdom of God and the household of our heavenly father, you have entered the house of peace. The foundation of the throne of God is righteousness, peace and justice. Peace means that everything is in the right place with nothing crooked. There is no decay and no lack; nothing missing, nothing broken. Enjoy this covenant of peace and don't allow anything to disturb the quietness of your spirit and tranquillity of your soul.

PRAYER

Thank you Jesus that by your sacrifice on the cross, you have made me a partaker of this covenant of peace. Holy Spirit, help me never to step out of this covenant.

Further reading: Ezekiel chapter 34

30th June
I AM WITH YOU

John 14:15-21

"If you love Me, keep My commandments. ¹⁶And I will pray the Father, and He will give you another Helper, that He may abide with you forever— ¹⁷the Spirit of truth, whom the world cannot receive, because it neither sees Him nor knows Him; but you know Him, for He dwells with you and will be in you. ¹⁸I will not leave you orphans; I will come to you.

¹⁹"A little while longer and the world will see Me no more, but you will see Me. Because I live, you will live also. ²⁰At that day you will know that I am in My Father, and you in Me, and I in you. ²¹He who has My commandments and keeps them, it is he who loves Me. And he who loves Me will be loved by My Father, and I will love him and manifest Myself to him."

The companionship of the Holy Spirit is one of the most exciting things of our new life in Jesus Christ. To be aware that the Holy Spirit is with you wherever you go and is there to help you wherever you go is comforting. We would not know Jesus Christ as he truly is but for the revelation of him that the Holy Spirit gives to us. We know we are not alone because the Spirit of God speaks with us and we speak to him. He has endowed us with the power and wisdom of heaven. The world cannot understand what makes us so joyful and hopeful. Without giving your life to Jesus Christ, you will not know the Holy Spirit. The bible tells us that the flesh cannot understand the things of the Spirit. No wonder some people mock spiritual things. We are not alone. 'I am' is with us wherever we go. We should introduce him wherever we go and say the things that he wants us to say. Jesus did that while he walked this earth and he turned his world upside down. Let us do the same and turn our world upside down.

PRAYER
Thank you Holy Spirit for always being there for me. I empty myself. Use me as a vessel. I pray that the world will know Jesus through me.

Further reading: John chapter 14

July
God is Love

Love is the foundation of everything God does. God is love. This is why understanding the subject of love is very important. The apostle John says that if you do not walk in love, you do not know God. It is only God who can give you real love. Jesus says that all the commandments of God can be summarised in the word, love.

Enjoy the love of God. God wants you to so flow in His love that others would also enjoy the overflow of His love from you. My prayer is that God's love will transform you into a distributor of love.

1st July
GOD GIVES HIS BEST

John 3:14-17

> And as Moses lifted up the serpent in the wilderness, even so must the Son of Man be lifted up, ¹⁵that whoever believes in Him should not perish but have eternal life. ¹⁶For God so loved the world that He gave His only begotten Son, that whoever believes in Him should not perish but have everlasting life. ¹⁷For God did not send His Son into the world to condemn the world, but that the world through Him might be saved.

How much a person is ready to give out to another shows the extent of one's love. Some gifts could be spectacular but may not be the result of deep love. Most people will give out of what they can conveniently do away with. If a thirsty man should come into your house and you give them a glass of water from your ever flowing tap, they would appreciate it but it cost you nothing. Such a gift is easy to give. If on the other hand a thirsty man meets you in the desert and you are down to your last bottle of water, there your love will be tested. God desired a sacrifice without blemish from the Israelites because it is not easy to give your best. Only love can give its best. God gave his best for the salvation of mankind. Think of the person or thing you love the most. Will you be ready to give it up to help someone else? Only deep love can do that. This is what God did for you when He gave up his only begotten son to pay the price of death for our sins. This is love in action. You can trust the love of the person who is ready to give up his best for you. Every other gift will be less than what he has already given so it will not be difficult to give it. You can count on God's love. He cares deeply for you.

PRAYER

Thank you father for the deep love and the price you paid for my salvation. Help me to return this love by giving my best in serving you.

Further reading: John chapter 3

2nd July
GOD HAS GIVEN US SALVATION

Romans 5:6-10

⁶For when we were still without strength, in due time Christ died for the ungodly. ⁷For scarcely for a righteous man will one die; yet perhaps for a good man someone would even dare to die. ⁸But God demonstrates His own love toward us, in that while we were still sinners, Christ died for us. ⁹Much more then, having now been justified by His blood, we shall be saved from wrath through Him. ¹⁰For if when we were enemies we were reconciled to God through the death of His Son, much more, having been reconciled, we shall be saved by His life.

Salvation is a gift of God. Anyone who has not met with God is walking in darkness and ignorance. The whole world would be walking in darkness if the love of God had not penetrated our darkness and opened our eyes to the goodness of God. Salvation means to be saved from a bad situation. Being in darkness is a bad situation. The bible calls it spiritual death. Walking in spiritual death is walking in ignorance about where you have come from, where you go after death, what life means and other questions that are impossible to answer without God. God could have left us in our ignorance to perish but His love for us would not allow that. His heart breaks when we suffer. He paid the price for our sins so we could be delivered from the penalty that sin brings. Isaiah 53:5 says the punishment for our peace was laid on him. Only love can make you take on another person's punishment. That is what Jesus did. He paid for your sins with His life. You don't have to face the anger of God any longer. The door has been open for you to enjoy living with God. Jesus qualifies to be called a real lover. You have a lover who has paid the price of death for you. You don't need to be lonely ever again.

PRAYER

Thank you father for this unmerited favour of salvation. I acknowledge your love. I also love you with my whole life

Further reading: Romans chapter 5

3rd July
GOD HAS MADE US ALIVE

Ephesians 2:1-5

And you He made alive, who were dead in trespasses and sins, ²in which you once walked according to the course of this world, according to the prince of the power of the air, the spirit who now works in the sons of disobedience, ³among whom also we all once conducted ourselves in the lusts of our flesh, fulfilling the desires of the flesh and of the mind, and were by nature children of wrath, just as the others. ⁴But God, who is rich in mercy, because of His great love with which He loved us, ⁵even when we were dead in trespasses, made us alive together with Christ (by grace you have been saved).

According to the scripture above, we who have received Jesus as our Lord have been made alive with him. It tells us that before we were made alive with Christ, we were dead in trespasses and sins. There are a lot of people who have closed their ears to this wonderful message of the kingdom of God. The scripture describes them as walking according to the course of this world. Many of the decisions such people make are made by the influence of the 'course of this world.' This world is greatly influenced by Satan who is described in the above scripture as the Prince of the power of the air. When you think you are making your own decisions, there are forces driving you to fulfill the lusts of your flesh and mind. Thank God for the cross of Jesus Christ which has exposed us to reality and revealed to us demonic deceptions that compel us. Love has exposed what is hidden. The bible assures us that whatever is hidden will come to light. All lies and deceptions will come to nothing. Truth is the only thing that has strength to survive. The great love of God has made us one with his truth. We have been given everlasting life. We have been born again by the incorruptible word of God. Our new life is not subject to corruption.

PRAYER
Thank you Jesus that through your death and resurrection I have received new life which cannot be corrupted.

Further reading: Ephesians chapter 2

4th July
GOD'S LOVE HAS RAISED US UP

Ephesians 2:4-8

> *4But God, who is rich in mercy, because of His great love with which He loved us, 5even when we were dead in trespasses, made us alive together with Christ (by grace you have been saved), 6and raised us up together, and made us sit together in the heavenly places in Christ Jesus, 7that in the ages to come He might show the exceeding riches of His grace in His kindness toward us in Christ Jesus. 8For by grace you have been saved through faith, and that not of yourselves; it is the gift of God,*

There is only one direction left for one who is on ground zero, upwards. We are of the earth (ground zero). No one from ground zero can lift us up. Only one from above can raise us up. Isaiah 55:9 tells us that God's thoughts and ways are as high above our thoughts and ways as the heavens are above the earth. How far is heaven from the earth? We may know the distance from the earth to the moon or other planets but it is impossible to know the distance from the earth to heaven. He who created all things including all galaxies and planets is above all. It was necessary for him who lives in heaven to come to our earth so he could expose heaven to us and take us to heavenly places. Imagine the greatest king on this earth descending to the dirtiest slum and bringing the lowest beggar to live with him in his palace. This example is nowhere near what Jesus has done for us. Only love can do that. We have been raised up with Christ. God is going to show you how much he loves you. As you receive this heavenly love, you will have no choice but to also go to the slums and bring people to your palace. The whole world without Jesus Christ is in a slum. There may be slum barons but they are still in a slum. Only love will raise them up.

PRAYER
Thank you for raising me up, my Lord and Saviour Jesus Christ.

Further reading: Ephesians chapter 2

5th July
JESUS CHRIST DIED FOR ME

Galatians 2:17-21

> [17]"But if, while we seek to be justified by Christ, we ourselves also are found sinners, is Christ therefore a minister of sin? Certainly not! [18]For if I build again those things which I destroyed, I make myself a transgressor. [19]For I through the law died to the law that I might live to God. [20]I have been crucified with Christ; it is no longer I who live, but Christ lives in me; and the life which I now live in the flesh I live by faith in the Son of God, who loved me and gave Himself for me. [21]I do not set aside the grace of God; for if righteousness comes through the law, then Christ died in vain."

Christ died that I may live. If Christ had not died, I would have remained dead. I would have been cut off from God. If you are cut from God, you do not know what life is really like. If his death opens me up to real life, it makes good sense to live for him. To live for him is to dedicate my life completely to him. He knows life more than I do. What I call life, he calls death. If he has opened me up to his life then I must cease living my own life. It is clear that I do not know what life is really like. I can only depend on him to show me real life. When God created Adam and Eve, he was in the process of teaching them about the world he had created. The bible said he would visit Adam in the cool of the day everyday and fellowship with them. This was an impartation of knowledge session. Adam and Eve decided to disobey God and by so doing cut themselves away from the life and knowledge of God. Jesus died to defeat death and Satan and bring all mankind back into fellowship with God. Enjoy your new life and refuse to be distracted by the deceitful influence of the world.

PRAYER

Thank you Jesus for dying for me and giving me a new life. The life that I live, I live to love and obey you.

Further reading: Galatians chapter 2

6th July
GOD REJOICES OVER YOU

Zephaniah 3:14-17

14Sing, O daughter of Zion! Shout, O Israel! Be glad and rejoice with all your heart, O daughter of Jerusalem! 15The Lord has taken away your judgments, He has cast out your enemy. The King of Israel, the Lord, is in your midst; You shall see disaster no more. 16In that day it shall be said to Jerusalem: "Do not fear; Zion, let not your hands be weak. 17The Lord your God in your midst, The Mighty One, will save; He will rejoice over you with gladness, He will quiet you with His love, He will rejoice over you with singing."

Love brings joy. When you love someone, you rejoice over their well-being. Love will do all in its power to bring joy to the object of their love. Where God is, there is fullness of joy and at God's right hand there is pleasure. One of the signs of identifying the presence of the Holy Spirit is joy. God loves us so much and rejoices over us. When you love someone, you even find dry jokes amusing. How a parent dotes over their little child and is amused at every turn of the child. God rejoices over us. The above prophecy to Israel is talking about how God will return to Israel and dwell in their midst. The promise to Israel is that God will rejoice over them with singing. God was not dwelling in their midst then. Today, Jesus Christ dwells in our midst. One of the names of Jesus Christ is Emmanuel, which means God with us. Jesus promised us the Holy Spirit who dwells with us forever. Today we have the Spirit of God in our midst. We should therefore not be afraid or let our hands be weak. He will save, rejoice over us with gladness, flood us with his love and rejoice over us with singing.

PRAYER

Thank you father for your love. I love you too with all my heart

Further reading: Zephaniah chapter 3

7th July
GOD IS LOVE

1 John 4:7-11

> *Beloved, let us love one another, for love is of God; and everyone who loves is born of God and knows God. ⁸He who does not love does not know God, for God is love. ⁹In this the love of God was manifested toward us, that God has sent His only begotten Son into the world, that we might live through Him. ¹⁰In this is love, not that we loved God, but that He loved us and sent His Son to be the propitiation for our sins. ¹¹Beloved, if God so loved us, we also ought to love one another.*

Every part of God is made up of love. That is the meaning of 'God is love'. Where God is, expect love. Love is selfless sacrifice for the benefit of others. This means that God is there for the benefit of others. God's love produces words like Grace, which means unmerited favour; Mercy – undeserving forgiveness; Intercession – standing in the gap for others. When you come close to God, expect compassion, sacrifice and blessing. He is love. Some ignorant commentators have called God a child molester for making Jesus go on the Cross of Calvary. God is love. When Jesus hung on the cross, it was God hanging there for the sake of the world. It was a sacrifice to bring the world to salvation. In the Old Testament, every time a prophet prophesied doom on Israel, it was because they had abandoned God. There was always a way out of doom. If Israel would repent and turn to God they would see a God of love who had gone nowhere and waiting for their love. This same love awaits you today. If you are frustrated, it is because you are not looking at God. Turn around and come to him to receive grace and mercy in your time of need. God cannot change. He is love. He can only love you. He can never hate you.

PRAYER
Father, it is so encouraging to be assured of your love forever. Holy Spirit, help me never to abandon this great love.

Further reading: 1 John chapter 4

8th July
GOD HAS PLACED HIS LOVE IN US

1 John 4:12-16

> *[12]No one has seen God at any time. If we love one another, God abides in us, and His love has been perfected in us. [13]By this we know that we abide in Him, and He in us, because He has given us of His Spirit. [14]And we have seen and testify that the Father has sent the Son as Saviour of the world. [15]Whoever confesses that Jesus is the Son of God, God abides in him, and he in God. [16]And we have known and believed the love that God has for us. God is love, and he who abides in love abides in God, and God in him.*

We can only truly confess Jesus as the Son of God in response to the revelation of God's love towards us. We only love him because he first loved us. Only a revelation of the love that Jesus displayed on the Cross of Calvary can bring us true repentance and salvation. God's message to the world is a message of the heart and not of the head. There are many head knowledgeable theologians who have never come face to face with the love of God. The truth is not for argument. Love gently instructs and intercedes. When we acknowledge Jesus Christ as our Lord and Saviour, He comes to live inside us. When we receive Jesus into our hearts, God has come to stay. When God comes to stay, love has come to stay. The first fruit of the Holy Spirit mentioned in Galatians 5:22 is love. The seed of love sown in you by the Holy Spirit has to produce a fruit of love that the world can eat. God wants to manifest who he is through you. Receive from his love and pass it on. The world will respond to the love of God. This is why you cannot preach any other gospel apart from the message of Jesus Christ and him crucified.

PRAYER
Father, as I drink of your love, may your love flow out of me wherever I am. May I fully represent you.

Further reading: 1 John chapter 4

9th July
LOVE MAKES US BOLD

1 John 4:17-19

¹⁷Love has been perfected among us in this: that we may have boldness in the day of judgment; because as He is, so are we in this world. ¹⁸There is no fear in love; but perfect love casts out fear, because fear involves torment. But he who fears has not been made perfect in love. ¹⁹We love Him because He first loved us.

One of Satan's greatest weapons is fear. Darkness produces fear. Ignorance is darkness. One of the most paralysing fears that hang around the necks of most people in the world is the fear of death. There is a saying: 'Death is an equalizer." This means that everyone must die at some stage where we all become equal. The ignorance of what happens after death brings different reactions from people. Thank God that the issue of death has been dealt with once and for all by the death and resurrection of Jesus Christ. We know that those of us who have received Jesus as our Lord and Saviour have inherited everlasting life. This means that death has been overcome for us and we shall never die. We may put this container of a body aside but we shall never see death. This takes away the tormenting fear of death out of our lives. We are free from this fear because of the love that Jesus displayed by paying the price of death for us. He has translated us from darkness into light. To be absent from this body is to be present with God. This is an exciting prospect and kills off every anxiety that death brings. The love of God shed abroad in our heart gives us hope. We are assured of the protection and provision of God. If God is on my side, no enemy will be able to stand against me. I pray that you will steadily grow in love and assurance and say bye to fear forever.

PRAYER

Thank you father for delivering me out of the torment of fear by flooding me with your love. I will walk boldly in your name

Further reading: 1 John chapter 5

10th July
GOD CARES FOR YOU

1 Peter 5:6-11

⁶Therefore humble yourselves under the mighty hand of God, that He may exalt you in due time, ⁷casting all your care upon Him, for He cares for you. ⁸Be sober, be vigilant; because your adversary the devil walks about like a roaring lion, seeking whom he may devour. ⁹Resist him, steadfast in the faith, knowing that the same sufferings are experienced by your brotherhood in the world. ¹⁰But may the God of all grace, who called us to His eternal glory by Christ Jesus, after you have suffered a while, perfect, establish, strengthen, and settle you. ¹¹To Him be the glory and the dominion forever and ever. Amen.

The Apostle Peter is exhorting us to humble ourselves under the mighty hand of God with the promise that he would exalt us. When we face challenges in life, we are often compelled to take matters in our own hands to deal with the situation. A lot of times we fall into an attitude of self-exaltation. If we can settle it in our spirits that God cares for us, it will make a whole lot of difference. God is able to take care of every situation. He is God. We must believe that God is powerful. We must also trust in his love for the world. This is the faith that will take us from every distraction and bring us in humility under the mighty hand of God. Peter promises perfection, establishment, strengthening and settlement after you endure challenges. God is watching over you as a mother hen watches over her chicks. Your enemy cannot have you if you would not allow him. Jesus said the enemy was coming but had nothing in Him. Make sure there is no landing place in your life for the enemy. If there is a sin or something you are convicted about, turn around from it to God and let Him exalt you because he cares.

PRAYER
Father, I completely submit myself under your mighty hand. Use me as you will.

Further reading: 1 Peter chapter 5

11th July
GOD IS COMPASSIONATE

Psalm 86:14-17

> O God, the proud have risen against me, And a mob of violent men have sought my life, And have not set You before them. But You, O Lord, are a God full of compassion, and gracious, Longsuffering and abundant in mercy and truth. Oh, turn to me, and have mercy on me. Give Your strength to Your servant, And save the son of Your maidservant. Show me a sign for good, That those who hate me may see it and be ashamed, Because You, Lord, have helped me and comforted me.

We live in a world of challenges. Jesus Christ tells us that we would face challenges and persecution as Christians. Yet he assures us that we should not be afraid because he would be with us. This prayer of David is drawing on the compassion of God to protect him against his enemies. Because God is made of pure love, you can count on his compassion and mercy. David lived a life of war. He had lots of enemies both within and outside his kingdom. David was a successful king because he trusted in the loving kindness of God. He drew a lot of strength from this. He called on God's mercy in his time of need. Many of the psalms of David are prayers and worship songs celebrating the goodness and loving kindness of God. Today, I am encouraging you to trust in the love and faithfulness of God. You may have done or said some wrong things for which you deserve the anger of God. If only you would recognize your wrongdoing and turn away from it to God asking for forgiveness, be assured of his embrace. He is a compassionate and longsuffering God. He will forgive you and cleanse you from all filth as if you never sinned. The blood of Jesus cleanses your inner man and makes you whiter than snow. Boldly approach Jesus today to obtain mercy and strength.

PRAYER

Thank you father for a compassionate heart that knows my weakness but still loves me. Your love is the greatest gift I have and I treasure it with all my heart.

Further reading: Psalm 86

12th July
WE ARE CHILDREN OF GOD

1 John 3:1-3

> *¹Behold what manner of love the Father has bestowed on us, that we should be called children of God! Therefore the world does not know us, because it did not know Him. ²Beloved, now we are children of God; and it has not yet been revealed what we shall be, but we know that when He is revealed, we shall be like Him, for we shall see Him as He is. ³And everyone who has this hope in Him purifies himself, just as He is pure.*

One of the things that really annoyed the religious leaders of Jesus day was the fact that Jesus called himself the Son of God. The Jews understood that to be the son of God is to be equal to God. John 5:18 says they sought to kill him because by claiming to be the son of God, he was making himself equal to God. Father and son relationship is a love bond that cannot be challenged. This is because the son is the product of the father. When it comes to God, the word son is not a gender issue. It is a position of inheritance. God is spirit and his children are spirit. Both male and female qualify to be called God's sons. If you have believed and received Jesus as your Saviour, you qualify as a son of God. John 1:12 says we are sons of God. If we are sons then there is a bond of love between us and God which cannot be broken. Except we choose to opt out of this covenant. God loves everyone. Every one who turns to him will drink from his love. By his loving kindness, he has paved the way through Jesus Christ for us to become sons. This locks us into a covenant with him that assures us of his ever-present love for us. This is for our benefit. Enjoy it.

PRAYER
Thank you father for making me a son and locking me in loving-kindness. I promise to stay in this warm embrace forever.

Further reading: 1 John chapter 3

13th July
GOD IS FAITHFUL

Deuteronomy 7:9-11

> ⁹"Therefore know that the Lord your God, He is God, the faithful God who keeps covenant and mercy for a thousand generations with those who love Him and keep His commandments; ¹⁰and He repays those who hate Him to their face, to destroy them. He will not be slack with him who hates Him; He will repay him to his face. ¹¹Therefore you shall keep the commandment, the statutes, and the judgments which I command you today, to observe them.

God is faithful. He is the source of all truth and all wisdom. He therefore cannot change his mind. What he says cannot be changed. As humans we may change our minds or direction because our original course was wrong. We might come by new information or forced into change. God does not make mistakes. He has all knowledge. There is no information that is new to God. You cannot force God to do anything. He is a faithful God; a covenant keeping God. When he says anything, he means what he has said. If he promises to be a father to you, he has the love, discipline and resources to be faithful to his word. It is impossible for God not to fulfill every good promise he gives. He gives his word out of his goodness. He promises mercy to a thousand generations to those who love him and keep his commandments. What are his commandments? To love God with everything you have and to love people with everything you have. If you walk in love with God and people, expect the faithful love of God for eternity. Stop counting the generations. A thousand generations simply means forever. If you hate God, you have taken yourself out of the kingdom of God and exposed to the wicked spirits of this world. These wicked spirits will steal, destroy and kill you. They will promise one thing and do the opposite. These spirits are as deceptive as God is faithful.

PRAYER

Thank you father that I can count on your faithfulness. The assurance of your faithful love as expressed in your word gives me peace. I will keep your word in my heart and mouth.

Further reading: Deuteronomy 7

14th July
GOD GIVES RICHES AND HONOUR

Proverbs 8:16-21

> [16] By me princes rule, and nobles, All the judges of the earth. [17] I love those who love me, And those who seek me diligently will find me. [18] Riches and honour are with me, Enduring riches and righteousness. [19] My fruit is better than gold, yes, than fine gold, And my revenue than choice silver. [20] I traverse the way of righteousness, In the midst of the paths of justice, [21] That I may cause those who love me to inherit wealth, That I may fill their treasuries.

One of the assignments of Jesus Christ is to baptize those who receive him with the Holy Spirit. When the Holy Spirit of God comes to rest on you through this baptism, you will have the following 7 spirits operating in your life: The Spirit of the Lord, the Spirit of Wisdom, Understanding, Counsel, Might, Knowledge and the Fear of the Lord (Isaiah 11:1-2). Proverbs 8 talks about the benefits of wisdom. Wisdom will bring you riches and honour. Riches refer to valuable and abundant resources which includes material wealth. The attitude of the rich people of the world has given riches a bad name. Many Christians run away from the word riches. Others make riches their sole ambition in life. The word of God warns us not to run after riches but to seek the kingdom of God and see his provision overtake us. God's creation is not for us to just observe but also enjoy. Real joy comes from recognizing the love of God for the world, receiving from this love and allowing this love to flow out of us to others. His word says that he has given us all that pertain to life and godliness. The wisdom of God brings honour, that is great respect and high esteem. The love of God has opened us to the heavenly lifestyle. Let's believe God for this heavenly lifestyle. Riches and honour in your hands is better than in any other's hand as more people will share in it.

PRAYER
Thank you for riches and honour, Father. I promise to share in every gift you have bestowed on me.

Further reading: Proverbs chapter 8

15th July
GOD HAS GOOD PLANS FOR YOU

Jeremiah 29:10-14

> *For thus says the Lord: After seventy years are completed at Babylon, I will visit you and perform My good word toward you, and cause you to return to this place. ¹¹For I know the thoughts that I think toward you, says the Lord, thoughts of peace and not of evil, to give you a future and a hope. ¹²Then you will call upon Me and go and pray to Me, and I will listen to you. ¹³And you will seek Me and find Me, when you search for Me with all your heart. ¹⁴I will be found by you, says the Lord, and I will bring you back from your captivity; I will gather you from all the nations and from all the places where I have driven you, says the Lord, and I will bring you to the place from which I cause you to be carried away captive.*

I do not know where you are now or how you feel. My assurance to you, if you are in God's kingdom, is that it will turn out well. God has very good plans for you. Weeping may endure for the night but joy is surely coming in the morning. The above scripture is an encouragement from God to the nation of Israel. Though they were in captivity which God allowed for their own discipline, God assures them of a safe return to the land of abundance. The foundation of our walk with God must be the assurance of God's unchanging love for us. God has very good plans for us because we are his children. God's discipline is not to destroy us but to straighten us out to enjoy the great love that he has for us. He is bringing us to the place of everlasting fellowship with him. This place of everlasting fellowship is also a place of everlasting peace. Trust his great love for you. It is yours for the taking. Let every anxiety leave now.

PRAYER

Father, I thank you for your good plans for me. I will always walk in hope because of your love for me

Further reading: Jeremiah chapter 29

16th July
LOVE ONE ANOTHER

John 13:31-35

³¹So, when he had gone out, Jesus said, "Now the Son of Man is glorified, and God is glorified in Him. ³²If God is glorified in Him, God will also glorify Him in Himself, and glorify Him immediately. ³³Little children, I shall be with you a little while longer. You will seek Me; and as I said to the Jews, 'Where I am going, you cannot come,' so now I say to you. ³⁴A new commandment I give to you, that you love one another; as I have loved you, that you also love one another. ³⁵By this all will know that you are My disciples, if you have love for one another."

God's love never stops with you. His love for us is so overwhelming and overflowing. It flows into us and overflows us into other people's lives. Jesus told the Samaritan woman in John 4:14 that the water he Jesus gives shall become a fountain of water springing up to everlasting life. The love of God springing up from us will bring everlasting life to others. Every gift Jesus gives to us does not only have us in mind, it has the whole world in mind. God will never ask you to give something you don't have. Only wicked taskmasters like Pharaoh will ask you to make bricks without supplying the straw. Jesus asked his disciples to love one another even as he has loved them. God knows we have love to give because he has given us this love. We love him because he first loved us. Jesus says the identification mark of a disciple is our love for one another. We know from the above scripture that it is the glory of God in us that makes us glorious. Jesus says he is glorified because God is glorified in him. When John describes the glory of Jesus in John 1, he described him as being full of grace and truth. Grace is the undeserving love of God. Walk in God's grace towards others.

PRAYER

Lord Jesus I promise to love others as you have loved me. Help me Holy Spirit.

Further reading: John chapter 13

17th July
HIS MERCY ENDURES FOREVER

Psalm 136:17-26

17 To Him who struck down great kings, For His mercy endures forever; 18 And slew famous kings, For His mercy endures forever— 19 Sihon king of the Amorites, For His mercy endures forever; 20 And Og king of Bashan, For His mercy endures forever— 21 And gave their land as a heritage, For His mercy endures forever; 22 A heritage to Israel His servant, For His mercy endures forever. 23 Who remembered us in our lowly state, For His mercy endures forever; 24 And rescued us from our enemies, For His mercy endures forever; 25 Who gives food to all flesh, For His mercy endures forever. 26 Oh, give thanks to the God of heaven! For His mercy endures forever.

His loving kindness endures forever. We can only give thanks for God's enduring love. The psalmist is recounting the many incidents when God has shown himself strong. Creation is by his enduring love. Look around at the beautiful sky and the glorious creation of God. Everything is made out of love. The mountains, the seas, man and animals are all the products of love. When we begin to see the world in its true perspective, it will change our lives. God did not create the world to harm us but as a loving gift for us to enjoy. In Genesis 1, it says all that God created was good. The ignorance of man because of our separation from God has made masters become slaves. Now circumstances drive man instead of man driving circumstances. Our reconciliation with the father through Jesus has changed this. God by his enduring mercy has saved us and given us his Holy Spirit. Man can now retake his position as master. The psalmists recount great moments of conquests for Israel because of the ever-present loving kindness of God. God's ever-present love is in you today. Walk in confidence.

PRAYER

Dear father, when I look at the good things you have done for me, I can only say thank you for your enduring love.

Further reading: Psalm 136

18th July
LOVE IS POURED IN OUR HEARTS

Romans 5:1-5

> *¹Therefore, having been justified by faith, we have peace with God through our Lord Jesus Christ, ²through whom also we have access by faith into this grace in which we stand, and rejoice in hope of the glory of God. ³And not only that, but we also glory in tribulations, knowing that tribulation produces perseverance; ⁴and perseverance, character; and character, hope. ⁵Now hope does not disappoint, because the love of God has been poured out in our hearts by the Holy Spirit who was given to us.*

Our hope in God cannot bring disappointment because it is backed by God's love. When the world uses the expression 'I hope so', what they mean is 'I wish so'. This type of hope is a 'maybe' hope. It is weak. Our hope in God is solid because the love of God is in our hearts. We know whom we have believed. The revelation of God has been poured in our spirits. We are in no doubt about his enduring love and the good plans he has in store for us. The faith we have is given to us through his word. It is his word that produces faith in us. Our faith is the indication of our love for him. His word is love. Our response of faith is love in action. This love in us is what gives us this solid hope. In the midst of challenges, we are not anxious. We are so sure of his love that we know every tribulation is working out for our good. The challenges we face produce strength in us which gives us heavenly character needed for this spiritual journey. God has poured so much love in us. You are a spring of love to a thirsty world. I have seen the delight on people's faces when a community experiencing drought receives rain or clean running water. The world is equally delighted when a Christian full of the love of God turns up in its midst. You are that Christian and the love the world is waiting for.

PRAYER

Thank you father for the love you have poured in my heart. I can't wait to pour it out into someone.

Further reading: Romans chapter 5

19th July
YOU ARE COMPLETE IN CHRIST

Colossians 2:6-10

> ⁶As you therefore have received Christ Jesus the Lord, so walk in Him, ⁷rooted and built up in Him and established in the faith, as you have been taught, abounding in it with thanksgiving. ⁸Beware lest anyone cheat you through philosophy and empty deceit, according to the tradition of men, according to the basic principles of the world, and not according to Christ. ⁹For in Him dwells all the fullness of the Godhead bodily; ¹⁰and you are complete in Him, who is the head of all principality and power.

If there is one thing everyone in this world needs, it is Jesus Christ. The kingdom of God is complete in Him. He is a one-stop shop. Colossians 1:17 says in Jesus Christ, all things consist. You do not need Jesus Christ and something else. Come to Jesus and you will have the Father and the Holy Spirit. The above scripture tells us that in Jesus dwelt the fullness of the Godhead bodily. No one has ever seen the Father. The Son has declared Him. No one has ever seen the Holy Spirit. Jesus Christ has baptized us with Him. Everything is in Jesus Christ. Paul said he came preaching no other message but Jesus Christ and his death on the Cross of Calvary. Don't be deceived by so called intelligent men and good sounding philosophies of the world. The love of Jesus Christ displayed on the cross is our only key to salvation. Salvation is into the kingdom of God. Anyone outside the kingdom of God is walking in ignorance and darkness. Jesus said the prophets and Moses spoke about him. The entire bible is centred on Jesus Christ. The father has given all authority in heaven and earth to Jesus Christ. Don't look for help or salvation anywhere else. You are complete in him. He is the light of the world, the Bread of Life, the Way, Truth and Life. You can have as much of Him as you want. Don't hold back.

PRAYER
Jesus, In you I am complete. I want to live totally for you.

Further reading: Colossians chapter 2

20th July
JESUS LOVE FOR YOU IS SETTLED

Romans 8:35-39

35Who shall separate us from the love of Christ? Shall tribulation, or distress, or persecution, or famine, or nakedness, or peril, or sword? 36As it is written: "For Your sake we are killed all day long; We are accounted as sheep for the slaughter." 37Yet in all these things we are more than conquerors through Him who loved us. 38For I am persuaded that neither death nor life, nor angels nor principalities nor powers, nor things present nor things to come, 39nor height nor depth, nor any other created thing, shall be able to separate us from the love of God which is in Christ Jesus our Lord.

The love of Jesus for us is going nowhere. He has come to stay. Except you run away from it, be sure God's love is going nowhere. Even if you take a walk away from God's love, you can be confident that you will come back to meet him where you left him. His love for you is settled. You have to make up your mind to stay permanently in this fellowship of love. We may go through tribulations, persecutions, hunger and other challenges. God's love for us goes nowhere. It is settled. God does not bring tribulation upon us to teach us anything. No good father will bring tribulation to teach his child. God teaches us through his word. John 8:31,32 says if we continue in God's word, we are his true disciples. We will know the truth and the truth will make us free. Our ignorance can make us step wrongly sometimes. Friend, continue in God's word and set your mind free one step at a time. If you are reading this devotional then you are a student of God's word. You are being set free as you grow in knowledge. As you press through to the price of God's higher calling, be assured of God's abiding love. Nothing shall separate you from the love of God.

PRAYER

Holy Spirit, help me never to depart from this amazing love of Jesus Christ.

Further reading: Romans chapter 8

21st July
LOVE BEYOND UNDERSTANDING

Ephesians 3:14-19

> *14For this reason I bow my knees to the Father of our Lord Jesus Christ, 15from whom the whole family in heaven and earth is named, 16that He would grant you, according to the riches of His glory, to be strengthened with might through His Spirit in the inner man, 17that Christ may dwell in your hearts through faith; that you, being rooted and grounded in love, 18may be able to comprehend with all the saints what is the width and length and depth and height— 19to know the love of Christ which passes knowledge; that you may be filled with all the fullness of God.*

The above scripture tells us that the love of Christ passes knowledge. For us to fully understand the love of Christ, we have to fully know Jesus Christ. To fully know Christ is to be filled with the fullness of God. What an exciting prospect. God, through his love has fully made himself available to us to possess and enjoy. We have the potential to walk in the fullness of God's ability and glory. The bible says that as we continue in fellowship with Jesus, we are being changed from one level of glory to another. With every time spent in fellowship with him and his word, we are becoming more and more like Jesus. We are assured that when we finally meet him on his return, we will be like him. God's love for us is beyond comprehension. He is an eternal God and his love cannot be measured. It is as deep as deep can be and as wide as wide can be. God's love for us is stronger and greater than anyone can think. He loves us exceedingly abundantly above what we can think or imagine. My prayer for you today is that the eyes of your understanding will be enlightened to know and enjoy more and more of his love. His love is freely there for us. Let us drink from it.

PRAYER

Dear father, as I draw nearer to you, open my understanding to receive from your abundant love.

Further reading: Ephesians chapter 3

22nd July
HE FIRST LOVED US

1 John 4:7-10

⁷Beloved, let us love one another, for love is of God; and everyone who loves is born of God and knows God. ⁸He who does not love does not know God, for God is love. ⁹In this the love of God was manifested toward us, that God has sent His only begotten Son into the world, that we might live through Him. ¹⁰In this is love, not that we loved God, but that He loved us and sent His Son to be the propitiation for our sins.

Our love for God is in response to the display of his love. God started everything with a lovely creation for man to enjoy. Our inability to return God's love by walking in obedience resulted in us not enjoying the fruit of God's love. Two cannot walk together unless they walk in agreement. If Adam and Eve had responded to the amazing love of God with their own love, we would not have needed a fresh start with God. They did not walk in obedience. God has offered as another chance. Jesus Christ went to the cross voluntarily to pave the way for another love affair with us. We must grab this new proposal of love with both hands and never let go. We are invited to a feast in the house of God. Many will respond to a love proposal from an earthly king. Jesus is a heavenly king and is proposing to you today. Respond now and be determined to walk in fellowship and obedience with him. He who possesses the heavens and the earth and is faithful and true is offering you his love on a silver platter. God is love and cannot deny himself. If you come to God, you are bound to swim in love. Loved one, let us love one another. Our love for others will show that we know God.

PRAYER

Thank you father for first loving me. Thank you Jesus for the cross. Thank you Holy Spirit for your faithful friendship.

Further Reading: Isaiah chapter 53

23rd July
THE LORD IS MERCIFUL

Psalm 103:1-8

¹ Bless the Lord, O my soul; And all that is within me, bless His holy name! ² Bless the Lord, O my soul, And forget not all His benefits: ³ Who forgives all your iniquities, Who heals all your diseases, ⁴ Who redeems your life from destruction, Who crowns you with lovingkindness and tender mercies, ⁵ Who satisfies your mouth with good things, So that your youth is renewed like the eagle's. ⁶ The Lord executes righteousness And justice for all who are oppressed. ⁷ He made known His ways to Moses, His acts to the children of Israel. ⁸ The Lord is merciful and gracious, Slow to anger, and abounding in mercy.

The Lord is slow to anger and full of mercy. In other words, God has not raised a rod of punishment waiting for you to take the wrong step so he can descend on you. Some people have this perception of God. Israel had this idea about God so would not dare approach him. The opposite is the truth. God through Jesus has demonstrated his love for us. Jesus makes an open invitation to all to come to him if you are burdened or heavily laden. He promises rest. God made the same appeal to Israel through his prophets. He promised to forgive their sins and make them as white as snow. He is a merciful God intent on saving the lost than driving people away with a heavy hand. Yes our actions may deserve a heavy hand according to divine justice. Yet our God of mercy has made mercy available if we will turn to him and desire his intervention. He is ready to forgive us as he is aware of human frailty. Mercy is available. The ball is in our court. If you don't need him, you cannot receive from him. You need him and you can trust him. Go boldly to him and obtain mercy for every need today.

PRAYER

Thank you father for your mercy which is new every morning. Holy Spirit, thank you for equipping me for my assignment today.

Further reading: Psalm 103

24th July
GOD HAS CHOSEN YOU

John 15:11-16

11 "These things I have spoken to you, that My joy may remain in you, and that your joy may be full. 12This is My commandment, that you love one another as I have loved you. 13Greater love has no one than this, than to lay down one's life for his friends. 14You are My friends if you do whatever I command you. 15No longer do I call you servants, for a servant does not know what his master is doing; but I have called you friends, for all things that I heard from My Father I have made known to you. 16You did not choose Me, but I chose you and appointed you that you should go and bear fruit, and that your fruit should remain, that whatever you ask the Father in My name He may give you.

Jesus reminds his disciples that he chose them. It is not the other way round. It is the same for you. God chose you. You did not choose him. Romans 8:29-30 says that he knew you before and planned for you to be conformed to the image of Jesus Christ. It says that he called you cleaned you up and equipped you for the assignment he had in mind for you. Your present position in the kingdom has very little to do with you. All you have done is respond to the call of God. You have been head hunted. You did not put in an application. What this means is that he who chose you is confident of your ability. You do not have to struggle to fill your shoes. You just have to take instructions from God and walk accordingly. Jesus tells the Pharisees at a point that no one can come to him Jesus except the father draws him. If you have received Jesus as your lord and Saviour, the Father himself has drawn you. He himself has justified you and is glorifying you. You can do all things by Gods anointing.

PRAYER
Thank you father for choosing me. You came into my darkness and plucked me out. Help me to walk in your glory fulfilling the assignment you have given me.

Further reading: John chapter 15

25th July
CALL ON JESUS AND BE SAVED

Romans 10:9-13

> *⁹That if you confess with your mouth the Lord Jesus and believe in your heart that God has raised Him from the dead, you will be saved. ¹⁰For with the heart one believes unto righteousness, and with the mouth confession is made unto salvation. ¹¹For the Scripture says, "Whoever believes on Him will not be put to shame." ¹²For there is no distinction between Jew and Greek, for the same Lord over all is rich to all who call upon Him. ¹³For "whoever calls on the name of the Lord shall be saved."*

The heart and the mouth are two very important parts of our body. Scripture tells us to protect our hearts from all filth. This is because the heart is the centre of your being and what you have in your heart is the real you. Scripture also admonishes us to be careful with what comes out of our mouths because our tongues have the power to release life or death. If we receive Jesus in our hearts we are made right with God. This means that our sins are forgiven and we don't have to pay the penalty of sin any longer. The penalty of sin is being separated from God. This separation from the light of God brings ignorance which leads to sickness, poverty and death. We must ensure that we have Jesus settled firmly in our hearts otherwise we become weak and wobbly, forever searching and not coming to truth. The scripture above tells us that we believe in our hearts unto righteousness and confess with our mouths unto salvation. There is a spiritual law that requires the testimony of at least two witnesses for a fact to be established. It is not enough to believe in your heart, you must confess with your mouth unto salvation. What you have in your heart must come out of your mouth. This establishes you and allows others to share in this truth. Call on Jesus today and experience salvation for every situation.

PRAYER

My Jesus I call on you today to be part of every situation. Bring salvation and deliverance wherever it is needed.

Further reading: Romans chapter 10

26th July
I AM WITH YOU ALWAYS

Isaiah 43:1-3

> But now, thus says the Lord, who created you, O Jacob, And He who formed you, O Israel: "Fear not, for I have redeemed you; I have called you by your name; You are Mine. When you pass through the waters, I will be with you; And through the rivers, they shall not overflow you. When you walk through the fire, you shall not be burned, Nor shall the flame scorch you For I am the Lord your God, The Holy One of Israel, your Saviour; I gave Egypt for your ransom, Ethiopia and Seba in your place.

God promises Israel that he would be with them through every challenge because they are his. How did Israel become God's? Israel is made up of the descendants of Abraham with whom God had a covenant. A covenant is an irrevocable promise. God had made a promise to Abraham that he would bless his seed. Israel had become a people that God had to take care of. God is not a covenant breaker. There were times that through misbehaviour, Israel would fall prey to its enemies and go through a period of suffering. God always promised restoration because there is no way God can go back on his word to Abraham. Although many in Israel do not accept Jesus Christ today as the Messiah, there is a promise waiting for them. They will accept Jesus and be restored. Friend, you have a better covenant with God than Israel. The covenant you have with God has Jesus Christ as the mediator. It is sealed with the blood of Jesus Christ. The blood of Jesus makes you part of the family of God. You are not just a friend or a servant to God but a son. You are just like Jesus Christ to the father. You may be in the fire or water now. Be assured that God is with you. He is a good father and you are being raised as a good son with a great destiny.

PRAYER

Thank you father for the assurance that you are with me wherever I go. I will continually acknowledge your presence with me. Thank you for this strong relationship you have offered me.

Further reading: Isaiah chapter 43

27th July
LOVE HAS PAID THE PRICE

Isaiah 53:4-6

Surely He has borne our griefs And carried our sorrows; Yet we esteemed Him stricken, Smitten by God, and afflicted. But He was wounded for our transgressions, He was bruised for our iniquities; The chastisement for our peace was upon Him, And by His stripes we are healed. All we like sheep have gone astray; We have turned, every one, to his own way; And the Lord has laid on Him the iniquity of us all.

What a beautiful love story between Jesus and his family which includes you and me. We commit all the sins and he pays for it all by his death on the cross. The grief, sorrow and death that we have to suffer for our sins have already been borne by Jesus Christ. We were separated from God but his desire to bring us to the same place where he is, made him offer his life as a complete payment for our sins. He defeated Satan and death. He has now offered a share in his kingdom to us. We can now share in his resurrection power if we would respond to his invitation. He has already paid the price. It is a done deal. He cannot go back and undo it. He is settled in everlasting life and is ready to share with whosoever shall respond to this invitation. You first have to believe that the price is paid for you. You then receive this salvation and live in it resisting any voice contrary to the invitation of Jesus Christ. God is love. Love has an object. There always has to be someone at the receiving end of love. You are the object of God's love. You are the reason why Jesus suffered. Who is the object of your love? Scripture commands us to love God and one another. Meditate on this and take action.

PRAYER

Thank you Jesus for paying the price of sin for me . I can confidently say I am free because of the price you have paid.

Further reading: Isaiah chapter 15

28th July
HE WILL WIPE AWAY YOUR TEARS

Revelation 21:1-4

¹Now I saw a new heaven and a new earth, for the first heaven and the first earth had passed away. Also there was no more sea. ²Then I, John, saw the holy city, New Jerusalem, coming down out of heaven from God, prepared as a bride adorned for her husband. ³And I heard a loud voice from heaven saying, "Behold, the tabernacle of God is with men, and He will dwell with them, and they shall be His people. God Himself will be with them and be their God. ⁴And God will wipe away every tear from their eyes; there shall be no more death, nor sorrow, nor crying. There shall be no more pain, for the former things have passed away."

God's plans for us are always beautiful. God's plan towards us is one of peace and an expected glorious end. We must rejoice in hope. God can never lose a fight. Jesus Christ has already settled the victory of life over death. The relationship between Jesus and his church is referred to as that of a bridegroom and his wife. The image of the groom and the bride represents fresh undying love. Jesus love of the church is like a groom anxiously waiting for the bride to finish adorning herself for the marriage ceremony to begin. Those of us who receive Jesus as our Lord and Saviour are the church. Jesus is beautifying his church and nothing can stop it. He is washing his church with his word. Revelation upon revelation is being poured upon the church. Every fresh revelation released to the church is like fresh perfumed oil poured and massaged into the church to produce new fragrance. The glory of the latter church shall be greater than the glory of the former. God is going to wipe away every tear. There shall be no more death, sorrow or crying. Pain shall pass away. That day is surely coming. Let us rejoice in hope.

PRAYER
Come Lord Jesus for your bride. I am looking forward to the marriage supper with you.

Further reading: Revelation chapter 21

29th July
YOU ARE BORN OF GOD

John 1:10-13

> He was in the world, and the world was made through Him, and the world did not know Him. *11*He came to His own, and His own did not receive Him. *12*But as many as received Him, to them He gave the right to become children of God, to those who believe in His name: *13*who were born, not of blood, nor of the will of the flesh, nor of the will of man, but of God.

Jesus is the Word of God. There is nothing that God made that he did not make through his word. He spoke the world into being. He ordered light to appear and it did. He created the heavens and the earth and all that are in it by his word. Scripture tells us that the Jesus who walked the earth in his flesh many years ago was God's word made flesh (John 1:14). Jesus is described as being full of grace and truth. God's word is true and full of love. When Jesus walked the earth, he only did good. He went about undoing the works of the devil. Many were set free from demonic oppression and sickness yet the people did not receive him. Isn't it interesting that the people in Jesus day shouted for a murderer to be released to them but asked for Jesus to be killed. Yet in the midst of this deprivation, there were some who received him. These he gave the power to become children of God. The few who received him transformed the world in their day. Even today when you receive Jesus you become a child of God. This is not just in name, you are born of God just like your father and mother gave birth to you. Except God is Spirit so you are born again by the spirit of God. You have become like Jesus. He is the first born of many children. God's love for us is the love of a father for his children.

PRAYER

Thank you father for counting me worthy to be part of your family. Holy Spirit, help me to forget my past and walk confidently as a child of God.

Further reading: John chapter 1

30th July
GOD IS OUR REFUGE

Psalm 62:5-8

> *My soul, wait silently for God alone, For my expectation is from Him. ⁶ He only is my rock and my salvation; He is my defense; I shall not be moved. ⁷ In God is my salvation and my glory; The rock of my strength, And my refuge, is in God. ⁸ Trust in Him at all times, you people; Pour out your heart before Him; God is a refuge for us.*

I like the way the psalmist singles out God. God is God and he is in a class of his own. He cannot be compared to anyone or anything. If you trust in anything more or the same as you trust God, it is an insult to God. He created all things. To trust in anything more than God is to make that thing your God. That breaks the first command of God not to have any other gods before him. It is easy to say you love God more than any other thing. In reality it may not be so. Do you put your job, family, entertainment before God? Jesus says that if you love father, mother or children more than you love me then you are not worthy of me. God is not telling you to ignore your family. He gave you your family. He is just asking you to get your priority right and you will get the right sort of love for your family. It is only God who can give you complete protection when you run to him. A refuge is a place you run to for security. In life, everyone will need a place of refuge one time or the other. No one and no place can give you complete security. Apart from God your total protection and provision cannot be guaranteed. Trust in his ability, faithfulness and love. He will never disappoint you or put you to shame. He is more solid than the hardest rock.

PRAYER

Father I join with the psalmist to say you alone are my total security. When you protect me, I feel totally protected. Thank you.

Further reading: Psalm 62

31st July
JESUS WAS MADE SIN FOR US

2 Corinthians 5:17-21

> [17]*Therefore, if anyone is in Christ, he is a new creation; old things have passed away; behold, all things have become new.* [18]*Now all things are of God, who has reconciled us to Himself through Jesus Christ, and has given us the ministry of reconciliation,* [19]*that is, that God was in Christ reconciling the world to Himself, not imputing their trespasses to them, and has committed to us the word of reconciliation.* [20]*Now then, we are ambassadors for Christ, as though God were pleading through us: we implore you on Christ's behalf, be reconciled to God.* [21]*For He made Him who knew no sin to be sin for us, that we might become the righteousness of God in Him.*

I don't know what crime you find most disgusting. Just imagine an accusation of child abuse is made against you and you have to serve a prison sentence for it though you are innocent. It would be the worst thing that could happen to you. To carry that stigma and serve the sentence for it would greatly affect you. This is what happened to Jesus. He was pure. Being God, he hated sin. He was righteous. Sin and righteousness cannot live together. Yet all sin was put on him. Not just one sin but all sin including rape and murder. The bible says he was led as a lamb to the slaughter but he did not open his mouth. He was to die for sins he had not committed yet he did not raise a protest. This was not an easy task. He had asked his father to let this cup pass him by but his father had not granted that request. He went through this horrible ordeal because it meant that others who had actually committed the offence did not have to suffer the consequence of it. He was made sin for you and me so we could be made righteous and be able to approach and share with God.

PRAYER
Thank you Jesus for this show of love that has given me right standing with God. I can now fully fellowship with God as my father.

Further reading: 2 Corinthians chapter 5

August

1st August
LOVE GOD AND LOVE PEOPLE

Matthew 22:35-40

Then one of them, a lawyer, asked Him a question, testing Him, and saying, ³⁶"Teacher, which is the great commandment in the law?" ³⁷Jesus said to him, "'You shall love the Lord your God with all your heart, with all your soul, and with all your mind.' ³⁸This is the first and great commandment. ³⁹And the second is like it: 'You shall love your neighbour as yourself.' ⁴⁰On these two commandments hang all the Law and the Prophets."

God's covenant with Israel was based on the law and the prophets. If Israel would obey God's commandments and receive his word through his prophets, they could count on the total provision and protection of God. The scripture says a lawyer tested Jesus by asking which is the greatest of the commandments. This lawyer probably had a good knowledge of the law and was ready to argue as lawyers do. Jesus answer simplified God's law into love. It is not a complicated issue for argument. Everything God does is motivated by love and designed for love. If you want to understand the law and prophets then think love. If you can walk in love towards God and your fellow man you have fulfilled your part in the covenant. A look at the ten commandments God gave to Israel through Moses shows that the first four are about our relationship with God and the last six about our relationship with others. God loves all people and desires for us to love all people. This is a difficult task as there are bad people around. We cannot love everyone without help from God. This help can only come as we love God and receive from his love to give to others. If you love God you will keep his word. If you stay in his word, you will have a revelation of the truth of the love of God. This will enable you to love even the unlovable. May you be filled with the love of God today.

PRAYER

Dear father, fill me with your love today that your love will flow out of me to others.

Further reading: Matthew chapter 22

2nd August
LOVE SHOWS OUR LEVEL OF SPIRITUALITY

1 Corinthians 13:1-3

Though I speak with the tongues of men and of angels, but have not love, I have become sounding brass or a clanging cymbal. ²And though I have the gift of prophecy, and understand all mysteries and all knowledge, and though I have all faith, so that I could remove mountains, but have not love, I am nothing. ³And though I bestow all my goods to feed the poor, and though I give my body to be burned, but have not love, it profits me nothing.

People in the world today are attracted to miracles and the extraordinary. Our television screens are filled with magical and talent shows. People are celebrated for doing extraordinary things. Real miracles belong to the Church. Extraordinary miracles of healing, raising the dead and commanding mountains to move only happen in the church. This is because only God has the power to perform lasting miracles. He has entrusted this power to his church. When the miracle is not from God, there is always a deception somewhere. Do not be deceived. Servants cannot make you king. Every spirit is subject to the authority of Jesus and only he can make you king. Jesus has given his church many gifts which include speaking the language of angels and men, prophesying, understanding mysteries and faith to remove mountains. He has even given us the gift to perform good works like helping the poor. These are gifts that many will applaud both in and out of the church. The apostle Paul is telling us by revelation that without love all these so called powerful gifts mean nothing. God has the power to change every situation. Love shows our closeness to God more than any of these gifts. Jesus rebuked his listeners for craving for miracles rather than the word of love he has brought them. Love can only come from God. Desire the sincere milk of God's love through his word today.

PRAYER

Father, I lift my cup to you today. Feed me with your love till it overflows. Thank you.

Further reading: *1 Corinthians chapter 13*

3rd August
LOVE IS PATIENT

1 Corinthians 13:4-7

> *Love suffers long and is kind; love does not envy; love does not parade itself, is not puffed up; [5]does not behave rudely, does not seek its own, is not provoked, thinks no evil; [6]does not rejoice in iniquity, but rejoices in the truth; [7]bears all things, believes all things, hopes all things, endures all things.*

An unseen force of impatience drives the world. A philosophy of "we have to achieve and achieve it now" drives people around like zombies or machines. Scripture tells us that when the end comes people will still be very busy running around chasing the wind. Scripture says destruction will suddenly come upon them like a thief in the night. This should not be so because the word of salvation is being declared day and night but many have not stopped to listen. Even in God's church, some are so busy running around trying to achieve something for God. God is quite capable of building his church and a little patience and separation to God will give us the heart of God and make us able to achieve more. Jesus is certainly not running around. He is seated and we are supposed to be seated right where he is with him. Love is never lazy. Love is compassionate and drives you to help where help is needed. Love is patient and long suffering. James 1:4 says patience brings perfection and we would lack nothing with patience. The oppression of age is one of the offshoots of the fear of death. A voice continually tells us that 'there is no time'. The message of God is completely different. Eternal life is life that will never end; endless life of quality. This is why God lovingly gave us Jesus Christ that whosoever believes in him will not perish but have everlasting life. Enjoy the patience of love and walk in perfection.

PRAYER

In the Name of Jesus, I command my body and soul to be patient. I choose to be still to enjoy the goodness of God. I silence every anxiety in me.

Further reading: 1 Corinthians chapter 13

4th August
LOVE NEVER FAILS

1 Corinthians 13:8-13

> *Love never fails. But whether there are prophecies, they will fail; whether there are tongues, they will cease; whether there is knowledge, it will vanish away. ⁹For we know in part and we prophesy in part. ¹⁰But when that which is perfect has come, then that which is in part will be done away. ¹¹When I was a child, I spoke as a child, I understood as a child, I thought as a child; but when I became a man, I put away childish things. ¹²For now we see in a mirror, dimly, but then face to face. Now I know in part, but then I shall know just as I also am known. ¹³And now abide faith, hope, love, these three; but the greatest of these is love.*

God never fails. He cannot fail because he is. You measure right by who he is and what he says. If the whole world should see something as white and God alone says it is black, then it is black. The whole world is wrong. This is why it is important to live by faith in the word of God and not by sight. He who created every part of our being and everything in the universe cannot possibly make mistakes. His word is the standard by which we measure right and wrong. The word righteousness simply means being right. Only God is righteous and only he can make others right. We have been made the righteousness of God through Christ Jesus. God is love and love is God. You cannot separate the two. Where you find love you find God and where you find God you find love. We are not talking about the world's definition of love which could be one of many things. We are talking about the agape love of God which is nothing short of who He is. This is the sacrificial love that went to the cross for the salvation of mankind. Love never fails.

PRAYER

Thank you father that you have never failed me. Thank you for your love for me which cannot stop. Help me to continually walk in this love.

Further reading: 1 Corinthians chapter 13

5th August
DO NOT BE QUICK TO CONDEMN

Romans 14:1-6

Receive one who is weak in the faith, but not to disputes over doubtful things. ²For one believes he may eat all things, but he who is weak eats only vegetables. ³Let not him who eats despise him who does not eat, and let not him who does not eat judge him who eats; for God has received him. ⁴Who are you to judge another's servant? To his own master he stands or falls. Indeed, he will be made to stand, for God is able to make him stand. ⁵One person esteems one day above another; another esteems every day alike. Let each be fully convinced in his own mind. ⁶He who observes the day, observes it to the Lord; and he who does not observe the day, to the Lord he does not observe it. He who eats, eats to the Lord, for he gives God thanks; and he who does not eat, to the Lord he does not eat, and gives God thanks.

Do not be quick to condemn. Scripture tells us that Jesus did not come to condemn but to save the world. Christians have not been anointed to condemn but save the world. Those who have not made Jesus the Lord of their lives are already condemned. Our responsibility is to use our gifts to rescue them. Satan is out to steal, kill and destroy as many as he can. Seek to draw people to salvation not to push them away. Scripture tells us to gently instruct the ignorant. There is nothing we have that we did not receive. The seed of God's righteousness and love sown in us produces fruits of righteousness. This is what others should eat. The fruit of the spirit is love, joy, peace, longsuffering, gentleness, kindness, faithfulness, humility and self-control. This is the power that will draw people to God. The devil laughs when division is created in the church as a result of condemnation. Seek to encourage the weak brother.

PRAYER

Lord Jesus, I thank you for the seed of love that you have freely sown in my heart. I will use the fruit of this seed to serve others in humility.

Further reading: Romans chapter 14

6th August
THE FRUIT OF LOVE IS ATTRACTIVE

Acts 9:36-39

At Joppa there was a certain disciple named Tabitha, which is translated Dorcas. This woman was full of good works and charitable deeds which she did. ³⁷But it happened in those days that she became sick and died. When they had washed her, they laid her in an upper room. ³⁸And since Lydda was near Joppa, and the disciples had heard that Peter was there, they sent two men to him, imploring him not to delay in coming to them. ³⁹Then Peter arose and went with them. When he had come, they brought him to the upper room. And all the widows stood by him weeping, showing the tunics and garments which Dorcas had made while she was with them.

Love produces good works. Tabitha was a disciple whose love had made her attractive amongst the people. When she died, the people around her felt she was too beneficial to them to be allowed to die. They cleaned her up and sent for the apostle Peter to come to them in emergency. Their faith in the power of God and respect for his apostle gave them hope that Peter could do something about the situation. Their trust paid off. Peter raised Tabitha from the dead. The desire on the people's hearts placed a demand on heaven to raise Tabitha from the dead. The love of God cannot bear the suffering of the people. As long as the people are drawing on the love of God in you for their survival, expect long life on this earth. The compassion of Jesus was also displayed when he met the funeral train of an only son. He raised him from the dead.. Today in many parts of the world, the dead are being raised in the Name of Jesus. Like Tabitha my prayer for you is that many will crave your presence when you are absent because your presence makes a difference to their lives. Let the love of God attract many to you and through you to Him.

PRAYER

When people see me, may they see you Lord Jesus. May I be a sweet well from which many will come and drink.

Further reading: Acts chapter 9

7th August
TURN THE OTHER CHEEK

Matthew 5:38-42

"You have heard that it was said, 'An eye for an eye and a tooth for a tooth.' ³⁹But I tell you not to resist an evil person. But whoever slaps you on your right cheek, turn the other to him also. ⁴⁰If anyone wants to sue you and take away your tunic, let him have your cloak also. ⁴¹And whoever compels you to go one mile, go with him two. ⁴²Give to him who asks you, and from him who wants to borrow from you do not turn away.

This revolutionary teaching on love by Jesus Christ would have been strange and challenging to his listeners. It sounded like one of those sermons that sound godly and good from the pulpit but to which you can close yourself and say: 'That is not for me. I cannot do that." Today, many Christians make fun of this scripture as they do of Jesus saying we should forgive seventy times seven. God does not play games with His Word. He will not ask us to do something we cannot do. Everything God would ask us to accomplish would be beyond our personal ability to do so. We need his empowering strength. It is never by our own might or power but by his spirit. God told King Jehoshaphat when he faced an enemy of three nations whose physical strength surpassed his that the battle is not Jehoshaphat's but God's. God supernaturally defeated King Jehoshaphat's enemies. Be ready to turn the other cheek and allow God to fight your battles. Our command is to walk in love. The world may look dangerous but Jesus encourages us not to be afraid because he is in control of the world. Jehoshaphat's father, King Asa made his own plans without consulting God in war. God told him that because he could fight his own wars, he would have many wars. Allow God to fight your battles for you.

PRAYER

Holy Spirit, help me to exercise patience when I am provoked. Help me to pray for my enemies.

Further reading: Matthew 5:1-20

8th August
LOVE YOUR ENEMY

Matthew 5:43-48

"You have heard that it was said, 'You shall love your neighbour and hate your enemy.' ⁴⁴But I say to you, love your enemies, bless those who curse you, do good to those who hate you, and pray for those who spitefully use you and persecute you, ⁴⁵that you may be sons of your Father in heaven; for He makes His sun rise on the evil and on the good, and sends rain on the just and on the unjust. ⁴⁶For if you love those who love you, what reward have you? Do not even the tax collectors do the same? ⁴⁷And if you greet your brethren only, what do you do more than others? Do not even the tax collectors do so? ⁴⁸Therefore you shall be perfect, just as your Father in heaven is perfect.

The word of God is telling us that if we love only those who love us we are not perfect. God desires for us to be perfect even as he is perfect. God does not allow us to hate our enemies. This tells you that God is not capable of hate. We must hate sin because sin will get you away from God. We must run away from sin. We cannot hate people if we want to be like our father who loves all equally. Jesus died for all. Whosoever shall respond to the invitation of God through Jesus Christ shall be saved. This offer is not to angels but to all people. We are therefore to love all people created by God. Many have mixed up their hatred for sin with their hatred of sinners. We are not allowed to hate sinners as our father loves everyone. Instead, we must do all in our power to bring sinners to repentance and salvation. When people curse you with their words, bless them with your words; return their evil deeds with good. Let God deal with his own.

PRAYER

Holy Spirit, help me to walk perfectly before my father in love. Give me the patience and self control not to revenge but to pray for my enemies.

Further reading: Matthew 5:21-47

9th August
FAITH MUST PRODUCE WORKS

James 2:14-18

> *What does it profit, my brethren, if someone says he has faith but does not have works? Can faith save him? ¹⁵If a brother or sister is naked and destitute of daily food, ¹⁶and one of you says to them, "Depart in peace, be warmed and filled," but you do not give them the things which are needed for the body, what does it profit? ¹⁷Thus also faith by itself, if it does not have works, is dead. ¹⁸But someone will say, "You have faith, and I have works." Show me your faith without your works, and I will show you my faith by my works.*

Scripture tells us that faith works by love. For you to have faith in God, you must trust him. Trust is a product of love. No one can truly confess that Jesus is Lord except by the revelation of the Holy Spirit. Faith in our day cannot bypass the lordship of Jesus Christ. If the Holy Spirit is in you then you must produce the fruit of the Holy Spirit. None of the fruit of the Holy Spirit listed in Galatians 5:22 – love, joy, peace, longsuffering, gentleness, faithfulness, kindness, humility and self-control – is passive. They are all fruit that produce works. You cannot have love or kindness and hide it. The scripture says by their fruit we will know the nature of the tree it has come from. If you say you have faith working through love then we need to see the works your faith has produced. The word used for the Holy Spirit in the bible is also translated wind. You cannot contain wind. If you have the faith of God, this faith cannot be contained. It has to produce works. Time to check yourself. How many people are praising God because of you? They may be praising you but has the fruit of humility in you given the glory to the source of your ability? Show me your works and I can tell of your faith.

PRAYER

Dear father, help me not to boast in my own works. May I give you the glory for all the work that your gift of faith has produced through me.

Further reading: James chapter 2

10th August
HELP THOSE IN NEED

James 1:22-27

But be doers of the word, and not hearers only, deceiving yourselves. ²³For if anyone is a hearer of the word and not a doer, he is like a man observing his natural face in a mirror; ²⁴for he observes himself, goes away, and immediately forgets what kind of man he was. ²⁵But he who looks into the perfect law of liberty and continues in it, and is not a forgetful hearer but a doer of the work, this one will be blessed in what he does.

²⁶If anyone among you thinks he is religious, and does not bridle his tongue but deceives his own heart, this one's religion is useless. ²⁷Pure and undefiled religion before God and the Father is this: to visit orphans and widows in their trouble, and to keep oneself unspotted from the world.

We are blessed today to have the word of God written down for us in the bible. We do not only have the Holy Spirit in us to convict us of what is right and wrong, we also have the bible to tell us truth. If what you are thinking cannot be supported by the written word of God then it cannot be from God. This means that we have to believe that the word we read from the bible is the inspired word of God. The bible tells us that if we have received Jesus Christ as our Lord and Saviour then we are children of God with full rights as Jesus. If you read this and you go away forgetting that you are under full protection and provision of God, you are like a mad person who doesn't know who he really is. If you don't know who you really are, you are bound to make the wrong decisions. You could also be bullied by Satan and you would think you deserve it. Instead God has anointed you with so much love and power to help those in need.

PRAYER

Father, my desire is to please you in every way. Thank you for saving me and giving me your Holy Spirit. I will use your gift to help those in need.

Further reading: James chapter 1

11th August
GIVE TO THE POOR

Matthew 19:16-21

Now behold, one came and said to Him, "Good Teacher, what good thing shall I do that I may have eternal life?" ¹⁷So He said to him, "Why do you call Me good? No one is good but One, that is, God. But if you want to enter into life, keep the commandments." ¹⁸He said to Him, "Which ones?" Jesus said, "'You shall not murder,' 'You shall not commit adultery,' 'You shall not steal,' 'You shall not bear false witness,' ¹⁹'Honour your father and your mother,' and, 'You shall love your neighbour as yourself.'" ²⁰The young man said to Him, "All these things I have kept from my youth. What do I still lack?" ²¹Jesus said to him, "If you want to be perfect, go, sell what you have and give to the poor, and you will have treasure in heaven; and come, follow Me."

God cares for the poor. If you were the ruler of the household and part of the household walked in lack, you would do your best to correct that. God loves us so much and would not want us to lack anything. He has enough to take care of every need of all men. Ignorance of the existence and heart of God has left many walking in lack. God channels his blessing through men who are ready to be obedient. God blessed the world through Jesus Christ who took on flesh to open up God to us. Jesus is building his church on the foundation of the apostles and prophets. He is blessing the world through his church. Scripture says the whole world is groaning waiting for the manifestation of the sons of God. The sons of God are those of us in the church. Jesus is not just wanting us to be religiously obedient to the letter of the law but to show love to the poor with our giving. The man above failed the test. He was obeying some commandments but not loving the poor as himself.

PRAYER

Father help me to worship you by loving what you love. You love the poor and so will I.

Further reading: Matthew chapter 19

12th August
BE HUMBLE

Matthew 18:1-6

At that time the disciples came to Jesus, saying, "Who then is greatest in the kingdom of heaven?" ²Then Jesus called a little child to Him, set him in the midst of them, ³and said, "Assuredly, I say to you, unless you are converted and become as little children, you will by no means enter the kingdom of heaven. ⁴Therefore whoever humbles himself as this little child is the greatest in the kingdom of heaven. ⁵Whoever receives one little child like this in My name receives Me. ⁶"Whoever causes one of these little ones who believe in Me to sin, it would be better for him if a millstone were hung around his neck, and he were drowned in the depth of the sea.

In the very competitive world we live in, everyone wants to be the greatest. The disciples were thinking along the same line when they asked the question above. Jesus response was as mind boggling as all his responses. The kingdom of God does not operate like the kingdom of the world. The humble reign in the kingdom of God. He encouraged the disciples to be converted to the innocence of a little child if they want to be great in the kingdom. Do not seek to be the greatest but seek to humble yourself to the obedience of God. True humility is putting aside your own reputation and coming to God in total trust and obedience. Scripture encourages us to see each other as better than ourselves. The place of humility is the place of great strength. You are not threatened by another's success. All you seek to do is to please God. Humility anchors your soul and fear is driven out. He who is down needs fear no fall and he who is down can only go up. Your trust in God makes you surrender everything to him in humility. Jesus went through the shame of the cross for our sake.

PRAYER

Holy Spirit, help me to be humble. Mold me into the shape you want me to be. I surrender all.

Further reading: Matthew chapter 18

13th August
PROTECT YOUR HEART

Proverbs 4:20-26

> My son, give attention to my words; Incline your ear to my sayings. ^{21} Do not let them depart from your eyes; Keep them in the midst of your heart; ^{22} For they are life to those who find them, And health to all their flesh. ^{23} Keep your heart with all diligence, For out of it spring the issues of life. ^{24} Put away from you a deceitful mouth, And put perverse lips far from you. ^{25} Let your eyes look straight ahead, And your eyelids look right before you. ^{26} Ponder the path of your feet, And let all your ways be established.

If you can put the word of God in the middle of your heart, scripture says it is life to those who find them. You will not only find God's kind of life, but others would benefit from these words in your heart as they flow through your mouth. It continues that this will bring health to your flesh. God's word in your mouth is good medicine with no side effect. If real life comes from the heart then it is important that we keep our heart clean. Evil things can also come from our hearts to defile us. In response to a query by the Pharisees about why his disciples do not go through ritual cleansing before eating, Jesus replies that it is not what you eat that defiles you but what comes out of you (Matthew 15:10-20). He explains that whilst your food goes through the digestive system and is expelled, evil thoughts, murders, fornication thefts, false witness and blasphemies proceed from the heart. The heart can therefore keep the word of God and bring life or harbour evil and bring death. Nothing can force itself into your heart. You will have to receive it. The enemy can get his way to your heart through deception and distraction. Don't allow it. Hold on to this truth and protect your heart.

PRAYER
Dear father, you are welcome to the centre of my heart. I will meditate on your word and allow only wholesome words out of my mouth.

Further reading: Proverbs chapter 4

14th August
CHECK YOUR WORDS

James 3:1-6

> ¹My brethren, let not many of you become teachers, knowing that we shall receive a stricter judgment. ²For we all stumble in many things. If anyone does not stumble in word, he is a perfect man, able also to bridle the whole body. ³Indeed, we put bits in horses' mouths that they may obey us, and we turn their whole body. ⁴Look also at ships: although they are so large and are driven by fierce winds, they are turned by a very small rudder wherever the pilot desires. ⁵Even so the tongue is a little member and boasts great things. See how great a forest a little fire kindles! ⁶And the tongue is a fire, a world of iniquity. The tongue is so set among our members that it defiles the whole body, and sets on fire the course of nature; and it is set on fire by hell.

The words of our mouth are very important to bring death or life. Scripture warns us in many places to watch what comes out of mouth. Jesus warns that we will give account for every idle word that comes out of our mouth. The heart is like the cartridge which holds the bullet before it is fired. The mouth is like the barrel of the gun that releases the bullet into the world. The moment the bullet is fired, it is too late to retrieve the bullet. You will have to live with the consequence of your shot. This is why it is important to release godly bullets than ungodly ones. James compares the tongue to the bridle with which you control a horse or the rudder with which you steer a ship. In other words, the rest of your body will turn in the direction of your words. The tongue is prone to boasting and lying in order to gain advantage. Check your tongue. Do not rush to teach if you are not equipped to teach. Teaching false doctrine will bring judgment on you. Check your words.

PRAYER

Holy Spirit, take control of my lips. I pray that no deceitful words will come out of my mouth. May the words of my mouth and meditation of my heart be acceptable to you.

Further reading: James chapter 3

15th August
IMITATE GOD

Ephesians 5:1-7

> *Therefore be imitators of God as dear children. ²And walk in love, as Christ also has loved us and given Himself for us, an offering and a sacrifice to God for a sweet-smelling aroma. ³But fornication and all uncleanness or covetousness, let it not even be named among you, as is fitting for saints; ⁴neither filthiness, nor foolish talking, nor coarse jesting, which are not fitting, but rather giving of thanks. ⁵For this you know, that no fornicator, unclean person, nor covetous man, who is an idolater, has any inheritance in the kingdom of Christ and God. ⁶Let no one deceive you with empty words, for because of these things the wrath of God comes upon the sons of disobedience. ⁷Therefore do not be partakers with them.*

God has come to live inside all of us who have received Jesus sacrifice on the Cross of Calvary. The Holy Spirit in us gives us direction and convicts us of right and wrong. In our world today filled with many deceptive voices, he has given us the written word of the bible as our companion. It is very helpful to ask yourself what Jesus would do in any circumstance and do likewise. I like the wise counsel of a preacher that if you are in doubt, don't do it. Do everything with faith. Imitate God. Almost everyone in this world imitates one person or the other. Our way of dressing, talking and buying are greatly influenced. Many imitate the wrong people. If you knew the lifestyles of some of the fashion designers or politicians and pop stars, we would not gladly dress or walk or speak like them. The only we can be sure of imitating the right person is to imitate God. Jesus told the Pharisees that when the blind lead the blind, they would both fall in a ditch. If you imitate God you will run away from sexual uncleanness, envy and greed, idolatry, foolish and deceitful talk. Flee youthful lust my friend and imitate God.

PRAYER
Holy Spirit, please help order my steps. It is only God I want to imitate and no one else.

Further reading: Ephesians chapter 5

16th August
RESPECT OTHERS

Ephesians 5:15-21

See then that you walk circumspectly, not as fools but as wise, ^{16}redeeming the time, because the days are evil. ^{17}Therefore do not be unwise, but understand what the will of the Lord is. ^{18}And do not be drunk with wine, in which is dissipation; but be filled with the Spirit, ^{19}speaking to one another in psalms and hymns and spiritual songs, singing and making melody in your heart to the Lord, ^{20}giving thanks always for all things to God the Father in the name of our Lord Jesus Christ, ^{21}submitting to one another in the fear of God.

There were times when we were ignorant and allowed the world to drive us. Thank God that in his mercy, he has delivered us from this darkness and given us the revelation of the light of God. Now that our eyes are open it will be foolish to continue to be driven by dark forces beyond our control. We have to rise up in wisdom and redeem the time. Time never stops. If you don't cease the time, all sorts of evil and fear will overtake you. Redeem the time. Get into prayer and know what the will of the father is. Do not be drunk with wine. Drunkenness could be a great distraction. Instead be filled with the Holy Spirit. Drunkenness has many side effects. Many use the example of Jesus drinking wine whilst he walked the earth as an excuse to get drunk. Alcohol drinking is not a sin in itself but it could be a big distraction. The bible says as Jesus is so are we now in this world. Jesus is definitely not getting drunk on alcohol now and I will encourage you to redeem the time. I am not giving a law here but encouraging you to try life without being drunk and see how it will help deliver some alcoholics. Be filled with the true Spirit of God, respecting one another and enjoying fellowship with each other.

PRAYER

Holy Spirit, help me to redeem the time as you direct me according to the purpose of God. Help me to respect others recognizing their gifts and submitting in humility.

Further reading: Ephesians chapter 5

17th August
HONOUR YOUR FATHER AND MOTHER

Ephesians 6:1-8

> *Children, obey your parents in the Lord, for this is right. ²"Honour your father and mother," which is the first commandment with promise: ³"that it may be well with you and you may live long on the earth." ⁴And you, fathers, do not provoke your children to wrath, but bring them up in the training and admonition of the Lord. ⁵Bondservants, be obedient to those who are your masters according to the flesh, with fear and trembling, in sincerity of heart, as to Christ; ⁶not with eyeservice, as men-pleasers, but as bondservants of Christ, doing the will of God from the heart, ⁷with goodwill doing service, as to the Lord, and not to men, ⁸knowing that whatever good anyone does, he will receive the same from the Lord, whether he is a slave or free.*

God is a master builder and knows where every stone fits. When Adam and Eve disobeyed God, they moved out of position and disturbed the entire building. Jesus Christ has become the foundation of God's new building. One of the assignments of Jesus Christ in his resurrection is to carry the government of God on his shoulder and to put the building of God back into shape. In a building, every stone rest on one and carries another stone. Jesus Christ is the corner or first stone as well as the cap or final stone. When you recognize the importance of the stone you are resting on as well as the one you are carrying, you will enjoy good rest. Children honour your father and mother. It pleased God for them to introduce you to the world. Honour the spiritual parents God has given you. Parents, fulfil the responsibility God has given to you towards your children. Guide and protect them. God is not condoning slavery but encouraging us to serve with diligence and love whether as employee or employer.

PRAYER

Thank you father for those you have put around me, older and younger. Help me to respect and discharge my responsibility towards them with much love.

Further reading: Ephesians chapter 6

18th August
LOOK OUT FOR THE INTEREST OF OTHERS

Philippians 2:1-4

> *Therefore if there is any consolation in Christ, if any comfort of love, if any fellowship of the Spirit, if any affection and mercy, ²fulfil my joy by being like-minded, having the same love, being of one accord, of one mind. ³Let nothing be done through selfish ambition or conceit, but in lowliness of mind let each esteem others better than himself. ⁴Let each of you look out not only for his own interests, but also for the interests of others.*

The word of God consistently assures us of God's love for us. The bible is full of his promises for us and the assurance that we are complete in him. In the same breath, his word encourages us to be concerned about the needs of others. We are asked to be concerned about the interest of others. Not many have the privilege of access to the provision of heaven. Through Jesus Christ, we have access to God's bountiful supply. There is enough there to serve the interest of all. The word of God therefore encourages us to share. There is a story in 2 Kings 7 where four lepers chance on treasure left behind by a fleeing army. This was a time of great famine in Samaria. Their initial instinct was to fill their pockets with as much of the treasure as they could. They focused on their own interest. They soon realized there was more than enough to get Samaria out of famine. They did the right thing and announced their find. All in Samaria shared in the booty. This brought prosperity to the land of Samaria. Take consolation in the fact that God has your interest at heart. Look out for the interest of others. Joy shared is joy multiplied. God created us to share with us. It is his desire that we share with others what we have received.

PRAYER

Father, forgive me for any selfishness I have displayed in the past. May I not seek my interest only but the interest of others. I have enough to share. Thank you.

Further reading: Philippians chapter 2

19th August
LIVE IN GOD'S LIGHT

1 John 2:7-11

Brethren, I write no new commandment to you, but an old commandment which you have had from the beginning. The old commandment is the word which you heard from the beginning. ⁸Again, a new commandment I write to you, which thing is true in Him and in you, because the darkness is passing away, and the true light is already shining.

⁹He who says he is in the light, and hates his brother, is in darkness until now. ¹⁰He who loves his brother abides in the light, and there is no cause for stumbling in him. ¹¹But he who hates his brother is in darkness and walks in darkness, and does not know where he is going, because the darkness has blinded his eyes.

The apostle John had a deep revelation of Jesus Christ. He shows a good understanding of the personality of Jesus Christ. He calls himself the disciple that Jesus loved. He was very close to Jesus and sat close to him. There was a time when Peter used him as a mediator to ask Jesus a question. He is the one Jesus gave the book of revelation to which talks about the end time. The letters of John have love as its central theme. In the above scripture he makes an emphatic statement that if you are not walking in love you are living in darkness. He is very clear that anyone who walks in love is living in God's light. My encouragement to you today is to live in God's light by walking in love. Jesus paid a heavy price to get us out of darkness into this light. Let's not go back to darkness by hating our brother. If you have lived in God's light, there is no way you would like to go back to the days of ignorance and fear. Do everything in your power to stay in love and light.

PRAYER

Dear father, you have given me the privilege of living in your light. I love it in your light. Help me never to take a step back into the torment of darkness.

Further reading: 1 John chapter 2

20th August
LOVE FROM A PURE HEART

1 Timothy 1:3-7

> As I urged you when I went into Macedonia—remain in Ephesus that you may charge some that they teach no other doctrine, ⁴nor give heed to fables and endless genealogies, which cause disputes rather than godly edification which is in faith. ⁵Now the purpose of the commandment is love from a pure heart, from a good conscience, and from sincere faith, ⁶from which some, having strayed, have turned aside to idle talk, ⁷desiring to be teachers of the law, understanding neither what they say nor the things which they affirm.

The gospel of the kingdom of God is pure love affair. This is about a loving God who creates man for a loving relationship. Man misuses the power given to him and in a moment of silly pride rejects God. It is the same offence Satan committed to lose heaven. Satan is not the same as man in status. Satan was created as a servant and lost his position in heaven forever. Man on the other hand was created in the image and likeness of God, He received the breath of God and therefore had the status of a son. Whilst a servant does not abide in the house forever, a son does. God would not give up on his son easily. Though man broke God's heart by jumping out of a relationship with God, God had a plan of rescue. Jesus Christ stood in the gap and paid the penalty for man's foolishness. Man could now return to a relationship of a son with God. Whosoever would choose to return could do so and receive a cleansing and a beautification. This is God's love story. It is the responsibility of the sons to announce this good news to every one on this earth. This is what we have been sent to announce: Love from a pure heart. We do this with sincere faith and a good conscience.

PRAYER
Dear Father I thank you for your love for me. You paid a great price to rescue me. I will not stray from this love affair to any other gospel.

Further reading: 1 Timothy 1:3-7

21st August
HONOUR ALL PEOPLE

1 Peter 2:17-21

Honour all people. Love the brotherhood. Fear God. Honour the king. ¹⁸Servants, be submissive to your masters with all fear, not only to the good and gentle, but also to the harsh. ¹⁹For this is commendable, if because of conscience toward God one endures grief, suffering wrongfully. ²⁰For what credit is it if, when you are beaten for your faults, you take it patiently? But when you do good and suffer, if you take it patiently, this is commendable before God. ²¹For to this you were called, because Christ also suffered for us, leaving us an example, that you should follow His steps:

Honour all people simply means value all people. Don't look down on anyone. One truth that will help you in this is to recognize that all people have been fearfully and wonderfully made by God. Don't devalue anything God has made. The devil may have deceived some for a period, Jesus has come to die for the sins and ignorance of all. Every person has the potential of being saved into the household of God. Every person in the whole world has the potential of becoming your brother or sister in the Lord. Don't undervalue anyone God puts such value on. Jesus Christ died for every single person on this earth. That is the value God puts on every soul irrespective of their present status. When they cross the line to become brothers and sisters in the Lord, you must love them deeply with the love you have for any blood brother or sister. The blood of Jesus makes you blood brothers. We must fear God. This means that we must have a reverential awe of God. He is God. Humility has made this most powerful God so easily accessible. He who created the heavens, the earth, all the planets, mountains and seas loves me so much and humbles himself to come and live in me. I enjoy this love and fellowship but I give maximum respect.

PRAYER

Dear Holy Spirit, give me the humility to value every one, to love the brotherhood, fear God and pray for those in authority.

Further reading: 1 Peter chapter 2

22nd August
MY GRACE IS SUFFICIENT FOR YOU

2 Corinthians 12:7-10

And lest I should be exalted above measure by the abundance of the revelations, a thorn in the flesh was given to me, a messenger of Satan to buffet me, lest I be exalted above measure. ⁸Concerning this thing I pleaded with the Lord three times that it might depart from me. ⁹And He said to me, "My grace is sufficient for you, for My strength is made perfect in weakness." Therefore most gladly I will rather boast in my infirmities, that the power of Christ may rest upon me. ¹⁰Therefore I take pleasure in infirmities, in reproaches, in needs, in persecutions, in distresses, for Christ's sake. For when I am weak, then I am strong.

Paul goes to God about a challenge he is facing and God tells him: "My grace is sufficient for you, for My strength is made perfect in weakness". In other words Jesus is assuring Paul that his love for him has not diminished and He is Lord over all circumstances. He has not intervened because it is working out for the good of Paul. The weakening of Paul's flesh will make the power of God stronger in him. Please note that God did not send this 'thorn in the flesh.' God does not test with evil. The scripture says it was brought by a messenger of Satan. As we press on to the high calling of God, our flesh is stripped away by the challenges we face. The assurance here is that God has not gone to sleep. He is Lord over the situation and his favour is on us. We should not panic. We will come out of it stronger. The revelation of the ever-present favour of God with Paul gave Paul new faith, boldness and endurance. He could confidently say that challenges make him happy because it makes him stronger. I pray that you will have the same confidence in God even in your most trying moments.

PRAYER
Lord Jesus, thank you for your grace even in my moments of trial. I will trust in you at all times. I will never be shaken.

Further reading: 2 Corinthians chapter 12

23rd August
COME TO GOD WITH CONFIDENCE

Hebrews 4:14-16

> *Seeing then that we have a great High Priest who has passed through the heavens, Jesus the Son of God, let us hold fast our confession. ^{15}For we do not have a High Priest who cannot sympathize with our weaknesses, but was in all points tempted as we are, yet without sin. ^{16}Let us therefore come boldly to the throne of grace, that we may obtain mercy and find grace to help in time of need.*

The role of the high priest was to present the sacrifice of the people before God. This sacrifice was for the forgiveness of their sins. In the Old Testament, they offered the blood of animals. We are blessed today to have Jesus as our high priest. He offered his own blood as a sacrifice for our sins. He is now seated in a position of power at the right hand of the father forever standing in the gap for us. Whilst before the time of Jesus, the high priest had to present this sacrifice every year, Jesus did it once and for all and is now permanently seated at the father's right hand as Lord and judge of all. Right hand represents power. All power in heaven and on earth is in the hands of Jesus. The great love of Jesus has opened the door for each one of us to share in this inheritance. Let us therefore approach his throne of grace to obtain mercy in our time of need. Our great high priest has gone through every temptation and trial that we can possibly go through. He therefore understands our struggles and sympathizes with our weaknesses. We should therefore not hold back but with all boldness approach him for help. He loves us dearly. His invitation is to bring our burdens and load to him. His promise is to give us rest from our struggles. He is God and cannot make promises he can't keep. He loves us too much to let us down.

PRAYER

I come to thee my God. No longer will I roam for I have looked for a home in the world and found none.

Further reading: Hebrews chapter 4

24th August
GRACE AND TRUTH HAS COME

John 1:14-18

And the Word became flesh and dwelt among us, and we beheld His glory, the glory as of the only begotten of the Father, full of grace and truth. ¹⁵John bore witness of Him and cried out, saying, "This was He of whom I said, 'He who comes after me is preferred before me, for He was before me.'" And of His fullness we have all received, and grace for grace. ¹⁷For the law was given through Moses, but grace and truth came through Jesus Christ. ¹⁸No one has seen God at any time. The only begotten Son, who is in the bosom of the Father, He has declared Him.

Grace is undeserving love. This is an exclusive attribute of God. John gives the revelation of Jesus as the word of God in flesh. When you met Jesus, you had met the word of God in action covered in flesh. It was impossible for Jesus to lie or be wrong. He could therefore confidently proclaim that he is the only way, truth and life. He testified to this by assuring his listeners that he only said what he heard the father say and did what he saw the father do. When he spoke in his hometown in Luke 4, the people marvelled at the gracious words that proceeded out of his mouth. He proclaimed the acceptable year of the Lord. He announced the age of grace and mercy where everyone who chooses could come to God and obtain forgiveness and favour. Moses had given Israel the law which was a great thing for them. It represented a written agreement with God. They were God's people. As long as they obeyed God's law, they could count on God's abundance and provision. John the Baptist represented the end of that era. In the River Jordan, John passed on the baton to Jesus who represented the age of grace. Truth and Love has come. The glory of God is here in the person of Jesus Christ.

PRAYER

Thank you for your love that has opened me up to grace and truth, big brother Jesus. You are the only truth.

Further reading: John chapter 1

25th August
GREAT GRACE WAS UPON THEM

Acts 4:32-35

> Now the multitude of those who believed were of one heart and one soul; neither did anyone say that any of the things he possessed was his own, but they had all things in common. ³³And with great power the apostles gave witness to the resurrection of the Lord Jesus. And great grace was upon them all. ³⁴Nor was there anyone among them who lacked; for all who were possessors of lands or houses sold them, and brought the proceeds of the things that were sold, ³⁵and laid them at the apostles' feet; and they distributed to each as anyone had need.

This description of the first church shows the love of God at work amongst the disciples. The same disciples who a few months before were arguing about who was the greatest were now showing the grace of God at work. The grace of God had increased their numbers. Two sermons from Peter had added five thousand souls to the church. The 'multitude' that made up the church were of one heart and one soul. They shared everything and no one lacked anything. This is the true acknowledgement that every gift we have has been freely given to us by God and is for the benefit of all. If your own ability has given you what you possess then you could keep it to yourself but if it is God then let's use it according to God's direction. Jesus said: "give to Caesar what belongs to Caesar and to God what belongs to God." As everyone selflessly shared in the grace of God in their lives, the whole church was under the heaviness of God's grace. This translated into the apostles giving great witness to the resurrection of Jesus Christ by the demonstration of great power. The church today will enjoy the fullness of this grace as our hearts and souls are knit together and we begin to share selflessly in the gift of God. This starts from you today.

PRAYER

Father, I pray for the unity of your church today. Help us to be of one heart and one soul and to share in the gift you have freely given to us.

Further reading: Acts chapter 4

26th August
GRACE PRODUCES SIGNS AND WONDERS

Acts 14:1-3

Now it happened in Iconium that they went together to the synagogue of the Jews, and so spoke that a great multitude both of the Jews and of the Greeks believed. ²But the unbelieving Jews stirred up the Gentiles and poisoned their minds against the brethren. ³Therefore they stayed there a long time, speaking boldly in the Lord, who was bearing witness to the word of His grace, granting signs and wonders to be done by their hands.

The church had chosen and sent Paul and Barnabas out to bring this message of the kingdom of grace to the nations. In Iconium, many had believed through their preaching. It takes grace for faith to be released. Yet they faced great opposition. Jesus had warned his disciples that they would face persecution but not to be discouraged because he would be with them all the time. As you declare the good news of the kingdom, the grace of God will bring in a harvest. In the midst of the harvest, expect persecution. Be assured that God will demonstrate the power of his grace in the midst of trials. Paul and Barnabas did not stop preaching. They spoke boldly in the Lord and Jesus bore witness to the word of his grace by granting signs and wonders at the hands of his apostles. Great miracles, signs and wonders are recorded in many parts of the world where the church faces strong opposition. The Lord is a good shepherd and is there to give us great help in our times of great need. He has assured the church that he is building his church and the gates of hell shall not prevail against it. Israel felt very afraid trapped between the sea and the formidable force of the Egyptian army. God opened the sea up for Israel to move on dry ground through the sea but used the same sea to bury the entire Egyptian army, destroying the formidable power of Egypt in one miracle. The grace of God includes his miracles.

PRAYER

Father your grace is sufficient for me. I will preach the good news of your kingdom with the assurance that you will give witness to your word with signs and wonders.

Further reading: Acts chapter 14

27th August
GOD'S WORD WILL BUILD YOU UP

Acts 20:32-35

> "So now, brethren, I commend you to God and to the word of His grace, which is able to build you up and give you an inheritance among all those who are sanctified. ³³I have coveted no one's silver or gold or apparel. ³⁴Yes, you yourselves know that these hands have provided for my necessities, and for those who were with me. ³⁵I have shown you in every way, by labouring like this, that you must support the weak. And remember the words of the Lord Jesus, that He said, 'It is more blessed to give than to receive.'"

The gospel of Jesus Christ is a gospel of love. It is an invitation to partake in an inheritance for which you have not laboured. The word of God's grace will build you up. The material that God's word is made of is power and love. When God sends his word, the power in it creates. God created the entire universe by the power of his word. He spoke the word and things were created. If his word of wisdom drops in your heart, wisdom is built. If his word of strength is released into you, strength will come to your body. The healing word will bring healing to your body. God's word is a word of grace. It does not tear you down but builds you up. It only tears down structures of Satan. Keep God's word in your mouth. When Moses died, Joshua took on the responsibility of leading about two million Israelites to possess their promised land. We know some of these lands were occupied by giants whilst others had strong fortification. It was a challenging task for Joshua. God encouraged him to be strong and courageous. God did not ask him to take any special weapons for this task. Instead he advised him to fill his heart and mouth with the word of God. This was God's recipe for good success. Do the same.

PRAYER

Thank you father for the power in your word that is able to build me up. I will fill my heart and mouth with the word of your grace.

Further reading: Joshua chapter 1

28th August
WE ARE SET APART BY GRACE

Romans 1:1-6

Paul, a bondservant of Jesus Christ, called to be an apostle, separated to the gospel of God ²which He promised before through His prophets in the Holy Scriptures, ³concerning His Son Jesus Christ our Lord, who was born of the seed of David according to the flesh, ⁴and declared to be the Son of God with power according to the Spirit of holiness, by the resurrection from the dead. ⁵Through Him we have received grace and apostleship for obedience to the faith among all nations for His name, ⁶among whom you also are the called of Jesus Christ;

Paul was set aside to be an apostle to the nations by the grace of God. Paul in his own strength was persecuting the followers of Jesus Christ. He thought he was doing a godly thing. Jesus before his death told his disciples that many will do wicked things and think they were working for God. Paul was one of such who persecuted the church of Jesus Christ. The grace of God entered his dark ignorant world and rescued him. God anointed him with much love. The persecutor became one of the great lovers of Jesus Christ. He was beaten, imprisoned, stoned and left for dead for the sake of the gospel. He said he enjoyed suffering for Jesus Christ because this type of suffering makes you strong. God's grace had called Paul out and made him a holy man. The Greek word translated church means the 'called out'. You have been separated to be empowered for good works. Holiness is an attribute of God. When God separates us to himself, he makes us holy. The only way to stay holy is to stay separated to him. You are no longer of the world. You are not part of the crowd. You have been chosen, separated and sanctified. You have been given the fragrance of God to represent him wherever you are. He has not done this because you are special. It is his grace that makes you special.

PRAYER
Thank you father for the love that separated me from the crowd and anointed me to represent you. I will not let you down.

Further reading: Romans chapter 1

29th August
DON'T SELL YOUR BIRTH RIGHT

Hebrews 12:12-17

> *Therefore strengthen the hands which hang down, and the feeble knees, ¹³and make straight paths for your feet, so that what is lame may not be dislocated, but rather be healed. ¹⁴Pursue peace with all people, and holiness, without which no one will see the Lord: ¹⁵looking carefully lest anyone fall short of the grace of God; lest any root of bitterness springing up cause trouble, and by this many become defiled; ¹⁶lest there be any fornicator or profane person like Esau, who for one morsel of food sold his birthright. ¹⁷For you know that afterward, when he wanted to inherit the blessing, he was rejected, for he found no place for repentance, though he sought it diligently with tears.*

The love of God has invited you to an inheritance that you must not treat lightly. You are now a child of God, born again by the Spirit of God. God does not give birth lightly. Unlike some earthly fathers, God does not give birth to abandon the child. He advises parents to train their children the way they should go. He tells parents not to provoke their children and not to deceive them out of their inheritance. If he advises this then you can be certain he is doing the same. Your inheritance is assured; he will train you the way you should go and he will not provoke you. Rise up today and stop behaving like an orphan. Strengthen the hands that hang down and straighten those feeble knees. You don't want to grow lame. You want to be healed. Don't replace God given destinies with fleshly fancies. That is what Esau did. As the first born of his father Isaac, the inheritance was his by right. He sold his birthright for food. God did not take his birthright from him, he simply gave it up for the joy of the flesh. He didn't seem to benefit from it in the present so he gave it up for the temporary thing he desired now. Be warned. Don't do the same and regret later as Esau did.

PRAYER

Holy Spirit please help me not to be as foolish as Esau. I desire eternal and spiritual things and refuse to be enticed by my senses.

Further reading: Hebrews chapter 12

30th August
YOU HAVE COME TO MOUNT ZION

Hebrews 12:18-24

For you have not come to the mountain that may be touched and that burned with fire, and to blackness and darkness and tempest, [19]and the sound of a trumpet and the voice of words, so that those who heard it begged that the word should not be spoken to them anymore. [20](For they could not endure what was commanded: "And if so much as a beast touches the mountain, it shall be stoned or shot with an arrow." [21]And so terrifying was the sight that Moses said, "I am exceedingly afraid and trembling.") [22]But you have come to Mount Zion and to the city of the living God, the heavenly Jerusalem, to an innumerable company of angels, [23]to the general assembly and church of the firstborn who are registered in heaven, to God the Judge of all, to the spirits of just men made perfect, [24]to Jesus the Mediator of the new covenant, and to the blood of sprinkling that speaks better things than that of Abel.

When Moses received the Law on Mount Horeb it was a fearful experience for the people. God was mysterious to them. They were so afraid of God that they would not even mention his name. There are many deeply religious Jews who would not even mention God's name today. On Mount Horeb, God was associated with fire, blackness, darkness, tempests and death. Even when an angel appeared to them, they expected to die as they were not qualified to meet with God. The description of Mount Zion is different. Mount Zion describes a city that is alive where angels mix with men. The church is with God. Perfect and just men fellowship with the great judge of all. It is not a place of revenge as Abel's blood cried for revenge. It is a place where the blood of Jesus speaks grace and forgiveness. You are at Mount Zion friend.

PRAYER
Lord Jesus, thank you for your blood of grace that has opened the way for me to confidently enjoy fellowship with my father. Thank you for the church and innumerable company of angels.

Further reading: Hebrews chapter 12

31st August
GOD HAS ANOINTED YOUR HEAD WITH OIL

Psalm 23

¹ The Lord is my shepherd; I shall not want. ² He makes me to lie down in green pastures; He leads me beside the still waters. ³ He restores my soul; He leads me in the paths of righteousness For His name's sake. ⁴ Yea, though I walk through the valley of the shadow of death, I will fear no evil; For You are with me; Your rod and Your staff, they comfort me. ⁵ You prepare a table before me in the presence of my enemies; You anoint my head with oil; My cup runs over. ⁶ Surely goodness and mercy shall follow me All the days of my life; And I will dwell in the house of the Lord Forever.

God has made you beautiful. God has anointed you with oil that smells good. Esther had to be specially beautified and prepared with all sorts of oil before she could appear before King Ahaseurus. In the case of the Lord, you come as smelly as you are. It is the king who cleans you up and anoints you with oil. This is sacrificial love. A good demonstration of this love can be seen in Zechariah chapter 3:1-5. The priest Joshua stood in dirty clothes before the Lord. Satan was also there accusing Joshua before the Lord. God himself rebuked Satan, reminded Joshua of his status as a brand plucked out of fire and clothed Joshua in new clothes. I don't know what voices have been whispering accusations into your ears. Rise up from your dejection today and stand before your father. He himself will rebuke the accuser for you, remind you of your identity and give you new clothes. He is your good shepherd who will guide and feed you. He will protect you even when you go through the territory of the enemy. He will make your enemy ashamed as he anoints you with the fragrance he loves.

PRAYER

Thank you Jesus for meeting every need of mine as my good shepherd. I am confident in your care.

Further reading: Psalm 91

September
Total Victory in Christ

The death and resurrection of Jesus Christ brought the whole world victory over the bad circumstances of life. It is only those who know and walk in this victory who experience the exciting life of the kingdom of God. The price has been paid for your total victory. Know, receive and walk in this revelation. Fear has been defeated forever. Do not allow fear to bully you any longer. My prayer is that as you walk through this part of the devotional, a new spirit of faith will rise in you and you will boldly display the power of God.

1st September
DEATH IS CONQUERED

1 Corinthians 15:51-58

> *Behold, I tell you a mystery: We shall not all sleep, but we shall all be changed—* ^{52}*in a moment, in the twinkling of an eye, at the last trumpet. For the trumpet will sound, and the dead will be raised incorruptible, and we shall be changed.* ^{53}*For this corruptible must put on incorruption, and this mortal must put on immortality.* ^{54}*So when this corruptible has put on incorruption, and this mortal has put on immortality, then shall be brought to pass the saying that is written: "Death is swallowed up in victory."* ^{55} *"O Death, where is your sting? O Hades, where is your victory?"* ^{56}*The sting of death is sin, and the strength of sin is the law.* ^{57}*But thanks be to God, who gives us the victory through our Lord Jesus Christ.* ^{58}*Therefore, my beloved brethren, be steadfast, immovable, always abounding in the work of the Lord, knowing that your labour is not in vain in the Lord.*

One of the deepest fears of man is the fear of death. Hebrews 2:15 tells us that all mankind is subject to the bondage of the fear of death. It was therefore necessary for Jesus Christ to openly defeat death by his death and resurrection. His death on the cross paid the price for all our sins. His resurrection from the dead openly demonstrated the conquest of death and the introduction to a new way of life without death - everlasting life. Everlasting life is available and present with us today to all who shall receive this truth of redemption. Walk in this victory today and know that death has no power over you. There is a future date at the end of God's harvest when death as we know it today will be completely done away with. There will not be another funeral. As for you who have received Jesus Christ, your victory over death has already begun. Enjoy it. When death threatens, command it to go far away from you and your family in the name of Jesus.

PRAYER

Thank you Jesus for defeating death on my behalf. I walk in the victory of your resurrection and know that the Holy Spirit in me renews my life everyday

Further reading: 1 Corinthians 15

2nd September
YOU ARE MORE THAN A CONQUEROR

Romans 8:35-39

³⁵Who shall separate us from the love of Christ? Shall tribulation, or distress, or persecution, or famine, or nakedness, or peril, or sword? ³⁶As it is written: "For Your sake we are killed all day long; We are accounted as sheep for the slaughter." ³⁷Yet in all these things we are more than conquerors through Him who loved us. ³⁸For I am persuaded that neither death nor life, nor angels nor principalities nor powers, nor things present nor things to come, ³⁹nor height nor depth, nor any other created thing, shall be able to separate us from the love of God which is in Christ Jesus our Lord.

Can you volunteer to die for someone? I don't know if I could. There are some people I love very much that I could possibly die for. Yet my thoughts may be mere thoughts of bravado as I have not been confronted with such a demand yet. One thing I am certain of is that there is one who has died for me to enable me share in his inheritance. No one has ever showed me such love. Jesus Christ did not need to pay the price of death on the cross for my sins because it was not his sin. He fought the fight and I get to enjoy the victory. That makes me more than a conqueror. If you have received Jesus into your life then you are indeed more than a conqueror. Don't live short of the victory that has been won for you. Man is so used to fighting his own battles that he has difficulty receiving the message of the finished work of the cross of Jesus Christ. Please accept the work that has already been done for you by Jesus Christ and enforce the result. If sin, sickness, pain, lack and other stealers of joy turn up at your door, command them away in the name of Jesus. The word of God in your mouth is the weapon to drive away the tormentor.

PRAYER
Father, I thank you that I am more than a conqueror. I will walk in this new authority entrusted to me by your love.

Further reading: Romans 8:18-39

3rd September
TRIUMPHANT IN CHRIST

2 Corinthians 2:14-17

> [14]*Now thanks be to God who always leads us in triumph in Christ, and through us diffuses the fragrance of His knowledge in every place.* [15]*For we are to God the fragrance of Christ among those who are being saved and among those who are perishing.* [16]*To the one we are the aroma of death leading to death, and to the other the aroma of life leading to life. And who is sufficient for these things?* [17]*For we are not, as so many, peddling the word of God; but as of sincerity, but as from God, we speak in the sight of God in Christ*

For those of us who have received the gift of forgiveness through the cross of Jesus Christ, when God sees us, he sees Jesus Christ. What does he see? He sees a resurrected son who has overcome death and is walking in triumph. We are the fragrance of Christ to God and he is our father as he is the father of Jesus Christ. As we are in the world, we will face challenges but always remember that you are victorious. You share fully in the victory of Christ over Satan and the world. You also have a father who is watching over you to ensure that this victory is not tampered with. If you have confidence in the finished work of the cross, it is called faith. Walk in confidence because this gospel is true. The enemy's strategy has always been to distract you from this liberating word and make what you see and feel in the world more real than God's word. Don't fall for it. Meditate on the word of God day and night and confess it with your mouth. Sometimes what you are saying may be contrary to what you are seeing but God's word is the truth. There is no other truth. The truth always wins. When it looks like defeat, still confess victory because you are triumphant in Christ.

PRAYER

Thank you father for making me share in the victory of Jesus Christ. Holy Spirit, help me walk confidently in this victory.

Further reading: 2 Corinthians 2

4th September
I CAN DO ALL THINGS

Philippians 4:8-13

8Finally, brethren, whatever things are true, whatever things are noble, whatever things are just, whatever things are pure, whatever things are lovely, whatever things are of good report, if there is any virtue and if there is anything praiseworthy—meditate on these things. 9The things which you learned and received and heard and saw in me, these do, and the God of peace will be with you. 10But I rejoiced in the Lord greatly that now at last your care for me has flourished again; though you surely did care, but you lacked opportunity. 11Not that I speak in regard to need, for I have learned in whatever state I am, to be content: 12I know how to be abased, and I know how to abound. Everywhere and in all things I have learned both to be full and to be hungry, both to abound and to suffer need. 13I can do all things through Christ who strengthens me.

Your confidence should never depend on your circumstances. If the circumstances of this world control your confidence then you are bound to have a miserable life. Your confidence should rest on the fact that the victorious Christ lives in you and will cause you to triumph. Paul encourages us to think about good and pure things because that is what the death and resurrection of Jesus Christ achieved for us. You may be under an attack of sickness and pain. Rather than make this sickness big in your eyes, make the triumphant Christ in your heart big in your eyes. Jesus Christ has overcome all sickness and disease on the cross. He that is in you is greater than he that is in the world.. Trust in the word of God and command that sickness out of your life in the name of Jesus. Even when the symptoms persist, they are only symptoms. The root has been defeated with God's word. Thank God for healing and enjoy your miracle. Do this for every challenge you face.

PRAYER

Thank you father for Christ in me. Holy Spirit, help me to resist any fear the world throws at me. I walk in the victory of Jesus Christ.

Further reading: Philippians chapter 4

5th September
SIN HAS NO POWER OVER YOU

Romans 6:12-18

> ^{12}Therefore do not let sin reign in your mortal body, that you should obey it in its lusts. ^{13}And do not present your members as instruments of unrighteousness to sin, but present yourselves to God as being alive from the dead, and your members as instruments of righteousness to God. ^{14}For sin shall not have dominion over you, for you are not under law but under grace.
>
> ^{15}What then? Shall we sin because we are not under law but under grace? Certainly not! ^{16}Do you not know that to whom you present yourselves slaves to obey, you are that one's slaves whom you obey, whether of sin leading to death, or of obedience leading to righteousness? ^{17}But God be thanked that though you were slaves of sin, yet you obeyed from the heart that form of doctrine to which you were delivered. ^{18}And having been set free from sin, you became slaves of righteousness.

In the past we have been tossed to and fro by the power of sin. Sin dominated us and drove us to do things we knew were not right. We had no way out. We would tell little lies just to get by. We would envy and covet what others had. We would wreak vengeance when we are offended and think of ourselves as better than others. These are just a few of what sin in us would drive us to. Thank God for Jesus Christ. He who had no sin in him was made sin for us and through the price he paid sin has been uprooted from us who have received him. Now, sin may knock at the door but we have the power to drive sin away. This is because the spirit of righteousness now resides in us. Now the excuse of "the devil made me do it" does not count . Jesus Christ has destroyed the power of the devil and you share in his victory. Let God make you do what he wants you to do rather than the devil.

PRAYER

Sin has no power over me. I walk in righteousness. Holy Spirit, please order my steps in righteousness today.

Further reading: Romans chapter 6

6th September
WE ARE SITTING WITH JESUS ON HIS THRONE

Ephesians 2:1-7

> *¹And you He made alive, who were dead in trespasses and sins, ²in which you once walked according to the course of this world, according to the prince of the power of the air, the spirit who now works in the sons of disobedience, ³among whom also we all once conducted ourselves in the lusts of our flesh, fulfilling the desires of the flesh and of the mind, and were by nature children of wrath, just as the others. ⁴But God, who is rich in mercy, because of His great love with which He loved us, ⁵even when we were dead in trespasses, made us alive together with Christ (by grace you have been saved), ⁶and raised us up together, and made us sit together in the heavenly places in Christ Jesus, ⁷that in the ages to come He might show the exceeding riches of His grace in His kindness toward us in Christ Jesus.*

Grace simply means unmerited favor. In a world where people do good to others because of what they can receive in return, grace is a difficult word. God's grace is explained by the fact that when the world was in sin and very much against God, God showed his love by paying a heavy price to reconcile man to himself. Christianity begins with the selfless love of death on the cross. Jesus loved the world so much that he paid the penalty for all our sins in order to get us to be family again and sit where he sits. For us not to receive this gift of grace and sit on the resurrection throne would make the hefty price paid ineffective. Where Jesus is, that is where we are. He is seated in heavenly places far above every devil and earthly enemy. Take your place right next to him. You did not do anything to deserve it so don't get into any false humility. Just sit down by God's grace.

PRAYER

Thank you Jesus for securing me a place next to you. Your love overwhelms me. Help me to exhibit this grace wherever I go.

Further reading: Ephesians chapter 2

7th September
NO MORE CONDEMNATION

Romans 8:1-4

> ¹*There is therefore now no condemnation to those who are in Christ Jesus, who do not walk according to the flesh, but according to the Spirit.* ²*For the law of the Spirit of life in Christ Jesus has made me free from the law of sin and death.* ³*For what the law could not do in that it was weak through the flesh, God did by sending His own Son in the likeness of sinful flesh, on account of sin: He condemned sin in the flesh,* ⁴*that the righteous requirement of the law might be fulfilled in us who do not walk according to the flesh but according to the Spirit.*

A great part of our thought and speech life is laced with words of condemnation. There always seems to be a voice running us down, telling us that we cannot achieve what is easily achievable. The voice of discouragement seems to be always louder than the voice of encouragement. The voice of condemnation always sows fear. Thank God for the cross of Jesus Christ which has reconciled us to God our father. We are now part of the household of God. We now hear another voice that tells us 'we can' through the Spirit of God that dwells in us. The voice that shouted 'guilty' and condemned us to a life of fear and uncertainty has been silenced once and for all. The voice of salvation and life now reigns in our life. We are no longer under condemnation and should therefore not tolerate the voice of condemnation. Let us receive the voice of deliverance and victory. Let our own voices echo victory because the price has been paid. Rejoice because life in Christ Jesus has replaced our condemned life. This is deliverance from a sentence of death. Imagine being transferred from a condemned cell in a prison to the house of the king as part of the king's family. It sounds like a fairy tale but that is what has happened to us in reality. Believe it.

PRAYER

Thank you father for delivering me from death and condemnation and welcoming me to your household. I rejoice in this spirit of life in Christ Jesus.

Further reading: Romans 8:1-7

8th September
ENJOY LIFE TO THE FULL

John 3:16-21

> ^{16}*For God so loved the world that He gave His only begotten Son, that whoever believes in Him should not perish but have everlasting life. ^{17}For God did not send His Son into the world to condemn the world, but that the world through Him might be saved. ^{18}"He who believes in Him is not condemned; but he who does not believe is condemned already, because he has not believed in the name of the only begotten Son of God. ^{19}And this is the condemnation, that the light has come into the world, and men loved darkness rather than light, because their deeds were evil. ^{20}For everyone practicing evil hates the light and does not come to the light, lest his deeds should be exposed. ^{21}But he who does the truth comes to the light, that his deeds may be clearly seen, that they have been done in God."*

God's love has made heavenly life available to each one of us who receives this free gift. Heavenly life is called everlasting life. This means life to the full. When the world uses the expression 'living life to the full' they often mean indulging the flesh to the extreme. Over-indulgence of the flesh leads to sickness and death. Everlasting life comes from being linked to heaven and living as God lives. It is for this reason that Jesus paid the price of the penalty of the cross. This was to remove anything that hindered us from approaching God with confidence. Satan, who is also called the accuser of the brethren, has always been whispering in our ears that we are not good enough to approach God. Jesus Christ has paid the penalty for every sin we have ever committed and will ever commit. He is now inviting us to reject the voice of the enemy and come on home to enjoy the full life with our father. Choose which voice you will listen to. Enjoy your full life.

PRAYER
Father, I thank you for your invitation. I choose everlasting life. Good-bye condemnation.

Further reading: John chapter 3

9th September
YOU ARE A NEW CREATION

Ephesians 2:8-13

> *⁸For by grace you have been saved through faith, and that not of yourselves; it is the gift of God, ⁹not of works, lest anyone should boast. ¹⁰For we are His workmanship, created in Christ Jesus for good works, which God prepared beforehand that we should walk in them. ¹¹Therefore remember that you, once Gentiles in the flesh—who are called Uncircumcision by what is called the Circumcision made in the flesh by hands— ¹²that at that time you were without Christ, being aliens from the commonwealth of Israel and strangers from the covenants of promise, having no hope and without God in the world. ¹³But now in Christ Jesus you who once were far off have been brought near by the blood of Christ.*

If you have responded to the invitation of Jesus Christ to come back home then you have been re-created anew. Being born again is difficult to receive with your mind. You accept with your heart. When Jesus told one of the wisest leaders in his day called Nichodemus about being born again, he was baffled as many people today are when you bring up the subject. He thought in the natural and asked Jesus how he as an adult could go back in his mother's womb and be born again. Jesus explained to him that the new birth is by the Spirit from heaven. When this Spirit from heaven comes, you are re-created in Jesus into the God class. Your life and aspirations become godly. God is a good God and every plan he has for the world is a good plan. Your new life is a life of doing good. You are recreated unto good works. You cannot live like God by obeying any set of rules. You can only live like God if you are recreated like God. I want to assure you, believer that you are the workmanship of God in Christ unto good works. Ignore all other distractions.

PRAYER

Father I thank you for your love that came into my darkness and brought me into your marvellous light. I am a new creation and will not let you down.

Further reading: Ephesians chapter 1

10th September
YOU ARE FREE FROM PUNISHMENT

Romans 5:8-15

⁸But God demonstrates His own love toward us, in that while we were still sinners, Christ died for us. ⁹Much more then, having now been justified by His blood, we shall be saved from wrath through Him. ¹⁰For if when we were enemies we were reconciled to God through the death of His Son, much more, having been reconciled, we shall be saved by His life. ¹¹And not only that, but we also rejoice in God through our Lord Jesus Christ, through whom we have now received the reconciliation. ¹²Therefore, just as through one man sin entered the world, and death through sin, and thus death spread to all men, because all sinned— ¹³(For until the law sin was in the world, but sin is not imputed when there is no law. ¹⁴Nevertheless death reigned from Adam to Moses, even over those who had not sinned according to the likeness of the transgression of Adam, who is a type of Him who was to come. ¹⁵But the free gift is not like the offense. For if by the one man's offense many died, much more the grace of God and the gift by the grace of the one Man, Jesus Christ, abounded to many.

The law of every good country is based on natural justice. This simply means that bad is punished and good rewarded. This is God's law. The important question remains, 'what is good?' Countries set out to define what is good and if you break any of these laws, you face the punishment prescribed for this law. The bible tells us that only God is good. When one man called Jesus 'good master', Jesus responded by saying only God is good. He said this because he was operating us the son of man. He wanted man to know the difference between God and man. Natural law is based on God's law. If you are in Jesus Christ and led by his spirit, you are operating as a good person. Expect reward and not punishment.

PRAYER
I thank you father for the privilege of walking under your forgiveness. I promise to remain in your house forever.

Further reading: Romans chapter 5

11th September
YOU ARE COMPLETELY SAVED

Hebrews 7:23-27

²³Also there were many priests, because they were prevented by death from continuing. ²⁴But He, because He continues forever, has an unchangeable priesthood. ²⁵Therefore He is also able to save to the uttermost those who come to God through Him, since He always lives to make intercession for them. ²⁶For such a High Priest was fitting for us, who is holy, harmless, undefiled, separate from sinners, and has become higher than the heavens; ²⁷who does not need daily, as those high priests, to offer up sacrifices, first for His own sins and then for the people's, for this He did once for all when He offered up Himself.

The comparison between the high priests of the Old Testament and Jesus our high priest is interesting. The role of the high priest was to stand as a mediator between man and God. God appoints the high priest as the one through whom he will receive the requests of man. In the Old Testament there were many high priests as they were men and therefore subject to sin and death. There was no continuity. They had to present a sacrifice of sin every year for themselves and for others. Jesus on the other hand has conquered sin once and for all. He does not need to make any further sacrifices for sin. He has risen from the dead to live forever. He is seated at the right hand of the father in an unchallenging position of authority. He knows you inside out and the salvation you have received is total. He will not allow the enemy to triumph over you. His position is to help you understand your new status in Christ. If you sin and turn to him, he is faithful and just to forgive you and turn you from all unrighteousness. The Holy Spirit in you and Jesus forever mediating between you and the father ensures your total salvation. Do not be afraid. Walk in this victory today.

PRAYER

I rejoice in my salvation. I will continue in the victory and joy of my salvation. Help me Holy Spirit.

Further reading: Hebrews chapter 7

12th September
GOD IS FOR YOU. NO ONE CAN WIN AGAINST YOU

Romans 8:28-32

> ^{28}And we know that all things work together for good to those who love God, to those who are the called according to His purpose. ^{29}For whom He foreknew, He also predestined to be conformed to the image of His Son, that He might be the firstborn among many brethren. ^{30}Moreover whom He predestined, these He also called; whom He called, these He also justified; and whom He justified, these He also glorified. ^{31}What then shall we say to these things? If God is for us, who can be against us? ^{32}He who did not spare His own Son, but delivered Him up for us all, how shall He not with Him also freely give us all things?

The above scripture always excites me. It makes me feel secure. Let this word of God give you rest in your spirit. God is assuring you that even before you were born he knew you. He had you in mind before he created you. He had a plan that would make you just like Jesus Christ. God does not fail in anything he plans to do. The only hindrance to God's good plan manifesting in your life is you. God will not force his will on you. What he does is to let you know his good plan for your life. Yours is to accept this good plan and walk in agreement with him. God is for you. Are you for him? If you are for him as he is for you, you are destined to walk in victory. People may come against you. The devil himself may plot against you. Be assured that no one will prevail against you. If you have agreed to walk with God, you are in covenant with him. This means that when they come against you, they come against him. If they contend with you, they contend with God. Walk in submission to Jesus and share in his victory.

PRAYER
Thank you father that you are for me. I am confident against any foe that rises against me. I submit my will completely to you.

Further reading: Galatians chapter 3

13th September
YOU ARE RESURRECTED WITH CHRIST

Romans 6:4-9

> ⁴Therefore we were buried with Him through baptism into death, that just as Christ was raised from the dead by the glory of the Father, even so we also should walk in newness of life. ⁵For if we have been united together in the likeness of His death, certainly we also shall be in the likeness of His resurrection, ⁶knowing this, that our old man was crucified with Him, that the body of sin might be done away with, that we should no longer be slaves of sin. ⁷For he who has died has been freed from sin. ⁸Now if we died with Christ, we believe that we shall also live with Him, ⁹knowing that Christ, having been raised from the dead, dies no more. Death no longer has dominion over Him.

Baptism is an act for us not for God. Baptism in water is an outward obedience of an inner decision to walk with Jesus in his resurrection power. Jesus does the actual dying and resurrection and offers it to us to share in it. Our response is to accept this offer by faith in our hearts and to demonstrate our acceptance by going through the physical act of baptism. Through the physical act of baptism, we go through an enactment of dying, burial and resurrection. By the two witnesses of faith in our hearts and baptism, we fully put our signature to this covenant agreement with Jesus. We are now fully resurrected as Jesus is resurrected. We are now empowered to live a resurrected life. Jesus empowers us by baptizing us with the Holy Spirit. The Holy Spirit baptism gives us the power to live like God. One of the names Jesus calls himself is the 'Resurrection and the Life.' He promises that all who would receive his resurrection would never die. Even when people die, he has the power to raise them from the dead. He demonstrated this in John chapter 11 when he raised Lazarus from the dead. You are resurrected with Christ. Live in victory with him.

PRAYER

Holy Spirit, help me to be conscious of the resurrection power you have given to me. Help me to bring life where there is death.

Further reading: John chapter 11

14th September
THE TRUTH HAS MADE YOU FREE

John 8:31-36

> ^{31}Then Jesus said to those Jews who believed Him, "If you abide in My word, you are My disciples indeed. ^{32}And you shall know the truth, and the truth shall make you free." ^{33}They answered Him, "We are Abraham's descendants, and have never been in bondage to anyone. How can You say, 'You will be made free'?" ^{34}Jesus answered them, "Most assuredly, I say to you, whoever commits sin is a slave of sin. ^{35}And a slave does not abide in the house forever, but a son abides forever. ^{36}Therefore if the Son makes you free, you shall be free indeed.

When Jesus spoke to the Jews about freedom, they responded that they were free because they were Abraham's descendants. Yet Jesus pointed out to them that they were not free. It is interesting how the enemy deceives us into slavery when we think we are free. There are many who think they are free because they live under western democracy and have freedom of speech. Yet many of these who are proud of their freedom are slaves to money, sensuality, pride and other forms of sin. There are many who are advocating the free use of drugs, alcohol and cigarettes as a sign of a free society. Yet their eyes are shut to the slavery these things bring. If you obey sin, you are a slave of sin. Sin leads to death and hell. Jesus gives us the recipe for true freedom – to abide in his word. To live in God's word is to know it, walk in obedience to it and not stray from it. This is true freedom. There are many who think submitting to Jesus and his word is losing your freedom. This is a lie. The opposite is true. When you become a slave to Jesus Christ, he will transfer you from being a slave to becoming a son of God. This is the only truth. Do not be deceived. The word of God has made you free.

PRAYER

Thank you father for your word that has made me free indeed. I will live in your word forever.

Further reading: John chapter 8

15th September
YOUR FAITH IS PRODUCING GODLY WORKS

James 2:20-26

> ²⁰But do you want to know, O foolish man, that faith without works is dead? ²¹Was not Abraham our father justified by works when he offered Isaac his son on the altar? ²²Do you see that faith was working together with his works, and by works faith was made perfect? ²³And the Scripture was fulfilled which says, "Abraham believed God, and it was accounted to him for righteousness." And he was called the friend of God. ²⁴You see then that a man is justified by works, and not by faith only. ²⁵Likewise, was not Rahab the harlot also justified by works when she received the messengers and sent them out another way? ²⁶For as the body without the spirit is dead, so faith without works is dead also.

There is a popular saying that 'God helps those who help themselves.' A lot of people use this saying as scripture but it is not. To help yourself is to reject God's offer to help you. If you can help yourself, you do not need God. I suppose this popular saying is aimed at lazy people who do nothing and use waiting on God as an excuse. God is certainly not lazy. The above scripture tells us that our faith cannot be hidden. Faith always produces godly works. Faith is too powerful to be dormant. I have heard many say their relationship with God is a private affair. I don't think you can ever hide God. The glory of God will make you shine. The power of God in in you will heal the sick, feed the poor and do other godly works. He who is producing nothing has no faith. Faith in a world of fear is light in darkness. You cannot hide it. Don't try to do too many things. Use your effort to build your faith. Your faith will do it easily for you. You have faith residing in you and you are already producing godly works. Keep strengthening your faith with the word of God.

PRAYER
Thank you father that I live by your faith. Thank you for the godly works that my faith is producing.

Further reading: James chapter 2

16th September
THE BREAD OF LIFE

John 6:46-51

> ⁴⁶*Not that anyone has seen the Father, except He who is from God; He has seen the Father. ⁴⁷Most assuredly, I say to you, he who believes in Me has everlasting life. ⁴⁸I am the bread of life. ⁴⁹Your fathers ate the manna in the wilderness, and are dead. ⁵⁰This is the bread which comes down from heaven, that one may eat of it and not die. ⁵¹I am the living bread which came down from heaven. If anyone eats of this bread, he will live forever; and the bread that I shall give is My flesh, which I shall give for the life of the world."*

If Jesus didn't speak the truth, then he was an outrageously boastful lunatic. I do not understand why anybody would call Jesus a good prophet or teacher and ignore the real claims he made in his word. The Jesus I know is not a mere above average godly person. He is either God or stark raving mad. Not even his opponents would admit to him being mad. Then he is God. His claim above is not a tame one. He says he is the bread of life and if you eat him you would never die. John describes Jesus as the word of God made flesh. Friend, let Jesus have the pride of place in the centre of your heart. Immerse yourself into Him big time and live a victorious life forever. Dedicate your life completely to the cause of Jesus Christ and understand what the 'Bread of Life' really means. Exchange your time, strength and possessions for his and experience the difference between heaven and earth. Jesus is indeed the bread of life. He has never disappointed anyone who has trusted in him. Eat from his table and let heaven explode in your heart. Righteousness, peace and joy in the Holy Spirit is what the kingdom of God has in store for you.

PRAYER
Bread of heaven, feed me till I want no more. Thank you for everlasting life.

Further reading: John chapter 6

17th September
HIS SPIRIT IN US GIVES LIFE

Romans 8:11-17

¹¹But if the Spirit of Him who raised Jesus from the dead dwells in you, He who raised Christ from the dead will also give life to your mortal bodies through His Spirit who dwells in you. ¹²Therefore, brethren, we are debtors—not to the flesh, to live according to the flesh. ¹³For if you live according to the flesh you will die; but if by the Spirit you put to death the deeds of the body, you will live. ¹⁴For as many as are led by the Spirit of God, these are sons of God. ¹⁵For you did not receive the spirit of bondage again to fear, but you received the Spirit of adoption by whom we cry out, "Abba, Father." ¹⁶The Spirit Himself bears witness with our spirit that we are children of God, ¹⁷and if children, then heirs—heirs of God and joint heirs with Christ, if indeed we suffer with Him, that we may also be glorified together.

Paul tells us that the Holy Spirit who dwells in us is the same Spirit that raised Jesus from the dead. Take your time to think about this. The Spirit that has come to live inside of you has a testimony. He raised Jesus up from the dead. If he raised Jesus up from the dead, what would his presence in you do? There is no part in you that is dead or dysfunctional that he cannot restore. I have used this scripture many times when I have been attacked physically or emotionally and I receive my deliverance. How have I used it? I have spent time meditating or thinking about it as well as confess it to myself. As I do this, I feel faith build in my spirit. I then command the pain or heaviness to leave my body in the name of Jesus. I always win. Do the same in your time of need and see the Holy Spirit jump into action for you. He is in you and he has the power to raise the dead.

PRAYER
Thank you Life of God for making your home in me. I am healed and strong in the name of Jesus.

Further reading: John chapter 15

18th September
GOD'S WORD WILL PROSPER YOU

Isaiah 55:10-13

> *"For as the rain comes down, and the snow from heaven, And do not return there, But water the earth, And make it bring forth and bud, That it may give seed to the sower And bread to the eater, So shall My word be that goes forth from My mouth; It shall not return to Me void, But it shall accomplish what I please, And it shall prosper in the thing for which I sent it. "For you shall go out with joy, And be led out with peace; The mountains and the hills Shall break forth into singing before you, And all the trees of the field shall clap their hands. Instead of the thorn shall come up the cypress tree, And instead of the brier shall come up the myrtle tree; And it shall be to the Lord for a name, For an everlasting sign that shall not be cut off."*

When God speaks,, his words are loaded with power that implements what he has said. The bible tells us that he spoke that light should appear at the beginning of creation and light appeared. He created everything in heaven and on earth by his words. God does not speak idle words. I have heard myself speak some idle words to get a laugh. I always end such statements with 'I was only joking'. As I have grown closer to God and known him better, I am steering away from such words. The bible says we will give account for every idle word spoken. When God speaks forth it has the power to bring to happen what he has spoken. He therefore cannot afford to be only joking. God's words are words to prosper us and except we reject his word, every received word is a word of prosperity. Receive every word of God with faith and enjoy prosperity. God lives in you so let your words be words that will bring prosperity to others.

PRAYER

Father, I receive your word like rain in my heart. May I overflow with prosperity that people will enjoy your prosperity through me.

Further reading: Isaiah chapter 55

19th September
JESUS VICTORY IS YOUR VICTORY

Colossians 2:15-19

> *15Having disarmed principalities and powers, He made a public spectacle of them, triumphing over them in it. 16So let no one judge you in food or in drink, or regarding a festival or a new moon or sabbaths, 17which are a shadow of things to come, but the substance is of Christ. 18Let no one cheat you of your reward, taking delight in false humility and worship of angels, intruding into those things which he has not seen, vainly puffed up by his fleshly mind, 19and not holding fast to the Head, from whom all the body, nourished and knit together by joints and ligaments, grows with the increase that is from God.*

Religion without Jesus Christ is one of the most enslaving things that can happen to anyone. The religion of most people is obeying a set of moral principles and laws. Whilst these moral laws seem the right thing to do, without the power to obey them, they are bound to enslave you. Due to our inability to obey these moral laws there is bound to be an attempt at an outward show of piety. Deceit can become the order of the day. Spiritual pride could be the highest form of pride. When you assume a deeper relationship with God because of your own ability to cut a path to him, this is the highest form of pride. This is what the Pharisees did in the days when Jesus walked the earth. Jesus described them as whitewashed graves. They showed the world their piety whilst inside they were wolves. True spirituality is inside out and only comes from Jesus coming to live inside your heart. The light that is on the inside manifests on the outside. There is no need of deceit. Jesus has won the victory over Satan and is Lord over all the earth. He has offered this lordship on a silver platter to you. Throw away your pride and enjoy the time of your life with Jesus.

PRAYER

Thank you Jesus for sharing your victory with me. In humility, I submit completely to you.

Further reading: Colossians chapter 2

20th September
BE STRONG IN THE LORD

Ephesians 6:10-18

> [10] Finally, my brethren, be strong in the Lord and in the power of His might. [11] Put on the whole armor of God, that you may be able to stand against the wiles of the devil. [12] For we do not wrestle against flesh and blood, but against principalities, against powers, against the rulers of the darkness of this age, against spiritual hosts of wickedness in the heavenly places. [13] Therefore take up the whole armor of God, that you may be able to withstand in the evil day, and having done all, to stand. [14] Stand therefore, having girded your waist with truth, having put on the breastplate of righteousness, [15] and having shod your feet with the preparation of the gospel of peace; [16] above all, taking the shield of faith with which you will be able to quench all the fiery darts of the wicked one. [17] And take the helmet of salvation, and the sword of the Spirit, which is the word of God; [18] praying always with all prayer and supplication in the Spirit, being watchful to this end with all perseverance and supplication for all the saints.

Jesus has won total victory for us over all the designs of the enemy. The enemy is completely defeated. Yet the enemy is still loose walking around and doing all he knows to do, deceiving people. Ignorant people could be deceived but not you and I who know the truth. God expects us to let the enemy show us the same respect he shows Jesus Christ. We know the truth of his defeated position. God has also given us the weapons of our salvation, righteousness, truth, the gospel of peace and the word of God as our sword. We are also endowed with the privilege of prayer. Be strong and don't be afraid another day of your life. You are hidden in Christ and the enemy cannot touch you. Boldly confront all situations with the word of God.

PRAYER
Thank you father for endowing me with your strength. I will boldly enforce the defeat of the devil wherever I go.

Further reading: Ephesians chapter 6

21st September
YOU BELONG TO GOD

1Peter 2:9-12

> ⁹*But you are a chosen generation, a royal priesthood, a holy nation, His own special people, that you may proclaim the praises of Him who called you out of darkness into His marvelous light;* ¹⁰*who once were not a people but are now the people of God, who had not obtained mercy but now have obtained mercy.* ¹¹*Beloved, I beg you as sojourners and pilgrims, abstain from fleshly lusts which war against the soul,* ¹²*having your conduct Honourable among the Gentiles, that when they speak against you as evildoers, they may, by your good works which they observe, glorify God in the day of visitation.*

Every human being is uniquely, fearfully and wonderfully made by God. It is rather unfortunate that many do not know this. Our ignorance has made us pick our identity from our culture, our looks and people's opinion of us. This is why it is important that all should know about the cross of Jesus Christ and the reconciliation it has brought between us and our maker. Knowing God will make us know who we really are. We are children of God if we would accept him as our father. If we are his children then we belong to God and all that he has belong to us. What a wonderful privilege. The above scripture answers a question that I had struggled with in the past.. I know I am unique just as you are. I have however always wanted to know why God made me come to the world at a time like this. The scripture tells me that our generation is a chosen generation. This means God had specifically chosen us for a time like this. His plan for us in this generation is that we would be kings and priests to him. By this we can show an intimacy with him and show off his power. He has chosen us to be separated to him as his own special people. People will give him praise because of us.

PRAYER
Thank you father, for making me part of this special generation. I will walk in the confidence of belonging to you as part of your family.

Further reading: 1 Peter chapter 2

22nd September
FAITH PRODUCES GOOD REPORT

Hebrews 11:1-6

[1] Now faith is the substance of things hoped for, the evidence of things not seen. [2] For by it the elders obtained a good testimony. [3] By faith we understand that the worlds were framed by the word of God, so that the things which are seen were not made of things which are visible. [4] By faith Abel offered to God a more excellent sacrifice than Cain, through which he obtained witness that he was righteous, God testifying of his gifts; and through it he being dead still speaks. [5] By faith Enoch was taken away so that he did not see death, "and was not found, because God had taken him"; for before he was taken he had this testimony, that he pleased God. [6] But without faith it is impossible to please Him, for he who comes to God must believe that He is, and that He is a rewarder of those who diligently seek Him.

Faith is to believe God. How do you believe someone? You believe in the person's word. To have faith in God is to believe in God's word. John gives an interesting revelation in John chapter 1 where he describes Jesus as the Word of God. By using the article 'the' word to describe Jesus, John is saying that Jesus Christ is the sum total of God's word. What we can also take from that is that to have faith in God you have to believe in Jesus Christ. You cannot have faith in God without Jesus Christ. Jesus describes himself as the only truth, the only way and the only life. There is no going around Jesus to God. As the Word of God, Jesus has been there before the foundation of the world. John tells us that the whole world was created through him. Jesus was there all through the Old Testament. He became flesh in the New Testament, so he could fulfill his assignment on the cross of paying the price for the sins of man. Faith in Jesus will always produce good report.

PRAYER

Father, thank you for your word that produces faith in me. May your faith in me continue to produce good report.

Further reading: John chapter 1

23rd September
YOU ARE MADE ALIVE BY THE HOLY SPIRIT

1 Peter 3:18-22

> [18]For Christ also suffered once for sins, the just for the unjust, that He might bring us to God, being put to death in the flesh but made alive by the Spirit, [19]by whom also He went and preached to the spirits in prison, [20]who formerly were disobedient, when once the Divine longsuffering waited in the days of Noah, while the ark was being prepared, in which a few, that is, eight souls, were saved through water. [21]There is also an antitype which now saves us—baptism (not the removal of the filth of the flesh, but the answer of a good conscience toward God), through the resurrection of Jesus Christ, [22]who has gone into heaven and is at the right hand of God, angels and authorities and powers having been made subject to Him.

As soon as Jesus died on the cross, the Holy Spirit went into action. From the above scripture we know that whilst the enemies of Jesus were rejoicing that they had finally defeated Jesus, he was actually preaching to some souls in prison. Isaiah prophesied that Jesus body would never experience corruption. We know that corruption sets in as soon as one dies. The Holy Spirit is the spirit of life and if he is in you, you will not see corruption either. Death has no power over Jesus. He laid down his life voluntarily to pay the price of sin for you and me. He immediately picked it up again with the help of the Holy Spirit. This same spirit that raised Jesus from the dead is in you. This spirit has made you alive. When we speak about life here, we are talking about God's kind of life. Life is more than just being able to breath. Scripture calls existence without God death. When you receive Jesus Christ, he brings to you everlasting life. The Holy Spirit in you has made you alive.

PRAYER

Dear Father, I thank you for the gift of Jesus. Dear Jesus, I thank you for the gift of the Holy Spirit. Dear Holy Spirit, I thank you for the gift of life.

Further reading: 1 Peter chapter 3

24th September
TO LIVE IS CHRIST

Philippians 1:19-25

> [19] For I know that this will turn out for my deliverance through your prayer and the supply of the Spirit of Jesus Christ, [20] according to my earnest expectation and hope that in nothing I shall be ashamed, but with all boldness, as always, so now also Christ will be magnified in my body, whether by life or by death. [21] For to me, to live is Christ, and to die is gain. [22] But if I live on in the flesh, this will mean fruit from my labour; yet what I shall choose I cannot tell. [23] For I am hard-pressed between the two, having a desire to depart and be with Christ, which is far better. [24] Nevertheless to remain in the flesh is more needful for you. [25] And being confident of this, I know that I shall remain and continue with you all for your progress and joy of faith,

I have tried living for myself when I thought my survival was paramount and I could depend on no one else. I have also tried living for others when their approval was important for my confidence. Thank God that now I can join Paul to say: "To live is Christ." This has given me a whole new sense of purpose. The presence of the Holy Spirit to help me live for Christ has given me greater confidence. I pray that if you are not living for Christ, you will begin to do so. This is 'buy one get two free'. When you begin to live for Christ you will see your needs met and be able to give out of your life to others. The motivation of living for Christ will give you strength to face the challenges of life. Paul actually encourages us to give God thanks for everything that comes our way as they work for our good. This is for those of us who love the Lord and are called according to his purpose. Jesus has prepared a place by his side when you finish your work here on earth.

PRAYER

Holy Spirit, help me not to be distracted but live for Christ in my life here on earth.

Further reading: Philippians chapter 1

25th September
YOU ARE AN HEIR OF GOD

Galatians 4:1-7

> [1] Now I say that the heir, as long as he is a child, does not differ at all from a slave, though he is master of all, [2] but is under guardians and stewards until the time appointed by the father. [3] Even so we, when we were children, were in bondage under the elements of the world. [4] But when the fullness of the time had come, God sent forth His Son, born of a woman, born under the law, [5] to redeem those who were under the law, that we might receive the adoption as sons. [6] And because you are sons, God has sent forth the Spirit of His Son into your hearts, crying out, "Abba, Father!" [7] Therefore you are no longer a slave but a son, and if a son, then an heir of God through Christ.

The inheritance has always been ours but we did not have the maturity to walk in it. I am talking about sharing in everything that belongs to God. At God's appointed time, Jesus came to pay the price to give us full access to our inheritance. You are an heir of God. What belongs to God belongs to you now. Walk in it. In our life here on earth, we fully enjoy our inheritance when the person giving us the inheritance dies. The good news is Jesus Christ has already died and risen from the dead. God is never going to die at a future date for you to begin enjoying your inheritance. Your total prosperity is now. Your life everlasting is now. Your freedom from death and sickness is now. You can enjoy as much of this as you believe you can. You will never overwhelm God with the size of your demand. Just make sure that your demand is not fuelled by greed but by love of God and his vision. God is waiting for people with faith like you.

PRAYER

Holy Spirit, please help me never to forget that I am an heir of God. Help me use your resources to reconcile the world to you.

Further reading: Galatians chapter 4

26th September
THE OLD YOU IS DEAD

Galatians 2:17-21

17"But if, while we seek to be justified by Christ, we ourselves also are found sinners, is Christ therefore a minister of sin? Certainly not! 18For if I build again those things which I destroyed, I make myself a transgressor. 19For I through the law died to the law that I might live to God. 20I have been crucified with Christ; it is no longer I who live, but Christ lives in me; and the life which I now live in the flesh I live by faith in the Son of God, who loved me and gave Himself for me. 21I do not set aside the grace of God; for if righteousness comes through the law, then Christ died in vain."

Many Christians think our new status in Christ is a continuation of our past life, only better. That is false. Our present status is a death and resurrection. Our past has nothing to do with our present. The blood of Jesus has cleansed us from our past. Our baptism has opened us up to a resurrected life. The enemy tries to tie us down to our past so we do not have the confidence to grab our present reality as part of the family of God and heirs of God by an irreversible covenant. Reject any word that refers to your life before the blood of Jesus came into your life. That is not who you are now. From the moment you received Jesus Christ, you have been crucified with Christ. The old life is gone. Embrace your new life. One of your greatest enemies is the distraction of this world. If you look at the world rather than the word of God, the lies and the ignorance of the world will become more real to you than the truth of God's word. Fill your mind, your eyes and your mouth with God's word. That is the only way you can be established in God's truth. Reject anything that is not God's word. It is a lie.

PRAYER

Thank you Lord Jesus. I no longer live for myself but for you. Help me Holy Spirit.

Further reading: Galatians chapter 2

27th September
NEVER GIVE UP

2 Corinthians 4:6-12

> ⁶For it is the God who commanded light to shine out of darkness, who has shone in our hearts to give the light of the knowledge of the glory of God in the face of Jesus Christ. ⁷But we have this treasure in earthen vessels, that the excellence of the power may be of God and not of us. ⁸We are hard-pressed on every side, yet not crushed; we are perplexed, but not in despair; ⁹persecuted, but not forsaken; struck down, but not destroyed— ¹⁰always carrying about in the body the dying of the Lord Jesus, that the life of Jesus also may be manifested in our body. ¹¹For we who live are always delivered to death for Jesus' sake, that the life of Jesus also may be manifested in our mortal flesh. ¹²So then death is working in us, but life in you.

Considering the high value of the gift of everlasting life that our father in heaven has given to us, the encouragement of 'never give up' would not be necessary. Yet the reality of our walk with God is that we are bound to face persecution and physical challenges. Paul explains that the purpose of these challenges is to make the excellence of the gift of God shine forth brighter. Our flesh stands in the way of the great power that is in our hearts. In Jesus Christ, death and resurrection are mixed up in a wonderful combination of power. That explains why Jesus who possesses the greatest authority anyone can imagine, can still be approached by the greatest sinners and they are not intimidated. We are used in this world to powerful people who flaunt their power and cannot be approached. Not so with Jesus. His mighty glory is powered by a love that is ready to die for you. Paul paid the price of suffering as the glory of God showed in him with great intensity. You are safe in the Father's hands. When you face challenges, never give up. It is working for your good.

PRAYER
Thank you father for this assurance that you are always with. Holy Spirit, continue to strengthen me never to fail.

Further reading: 2 Corinthians chapter 4

28th September
VICTORY IS IN YOUR MOUTH

John 1:1-9

¹In the beginning was the Word, and the Word was with God, and the Word was God. ²He was in the beginning with God. ³All things were made through Him, and without Him nothing was made that was made. ⁴In Him was life, and the life was the light of men. ⁵And the light shines in the darkness, and the darkness did not comprehend it. ⁶There was a man sent from God, whose name was John. ⁷This man came for a witness, to bear witness of the Light, that all through him might believe. ⁸He was not that Light, but was sent to bear witness of that Light. ⁹That was the true Light which gives light to every man coming into the world.

The two things that come to our mind when we think about the uses of the mouth are speaking and eating. These are 2 very important functions. Scripture tells us that the words that come from our mouth are very important because they can bring life or death. In Matthew 15, when the Jews questioned Jesus about why his disciples do not wash their hands before eating, Jesus responded that it is not the food that goes into them that defiles them but it is the words that come from their hearts. When the devil tempted Jesus with food at the time of hunger, Jesus gave him the scripture that 'man shall not live by bread alone but by every word that comes from the mouth of God. God's word in our mouth is very important to God. Let us keep the victory of Jesus in our mouths. That is the gospel. Jesus through his death and resurrection has defeated the devil and freed all of us from the bondage of sin, hell and death. Do you believe this? If you do, then keep it in your mouth. If you believe this then any thought of defeat is a lie. Do not confess lies in spite of what you see.

PRAYER

Thank you father for giving me a sure word of victory in my mouth. With the help of the Holy Spirit, I will only say what I hear you say.

Further reading: James chapter 3

29th September
THE DEVIL MUST OBEY YOU

Luke 10:17-22

17Then the seventy returned with joy, saying, "Lord, even the demons are subject to us in Your name." 18And He said to them, "I saw Satan fall like lightning from heaven. 19Behold, I give you the authority to trample on serpents and scorpions, and over all the power of the enemy, and nothing shall by any means hurt you. 20Nevertheless do not rejoice in this, that the spirits are subject to you, but rather rejoice because your names are written in heaven." 21In that hour Jesus rejoiced in the Spirit and said, "I thank You, Father, Lord of heaven and earth, that You have hidden these things from the wise and prudent and revealed them to babes. Even so, Father, for so it seemed good in Your sight. 22All things have been delivered to Me by My Father, and no one knows who the Son is except the Father, and who the Father is except the Son, and the one to whom the Son wills to reveal Him."

One of the powers the Holy Spirit gives to the believer is to cast out demons. I have met so called Christians who think demons don't exist or should be ignored. The bible teaches otherwise. Jesus cast out many demons when he walked the earth. He mentioned the signs that will follow those of us who believe. The first sign is that we will cast out demons in His name. Demons are deceiving spirits that enslave people. They are spirits who act contrary to the freedom Jesus has brought. They lead you to sin whilst Jesus leads you to righteousness. They bring sickness whilst Jesus heals; poverty whilst Jesus has brought abundant provision. The world is manipulated by these dumb spirits. Jesus has openly defeated them and given us the power to drive them out. They have no choice but to bow to your command if you come in the name of Jesus. Speak boldly to these defeated spirits and drive them out of situations.

PRAYER
If you know of any chronic illness or addiction in your family, it could be a demon. Command it out in the name of Jesus.

Further reading: Luke chapter 10

30th September
YOU ARE A KING AND A PRIEST

Revelation 1: 4-8

⁴John, to the seven churches which are in Asia: Grace to you and peace from Him who is and who was and who is to come, and from the seven Spirits who are before His throne, ⁵and from Jesus Christ, the faithful witness, the firstborn from the dead, and the ruler over the kings of the earth. To Him who loved us and washed us from our sins in His own blood, ⁶and has made us kings and priests to His God and Father, to Him be glory and dominion forever and ever. Amen. ⁷Behold, He is coming with clouds, and every eye will see Him, even they who pierced Him. And all the tribes of the earth will mourn because of Him. Even so, Amen. ⁸"I am the Alpha and the Omega, the Beginning and the End," says the Lord, "who is and who was and who is to come, the Almighty."

When Jesus told his disciples in Matthew 28 that all authority in heaven and earth are his, he was telling the disciples that no power surpasses his. That gives great confidence to us who have been assigned responsibilities by him. This means that he has the power to back us in the assignment he has given to us. That is why we can drive out devils, heal the sick and perform miracles in his name. From the above scripture, we know that he has not only given us his power, he has actually appointed us as kings and priests. As kings, we have the power to command and see it come to pass. We have authority over our environment. The truth is, if the real kings do not step into their roles, false kings will reign. We have power to put things in God's order. As priests, we have been given a position of trust to stand between a sinful world and a righteous God. We can plead on behalf of the people and obtain mercy from God. Use your authority to change the world.

PRAYER

Thank you father for this trust you have given to me. Holy Spirit, help me never to abandon my responsibility.

Further reading: Revelation chapter 1

Be Strong Devotional

October

1st October
YOU ARE LIKE JESUS

1 John 3:1-5

¹Behold what manner of love the Father has bestowed on us, that we should be called children of God! Therefore the world does not know us, because it did not know Him. ²Beloved, now we are children of God; and it has not yet been revealed what we shall be, but we know that when He is revealed, we shall be like Him, for we shall see Him as He is. ³And everyone who has this hope in Him purifies himself, just as He is pure. ⁴Whoever commits sin also commits lawlessness, and sin is lawlessness. ⁵And you know that He was manifested to take away our sins, and in Him there is no sin.

Many Christians today readily accept the title of child of God. Yet not many know what a child of God looks like. If you are a child of God, you are just like Jesus. The moment you turned away from your sins and received Jesus into your life. God re-created you to be like Jesus. This simply means that you look like Jesus and you are in the same class as Jesus. Many find it difficult to accept this but it is the truth. Jesus himself confirmed this by saying that we as his brethren will do more than we had seen him do when he walked the earth. I must confess that this statement challenged me greatly. I never envisaged doing even a tenth of what Jesus did when he walked the earth. That was way beyond my spiritual ambition. We know Jesus cannot lie and he is clearly telling us that we have the capacity and the power to do what he did. You can change the world as Jesus did. Just believe God's word and rise up in faith today. Stay away from sin and distraction and be consumed by God's word. Faith will arise in you. You would operate like God above physical laws, driving out demons, healing the sick and setting people free.

PRAYER

I thank you Jesus for sharing yourself with me. I fully receive you and will operate like you.

Further reading: 1 John chapter 3

2nd October
YOU ARE BORN AGAIN TO A LIVING HOPE

1 Peter 1:3-6

> ³Blessed be the God and Father of our Lord Jesus Christ, who according to His abundant mercy has begotten us again to a living hope through the resurrection of Jesus Christ from the dead, ⁴to an inheritance incorruptible and undefiled and that does not fade away, reserved in heaven for you, ⁵who are kept by the power of God through faith for salvation ready to be revealed in the last time. ⁶In this you greatly rejoice, though now for a little while, if need be, you have been grieved by various trials,

The inheritance to which our faith in Jesus Christ has brought us is permanently glorious. It cannot be corrupted. We have been endowed with a glory that cannot perish. We are born again to this imperishable glory. Our mind must accept this otherwise there is the tendency of living like paupers when we are kings. In Romans 12:1-2, Paul encourages us not to conform to this world but be transformed by the renewing of our mind. This is the only way we can enjoy this perfection that our big brother has invited us to. The world is so real around us and influences us greatly in our decision-making and thought life. Jesus, coming to the world has brought a new reality which is the truth. In other words, the reality of the kingdom of God is more powerful than the world we see around us. The more we shut our naked senses to the world we see around us and open our eyes to the greater reality of the word of God, the more successful we are bound to be. God cannot be contaminated. His glory cannot fade or be defiled. We can shut him out and therefore not enjoy him. That would be the greatest mistake anyone could make. Enjoy your new reality by meditating on the word of God and using it as a weapon against what your senses tell you.

PRAYER

Thank you father for this living hope that you have brought me to. Holy Spirit, help me to get my priorities right by meditating and renewing my mind with the word of God.

Further reading: 1 Peter chapter 1

3rd October
YOUR FAITH WILL BE TRIED

1 Peter 1:3-9

³Blessed be the God and Father of our Lord Jesus Christ, who according to His abundant mercy has begotten us again to a living hope through the resurrection of Jesus Christ from the dead, ⁴to an inheritance incorruptible and undefiled and that does not fade away, reserved in heaven for you, ⁵who are kept by the power of God through faith for salvation ready to be revealed in the last time. ⁶In this you greatly rejoice, though now for a little while, if need be, you have been grieved by various trials, ⁷that the genuineness of your faith, being much more precious than gold that perishes, though it is tested by fire, may be found to praise, Honour, and glory at the revelation of Jesus Christ, ⁸whom having not seen you love. Though now you do not see Him, yet believing, you rejoice with joy inexpressible and full of glory, ⁹receiving the end of your faith—the salvation of your souls.

Your faith in God will be tried. The purpose of the trial of your faith, is to show you how much stronger your faith is than the circumstances around you. The trial of your faith will expose you to your fears. God is faithful and will never abandon you to defeat. As a member of God's family, he has an obligation to ensure your happiness. Gold is refined by fire. It takes fire to bring out the real quality of gold. When you put fire to gold, you are not harming gold. Instead you are purifying it and making it better. Our faith is more valuable than gold. When we go through the fire of temptation and trial, our faith comes out stronger. Except we give up God in our times of trial, our faith will always win. When we go through hell, let us take our eyes of our circumstances and fix them on God who is in heaven and has seated us with himself in heaven.

PRAYER

Dear father, may I never lose sight of who you have made me. Thank you that my trials are strengthening me.

Further reading: James chapter 1

4th October
LOOK IN THE MIRROR OF GOD

James 1:22-26

> *²²But be doers of the word, and not hearers only, deceiving yourselves. ²³For if anyone is a hearer of the word and not a doer, he is like a man observing his natural face in a mirror; ²⁴for he observes himself, goes away, and immediately forgets what kind of man he was. ²⁵But he who looks into the perfect law of liberty and continues in it, and is not a forgetful hearer but a doer of the work, this one will be blessed in what he does. ²⁶If anyone among you thinks he is religious, and does not bridle his tongue but deceives his own heart, this one's religion is useless.*

I know you trust God. If you do, act on his word. His word for you is really about you. The foundation of his word is that he has paid the price for you to come in and enjoy a godly life with him as part of his family. Even when he talks about himself, it is meant for you. His power and love are for your benefit. The scripture above describes the word of God as a mirror. What you see in the word of God is really who you are. When the word of God says Jesus has borne your sickness and pain and you are healed, that is who you are. You are healed. Your healing is not in the future. As you see in the mirror of the word now, so are you. Do not allow the symptoms of pain and sickness make you forget who you really are. You are part of the family of a loving and all powerful father. He will not allow any defeat to come your way. James encourages us to continue in the word of God which he calls the perfect law of liberty. The word of God will set you free if you do not allow trials and distractions to steal it away.

PRAYER

Thank you father for your word which is my perfect law of liberty. Holy Spirit, help me to continue in the word and not be distracted in any way.

Further reading: James chapter 1

5th October
YOU POSSESS THE SHARPEST SWORD

Hebrews 4:12-16

> ^{12}For the word of God is living and powerful, and sharper than any two-edged sword, piercing even to the division of soul and spirit, and of joints and marrow, and is a discerner of the thoughts and intents of the heart. ^{13}And there is no creature hidden from His sight, but all things are naked and open to the eyes of Him to whom we must give account. ^{14}Seeing then that we have a great High Priest who has passed through the heavens, Jesus the Son of God, let us hold fast our confession. ^{15}For we do not have a High Priest who cannot sympathize with our weaknesses, but was in all points tempted as we are, yet without sin. ^{16}Let us therefore come boldly to the throne of grace, that we may obtain mercy and find grace to help in time of need.

The sharpest sword known to man can do amazing things to the body of man. When you talk about a sword that can divide between the soul and the spirit, that is another level. The soul of man is made up of the mind, emotion and the will. As real as this is, it is not tangible. We all possess a mind, emotion and a will but we cannot really hold these in our hand. In the same way, you cannot hold your spirit in your hands. You could cut my head or hand off with a sword but how do you possibly cut my spirit off. The word of God above tells us that there is a sword that can actually separate the soul and the spirit. This sword is the word of God. Not only can the word of God divide between the marrow and the joints, it can also divide between the soul and spirit. The word of God can perform both physical and spiritual miracles. The word of God has eyes to see what is in people's hearts and can minister to them accordingly. This sharp sword is in your hands. Use it.

PRAYER
Thank you father for giving me the sword of your word. I will use it to defeat the enemy at every turn.

Further reading: Hebrews chapter 4

6th October
THE DEVIL IS RENDERED POWERLESS AGAINST YOU

Hebrews 2:14-18

¹⁴Inasmuch then as the children have partaken of flesh and blood, He Himself likewise shared in the same, that through death He might destroy him who had the power of death, that is, the devil, ¹⁵and release those who through fear of death were all their lifetime subject to bondage. ¹⁶For indeed He does not give aid to angels, but He does give aid to the seed of Abraham. ¹⁷Therefore, in all things He had to be made like His brethren, that He might be a merciful and faithful High Priest in things pertaining to God, to make propitiation for the sins of the people. ¹⁸For in that He Himself has suffered, being tempted, He is able to aid those who are tempted.

The devil is a wicked spirit. His advantage over fleshly man is the fact that he is spirit. His understanding of spiritual things gives him an advantage over physical man. Death is a mystery to physical man. Ignorance produces fear. The devil has used this advantage to frighten man. His greatest weapon has been the fear of death. Jesus, the Son of God had always known the weak position of Satan in the spirit. He was there when the devil was thrown out of heaven. The only influence the devil can have is through deception. Jesus needed to come and show the world the powerlessness of Satan. He took on the flesh of man and used the authority of the Holy Spirit to defeat Satan and death. We are all witnesses of this. We can testify that Jesus is alive and lives to die no more. Jesus has invited us to share in this victory. This is resurrection life offered to us. We have been born again by the Spirit of God. The devil can no longer deceive us. He has no status in the spirit realm. Let us cast his deception away from our lives.

PRAYER

Lord Jesus, thank you for defeating Satan and death for us. We refuse to be deceived. Satan, we command you to bow in every area of our lives.

Further reading: Hebrews chapter 2

7th October
BE STRONG IN THE GRACE OF CHRIST

1 Timothy 2:1-7

> ¹You therefore, my son, be strong in the grace that is in Christ Jesus. ²And the things that you have heard from me among many witnesses, commit these to faithful men who will be able to teach others also. ³You therefore must endure hardship as a good soldier of Jesus Christ. ⁴No one engaged in warfare entangles himself with the affairs of this life, that he may please him who enlisted him as a soldier. ⁵And also if anyone competes in athletics, he is not crowned unless he competes according to the rules. ⁶The hardworking farmer must be first to partake of the crops. ⁷Consider what I say, and may the Lord give you understanding in all things.

The encouragement Paul gives to Timothy to be strong in the grace of Christ is for each one of us who has received the salvation of Christ. We are saved by grace. Grace is the favour of God. We have done nothing to deserve this grace. If we had to do anything to be saved, then salvation will be God's payment for our good works. God will be merely paying us for what we have done. God owes no one. We were ignorant walking in sin and death. There was nothing we could give to God in our sorry state. Rather, his compassion made him pay the price to free us from bondage. Jesus paid the price for our sins and opened the way for us to enjoy his righteousness. Our salvation is a response to an invitation of unmerited favour. The heart with which Jesus made this invitation is still there for us. The love, compassion and grace of Jesus Christ has gone nowhere. Strengthen yourself with this knowledge. If when we were enemies, he could come into our darkness and bring us home, it is impossible for him to abandon us now that we are family. Be strong in the grace of Christ.

PRAYER

Thank you Jesus for this grace with which you have saved me. I know you are with me all the way. I will not be afraid.

Further reading: 2 Timothy chapter 2

8th October
YOU HAVE GOD'S POWER

2 Timothy 1: 7-11

[7]For God has not given us a spirit of fear, but of power and of love and of a sound mind. [8]Therefore do not be ashamed of the testimony of our Lord, nor of me His prisoner, but share with me in the sufferings for the gospel according to the power of God, [9]who has saved us and called us with a holy calling, not according to our works, but according to His own purpose and grace which was given to us in Christ Jesus before time began, [10]but has now been revealed by the appearing of our Saviour Jesus Christ, who has abolished death and brought life and immortality to light through the gospel, [11]to which I was appointed a preacher, an apostle, and a teacher of the Gentiles.

Ignorance brings fear. A great majority of people know there is God. The bible actually says no one has an excuse for believing there is no God. The signs for the existence of God are all around us. The problem of man has always been the absence of any relationship with God. Many refer to God as a mysterious God. When God released Jesus for our salvation, he was telling the world that he was not mysterious. He displayed who he was through Jesus Christ for all to see. Jesus did not only come to show who God was but also to make the power of God available to all who would receive him. He has taken away the spirit of fear in us and replaced it with power, love and a sound mind. You therefore have the power of God, his sound mind and love. If you have fear in your life, God did not give you that. Give it back to whoever gave you that and receive love, power and a sound mind from God. The reason God has given you his power is for you to undo the works of the devil. The world needs a lot of help and God has chosen you as his agent.

PRAYER

Thank you father for endowing me with such wonderful attributes. I will use your power, love and a sound mind to undo the works of the devil.

Further reading: 2 Timothy chapter 1

9th October
FIGHT THE GOOD FIGHT OF FAITH

1 Timothy 6:10-16

¹⁰For the love of money is a root of all kinds of evil, for which some have strayed from the faith in their greediness, and pierced themselves through with many sorrows. ¹¹But you, O man of God, flee these things and pursue righteousness, godliness, faith, love, patience, gentleness. ¹²Fight the good fight of faith, lay hold on eternal life, to which you were also called and have confessed the good confession in the presence of many witnesses. ¹³I urge you in the sight of God who gives life to all things, and before Christ Jesus who witnessed the good confession before Pontius Pilate, ¹⁴that you keep this commandment without spot, blameless until our Lord Jesus Christ's appearing, ¹⁵which He will manifest in His own time, He who is the blessed and only Potentate, the King of kings and Lord of lords, ¹⁶who alone has immortality, dwelling in unapproachable light, whom no man has seen or can see, to whom be Honour and everlasting power. Amen.

One battle that is worth fighting is the good fight of faith. You will have to fight with your faith to enforce God's kingdom on this earth. There is an enemy, the devil, who hates your faith. Scripture says that nothing is impossible with those who walk in faith. Faith is believing in God and the lordship of Jesus Christ. When people accept the truth of Jesus Christ, the deception of the devil is defeated. Satan does not want to lose this deceptive influence he has over the world. He will do all in his power to kill the vision of the spread of the gospel of Jesus Christ. It is impossible for him to succeed in this quest and he knows it. You cannot defeat faith. A Christian without faith is only a Christian in name. He is easy prey for the devil. A Christian with faith is the devil's worst nightmare. You have faith. Fight the good fight of faith and give the devil a nightmare.

PRAYER
Thank you father for the faith you have given to me. I will fight with it to establish your kingdom wherever I go.

Further reading: 1 Timothy chapter 6

10th October
YOU ARE CHOSEN FOR GOD'S GLORY

2 Thessalonians 2:13-17

> ^{13}But we are bound to give thanks to God always for you, brethren beloved by the Lord, because God from the beginning chose you for salvation through sanctification by the Spirit and belief in the truth, ^{14}to which He called you by our gospel, for the obtaining of the glory of our Lord Jesus Christ. ^{15}Therefore, brethren, stand fast and hold the traditions which you were taught, whether by word or our epistle. ^{16}Now may our Lord Jesus Christ Himself, and our God and Father, who has loved us and given us everlasting consolation and good hope by grace, ^{17}comfort your hearts and establish you in every good word and work.

Jesus Christ paid the price of death for every human being on this earth. Our gain from his death is to enjoy a resurrected life with him. This is one reason why every soul on this earth has to hear the true gospel of Jesus Christ. There are some in this world today who have not heard this good news. The kingdom of God however is expanding and many are hearing the gospel and being set free. It started with Jesus Christ alone, it increased to the 120 in the Upper Room who were baptized with the Holy Spirit. Today, there are at least a billion spirit filled believers. You may be one of these spirit filled believers. Don't take this special gift for granted. You are chosen by God. He has chosen you to glorify you. This means that you have been selected to look increasingly like God. God wants you to be to the praise of his glory. In other words, God wants people to see you and know him. When they see him through you they will praise him. Please don't be distracted by the trivial things in life. This is a noble calling and God has placed his trust on you. He loves you and has chosen you.

PRAYER

Thank you father for choosing me to manifest your glory. May the people praise your holy name as they encounter me.

Further reading: 2 Thessalonians chapter 2

11th October
BE SOBER

1 Thessalonians 5:5-11

> *⁵You are all sons of light and sons of the day. We are not of the night nor of darkness. ⁶Therefore let us not sleep, as others do, but let us watch and be sober. ⁷For those who sleep, sleep at night, and those who get drunk are drunk at night. ⁸But let us who are of the day be sober, putting on the breastplate of faith and love, and as a helmet the hope of salvation. ⁹For God did not appoint us to wrath, but to obtain salvation through our Lord Jesus Christ, ¹⁰who died for us, that whether we wake or sleep, we should live together with Him. ¹¹Therefore comfort each other and edify one another, just as you also are doing.*

When we did not know God, we were like drunken people reeling from left to right under the influence of the intoxicating spirit of alcohol. A drunken man has no control over his speech or movement. One who has no purpose in life can afford to be distracted by drunkenness. You cannot afford to be drunk. You are on an important assignment. Scripture says Jesus woke up at dawn early before everyone to spend time in prayer. He needed this because he had a gospel to preach, sicknesses to heal, a devil to defeat. He needed the power of heaven to accomplish this. He could not do this by waking up tired with a hang over. He needed to be sober and equipped. He has entrusted this responsibility to us. We need to be sober and equipped. Jesus admonished his disciples to watch and pray in order not to fall into temptation. You are of the day so don't sleep or get drunk. Your eyes are open to the reality of spiritual warfare. You cannot enforce the kingdom of God without discipline. The enemy is looking for a sign of weakness in you to exploit for your defeat. Don't give him any. Watch and pray. Be sober.

PRAYER

Thank you Jesus for opening my eyes to the reality of the spiritual battle I face. I am grateful that you have fully equipped me for it. I promise to remain sober in prayer.

Further reading: 1 Thessalonians 5

12th October
YOU ARE PROTECTED IN CHRIST

Colossians 3:1-7

> *¹If then you were raised with Christ, seek those things which are above, where Christ is, sitting at the right hand of God. ²Set your mind on things above, not on things on the earth. ³For you died, and your life is hidden with Christ in God. ⁴When Christ who is our life appears, then you also will appear with Him in glory. ⁵Therefore put to death your members which are on the earth: fornication, uncleanness, passion, evil desire, and covetousness, which is idolatry. ⁶Because of these things the wrath of God is coming upon the sons of disobedience, ⁷in which you yourselves once walked when you lived in them.*

We have been raised with Christ into the god class. We must therefore live by the rules of our new status. The followers of John the Baptist tried to draw John into competition with Jesus. John who had a revelation of who Jesus was, shut them up by revealing the great difference between him and Jesus. He said Jesus was from heaven and he John from the earth. There is a great difference between heaven and earth. Jesus has raised us up from the earth to sit with him in heavenly places. We should recognize where we are and seek those things which are heavenly. We must relinquish those things which are earthly. Our protection in Christ is guaranteed. The scripture above assures us that our new life is hidden with Christ in God. Nothing can really touch us where we are. When we are confronted with challenges, God would have allowed it. If we are hidden in God then for you to get to us, you must come through God. If God allows the challenge, he wants you to defeat the challenge with your faith. In the story of Job, Satan comes to God to challenge him that Job is loyal to God because of his pampering of Job. God allows Job to defeat the devil's argument by remaining faithful even in the greatest trials. Remain faithful. You are protected.

PRAYER

Thank you father for my protection in you. I will not be anxious another day in my life. ***Further reading: Colossians chapter 3***

13th October
YOU ARE PRODUCING GOOD FRUIT

Galatians 5:16-23

> [16] I say then: Walk in the Spirit, and you shall not fulfill the lust of the flesh. [17] For the flesh lusts against the Spirit, and the Spirit against the flesh; and these are contrary to one another, so that you do not do the things that you wish. [18] But if you are led by the Spirit, you are not under the law. [19] Now the works of the flesh are evident, which are: adultery, fornication, uncleanness, lewdness, [20] idolatry, sorcery, hatred, contentions, jealousies, outbursts of wrath, selfish ambitions, dissensions, heresies, [21] envy, murders, drunkenness, revelries, and the like; of which I tell you beforehand, just as I also told you in time past, that those who practice such things will not inherit the kingdom of God. [22] But the fruit of the Spirit is love, joy, peace, longsuffering, kindness, goodness, faithfulness, [23] gentleness, self-control. Against such there is no law.

If you walk in the spirit, you will not fulfill the lusts of the flesh. You walk in the spirit by staying in the word of God. You must be consumed by being kingdom of God minded. Stay in the word, prayer and fellowship with other Christians. If you do not, the lust of the flesh will lead you to the works of the flesh as listed above. You will see yourself doing things that you know God does not approve. These works of the flesh ultimately lead to death. You are not of those who would allow the flesh to overtake them. Rather you belong to the Holy Spirit. As long as you acknowledge the Holy Spirit in you and reverence his presence, you will naturally produce the fruit of the spirit which will bring fulfilment to many. When the Holy Spirit is at work in you, you will not strive to be good. Good will naturally flow out of you. You become a spring of life and many will come to drink at your spring. You are already producing good fruit.

PRAYER

Thank you father for making me a fruitful tree. I pray that people will eat of my tree wherever I go.

Further reading: Galatians chapter 5

14th October
JESUS WILL BREAK THROUGH EVERY BARRIER

John 20:19-22

¹⁹Then, the same day at evening, being the first day of the week, when the doors were shut where the disciples were assembled, for fear of the Jews, Jesus came and stood in the midst, and said to them, "Peace be with you." ²⁰When He had said this, He showed them His hands and His side. Then the disciples were glad when they saw the Lord. ²¹So Jesus said to them again, "Peace to you! As the Father has sent Me, I also send you." ²²And when He had said this, He breathed on them, and said to them, "Receive the Holy Spirit.

Before his death and resurrection, Jesus was limited by how far he could go in the human flesh. The Holy Spirit working in him had no limits. The Holy Spirit in him could raise the dead and do all sorts of exploits. Even in his physical flesh, the Holy Spirit could make him walk on the sea. However, after his resurrection, his resurrected body broke physical laws at every turn. In the scripture above, he was able to gatecrash a meeting of the disciples behind closed doors. He came through the walls. He lived this superior life on earth for thirty days before ascending to heaven to take his place at the right hand of the father. You may be limited by your physical flesh to go through walls but Jesus has no such limitation. He will go through walls into offices for your sake. He can plant thoughts in people's hearts that favor you. Scripture says the heart of kings are in the hands of God and he turns them the way he wills as he does with rivers. God will turn the hearts of kings to favor you because he loves you. In life, there are some friendships you have to protect at all cost because of its value to you. Your covenant with Jesus will break through every barrier.

PRAYER

Thank you Jesus that because of your love and limitless power, every anxiety is removed from me, I promise to be faithful to our covenant and friendship.

Further reading: John chapter 20

15th October
JESUS HAS OVERCOME THE WORLD

John 16:28-33

²⁸I came forth from the Father and have come into the world. Again, I leave the world and go to the Father." ²⁹His disciples said to Him, "See, now You are speaking plainly, and using no figure of speech! ³⁰Now we are sure that You know all things, and have no need that anyone should question You. By this we believe that You came forth from God." ³¹Jesus answered them, "Do you now believe? ³²Indeed the hour is coming, yes, has now come, that you will be scattered, each to his own, and will leave Me alone. And yet I am not alone, because the Father is with Me. ³³These things I have spoken to you, that in Me you may have peace. In the world you will have tribulation; but be of good cheer, I have overcome the world."

The idea of defeating the world is unimaginable. The world looks so powerful with all its powerful countries and institutions , big business, skyscrapers and banks, politicians, billionaires and smart suits. Yet Jesus assures us that he has overcome the world. He did not say he would overcome the world but that he had already overcome the world. Not many know this. People blaspheme the name of Jesus. Some people behave as if it is the foolish and gullible who believe in Jesus. We know that Jesus Christ has indeed overcome the world. He has given his church the authority to enforce this victory and the church is gradually doing this. At his appointed time, Jesus Christ himself will appear and finish off this assignment. Every thing that is named on this earth must bow to the name of Jesus. We must take territory in the name of Jesus. With faith and love in our hearts and the word of God on our lips, the world would bow to superior authority. Don't be intimidated by the world. Jesus has already overcome the world.

PRAYER

Thank you Jesus for doing all the hard work for us. Holy Spirit, help us to boldly declare the lordship of Jesus Christ wherever we go so that an ignorant world may enjoy the benefits of the kingdom of God.

Further reading: John chapter 16

16th October
SLEEP IN PEACE

Psalm 4

Hear me when I call, O God of my righteousness! You have relieved me in my distress; Have mercy on me, and hear my prayer. How long, O you sons of men, Will you turn my glory to shame? How long will you love worthlessness And seek falsehood? Selah But know that the Lord has set apart for Himself him who is godly; The Lord will hear when I call to Him. Be angry, and do not sin. Meditate within your heart on your bed, and be still. Selah Offer the sacrifices of righteousness, And put your trust in the Lord. There are many who say, "Who will show us any good?" Lord, lift up the light of Your countenance upon us. You have put gladness in my heart, More than in the season that their grain and wine increased. I will both lie down in peace, and sleep; For You alone, O Lord, make me dwell in safety.

God grants his beloved sleep. One of the punishments of being separated from God is that we lose our peace. The whole world became chaotic when Adam and Eve disobeyed God and we lost the light of heaven. I asked a little boy what happens when there is darkness. His answer was quick and forthright. You do not see where you are going, you bump into things and you become afraid. That is exactly what happened to us when we lost the light of the world. We could not see where we were going and we bumped into things. Fear and anxiety set in. Worry takes sleep away from you. When you lose sleep, you lose the body's natural way of restoring freshness. Scripture says the devil has come to steal, kill and destroy. If he can make you lose your sleep, his work is done. The night is meant for sleep but a massive night industry has been developed that keeps people away from their beds. In almost every city today, there are parts where demonic and carnal activities go on through the night. The light of God has come through Jesus. Sleep in Peace.

PRAYER
Thank you father for giving me peace. I will sleep in peace.

Further reading: Psalm 4

17th October
THE LORD IS YOUR STRONGHOLD

Psalm 27:1-5

> The Lord is my light and my salvation ;Whom shall I fear? The Lord is the strength of my life; Of whom shall I be afraid? When the wicked came against me To eat up my flesh, My enemies and foes, They stumbled and fell. Though an army may encamp against me, My heart shall not fear; Though war may rise against me, In this I will be confident. One thing I have desired of the Lord, That will I seek: That I may dwell in the house of the Lord All the days of my life, To behold the beauty of the Lord, And to inquire in His temple. For in the time of trouble He shall hide me in His pavilion; In the secret place of His tabernacle He shall hide me; He shall set me high upon a rock.

If we trust in the Lord, we would enter his rest. He is all powerful, all knowing and ever present. He has promised to take care of us so we should not be anxious about anything. We should go to sleep in peace. Jesus is called the Prince of Peace. Wherever he governs, there is peace. If he is the lord of your life, then expect peace. If you can hide in him, your peace is guaranteed. Peace simply means that you cannot be shaken by any circumstance. The Lord is your light and salvation so you cannot be shaken. The psalmist declares that his desire is to dwell in the house of the Lord all the days of his life. That should be our desire too. Our guarantee of protection is within the fortress not outside of it. We must endeavour through our study of the word of God, continuous prayer and fellowship to be in Christ all the time to guarantee our full protection. The ball is in your court.

PRAYER

Thank you Jesus for the full protection you have guaranteed me in you. Holy Spirit, help me to stay focused and not stray.

Further reading: Psalm 27

18th October
HE TURNS OUR MOURNING INTO DANCING

Psalm 30:8-12

I cried out to You, O Lord; And to the Lord I made supplication: "What profit is there in my blood, When I go down to the pit? Will the dust praise You? Will it declare Your truth? Hear, O Lord, and have mercy on me; Lord, be my helper!" You have turned for me my mourning into dancing; You have put off my sackcloth and clothed me with gladness, To the end that my glory may sing praise to You and not be silent. O Lord my God, I will give thanks to You forever.

God would rather have you alive bringing praise to his name than dead. This is why Jesus paid the price of death for every one. Everyone who calls on the name of Jesus shall be saved. Scripture tells us that without Jesus, we are already condemned to death. The wages of sin is death. We are privileged to be confronted with the wonderful choice of salvation in the name of Jesus. I have received this salvation which has completely transformed my life. If you haven't received salvation then do so today. The bible says that if you believe Jesus is risen from the dead and confess Jesus as Lord, you shall be saved (Romans 10:9). Jesus promises that if you come to him, he will not drive you away. One assurance I can give to you is that Jesus will turn your mourning into dancing. He has turned my mourning into dancing. So has he done for many. It is God's desire that people will see you and give glory to his name. He has made provision for this by giving us the Holy Spirit who is changing us every day to be like God. The more you become like God, the greater your love, joy and peace; the less your anxiety and sorrow. Dance, for the time of your dance has come.

PRAYER

Thank you father for turning my mourning to Joy. I will continually dance to the glory of your name.

Further reading: Psalm 30

19th October
I WILL NEVER BE AFRAID AGAIN

Psalm 62:1-5

Truly my soul silently waits for God; From Him comes my salvation. He only is my rock and my salvation; He is my defense; I shall not be greatly moved. How long will you attack a man? You shall be slain, all of you, Like a leaning wall and a tottering fence. They only consult to cast him down from his high position They delight in lies; They bless with their mouth, But they curse inwardly. Selah My soul, wait silently for God alone, For my expectation is from Him.

Hope drives away fear. If the source of your hope is as solid as the faithfulness of God then you can go to sleep in peace and be afraid of nothing. Your enemies may plan against you but they will not succeed because God is your protection. The giants of this world may rise against you but you will not be afraid because he that is in you is greater than he that is in the world. He who protects you is stronger than the whole world put together. You are in good solid hands. Do not be afraid another day in your life. The financial threats will not win against you. God who created all the gold and silver is your father and will not allow you to see shame. The threat of disease will not prevail against you because Jesus has already paid the price for your total healing. You may have come from the 'wrong' family in the 'wrong' part of the world but Jesus has come to change everything. You now belong to the family of God. Jesus is your big brother and you are a citizen of heaven. How people pride themselves on how developed and rich their country is. Certainly, no country is more developed and richer than heaven which is your country. Don't be afraid another day of your life.

PRAYER

Thank you father for saving me and making me part of your household and kingdom. I am afraid of nothing.

Further reading: Psalm 62

20th October
JESUS THE POWER AND WISDOM OF GOD

1 Corinthians 1:20-24

^{20}Where is the wise? Where is the scribe? Where is the disputer of this age? Has not God made foolish the wisdom of this world? ^{21}For since, in the wisdom of God, the world through wisdom did not know God, it pleased God through the foolishness of the message preached to save those who believe. ^{22}For Jews request a sign, and Greeks seek after wisdom; ^{23}but we preach Christ crucified, to the Jews a stumbling block and to the Greeks foolishness, ^{24}but to those who are called, both Jews and Greeks, Christ the power of God and the wisdom of God.

Paul's audience is divided into two categories – Jews and Greeks. The Jews were those from Israel and the Greeks were those who were not Jews mainly in Europe and Asia where Paul preached. Greek was the common language used then. Because of the Jewish historical connection with God, they liked to see miracles. The Greeks on the other hand liked the use of the mind. In today's world, you will still find these two categories of people – people emotionally driven by what they see and feel and people locked up in their intellect trying to out do each other in wisdom. Paul brought to them the message of Jesus Christ which is the power and wisdom of God. Do you want the power of God? Then what you need is Jesus Christ. Do you want to operate in the wisdom of God? Your answer lies in Jesus Christ. Scripture tells us that in Jesus Christ all things consist. Scripture also tells us that he fills all things. You cannot have anything outside of Jesus. It is a great privilege to have Jesus living in us. By being born again, we have also become part of the church which is the body of Christ. You are therefore in him. You walk in the power and wisdom of God

PRAYER

Thank you my father for opening my eyes to know that all power and wisdom reside in Jesus Christ. Jesus, you are all I need.

Further reading: 1 Corinthians chapter 1

21st October
YOU ARE A WITNESS

Acts 1:7-11

⁷And He said to them, "It is not for you to know times or seasons which the Father has put in His own authority. ⁸But you shall receive power when the Holy Spirit has come upon you; and you shall be witnesses to Me in Jerusalem, and in all Judea and Samaria, and to the end of the earth."

⁹Now when He had spoken these things, while they watched, He was taken up, and a cloud received Him out of their sight. ¹⁰And while they looked steadfastly toward heaven as He went up, behold, two men stood by them in white apparel, ¹¹who also said, "Men of Galilee, why do you stand gazing up into heaven? This same Jesus, who was taken up from you into heaven, will so come in like manner as you saw Him go into heaven."

The times and seasons are in God's hands. Jesus however promises the disciples the Holy Spirit who will give them power and make them his witnesses. This was in answer to a question about God's plans for them as disciples. They were looking for what God would do for their country to change their lives. Jesus answer was not to worry about what God was going to do or when he was going to do it. Instead he promises the baptism of the Holy Spirit which will make them live like God. The Holy Spirit they were going to receive would make them witnesses. People would watch them in operation and believe in God. Many spirit filled people like you are not aware that even in your every day speech and action people are seeing the true nature of Jesus and desiring to be his disciple. You are a witness of Jesus Christ. You already are. This is a present reality. The new wine of the Holy Spirit is breaking down the old flesh of your body and spilling out for others to enjoy.

PRAYER

Dear Jesus, it is a great honour to be your witness. I pray that my life will reflect who you are wherever I go.

Further reading: Acts chapter 1

22nd October
WE HAVE VICTORY OVER SIN

Isaiah 53:10-12

Yet it pleased the Lord to bruise Him; He has put Him to grief. When You make His soul an offering for sin, He shall see His seed, He shall prolong His days, And the pleasure of the Lord shall prosper in His hand. He shall see the labour of His soul, and be satisfied. By His knowledge My righteous Servant shall justify many, For He shall bear their iniquities. Therefore I will divide Him a portion with the great, And He shall divide the spoil with the strong, Because He poured out His soul unto death, And He was numbered with the transgressors, And He bore the sin of many, And made intercession for the transgressors.

The primary reason for which Jesus Christ left heaven to come and face the cross on this earth was to deal with the issue of sin once and for all. Sin had cut us away from God. Sin and righteousness cannot dwell together. Righteousness is completely clean and pure. To bring sin next to righteousness is to contaminate righteousness. Righteous God needed man with him. The sin of man would not make this possible except the issue of man's sin was dealt with. Jesus therefore set out to deal with sin by paying for all our sins, committed and yet to be committed, on the cross. The punishment of sin is death so Christ died for us. He was the sacrifice of the lamb without blemish. By dying on the cross, he has paid the price for sin once and for all. The blood of Jesus has paved the way for us to step into the righteousness of God. He has taken all our sins on himself. We are no longer sinners. We are righteous through Christ who took our sins. The power of sin over us is broken in the name of Jesus. Live without condemnation and approach the righteous presence of God freely because you are righteous.

PRAYER

Thank you Jesus for the victory we have over sin. In righteousness, I will confidently bring the beauty of God wherever I go.

Further reading: Isaiah chapter 53

23rd October
YOUR FRUIT WILL LAST

John 15:11-17

> [11]"These things I have spoken to you, that My joy may remain in you, and that your joy may be full. [12]This is My commandment, that you love one another as I have loved you. [13]Greater love has no one than this, than to lay down one's life for his friends. [14]You are My friends if you do whatever I command you. [15]No longer do I call you servants, for a servant does not know what his master is doing; but I have called you friends, for all things that I heard from My Father I have made known to you. [16]You did not choose Me, but I chose you and appointed you that you should go and bear fruit, and that your fruit should remain, that whatever you ask the Father in My name He may give you. [17]These things I command you, that you love one another.

When God gives you a gift it is forever. The fruit of God is imperishable, undefiled and unfading. If we are connected to the vine of Jesus Christ then we must expect to produce fruit that will last. God already had a plan that you should produce fruit that would remain. He chose you to go and bear fruit that will remain. As you bear this lasting fruit, Jesus promises that whatever you ask the father in his name, you shall receive. As you make yourself available for this joint assignment with Jesus, you are opening yourself for abundant blessing. Remember that your fruit is not for your own consumption. Others will eat your fruit. God's will is to bless the whole world with his godliness. All must eat of the fruit of heaven. You have been chosen as one of the vessels for this assignment. If you will make yourself available for this responsibility, you have set yourself as a co-worker of the prince of heaven himself. Expect great reward. Your fruit will last.

PRAYER

Thank you Jesus for producing through me fruit that will last. I am privileged to be working with you to bless the world. Help me Holy Spirit

Further reading: John chapter 15

24th October
DEVELOP A ZEAL FOR GOOD WORKS

Titus 2:11-15

> *¹¹For the grace of God that brings salvation has appeared to all men, ¹²teaching us that, denying ungodliness and worldly lusts, we should live soberly, righteously, and godly in the present age, ¹³looking for the blessed hope and glorious appearing of our great God and Saviour Jesus Christ, ¹⁴who gave Himself for us, that He might redeem us from every lawless deed and purify for Himself His own special people, zealous for good works. ¹⁵Speak these things, exhort, and rebuke with all authority. Let no one despise you.*

Jesus is purifying for himself his own special people who have a zeal for good works. There are many who do not understand that Jesus, through his death and resurrection has already met every need of ours. By making us part of God's family and baptizing us in the Holy Spirit, he has given us an inheritance of peace that covers every need of ours. We should thank him for divine health, strength, provision and contentment. Our father is a good God who wants people to enjoy his goodness. To have the heart of God is to have a zeal for good works. The Holy Spirit in us is to help us provide solution to the world's needs. Scripture tells us in Acts 10:38 that God anointed Jesus Christ with the Holy Spirit and power and he went about doing good and healing all who were oppressed of the devil because God was with him. You have been anointed with the same Holy Spirit and power and you can go around doing good and healing all who are oppressed of the devil. God is with you. Forgiving someone who offends you is good works. Showing mercy is also good work. Healing the sick and feeding the hungry are all good works. The Holy Spirit in you is to help bind the broken hearted and free the oppressed. Step out in the name of Jesus with a zeal for good works and see people praise God for your presence.

PRAYER

Thank you Holy Spirit for giving me a zeal for good works. May every one who comes around me experience your goodness through me.

Further reading: Titus chapter 2

25th October
DRIVE OUT DEVILS

Mark 16:15-20

¹⁵And He said to them, "Go into all the world and preach the gospel to every creature. ¹⁶He who believes and is baptized will be saved; but he who does not believe will be condemned. ¹⁷And these signs will follow those who believe: In My name they will cast out demons; they will speak with new tongues; ¹⁸they will take up serpents; and if they drink anything deadly, it will by no means hurt them; they will lay hands on the sick, and they will recover." ¹⁹So then, after the Lord had spoken to them, He was received up into heaven, and sat down at the right hand of God. ²⁰And they went out and preached everywhere, the Lord working with them and confirming the word through the accompanying signs. Amen.

Before the appearance of Jesus Christ, demons had freedom to torment people. No one was driving them out. Those who tried were just deceiving others. You can only drive out devils by the finger of God because a house divided against itself cannot stand. In the world today, there are many who have experienced demonic attack but have no antidote due to ignorance. The world in its ignorance has treated many demonic attacks with physical drugs. Thank God for Jesus who has exposed us to spiritual things. One of the gifts of the Holy Spirit is 'discerning of spirits.' This gift enables us to discern what is spiritual from the physical. Jesus has also given us the authority to drive out devils in the name of Jesus. Armed with this authority, nobody needs to suffer demonic oppression around us. We have the power to drive out devils in the name of Jesus. Let us use it. When Jesus entered a place where there are devils, they begin to shriek acknowledging him. He sets the people free by driving the devils out. Let the devils recognize us as we drive them out. We have the same Holy Spirit Jesus had.

PRAYER

Thank you Jesus for the authority to drive out the devils. I will obey your command to drive them out. No demon will be comfortable around me.

Further reading: Mark chapter 16

26th October
SPEAK TO THE MOUNTAIN

Mark 11:22-24

²²So Jesus answered and said to them, "Have faith in God. ²³For assuredly, I say to you, whoever says to this mountain, 'Be removed and be cast into the sea,' and does not doubt in his heart, but believes that those things he says will be done, he will have whatever he says. ²⁴Therefore I say to you, whatever things you ask when you pray, believe that you receive them, and you will have them.

One of the peculiar things in Jesus ministry that amazed his followers was that he spoke to trees, storms and dead bodies and they heard him and responded to his command. That separated him as God. By being born again into the god class, we have been endowed with this ability to speak to things alive or dead and see them respond. In the scripture above, Jesus tells his disciples which includes you and I that if we would believe, we could speak to a physical mountain and see it respond in obedience. Though he was using a specific mountain near to them as an example, a mountain could also metaphorically stand for any high impregnable problem standing before us. You may never need to command a stone mountain to be removed and thrown into the sea but you could be facing a mountain of debt that would not go away. You have the power in your mouth to command that debt out of your way into the sea. Your words backed by the breath of God will cause the mountain to obey. It could be the mountain of an incurable disease diagnosed by your doctor. Speak to it today without doubting and prepare yourself to celebrate the miracle that will follow. Jesus will not give us an instruction that will not work. His word is a mirror to us telling us who we really are. You are a mountain=moving powerhouse. Move the mountain that stands in your way and go on to move the mountain in other people's way.

PRAYER

I thank you father for the power to move mountains. I command every mountain in my life to be removed and thrown in the sea.

Further reading: Mark chapter 11

27th October
POWER TO DESTROY EVIL AND ESTABLISH GOOD

Jeremiah 1:7-10

But the Lord said to me: "Do not say, 'I am a youth,' For you shall go to all to whom I send you, And whatever I command you, you shall speak. Do not be afraid of their faces, For I am with you to deliver you," says the Lord. ⁹Then the Lord put forth His hand and touched my mouth, and the Lord said to me: "Behold, I have put My words in your mouth. ¹⁰See, I have this day set you over the nations and over the kingdoms, To root out and to pull down, To destroy and to throw down, To build and to plant."

God demonstrates his kingdom with power. God never intended to establish his kingdom through arguments and debates. Other religions may use mere words of wisdom to defend their legitimacy. Christianity is proved by supernatural power. Christianity without the demonstration of power becomes another religion. The Holy Spirit is the breath of Christianity. The Holy Spirit is God's power at work. Jesus told the disciples that they shall receive power when the Holy Spirit comes upon them and they shall be his witnesses wherever they went. When the Holy Spirit came upon them in Acts chapter 2, they burst out of the upper room speaking in other tongues and everyone heard them in their own language. One little sermon from Peter brought conviction and salvation to 3000 people, A thirty eight year old man who had been lame from birth is completely healed. When God's people come to town the work of the enemy is undone and God's work is established. When God appointed Jeremiah as his messenger to the nations, he told him he had put his word in his mouth. Friend, God has put his word in your mouth. He also gave him power to destroy what was wrong and plant what is right. You have been given the same authority to root out and to plant.

PRAYER

In the name of Jesus, I root out every plant of the enemy in my family, church and city. I declare the kingdom of God planted over my city.

Further reading: Jeremiah chapter 1

28th October
POWER TO BIND AND LOOSE

Matthew 16:13-19

> ¹³When Jesus came into the region of Caesarea Philippi, He asked His disciples, saying, "Who do men say that I, the Son of Man, am?" ¹⁴So they said, "Some say John the Baptist, some Elijah, and others Jeremiah or one of the prophets." ¹⁵He said to them, "But who do you say that I am?" ¹⁶Simon Peter answered and said, "You are the Christ, the Son of the living God." ¹⁷Jesus answered and said to him, "Blessed are you, Simon Bar-Jonah, for flesh and blood has not revealed this to you, but My Father who is in heaven. ¹⁸And I also say to you that you are Peter, and on this rock I will build My church, and the gates of Hades shall not prevail against it. ¹⁹And I will give you the keys of the kingdom of heaven, and whatever you bind on earth will be bound in heaven, and whatever you loose on earth will be loosed in heaven."

Israel had been waiting for the Messiah. God had promised them a deliverer. Their hope was in the deliverance the Messiah was bringing. The Messiah was in their midst but they did not recognize him. They had mindsets of how the Messiah was going to appear. Jesus did not appear the way they had thought he would so they did not recognize him. The miracles he did and all the gracious words from him did not remove the scales from their eyes. Many Christians pray to God about a situation and fail to recognize the answer because God does not answer the way they expected him to answer. May God open our eyes to discern his ways and give us the humility to submit to his timing and style. When Peter recognized Jesus as the Messiah, it was a revelation on which great power rest. Christ is Greek for Messiah. The revelation of Jesus as the Christ is going to give the Church the power to bind and loose. This means we have the power to decree and see it come to pass.

PRAYER

In the name of Jesus, I bind up every foul spirit that is loose in my family and community and loose the power of heaven.

Further reading: Matthew chapter 16

29th October
THE POWER OF AGREEMENT

Matthew 18:18-22

18"Assuredly, I say to you, whatever you bind on earth will be bound in heaven, and whatever you loose on earth will be loosed in heaven. 19"Again I say to you that if two of you agree on earth concerning anything that they ask, it will be done for them by My Father in heaven. 20For where two or three are gathered together in My name, I am there in the midst of them." 21Then Peter came to Him and said, "Lord, how often shall my brother sin against me, and I forgive him? Up to seven times?" 22Jesus said to him, "I do not say to you, up to seven times, but up to seventy times seven.

There is power in agreement. When man agrees with God, that is faith. Formidable power is released. That is why Jesus had to go through paying the penalty of sin. This brought us close to God. Scripture says that Jesus was made sin for us so we could be made the righteousness of God through Christ Jesus. This means that Jesus took our sins which separated us from God on himself. It was our sins on him which killed him. If he has died for our sins then we should no longer live under the condemnation of sin. We are reconciled with God and can walk in agreement with him. Agreement between two sinners can release a demonic force greater than that of one. The anointing of God scatters bad and unites good. To ensure good results, your first point of agreement should always be God. You must be born again. The dividing wall between you and God must be removed by you acknowledging and receiving the price paid on the cross by Jesus Christ. Agree with every promise of God and see it come to pass in your life. Don't follow the counsel of the ungodly. A prayer of agreement between two godly people is powerful. Walk in love and forgiveness so you can walk in agreement.

PRAYER

Dear father, I thank you for paving the way for me to be able to stand in agreement with you. I agree with every word that comes from you. It is truth.

Further reading: Matthew chapter 18

30th October
YOU ARE ON THE WINNING TEAM

Revelation 19:11-16

11Now I saw heaven opened, and behold, a white horse. And He who sat on him was called Faithful and True, and in righteousness He judges and makes war. 12His eyes were like a flame of fire, and on His head were many crowns. He had a name written that no one knew except Himself. 13He was clothed with a robe dipped in blood, and His name is called The Word of God. 14And the armies in heaven, clothed in fine linen, white and clean, followed Him on white horses. 15Now out of His mouth goes a sharp sword, that with it He should strike the nations. And He Himself will rule them with a rod of iron. He Himself treads the winepress of the fierceness and wrath of Almighty God. 16And He has on His robe and on His thigh a name written: KING OF KINGS AND LORD OF LORDS.

You are part of 'Team Jesus'. That is a winning team. He has overcome the world and conquered death. He holds the keys of death and hell in his hands. All authority in heaven and earth has been given to him. He is the king of all kings and lord of all lords. He has chosen you to be part of his team. As long us you remain part of his team, you are on the winning side. My heart weeps for many who have had a 'good' life here on this earth, enjoying all that money can buy. Yet without Jesus in their lives. As this person draws closer to death, it must be frightening. Jesus offers everlasting life. He has conquered death and lives to reign forever more with you. Friend, lay your burden at the feet of Jesus and take on his easy yoke. He has already won the war so you are on the winning side. Everything we see will pass away but the word of God lives forever. Jesus reigns forever.

PRAYER

Dear Jesus, thank you for accepting me on the winning team. This is where I belong and nothing will distract me.

Further reading: Revelation chapter 19

31st October
JESUS HAS CONQUERED

Revelation 19:16-21

¹⁶And He has on His robe and on His thigh a name written: KING OF KINGS AND LORD OF LORDS. ¹⁷Then I saw an angel standing in the sun; and he cried with a loud voice, saying to all the birds that fly in the midst of heaven, "Come and gather together for the supper of the great God, ¹⁸that you may eat the flesh of kings, the flesh of captains, the flesh of mighty men, the flesh of horses and of those who sit on them, and the flesh of all people, free and slave, both small and great." ¹⁹And I saw the beast, the kings of the earth, and their armies, gathered together to make war against Him who sat on the horse and against His army. ²⁰Then the beast was captured, and with him the false prophet who worked signs in his presence, by which he deceived those who received the mark of the beast and those who worshiped his image. These two were cast alive into the lake of fire burning with brimstone. ²¹And the rest were killed with the sword which proceeded from the mouth of Him who sat on the horse. And all the birds were filled with their flesh.

We know the end of the story because God has revealed it to us. Evolutionists have been struggling unsuccessfully to tell us how the world came to be. It will be a greater struggle to let us know how things will be at the end. They can only speculate as they have always done. We know the beginning and the end because God has revealed it to us in his word. God created the heavens and the earth by his word and he will remove all evil and take over and rule the heavens and the earth by his word. We shall rule with him eternally. This was his original intention and it shall come to pass. God never fails. There may have been some twists and turns due to the ignorance of men, the purpose of God shall prevail.

PRAYER

Thank you father that your good purpose for my life shall prevail in spite of the turns I am going through now. I love you.

Further reading: Revelation chapter 22

November

Thanksgiving, Praise and Harvest

God created us to enjoy everything He has made. He does all things beautifully. Our part is to enjoy His goodness. Our response is to show gratitude through our thanksgiving and praise. Thanksgiving and Praise is a sign of our faith in God. Let us recognise the goodness of God and let Him know that we appreciate Him greatly. Enjoy some beautiful moments of Praise in the word of God. My prayer is for you to reap a mighty harvest of God's bounty as praise makes its home in your heart.

1st November
ENTER HIS GATES WITH THANKSGIVING

Psalm 100

Make a joyful shout to the Lord, all you lands! Serve the Lord with gladness; Come before His presence with singing. Know that the Lord, He is God; It is He who has made us, and not we ourselves; We are His people and the sheep of His pasture. Enter into His gates with thanksgiving, And into His courts with praise. Be thankful to Him, and bless His name. For the Lord is good; His mercy is everlasting, And His truth endures to all generations.

A couple of days ago, my wife said something that plunged me into deep laughter. As soon as I stopped laughing, another shriek of laughter would explode from my inner being. Tears were running down my cheeks. This laughter was such that it would stop me as I walked down the street and make me bend over. When the psalmist exhorts us to make a joyful shout to the Lord, he was talking about an uncontrollable shout of joy coming from our inner being. A joy released by a heart of gratitude. An experience of the Lord's goodness and generosity of bringing us into his family deserves a shout. I don't know about you but the Lord has been good to me. I was ignorant and miserable but his love has rescued me. He has turned my mourning into dancing. If you are not experiencing his joy then you need to draw closer to him and know him better. Jesus has paid the ultimate price of dying on the cross and opening the way for us to be part of the family of God. This is a joyful family. You can be part of the family if you desire. Call on the name of Jesus today. Enter His gates with Thanksgiving for the Lord is good and his mercy and truth endure forever.

PRAYER

Thank you father for thinking about me. You have saved me to be part of your family I will forever be grateful and give you praise.

Meditation: *Think about all the good things God has done for you and thank him for each one.*

2nd November
IN EVERYTHING GIVE THANKS

1 Thessalonians 5:16-18

[16]Rejoice always, [17]pray without ceasing, [18]in everything give thanks; for this is the will of God in Christ Jesus for you.

"Rejoice always" sounds like an impossible demand. How can anyone rejoice always? In a world of ups and downs, there is a natural expectation to be down and sad at times and be joyful at other times. I believe Paul, the writer of this letter was very aware of this. I am in no doubt that there were moments in Paul's life when we he felt disappointed and discouraged. Yet he had found a key to overcoming discouragement – Rejoice. It is possible to rejoice in the midst of trouble. I don't know where you are now or what condition you are in. Why don't you make a decision to rejoice now? Command your spirit and your emotions to rise up in joy. Things may happen on the outside that you have no control over. Your body, however, is your possession and you have a right to command it to do what you want it to do. Paul tells us other things that we can do to help ourselves. He says in verse 17: "Pray without ceasing." This simply means that you should keep talking and listening to God all the time. Prayer should be like breath to us. To stay in communication with God is to acknowledge his presence. To know that God is with you is a battle winner. He is forever present with us. He promises that he would never leave nor forsake us. Acknowledge him by talking to him all the time. You must also learn to listen to him. Continuous practice will make you hear him better. Know that God wants you to hear him and he will help you to hear his voice. Another key Paul releases is to give him thanks in all things. In other words, it is well with you so thank him. He is in absolute control.

PRAYER

I thank you father for every circumstance (name them) I am in now. I thank you for being in absolute control.

Further reading: 1 Thessalonians chapter 5

3rd November
HIS MERCY ENDURES FOREVER

1 Chronicles 16:29-34

Give to the Lord the glory due His name; Bring an offering, and come before Him. Oh, worship the Lord in the beauty of holiness! ³⁰Tremble before Him, all the earth. The world also is firmly established, It shall not be moved. ³¹ Let the heavens rejoice, and let the earth be glad; And let them say among the nations, "The Lord reigns." ³² Let the sea roar, and all its fullness; Let the field rejoice, and all that is in it. ³³Then the trees of the woods shall rejoice before the Lord, For He is coming to judge the earth. ³⁴Oh, give thanks to the Lord, for He is good! For His mercy endures forever.

The loving kindness and forgiveness of the Lord is forever. You can count on it anytime, anywhere. One day Peter asked Jesus how many times a person should forgive one who keeps offending him. Jesus responded with an answer of 'seventy times seven.' Jesus was telling Peter that forgiveness should be continuous and never ceasing. Jesus would not give such an answer if he was not practicing same. You can go to bed on God's goodness and mercy. When you think about his everlasting love, all one can do is to thank and praise him. David sang this song of gratitude when God made him king in Israel. He brought the ark of God back to Jerusalem and was overwhelmed with gratitude for the goodness of God. May the goodness of God overwhelm you and fill your heart and mouth with spontaneous thanksgiving and praise. There is no reason why you should not enjoy God's goodness. It is available to everyone. Even if you feel condemned, be assured that his mercy endures forever. Approach his throne of grace with confidence and obtain forgiveness in your time of need. His loving kindness is waiting for you.

PRAYER

Thank you father for saving me. I am so grateful that you have been so good to me. The assurance that I can return to your mercy even when I stray fills me with such joy. I will forever praise you.

Further reading: 1 Chronicles 16

4th November
TELL THE WORLD ABOUT GOD

Psalm 105:1-9

> Oh, give thanks to the Lord! Call upon His name; Make known His deeds among the peoples! ²Sing to Him, sing psalms to Him; Talk of all His wondrous works! ³Glory in His holy name; Let the hearts of those rejoice who seek the Lord! ⁴Seek the Lord and His strength; Seek His face evermore! ⁵Remember His marvellous works which He has done, His wonders, and the judgments of His mouth, ⁶ O seed of Abraham His servant, You children of Jacob, His chosen ones! ⁷ He is the Lord our God; His judgments are in all the earth. ⁸ He remembers His covenant forever, The word which He commanded, for a thousand generations, ⁹ The covenant which He made with Abraham, And His oath to Isaac,

When you love someone, you enjoy talking about them. It is difficult to stop that doting mother or father from talking about their child. The proud son always wants to talk about his father. God announced to the whole world how proud he was of Jesus. He said loudly: "You are my Beloved Son; in You I am well pleased." If you have given your life to Jesus, you are a child of God. Your father is proud of you and wants to boast about you to the world. He has glorified you and the world must notice it. Are you proud of him? Are you ready to tell the world about how good God is? This is our praise. This is an indication of a son's love for the father. Praising God before men pleases him. It is a display of your gratitude before men. Why don't you tell someone today about what God has done for you? What about telling another person tomorrow about what God has done for you? You can make it a lifestyle of telling others how great God is. Imagine how happy that will make your father in heaven. Make known his deeds among the people.

PRAYER

Thank you father that you are so proud of me that you want the whole world to know I am yours. I will also tell all about your goodness.

Further reading: Psalm 105

5th November
PRAISE HIM IN THE ASSEMBLY OF ELDERS

Psalm 107:29-38

He calms the storm, So that its waves are still. ³⁰Then they are glad because they are quiet; So He guides them to their desired haven. ³¹Oh, that men would give thanks to the Lord for His goodness, And for His wonderful works to the children of men! ³²Let them exalt Him also in the assembly of the people, And praise Him in the company of the elders. ³³He turns rivers into a wilderness, And the watersprings into dry ground; ³⁴A fruitful land into barrenness, For the wickedness of those who dwell in it. ³⁵He turns a wilderness into pools of water, And dry land into watersprings. ³⁶There He makes the hungry dwell, That they may establish a city for a dwelling place, ³⁷And sow fields and plant vineyards, That they may yield a fruitful harvest. ³⁸He also blesses them, and they multiply greatly; And He does not let their cattle decrease.

When we praise God, it makes him real to us and all who hear the praise. God is everywhere. God is right there with you now. If only you would acknowledge him, your eyes would be open to see him. Psalm 22:3 says he is enthroned on the praises of Israel. The world seems unjust. When the wicked seem to prosper and the good seem to suffer, it is not just. It is only the God of righteousness who establishes justice. Righteousness means justice. He is the God of order. Wherever there is rebellion against God, injustice prevails. The elders and rulers need to hear you lift God high. He is the only one who can establish true justice. David always praised God in the family and even with Saul the king. He praised God before Goliath. His praise always drove fear away, brought hope and established the supremacy of God. Today make a decision to praise God everywhere, even before the elders.

PRAYER
I will praise you Lord with every breath I take. I will praise you in the assembly of elders.

Further reading: Psalm 107

6th November
BLESS THE LORD AT ALL TIMES

Psalm 34:1-6

I will bless the Lord at all times; His praise shall continually be in my mouth. ²My soul shall make its boast in the Lord; The humble shall hear of it and be glad. ³Oh, magnify the Lord with me, And let us exalt His name together. ⁴I sought the Lord, and He heard me, And delivered me from all my fears. ⁵They looked to Him and were radiant, And their faces were not ashamed. ⁶This poor man cried out, and the Lord heard him, And saved him out of all his troubles.

The world and all that is in it did not happen by accident. The Lord God created them all. The change in my life from ignorance, suffering and defeat to knowledge, contentment and peace is not just a stroke of luck. The Lord God made them all. I know this because by a deliberate decision, I responded to the call of Jesus Christ and invited him into my life. True to his faithfulness, Jesus has transformed my life. He now leads me in the path of righteousness. I will therefore praise his name at all times. Friend, continually bless his name. He who has taken you out of darkness into his marvellous light deserves to be praised. We all have a choice between a life of uncertainty and a life of truth. A life of uncertainty is when you set out for the day not knowing how your day is going to turn out. If you are lucky, things will turn out well. If you are not, expect the worse. A life of truth is when you are born again into the kingdom of God. Your eyes of understanding are opened wide. You therefore occupy a position of rule with Jesus Christ. Praise the Lord at all times for he who has saved you will never abandon you. He is always by you to lead you.

PRAYER
I will bless you at all times my dear Lord and Saviour. Your praise shall continually be in my mouth.

Further reading: Psalm 34

7th November
SALVATION IS FROM GOD

Jonah 2:4-10

Then I said, 'I have been cast out of Your sight; Yet I will look again toward Your holy temple.' ^{5} *The waters surrounded me, even to my soul; The deep closed around me; Weeds were wrapped around my head.* ^{6}*I went down to the moorings of the mountains; The earth with its bars closed behind me forever; Yet You have brought up my life from the pit, O Lord, my God.* ^{7}*"When my soul fainted within me, I remembered the Lord; And my prayer went up to You, Into Your holy temple.* ^{8}*"Those who regard worthless idols Forsake their own Mercy.* ^{9}*But I will sacrifice to You With the voice of thanksgiving; I will pay what I have vowed. Salvation is of the Lord."* ^{10}*So the Lord spoke to the fish, and it vomited Jonah onto dry land.*

There are times that we may find ourselves in such desperate situations that we wonder if anyone could rescue us. This could be due to a bad decision in business, a family or relationship challenge. It could even be a frightening report from your bank manager or doctor. In every situation, there is only one Saviour and that is Jesus Christ. Praise him even in your midnight hour. I don't know what challenges you have been in, yet I can safely say you have never been swallowed by a fish. The scripture of praise above is from Jonah who was swallowed by a fish. He was praising God from the belly of a giant fish. Scientists have argued about how impossible it is for a whale to swallow a man and for either party to survive. I wish scientists knew everything. The world would be a better place. I believe in a supernatural God of deliverance. When Jonah praised God, he was delivered from his fish prison. Rather than argue with your creator and try to be more knowledgeable than he who made you, praise him out of your confusion. He who saves is ready to save you now.

PRAYER

Nothing is impossible to you, creator of the universe. As you so easily delivered Noah from the belly of the whale, I know you will deliver me from all my troubles.

Further reading: Jonah chapter 2

8th November
THANK YOU FOR THE EARTH

Psalm 65:9-13

> You visit the earth and water it, You greatly enrich it; The river of God is full of water; You provide their grain, For so You have prepared it. ^{10}You water its ridges abundantly, You settle its furrows; You make it soft with showers, You bless its growth. ^{11}You crown the year with Your goodness, And Your paths drip with abundance. ^{12}They drop on the pastures of the wilderness, And the little hills rejoice on every side. ^{13}The pastures are clothed with flocks; The valleys also are covered with grain; They shout for joy, they also sing.

People admire good landscape drawing and hail it as great work of art. Some are ready to pay a high price to own such works of art. Stop and think for a moment that this is just a representation on canvas of a minute part of God's creation. The earth on its whole is an amazing piece of creation in its beauty and function. The earth provides a habitation for all people and innumerable variety of animals, vegetation, rivers and seas to live side by side. There is food in abundance, sleeping places and recreational grounds for all. The Lord God made them all. When I look at the work of your hands, Father God, I can only marvel and say thank you Lord. When you have the opportunity, look around you at the mountains, rivers, trees, birds, insects and all God's creation and shout a loud thank you to the Lord. Scripture tells us that he created everything with man in mind. But for the distraction and disobedience of the first man Adam, we would all be enjoying more of the earth than we are enjoying. Men are crowded in cities trying to make a living whilst 90% of the earth is unexplored and unutilized. May the Lord open your eyes to see this great creation called earth and may you thank the Lord as you enjoy it.

PRAYER

I thank you father for the gift of the earth. Please open my eyes to see your beauty and give me wisdom to enjoy this creation.

Further reading: Psalm 65

9th November
THE LORD IS GREAT GOD ABOVE ALL

Psalm 95:1-7

Oh come, let us sing to the Lord! Let us shout joyfully to the Rock of our salvation. ²Let us come before His presence with thanksgiving; Let us shout joyfully to Him with psalms. ³For the Lord is the great God, And the great King above all gods. ⁴In His hand are the deep places of the earth; The heights of the hills are His also. ⁵The sea is His, for He made it; And His hands formed the dry land. ⁶Oh come, let us worship and bow down; Let us kneel before the Lord our Maker. ⁷For He is our God, And we are the people of His pasture, And the sheep of His hand.

The world is fond of gods. A god is anything you hold as supreme possessing supernatural powers. Some cultures make gods out of people they perceive as having extraordinary attributes. The Romans saw their emperors as gods so did the Egyptians in ancient times. Some animist societies today see a god in everything they can't explain. Mountains, rivers and trees are gods to them. Disasters as well as good fortunes are attributed to them. Sacrifices are made to them. All these creatures are not gods. There is a supreme God above all 'gods'. It does not matter who your god is. The creator of all things is the supreme God above all. Some people say they do not believe in any god. They are their own god. If man is god then god must be very weak. We know better. The Lord is great God above all. We need to let the world know about the real God. God has promised to prove himself to the world if we would talk about him. The way God will prove himself to the world is through miracles, signs and wonders. Expect the great God above all to prove himself as Lord as you praise him before others. Every other god will bow before our great God. Confidently introduce your father to the world.

PRAYER

Mighty God above all gods, I am grateful that you have made me your son. All other gods are the work of men. You are the only true God and there is none like you.

Further reading: Psalm 95

10th November
GOD IS GRACIOUS

Psalm 136:1-9

> Oh, give thanks to the Lord, for He is good! For His mercy endures forever. ²Oh, give thanks to the God of gods! For His mercy endures forever. ³Oh, give thanks to the Lord of lords! For His mercy endures forever: ⁴To Him who alone does great wonders, For His mercy endures forever; ⁵To Him who by wisdom made the heavens, For His mercy endures forever; ⁶To Him who laid out the earth above the waters, For His mercy endures forever; ⁷To Him who made great lights, For His mercy endures forever— ⁸The sun to rule by day, For His mercy endures forever; ⁹The moon and stars to rule by night, For His mercy endures forever.

A kind, rich friend will be the dream for most poor people. Need is like a hole that desires to be filled. This is why a gracious God is the greatest gift anyone can have. Every person in this world has a need, one way or the other. God can meet every need there is. God is the creator of all things. He is rich multiplied by infinity. You cannot exaggerate God's glory. In him all things consist. The earth is the Lord's and everything in it. Not only is God super rich. He is also gracious. He is a kind friend. You are marked for favor. Rejoice in God for he cares for you and desires to show you favor. But for the grace of God, we would have been left in our darkness and ignorance. God so loved the world that he gave us his only begotten son to die to pay for our sins. He has promised that anyone who believes in him will be saved from death and translated to life. That is you. The grace of God has made you a child of God open to enjoy everything he has. He deserves our thanksgiving for he has made us sharers of everything he has created. Sing him a song of praise.

PRAYER
Thank you for your love father God. I love you too.

Further reading: Psalm 136

11th November
HE GIVES FOOD TO THE BEAST

Psalm 147:7-12

Sing to the Lord with thanksgiving; Sing praises on the harp to our God, ⁸Who covers the heavens with clouds, Who prepares rain for the earth, Who makes grass to grow on the mountains. ⁹He gives to the beast its food, And to the young ravens that cry. ¹⁰He does not delight in the strength of the horse; He takes no pleasure in the legs of a man. ¹¹The Lord takes pleasure in those who fear Him, In those who hope in His mercy. ¹²Praise the Lord, O Jerusalem! Praise your God, O Zion!

When God feeds you, he gives you the best. It is every good father's desire to feed his children with the best. God is the best father anyone can have. He feeds us with good things. There is a place in scripture when Jesus tells his listeners not to be anxious about what they will eat or drink. He promises that just as the father feeds the birds and clothes the lilies so will he faithfully feed and clothe them. Man has struggled to feed and clothe himself whilst God has promised the best food and clothing if we would trust in him. You can never go hungry if you would trust in him who created the heavens and the earth and all that are in it. In ignorance, people have killed, stolen, deceived and fought in order to eat. The time of ignorance is over. He who feeds the beast of the forest is standing by to feed you his child created in his image. In our ignorance and pride we have been deaf to a loud invitation to dinner at the Lord's table. Shout aloud in praise to our God and dance in response to this invitation. Man has tried to cage and feed animals. They are better off fed by God who has made provision for all. We try to cage ourselves as we do animals. Break free and sing to the Lord who will feed you as he feeds the beast.

PRAYER
Thank you father for food and for meeting all my needs.

Further reading: Psalm 147

12th November
THE LORD IS COMPASSIONATE

Psalm 145:1-8

I will extol You, my God, O King; And I will bless Your name forever and ever. ²Every day I will bless You, And I will praise Your name forever and ever. ³Great is the Lord, and greatly to be praised; And His greatness is unsearchable. ⁴One generation shall praise Your works to another, And shall declare Your mighty acts. ⁵I will meditate on the glorious splendour of Your majesty, And on Your wondrous works. ⁶ Men shall speak of the might of Your awesome acts, And I will declare Your greatness. ⁷They shall utter the memory of Your great goodness, And shall sing of Your righteousness. ⁸The Lord is gracious and full of compassion, Slow to anger and great in mercy.

Man-made religion makes God like man only more powerful. In other words, God gets angry with you when you don't do what he likes. The truth is that God is love. He desires for us to walk in obedience to him and reap the good harvest of obedience. He is, however, not a wicked taskmaster who is waiting for you to take a step wrong so he can descend on you with a hammer. The Lord is full of compassion; slow to anger and great in mercy. The bible tells us that a good parent teaches his children the way to go. God's purpose in disciplining us is to teach us the way to go. He disciplines us in love. Jesus paid a heavy price to bring us back home and he will do all in his power to keep us home. We can count on his compassion. There is no condemnation for you if you are in Jesus Christ and led by the Holy Spirit. God in his love is waiting for you with open arms. Approach his throne of grace with confidence and obtain mercy in your time of need. God knows every challenge we face and looks on with compassion. Give him praise in every situation and see him rise up on your behalf.

PRAYER

I praise you for your love, compassion and patience. Holy Spirit, help me to walk in these same qualities.

Further reading: Psalm 145

13th November
PROCLAIM HIS LOVE IN THE MORNING

Psalm 92:1-5

> *It is good to give thanks to the Lord, And to sing praises to Your name, O Most High; ²To declare Your loving kindness in the morning, And Your faithfulness every night, ³On an instrument of ten strings, On the lute, And on the harp, With harmonious sound. ⁴For You, Lord, have made me glad through Your work; I will triumph in the works of Your hands. ⁵O Lord, how great are Your works! Your thoughts are very deep.*

Every time we wake up, we should praise the Lord for his loving kindness. I praise the Lord in the morning for my uniqueness. Scripture tells me that he thought about me and made me. To be alive is a great reason to praise the Lord. You are unique. There is no one else like you. You may have an identical twin who looks exactly like you on the outside but on the inside you are unique. Scripture tells us that each one of us is fearfully and wonderfully made. That is a good reason to praise the Lord for his loving kindness every morning. When I wake up and know that I have the capacity to steer away from evil and to have dominion over my surroundings, praise rises in my heart. When I remember that God lives in me and I can confidently enjoy the earth as an heir with Jesus Christ, a praise dance comes to my feet. Walking in faith with Jesus Christ is a beautiful life. Praise the Lord with every part of your being. Sleep is a gift of God. It gives you rest and brings restoration to your body. Scripture says God gives his beloved sleep. Your strength is refreshed every morning. Praise him. His mercies are new every morning. Praise him. Some go to sleep and never wake up. You are awake. Praise him. I pray that when you wake up every morning the first thing you will see is the face of God looking lovingly at you. He loves you.

PRAYER

I will praise your loving kindness every morning. You are a good God and I love you very much.

Further reading: **Psalm 92**

14th November
LET THE REDEEMED OF THE LORD SAY SO

Psalm 107:1-8

Oh, give thanks to the Lord, for He is good! For His mercy endures forever. ² Let the redeemed of the Lord say so, Whom He has redeemed from the hand of the enemy,³ And gathered out of the lands, From the east and from the west, From the north and from the south. ⁴They wandered in the wilderness in a desolate way; They found no city to dwell in. ⁵Hungry and thirsty, Their soul fainted in them. ⁶ Then they cried out to the Lord in their trouble, And He delivered them out of their distresses. ⁷And He led them forth by the right way, That they might go to a city for a dwelling place. ⁸ Oh, that men would give thanks to the Lord for His goodness, And for His wonderful works to the children of men!

There is something special about everyone who has made Jesus the Lord of their lives. This is because the Holy Spirit lives in you. The Holy Spirit is God. When God lives in you, his glory shines through you. Others see it even if you don't. You are not supposed to see it. You are just to believe that God lives in you because scripture says so. You are also to declare who you are. The people around you are wondering what makes you so strong, gentle and patient. Scripture says that you should give them the reason for your hope when they ask you. Let the redeemed of the Lord say so. You are redeemed by the blood of Jesus Christ. Redeemed means that you have been bought back. Yes you have been redeemed from spiritual death and ignorance. Let the world know. Jesus said that when he is lifted up, he will draw all men to himself. Lift the name of Jesus high before all men. This pleases him.

PRAYER
I will praise you Lord with every breath I take. I will make the whole world know what you have done for me.

Further reading: Psalm 107

15th November
PRAISE HIM FOR HIS GREAT BENEFITS

Psalm 103:1-8

> *Bless the Lord, O my soul; And all that is within me, bless His holy name! ²Bless the Lord, O my soul, And forget not all His benefits: ³Who forgives all your iniquities, Who heals all your diseases, ⁴Who redeems your life from destruction, Who crowns you with loving kindness and tender mercies, ⁵Who satisfies your mouth with good things, So that your youth is renewed like the eagle's. ⁶ The Lord executes righteousness And justice for all who are oppressed. ⁷ He made known His ways to Moses, His acts to the children of Israel. ⁸The Lord is merciful and gracious, Slow to anger, and abounding in mercy*

The psalmist commands his soul to bless the Lord. The soul is made up of your mind, will and emotions. He is asking his will, mind and emotions to rise up and praise the Lord. They have no right to go to sleep. Command your mind, emotions and will to praise the Lord. When we think of certain situations we feel down in our emotions and there is no will to praise the Lord. The psalmist here is giving us a way out. Command your soul and everything in you to praise the Lord. His benefits to us are so great that we cannot afford not to praise him. He has forgiven us all our sins. This is the greatest reason to thank the Lord. We were separated from God because of our sins. Jesus has reconciled us to the father by sacrificially paying for our sins on the cross. Today you are a child of God. Shout with Joy. He has also healed all our diseases. I have seen many diseases healed by the power of God. This promise goes beyond that. It promises healing for all diseases. Don't argue. Just receive the word of God and your healing without complacency. You are crowned with loving kindness.

PRAYER
Let everything in me praise the Lord. My mind praises you Lord. My emotions praise the Lord. I will praise the Lord with everything I have.

Further reading: Psalm 103

16th November
ALL NATIONS MUST PRAISE THE LORD

Psalm 117:1-2

Praise the Lord, all you Gentiles! Laud Him, all you peoples! ²For His merciful kindness is great toward us, And the truth of the Lord endures forever. Praise the Lord!

In Old Testament thinking, the world was divided into two groups: Jews and Gentiles. The Jews knew and had a covenant with God through their ancestors Abraham, Isaac and Jacob. The rest of the world, also known as the nations did not have a covenant with God. They were called gentiles. Today the cross of Jesus Christ has opened the rest of the world (gentiles, nations) to a relationship with God. Scripture tells us that by the cross of Jesus Christ, there is no longer Jew or gentile. In Jesus Christ, both Jews and gentiles are united into one. Whosoever shall call on the name of Jesus shall be saved. What is interesting about today's reading is the fact that the writer is calling on even those who do not have a relationship with God to praise the Lord. Everyone benefits from the loving kindness of God. Each person on this earth has been fearfully and wonderfully made by God. Many are ignorant of this fact. Our ignorance does not change who God is. He loves everyone and his desire is that all would know about him. The good news of Jesus Christ has to be proclaimed everywhere. The psalmist is calling even unbelievers to praise the Lord. All people, irrespective of faith enjoy his sun and rain. Scripture says that no one has any excuse not to acknowledge God. His attributes clearly show in his creation. Many have turned this revelation into serving false gods created by their imagination. The true God is our father in heaven and all creation must give him praise. All creation shall give him praise because of you. They will see the glory in you. You will direct them to the source of all glory and they will have no choice but to give him praise.

PRAYER

Thank you father for your beautiful creation. Thank you for all the people you have made everywhere. All shall praise your holy name.

Sing songs of Praise to the Lord.

17th November
GOD LOVES MUSIC

Psalm 98:1-8

Oh, sing to the Lord a new song! For He has done marvellous things; His right hand and His holy arm have gained Him the victory. ²The Lord has made known His salvation; His righteousness He has revealed in the sight of the nations. ³He has remembered His mercy and His faithfulness to the house of Israel; All the ends of the earth have seen the salvation of our God. ⁴Shout joyfully to the Lord, all the earth; Break forth in song, rejoice, and sing praises. ⁵Sing to the Lord with the harp, With the harp and the sound of a psalm, ⁶With trumpets and the sound of a horn; Shout joyfully before the Lord, the King. ⁷Let the sea roar, and all its fullness, The world and those who dwell in it; ⁸Let the rivers clap their hands; Let the hills be joyful together before the Lord,

Music is a powerful gift of God. God created music. Everything that God created is good. Beautiful singing and instrumentation is sweet to the soul. Everything God created was for the benefit of both God and man. Music was created to bring joy to God and man. The devil exploiting our ignorance has corrupted many of the good things God created for our benefit. Today, the power of music is used negatively in many places. People have used music to seduce, incite and hypnotize. Scripture says that if you feed the flesh, you will reap corruption. However if you feed the spirit, you will reap life. I endeavor not to sing or be entertained by music that only feeds the flesh. I would rather sing songs or listen to music that build my spirit. If the spirit gives life then I want to build my spirit. I would encourage you to do the same. Galatians 5:17 says that the flesh and the spirit fight against each other. Build the spirit to defeat the flesh. God loves music. If you will allow God he will give you the best music.

PRAYER

Holy Spirit, help me to make the best music to my father as I know he loves music.

Compose your own music of praise to the Lord.

18th November
THE LORD IS ON YOUR SIDE

Psalm 118:1-9

Oh, give thanks to the Lord, for He is good! For His mercy endures forever. ²Let Israel now say ,"His mercy endures forever." ³Let the house of Aaron now say ,"His mercy endures forever." ⁴Let those who fear the Lord now say, "His mercy endures forever." ⁵I called on the Lord in distress ;The Lord answered me and set me in a broad place. ⁶The Lord is on my side; I will not fear. What can man do to me? ⁷The Lord is for me among those who help me Therefore I shall see my desire on those who hate me.⁸It is better to trust in the Lord Than to put confidence in man. ⁹It is better to trust in the Lord Than to put confidence in princes.

It is better to trust in the Lord than to put your confidence in princes. Princes represent the most powerful people in society. They have armies, wealth and make the rules. If you have a prince on your side, there is an obvious advantage. The scripture above is telling us that these princes are nothing compared to the companionship of God. The creator of heaven and earth is on your side. If God is for you, no desire of man shall prevail over you. He is your protector against any plan of the enemy. David used this understanding of God on his side to defeat Goliath. God was on the side of all Israel but none of them had grasped this fact. Goliath was therefore able to bully Israel for forty days and nights. When David appeared on the scene, he came with the knowledge of God on his side and Goliath was no match. The challenges of this world seem like Goliaths till you recognize the presence of God with you. The Holy Spirit is with you and in you. Tell Goliath who is king and kill him with the sword of the spirit which is the word of God. Rejoice, you are more than a conqueror.

PRAYER

Dear father, I thank you for being on my side. I will fear no foe. Because you are for me, I can boldly face my enemies.

Further reading: Psalm 118

19th November
GOD PROVIDES FOOD

Psalm 111:1-5

Praise the Lord! I will praise the Lord with my whole heart, In the assembly of the upright and in the congregation. ²The works of the Lord are great, Studied by all who have pleasure in them. ³His work is Honourable and glorious, And His righteousness endures forever. ⁴He has made His wonderful works to be remembered; The Lord is gracious and full of compassion. ⁵He has given food to those who fear Him; He will ever be mindful of His covenant.

God created us. He made us in a way that we need food to survive. Because God did not create us to die, he is obliged to provide us with food and he has promised to feed us. Jesus says in Matthew 6:26 that God feeds the birds of the air without much effort. He will therefore definitely provide food for us as we are more important than birds. In Deuteronomy 28, God promises to bless the crops, baskets, kneading bowls and storehouses of those who would walk with him in obedience.. As you are in Christ, you qualify to be part of this promise. He will give you food. If you allow God to feed you, he will give you the best. Thank him for every food you eat. He took Israel through the desert for forty years and fed them with manna. His word says that none of them was sick during the time. Not even their foot was swollen during forty years of wilderness walking. Israel did not know about manna before God gave it to them. All they knew was bread. God said he did this to show Israel that man shall not live by bread alone. God is able to give you food that you have never known. Jesus said he is the bread of life and if you eat him, you would never be hungry. David said that in his long experience with God, he had never seen the righteous forsaken nor his children beg for bread. God will provide.

PRAYER
Thank you for always providing healthy food for me. Holy Spirit, help me to trust in the provision of my father.

Further reading: Psalm 111

20th November
GOD RIDES ON THE WIND

Psalm 104:1-5

Bless the Lord, O my soul! O Lord my God, You are very great: You are clothed with Honour and majesty ,²Who cover Yourself with light as with a garment, Who stretch out the heavens like a curtain. ³He lays the beams of His upper chambers in the waters, Who makes the clouds His chariot, Who walks on the wings of the wind, ⁴Who makes His angels spirits, His ministers a flame of fire. ⁵You who laid the foundations of the earth, So that it should not be moved forever,

When you see the clouds, God is there. When the wind blows, God is there. He rides the winds. He stretched out the heavens and he fixed the earth in such a way that it cannot be moved. Three expressions have been used to describe God: 'All powerful', 'All knowing', 'Present everywhere'. These three attributes are captured in the psalm above. In him all things consists and he fills all things. There is no way that you can hide from his presence. Nothing is too difficult for him. If such a God can humble himself to become a man so he could pay for our sins and reconcile us to himself, then he deserves our praise. We should forever be thankful for this show of love. My loyalty to this God who has taken me from darkness into his marvellous light cannot be disturbed. Never allow thanksgiving and praise to be absent from your lips. He has given you life where there was death. You can count on the faithfulness of this powerful God. His humility matches his power. Majesty and meekness, deity and manhood walking hand in hand and side by side. You are a part of this indescribable communion. The knowledge of this fills me with reverential awe. Gratitude explodes in my heart and praise gushes out of my heart. That should be your natural response to this awesome life that we have been made partakers of. Never take your eyes of this glory as you are changed from one level of glory to another. Praise him with everything you have.

PRAYER
I will hold nothing back as you have held nothing back. Father, I come into your warm embrace in full assurance of your love and faithfulness.

Further reading: Psalm 104

21st November
GIVE THANKS FOR HELPERS

Romans 16:1-10

¹I commend to you Phoebe our sister, who is a servant of the church in Cenchrea, ²that you may receive her in the Lord in a manner worthy of the saints, and assist her in whatever business she has need of you; for indeed she has been a helper of many and of myself also. ³Greet Priscilla and Aquila, my fellow workers in Christ Jesus, ⁴who risked their own necks for my life, to whom not only I give thanks, but also all the churches of the Gentiles. ⁵Likewise greet the church that is in their house. Greet my beloved Epaenetus, who is the firstfruits of Achaia to Christ. ⁶Greet Mary, who Laboured much for us. ⁷Greet Andronicus and Junia, my countrymen and my fellow prisoners, who are of note among the apostles, who also were in Christ before me. ⁸Greet Amplias, my beloved in the Lord. ⁹Greet Urbanus, our fellow worker in Christ, and Stachys, my beloved. ¹⁰Greet Apelles, approved in Christ. Greet those who are of the household of Aristobulus.

God never leaves us without help. He ensures that we always have all the help we need to accomplish his purpose. The Holy Spirit lives in us to empower us to live godly lives. Angels are available to serve us in our time of need. Hebrews 1:14 tells us that angels are serving spirits sent for to serve us who are heirs of salvation. We are blessed in this generation to have the word of God in the form of the bible to be the light of our path and a lamp to our feet. God gives us human helpers as well. We have to be grateful to the people he brings alongside to help us on our journey of life. We must thank God for our parents, spouses, family, co-workers and everyone God uses to help us. May the Lord open your eyes to see the helpers he has made available to you. Thank him for each one of them.

PRAYER

Thank you father that you have given me people to help me on my journey. I thank you for each of them. Continue to bless them on their own journeys.

Further reading: Romans chapter 16

22nd November
THE EARTH BELONGS TO THE LORD

1 Corinthians 10:23-31

All things are lawful for me, but not all things are helpful; all things are lawful for me, but not all things edify. ^{24}Let no one seek his own, but each one the other's well-being. ^{25}Eat whatever is sold in the meat market, asking no questions for conscience' sake; ^{26}for "the earth is the Lord's, and all its fullness." ^{27}If any of those who do not believe invites you to dinner, and you desire to go, eat whatever is set before you, asking no question for conscience' sake. ^{28}But if anyone says to you, "This was offered to idols," do not eat it for the sake of the one who told you, and for conscience' sake; for "the earth is the Lord's, and all its fullness." ^{29}"Conscience," I say, not your own, but that of the other. For why is my liberty judged by another man's conscience? ^{30}But if I partake with thanks, why am I evil spoken of for the food over which I give thanks? ^{31}Therefore, whether you eat or drink, or whatever you do, do all to the glory of God.

No one can lay any claim to the ownership of the earth except he who created it. Individuals, corporations as well as nations claim ownership of portions of this earth. They claim ownership through conquests, purchase or gifts. Man may enjoy ownership of parts of this earth but this is only temporary. The earth is the Lord's and all the people in it. Psalm 24 tells us that this is so because he created them. The Lord can give any portion of land to whoever he chooses. That is why he chose to give the Promise Land to Israel. In Genesis he gave the earth to man to dominate it. Man, however, had selfish plans and lost this fruitful partnership. Jesus has come to take back ownership of the earth and shares it with all who would come to him. Praise his name forever.

PRAYER
Thank you Jesus, for making me co-heir with you. I will never leave your side. Please order my steps.

Further reading: Psalm 24

23rd November
THANK GOD FOR HIS GREAT POWER

Ephesians 1:15-21

> *Therefore I also, after I heard of your faith in the Lord Jesus and your love for all the saints, [16]do not cease to give thanks for you, making mention of you in my prayers: [17]that the God of our Lord Jesus Christ, the Father of glory, may give to you the spirit of wisdom and revelation in the knowledge of Him, [18]the eyes of your understanding being enlightened; that you may know what is the hope of His calling, what are the riches of the glory of His inheritance in the saints, [19]and what is the exceeding greatness of His power toward us who believe, according to the working of His mighty power [20]which He worked in Christ when He raised Him from the dead and seated Him at His right hand in the heavenly places, [21]far above all principality and power and might and dominion, and every name that is named, not only in this age but also in that which is to come.*

The prayer of Paul above is one prayer that we should continually pray for all the saints. We need to pray for the salvation of those who have not met Jesus Christ. For those of us who have received Jesus as our Lord and Saviour, my prayer for all of us is Paul's prayer above that our spiritual eyes will be open to really grasp the great salvation we have received. May our eyes be open to the great might of our God. Nothing is impossible to him and he is our father. May his name be praised forever. For us to understand his power, we have to grasp what it takes to raise the dead. This he accomplished in the death and resurrection of our Saviour Jesus Christ. Human knowledge ends with death. Anything beyond death is a mystery. We are not talking about resuscitation from what looks like death. We are talking about resurrection from the dead. All hail the power of our God.

PRAYER

Thank you father for opening my eyes to understand your power and love. I pray this revelation and understanding for every Christian brother and sister.

Further reading: Ephesians chapter 1

24th November
BE FRUITFUL IN EVERY GOOD WORK

Colossians 1:3-9

> *We give thanks to the God and Father of our Lord Jesus Christ, praying always for you, ⁴since we heard of your faith in Christ Jesus and of your love for all the saints; ⁵because of the hope which is laid up for you in heaven, of which you heard before in the word of the truth of the gospel, ⁶which has come to you, as it has also in all the world, and is bringing forth fruit, as it is also among you since the day you heard and knew the grace of God in truth; ⁷as you also learned from Epaphras, our dear fellow servant, who is a faithful minister of Christ on your behalf, ⁸who also declared to us your love in the Spirit. ⁹For this reason we also, since the day we heard it, do not cease to pray for you, and to ask that you may be filled with the knowledge of His will in all wisdom and spiritual understanding;*

Since I tasted of life with Jesus Christ in his kingdom, it has become so clear to me how wasteful life outside the kingdom of God is. The only real satisfaction comes from walking with Jesus Christ and producing fruit for his glory. Producing fruit in the kingdom is seeing the poor saved through your preaching; comforting the broken hearted; making the blind see and bringing deliverance to those in captivity. Outside this, life is eating, drinking, work, accumulation of goods and sleep. These activities can never bring fulfilment. Being born again by the Spirit of God puts you in the God class. The glory of God in you will produce good works. The bible says we are created in Christ Jesus to do good works. If the little seed that is planted could see the tree, fruits and many seeds it produces, it would overwhelm it with joy. That is the joy of harvest God has given to us as we see the fruit of our Labour. Praise him without ceasing.

PRAYER
Thank you father for making me produce fruit that will last. I praise you for giving me the joy of harvest.

Further reading: Colossians chapter 1

25th November
YOU ARE ELECTED BY GOD

1 Thessalonians 1:2-8

> We give thanks to God always for you all, making mention of you in our prayers, ³remembering without ceasing your work of faith, Labour of love, and patience of hope in our Lord Jesus Christ in the sight of our God and Father, ⁴knowing, beloved brethren, your election by God. ⁵For our gospel did not come to you in word only, but also in power, and in the Holy Spirit and in much assurance, as you know what kind of men we were among you for your sake. ⁶And you became followers of us and of the Lord, having received the word in much affliction, with joy of the Holy Spirit, ⁷so that you became examples to all in Macedonia and Achaia who believe. ⁸For from you the word of the Lord has sounded forth, not only in Macedonia and Achaia, but also in every place. Your faith toward God has gone out, so that we do not need to say anything.

Paul commends the Christians in Thessalonica. Their faith is producing works. They are Labouring in love and are patient in hope. He is not surprised because they are chosen of God. You have been chosen by God. The word elected drives the point home even more clearly. In our democracies, elections are held and a person is elected from a line of candidates. Imagine the number of people God could have chosen to undertake your assignment. God elected you. That is special and you have to show your gratitude through praise. I ask myself sometimes: Why me? God's personal love for me always answers this question. To know that he personally knows me and has chosen me overwhelms my heart with gratitude and praise. As Paul describes above, he demonstrates his power through his chosen. God's power is demonstrated by miracles, signs and wonders. Expect miracles in your life because you are chosen. People will recognize your elected status by your fruit. Praise the Lord.

PRAYER
Thank you father that you know me and have chosen me. I am so grateful that I am special to you.

Further reading: 1 Thessalonians chapter 1

26th November
YOU ARE CHOSEN

2 Thessalonians 2:13-17

> *But we are bound to give thanks to God always for you, brethren beloved by the Lord, because God from the beginning chose you for salvation through sanctification by the Spirit and belief in the truth, ^{14}to which He called you by our gospel, for the obtaining of the glory of our Lord Jesus Christ. ^{15}Therefore, brethren, stand fast and hold the traditions which you were taught, whether by word or our epistle. ^{16}Now may our Lord Jesus Christ Himself, and our God and Father, who has loved us and given us everlasting consolation and good hope by grace, ^{17}comfort your hearts and establish you in every good word and work.*

Paul tells us that we have been chosen from the beginning. That is interesting. This means that God chose you and me from among those who have ever lived including all the people in the days of Noah, Abraham and David. Our minds cannot completely grasp this reality but God is God. He knows the end from the beginning. He knows the number of hairs on your head and the number of sand particles on the seashore. Scripture calls our generation, the chosen generation. No temporary challenges in life will distract me from the immeasurable love of God for me. I pray that you take the same attitude. Scripture says that our light affliction is but for a moment. Our affliction is working out the glory of the Lord Jesus Christ in us. Paul says in Romans 8:29-30 that God chose us to be conformed to the image of Jesus Christ. His process, as we respond to his call, is to justify us with the blood of Jesus Christ and glorify us with his Holy Spirit. What an awesome privilege to belong to such an elite group. He loves you more than you can ever imagine so never let his praise be absent from your mouth. You have been chosen from a great number of people to be beautified.

PRAYER

I am so privileged to be part of your family and I am so grateful. Holy Spirit, help me to give back in praise this great love my father has given me.

Further reading: 2 Thessalonians chapter 2

27th November
ALL CREATURES PRAISE HIM

Revelation 4:6-11

Before the throne there was a sea of glass, like crystal. And in the midst of the throne, and around the throne, were four living creatures full of eyes in front and in back. ⁷The first living creature was like a lion, the second living creature like a calf, the third living creature had a face like a man, and the fourth living creature was like a flying eagle. ⁸The four living creatures, each having six wings, were full of eyes around and within. And they do not rest day or night, saying: "Holy,holy, holy, Lord God Almighty, Who was and is and is to come!" ⁹Whenever the living creatures give glory and Honour and thanks to Him who sits on the throne, who lives forever and ever, ¹⁰the twenty-four elders fall down before Him who sits on the throne and worship Him who lives forever and ever, and cast their crowns before the throne, saying: ¹¹"You are worthy, O Lord, To receive glory and Honour and power; For You created all things, And by Your will they exist and were created."

The apostle John had a revelation of the throne room of God where praise and worship does not stop. God showed him four living creatures who represent creation and twenty four elders who represent the church consistently falling before him in worship. True worship arises when we encounter God's glory. When John encountered Jesus Christ in his glory at the beginning of the book of Revelation, he fell down as dead. Someone said heaven will be boring if we have no work to do but just praising God. There is nothing boring about encountering the glory of God. The times that I have personally encountered the glory of God, I never wanted it to cease. True intimacy with God happens which you never want to let go. Desire to experience more of the glory of God and you will cease from your own works. Worship the Lord.

PRAYER

All creatures you have created will give you praise because you deserve praise. I worship you in the beauty of your holiness.

Further reading: Revelation chapter 4

28th November
GOD IS THE GREAT JUDGE

Revelation 11:15-19

Then the seventh angel sounded: And there were loud voices in heaven, saying, "The kingdoms of this world have become the kingdoms of our Lord and of His Christ, and He shall reign forever and ever!" ¹⁶And the twenty-four elders who sat before God on their thrones fell on their faces and worshiped God, ¹⁷saying: "We give You thanks, O Lord God Almighty, The One who is and who was and who is to come, Because You have taken Your great power and reigned. ¹⁸The nations were angry, and Your wrath has come, And the time of the dead, that they should be judged, And that You should reward Your servants the prophets and the saints, And those who fear Your name, small and great, And should destroy those who destroy the earth. ¹⁹Then the temple of God was opened in heaven, and the ark of His covenant was seen in His temple. And there were lightnings, noises, thunderings, an earthquake, and great hail.

Our God is going to judge all things in the fullness of time. One of the names of God is Alpha and Omega, which means 'The beginning and End'. He created all things and will end all things. All things will be judged by his standard. The old word 'Righteousness' is a peculiar attribute of God. It simply means that he is right. If he started everything, he has all wisdom concerning what he started. He can heal all diseases because he knows the material he used for creation and how to manufacture it. He is the only one who can determine whether we lived right or not. He does not only give justice, he is justice. When we become part of his family through Jesus Christ, we take on the quality of righteousness. We have already been justified. In other words, we have been judged and found innocent because of the intervention of Jesus Christ. The great judge is family. Praise the Lord.

PRAYER

Thank you Jesus for bringing me salvation. The great judge is my father and I am filled with gratitude.

Further reading: Revelation chapter 11

29th November
THANK GOD FOR HIS RIGHTEOUSNESS

Psalm 7:10-17

> My defense is of God, Who saves the upright in heart. ^{11}God is a just judge, And God is angry with the wicked every day. ^{12}If he does not turn back, He will sharpen His sword; He bends His bow and makes it ready. ^{13}He also prepares for Himself instruments of death; He makes His arrows into fiery shafts. ^{14}Behold, the wicked brings forth iniquity; Yes, he conceives trouble and brings forth falsehood. ^{15}He made a pit and dug it out, And has fallen into the ditch which he made ^{16}His trouble shall return upon his own head, And his violent dealing shall come down on his own crown. ^{17}I will praise the Lord according to His righteousness, And will sing praise to the name of the Lord Most High.

God is light. In him is no darkness at all. This assertion goes for every attribute of God. God is truth and there can be no lie in him. God is holy and there can be no sin in him. God is just and there can be no injustice in him. There is going to be a final judgment of all people. Everyone will receive their reward according to the judgment of God. The good news is that in Jesus Christ, God's mercy for our shortfall has been made available. Jesus has paid the price for our sins and rescued all who will receive him from condemnation. God deserves our gratitude for his righteousness, grace and mercy. Scripture warns us not to take this expensive salvation for granted. We should protect our salvation with fear and trembling. John encourages us to receive this salvation of God. Jesus did not come to condemn the world but that the world will be saved through him. He goes on to warn that he who does not receive this salvation is condemned already. The judgment of God without his mercy is severe. Let us latch on to his mercy. Don't let go.

PRAYER

Thank you father for uniting me with your righteousness. Thank you Jesus for serving my sentence for me. Thank you Holy Spirit for revealing God to me.

Further reading: Psalm 7

30th November
SING TO THE LORD

Psalm 28:6-9

Blessed be the Lord, Because He has heard the voice of my supplications! ⁷The Lord is my strength and my shield; My heart trusted in Him, and I am helped; Therefore my heart greatly rejoices, And with my song I will praise Him. ⁸The Lord is their strength, And He is the saving refuge of His anointed. ⁹Save Your people, And bless Your inheritance; Shepherd them also, And bear them up forever.

A good love poem for a loved one is always desirable. It does not need to rhyme in couplets or have any special poetic technical details. What is needed is a genuine heart and true meaningful expression. If melody is added to this poem to turn it into a song, it adds an extra dimension to it. God also appreciates a good, truthful song of praise from his children. The church has many beautiful praise songs filled with lovely words that we sing to the Lord. As helpful as these songs are in praising God, there is something special about composing your own love song to the father. Everyone can make love music to God. You do not have to be an accomplished musician to sing to your lover. You may be out of tune but God is not listening to your tune. He is listening to your heart and the genuineness of your love song to him. Many times we are hindered by our fears. Many refuse to sing with the excuse that they can't carry a tune. Moses gave that same excuse when God gave him an assignment to go and rescue Israel out of Egypt. He said he couldn't speak. God reminded him that he was the one who created the mouth that is used for speech. In other words, if you are with the creator of all things, he is able to make you do things that you could not do naturally. I have seen many who thought they could not sing transformed into great singers as they trusted in God. God loves a song.

PRAYER
Thank you father for the gift of song. I will use my voice to sing for you.

Compose your own love song to the Lord.

Be Strong Devotional

Be Strong Devotional

December

1st December
ABRAHAM BUILT AN ALTAR

Genesis 13:14-18

And the Lord said to Abram, after Lot had separated from him: "Lift your eyes now and look from the place where you are--northward, southward, eastward, and westward; [15] for all the land which you see I give to you and your descendants forever. [16] And I will make your descendants as the dust of the earth; so that if a man could number the dust of the earth, then your descendants also could be numbered. [17] Arise, walk in the land through its length and its width, for I give it to you." [18] Then Abram moved his tent, and went and dwelt by the terebinth trees of Mamre, which are in Hebron, and built an altar there to the Lord.

Our covenant relationship with God is one of promise and obedience. God makes a promise. We have to believe and receive this promise. One practice we see with Abraham is the building of an altar whenever he has a special encounter with God. An altar is used for a sacrifice. Whenever Abraham receives a special word from God, he confirms his faith with a sacrifice. Today, we do not kill animals as sacrifice but there are other things we could do to show our gratitude to God's generosity. The first of this is thanksgiving and praise. Expression of gratitude is your first act of acceptance of a gift. It gives the receiver the contentment of returning the favour bestowed on him. A grateful receipt of a gift satisfies the giver because the whole purpose of giving is for someone to receive it gratefully and put it to good use. God is the creator of all things and has a lot to give. We must be ready to receive his gifts with gratitude. The greatest gift our Father in heaven has given to us is the gift of the Holy Spirit. He has given himself to us. If you have received the Holy Spirit then give him praise today. If you haven't, receive the Holy Spirit today.

PRAYER

Thank you father for the Holy Spirit. Holy Spirit, I receive you fully in my life this day. With your help I will do the works of God.

Further reading: Genesis 13

2nd December
ABRAHAM FELL ON HIS FACE

Genesis 17:1-8

When Abram was ninety-nine years old, the Lord appeared to Abram and said to him, "I am Almighty God; walk before Me and be blameless. ² And I will make My covenant between Me and you, and will multiply you exceedingly." ³ Then Abram fell on his face, and God talked with him, saying: ⁴ "As for Me, behold, My covenant is with you, and you shall be a father of many nations. ⁵ No longer shall your name be called Abram, but your name shall be Abraham; for I have made you a father of many nations. ⁶ I will make you exceedingly fruitful; and I will make nations of you, and kings shall come from you. ⁷ And I will establish My covenant between Me and you and your descendants after you in their generations, for an everlasting covenant, to be God to you and your descendants after you. ⁸ Also I give to you and your descendants after you the land in which you are a stranger, all the land of Canaan, as an everlasting possession; and I will be their God."

What awesome promises God gives to Abraham. These were the promises he gave to Adam when he first created man. He promised Adam the earth, fruitfulness and total dominion. God does not change. Neither does he show favouritism. These promises are not just for Abraham. By the grace of our Lord Jesus Christ, these promises are for all who will receive it. Fruitfulness and dominion is your portion. The devil deceived us into a life of fear but Jesus Christ has delivered us into a life of faith, hope and love. Abraham fell on his face before the Lord. To fall on your face is an act of humility and acknowledgement of the total superiority of the person you fall before. It is an act of worship. Fall before your God today and acknowledge him as God. He has invited you into a covenant where he provides and you receive.

PRAYER

Father, I fall before you today to acknowledge your greatness and my nothingness. To make me your child is a great gift for me. Thank you.

Lie before God today and worship him from your heart.

3rd December
THE COVENANT OF CIRCUMCISION

Genesis 17:9-14

> And God said to Abraham: "As for you, you shall keep My covenant, you and your descendants after you throughout their generations. ¹⁰ This is My covenant which you shall keep, between Me and you and your descendants after you: Every male child among you shall be circumcised; ¹¹ and you shall be circumcised in the flesh of your foreskins, and it shall be a sign of the covenant between Me and you. ¹² He who is eight days old among you shall be circumcised, every male child in your generations, he who is born in your house or bought with money from any foreigner who is not your descendant. ¹³ He who is born in your house and he who is bought with your money must be circumcised, and My covenant shall be in your flesh for an everlasting covenant. ¹⁴ And the uncircumcised male child, who is not circumcised in the flesh of his foreskin, that person shall be cut off from his people; he has broken My covenant."

A covenant involves two parties. Each party brings something to the table and the two agree to share in all things equally. God gives Abraham wonderful promises of fruitfulness and dominion. He demands circumcision from Abraham. Circumcision stands for the giving up of the flesh. The one thing that blinds the world from the goodness of God is the flesh. Without the Spirit of God, the world lives by the flesh. The world lives by the five senses. We make our decisions from what we see, hear, smell, taste and feel. As long as there is colour blindness and the eyes can be weak, we could be seeing wrongly. As long as the ear can be weakened, we could be hearing wrongly. It is therefore important that we give up our flesh for the Spirit of God. What a beautiful exchange. Fill yourself with the word of God. Separate yourself to hearing from God. This is the only truth.

PRAYER

Thank you father for bringing your all and exchanging it for my nothingness. I love this covenant. I promise to walk in the circumcision of my heart. Thank you.

Further reading: Genesis chapter 17

4th December
ABRAHAM WAS GENEROUS

Genesis 18:1-10

Then the Lord appeared to him by the terebinth trees of Mamre, as he was sitting in the tent door in the heat of the day. ² So he lifted his eyes and looked, and behold, three men were standing by him; and when he saw them, he ran from the tent door to meet them, and bowed himself to the ground, ³ and said, "My Lord, if I have now found favour in Your sight, do not pass on by Your servant. ⁴ Please let a little water be brought, and wash your feet, and rest yourselves under the tree. ⁵ And I will bring a morsel of bread, that you may refresh your hearts. After that you may pass by, inasmuch as you have come to your servant." They said, "Do as you have said." ⁶ So Abraham hurried into the tent to Sarah and said, "Quickly, make ready three measures of fine meal; knead it and make cakes." ⁷ And Abraham ran to the herd, took a tender and good calf, gave it to a young man, and he hastened to prepare it. ⁸ So he took butter and milk and the calf which he had prepared, and set it before them; and he stood by them under the tree as they ate. ⁹ Then they said to him, "Where is Sarah your wife?" So he said, "Here, in the tent." ¹⁰ And He said, "I will certainly return to you according to the time of life, and behold, Sarah your wife shall have a son." (Sarah was listening in the tent door which was behind him.)

One of the things that please God is to be hospitable. Scripture tells us that some by being hospitable have hosted angels. Abraham was hospitable and received the promise of a son. God wants us to be kind. He loves everyone. He fearfully and wonderfully created everyone. Don't let the ignorance of man put you off being generous. Walk in love. Love others even as your Father has loved you.

PRAYER
Dear father, thank you for being so generous to me. Holy Spirit, help me to be generous to others.

Further reading: Genesis chapter 18

5th December
GOD HAS BROUGHT LAUGHTER

Genesis 21:1-8

And the Lord visited Sarah as He had said, and the Lord did for Sarah as He had spoken. ² For Sarah conceived and bore Abraham a son in his old age, at the set time of which God had spoken to him. ³ And Abraham called the name of his son who was born to him--whom Sarah bore to him--Isaac. ⁴Then Abraham circumcised his son Isaac when he was eight days old, as God had commanded him. ⁵ Now Abraham was one hundred years old when his son Isaac was born to him. ⁶ And Sarah said, "God has made me laugh, and all who hear will laugh with me." ⁷ She also said, "Who would have said to Abraham that Sarah would nurse children? For I have borne him a son in his old age." ⁸ So the child grew and was weaned. And Abraham made a great feast on the same day that Isaac was weaned.

Every good gift comes from God. God's presence in your life has brought you laughter. If you are not laughing now then prepare to laugh. One of the fruits of the Holy Spirit is joy. Sarah's life was filled with laughter after the fulfilment of God's promise in her life. She had not been able to have her own children for 90 years. She and her husband were well past the age of child bearing. There is no limit to the power of God. God is able to raise the dead. Men in our limited wisdom can put time limits. God lives in eternity and is not limited by time. Do not let time or age oppress you. Rise up and laugh. Moses was sent by God on the great assignment of leading two million Jews from Egypt at the age of 80 years. He performed this task vigorously for forty years. The bible describes him as strong and with perfect eyesight at the age of 120 years. It is not late. Rise up and enjoy the beautiful promises of God.

PRAYER
Thank you father for filling my heart with joy and my mouth with laughter. I love you too.

Further reading: Genesis chapter 21

6th December
YOU ARE BLESSED

Genesis 22:15-18

> *Then the Angel of the Lord called to Abraham a second time out of heaven, ^{16} and said: "By Myself I have sworn, says the Lord, because you have done this thing, and have not withheld your son, your only son-- ^{17} blessing I will bless you, and multiplying I will multiply your descendants as the stars of the heaven and as the sand which is on the seashore; and your descendants shall possess the gate of their enemies. ^{18} In your seed all the nations of the earth shall be blessed, because you have obeyed My voice."*

God's word is as good as done. When he speaks, there is power in his word to go and do what he has sent it to do. In the scripture above, he does not only release his indestructible word. He swears to it. He did not need to but he did and Abraham would have understood this double emphasis. God did this in response to what Abraham had done. Abraham had obeyed God in offering up Isaac to God. Although God did not allow Abraham to sacrifice Isaac, Abraham had sacrificed Isaac in every way apart from the actual act of Isaac physically dying. Isaac was the most valuable asset Abraham had. He was ready to forfeit it in obedience to God. He therefore received a blessing that has benefited the whole world including you and me. Jesus Christ came from the lineage of Abraham. Abraham gave his best and God also gave his best for the salvation of mankind. Are you ready to give your best to God? Your best includes your heart, mind and body. You are blessed my friend. You are in an elite group of chosen and separated to God. We who had no hope now have hope. Rejoice in the Lord always. Through the death of Jesus Christ on the cross, he has sworn to you and me that we are part of his family. We can walk in his blessing as a covenant right. Again I say, rejoice.

PRAYER

Thank you father that I am blessed for being part of your family. Holy Spirit, help me to give my best always.

Further reading: Genesis chapter 22

7th December
YOU SHARE IN ABRAHAMS PROMISE

Galatians 3:26-29

For you are all sons of God through faith in Christ Jesus. [27] For as many of you as were baptized into Christ have put on Christ. [28] There is neither Jew nor Greek, there is neither slave nor free, there is neither male nor female; for you are all one in Christ Jesus. [29] And if you are Christ's, then you are Abraham's seed, and heirs according to the promise.

In a world of so much division and racism, Jesus Christ remains our hope for unity and love. As many as have been baptized into Christ, have put on Christ. This buries our old divisions. We must now see each other as clothed in Christ. There is no black, white or Asian church. We are all the church of Christ. We are all free in Jesus Christ. There are no slaves. We must treat each other with mutual respect. Through Jesus Christ, we are all partakers of the blessing of Abraham. True humility is receiving what God says about you in his word and walking in it. God will surely back his word without fail. Many times we do not receive what is rightly ours. This is because we would go into false humility of 'I am not worthy'. Of course no one was worthy as we had all sinned and fallen short of the glory of God. The love of God did not leave us in our sin. He could do something about it and he did. Jesus Christ on the cross paid for all our sins and delivered us from our begging unworthy state. We are now part of the family of God and share in Abraham's blessing. We are blessed in every area of our lives. Shout Halleluiah! You can count on God's protection and provision. Shut off the belittling negative voices that are constantly shouting to us and making us feel like grasshoppers. You are more than a conqueror through Jesus Christ.

PRAYER

I thank you father that through Jesus Christ, I share in the wonderful blessings of Abraham. May I never lose sight of this fact.

Further reading: Galatians chapter 3

8th December
SEEDTIME AND HARVEST

Genesis 8:20-22

Then Noah built an altar to the Lord, and took of every clean animal and of every clean bird, and offered burnt offerings on the altar. [21] And the Lord smelled a soothing aroma. Then the Lord said in His heart, "I will never again curse the ground for man's sake, although the imagination of man's heart is evil from his youth; nor will I again destroy every living thing as I have done. [22] "While the earth remains, Seedtime and harvest, Cold and heat, Winter and summer, And day and night Shall not cease."

All through the bible, whenever men offered a sacrifice from a grateful heart, there was response from God. Noah offered a sacrifice after the flood and it pleased God. God cut a covenant with Noah. This shows us the importance of sacrificing to God. A sacrifice is when you give to God at your expense something that belongs to you. If you give to God your best lamb of the flock, you are showing your love. You could have enjoyed a lamb barbecue. You however chose to present it as a burnt offering to God. These days we do not burn animals to God but our sense of gratitude still demands a sacrifice. This could be expressed in our public acknowledgement of the goodness of God. It is also well expressed in our financial generosity to his church and work. You can never out-give God. This eternal law of seedtime and harvest puts our prosperity in our own hands. When you sow, you will reap. A farmer sows a small quantity of seed compared to the great harvest of crop he reaps. God supernaturally gave manna to the Israelites in the desert but when they reached the promise land, they were mature enough to eat from their own seed. When you see what you have as seed rather than food, then you are in for a great harvest. A good seed from a cheerful heart will always reap a good harvest.

PRAYER

Thank you for the law of seedtime and harvest. I expect a harvest as I generously sow seed.

Further reading: Genesis chapter 8

9th December
YOUR SEED WILL BEAR FRUIT

Mark 4:24-28

Then He said to them, "Take heed what you hear. With the same measure you use, it will be measured to you; and to you who hear, more will be given. ^{25} For whoever has, to him more will be given; but whoever does not have, even what he has will be taken away from him." ^{26} And He said, "The kingdom of God is as if a man should scatter seed on the ground, ^{27} and should sleep by night and rise by day, and the seed should sprout and grow, he himself does not know how. ^{28} For the earth yields crops by itself: first the blade, then the head, after that the full grain in the head.

Your seed will bear fruit. No farmer sows a seed and goes later to open the hole up to check if the seed is growing. He expects his seed to produce fruit if the weather is right. God in his word has promised to give us rain to water our seeds. He who controls the weather is the one who has promised us that our seed will bear fruit. There is a warning in the scripture above. Be careful what you hear. The word you receive is like a seed sown in you. It will bear fruit. Corrupt seed gives birth to corrupt fruit. Good seed gives birth to good fruit. Be good stewards of the gift God has given to you. Sow righteous seeds and reap a bountiful harvest of righteousness. Every word you speak is a seed. Avoid discouraging words as they will produce fruits of discouragement. Speak the word of God as it will produce fruits of righteousness. Sow your time, strength and treasure into God's kingdom. You can never out-give God. All things were made by him and for him. He is a generous rewarder. Understand your covenant with Jesus. He wants to bless the world through you and he will not muzzle your mouth while you distribute his goodness.

PRAYER

I am grateful for the assurance that my seed will definitely bear fruit. Holy Spirit, help me to sow righteous seed that will bear righteous fruit.

Further reading: Mark chapter 4

10th December
REAP EVERLASTING LIFE

Galatians 6:7-10

Do not be deceived, God is not mocked; for whatever a man sows, that he will also reap. ⁸ For he who sows to his flesh will of the flesh reap corruption, but he who sows to the Spirit will of the Spirit reap everlasting life. ⁹ And let us not grow weary while doing good, for in due season we shall reap if we do not lose heart. ¹⁰ Therefore, as we have opportunity, let us do good to all, especially to those who are of the household of faith.

I love music. Over the years, I had a good collection of musical records. I had to get rid of many of them because I realized that they fed my flesh. If what you are enjoying is not feeding your spirit, it is probably feeding your flesh. Do not feed on anything that raises your flesh to the detriment of your spirit. There should not be a moment in your walk when you are not conscious of the Holy Spirit with you because he has promised he will forever be with you. Feed the Spirit with the word of God. Separating yourself in prayer makes the Holy Spirit real to you. When you become conscious of the presence of the Holy Spirit, you will show him the reverence due him. Sow to the Spirit and reap everlasting life. Fleshly things may seem enjoyable for the moment but have eternal corruption. Fleshly enticement does not allow you time to think. You just desire it now. You also get the hangover very quickly. Spiritual seed would require a deliberate effort on your side to systematically sow to the spirit. I assure you that you will definitely reap everlasting life. Everlasting life is not just length of days. It is also good quality life. This is life without negative hangovers. As you sow to the Spirit, expect to reap some positive hangovers like joy, peace and love. As a member of the family of God, expect all God's goodness. Rejoice.

PRAYER

Thank you Jesus for everlasting life. I promise to use every gift you have given me as a seed to reap this glorious harvest.

Further reading: Galatians chapter 6

11th December
YOU ARE BLESSED LIKE A KING

Psalm 21:1-7

> The king shall have joy in Your strength, O Lord; And in Your salvation how greatly shall he rejoice! ² You have given him his heart's desire, And have not withheld the request of his lips. Selah ³ For You meet him with the blessings of goodness; You set a crown of pure gold upon his head. ⁴ He asked life from You, and You gave it to him-- Length of days forever and ever. ⁵ His glory is great in Your salvation; Honour and majesty You have placed upon him. ⁶ For You have made him most blessed forever; You have made him exceedingly glad with Your presence. ⁷ For the king trusts in the Lord, And through the mercy of the Most High he shall not be moved

David knew how to praise his maker. He was honoured because he showed gratitude. His seed produced tremendous blessing. He used his harvest as seed even unto greater harvest. Friend, we have an inheritance of blessing that is greater than what David had. He was a king over Israel. We are co-heirs with the King of kings over the whole universe. If we could learn to praise God like David did, it will stand us in good stead with God. Even before David met Goliath, he was known for the anointing on him when he played the harp. I am in no doubt that David's harp playing was in praise of God. We know that only the presence of God can drive away demons. When David played his harp, the evil spirits in Saul had to flee. Read every blessing that is in the scripture above and make it yours. Add everlasting life and the baptism of the Holy Spirit. You are in a position to shout praise to God. We may not be able to play the harp like David but we could sing to the Lord. We could clap our hands, shake the tambourine or play the drum. Let us praise the Lord.

PRAYER

Thank you Lord for the Holy Spirit. This puts me in the God and king class like my brother Jesus.

Further reading: Psalm 21

12th December
YOUR HARVEST WILL RUN OVER

Luke 6:37-38

"Judge not, and you shall not be judged. Condemn not, and you shall not be condemned. Forgive, and you will be forgiven. ³⁸ Give, and it will be given to you: good measure, pressed down, shaken together, and running over will be put into your bosom. For with the same measure that you use, it will be measured back to you."

Jesus is the great judge. He is also the great Saviour. His first offer to the world is salvation. This is the acceptable year of the Lord. Scripture tells us that Jesus did not come to condemn the world but he came so that the world would be saved through him. We know that his death on the cross was for the sins of the whole world. Everyone who calls on the name of Jesus shall be saved. Unfortunately, in the face of the overwhelming evidence of the good news of Jesus Christ, not everyone will use their freewill wisely and opt for salvation. Some would choose eternal damnation. Jesus would have to sit as a reluctant judge and grant everyone their heart's desire. As brothers and sisters of Jesus Christ, our responsibility is to bring the world to salvation not to judge them. Judgment is not yet. Instead let us give out of the love that has been poured out in our hearts. The world would respond to the nature of Jesus Christ that is in us. Jesus did not highlight our shortcomings. He forgave us our sins. Let us not highlight the sins of the world. Let us tell them more about the grace that is available to forgive their sins. Without the love that is displayed on the cross of Calvary, the world is doomed. Let us tell them about the cross of Jesus Christ. He who shows mercy shall receive mercy. Walk in forgiveness and love towards others and see your harvest overflow. Many shall drink from your overflow. Expect a big harvest in every area of your life.

PRAYER

Father, I will continually praise you as you give me a harvest of good measure, pressed down, shaken together and running over. Thank you.

Further reading: Luke chapter 6

13th December
YOUR EYES ARE OPEN TO SEE

Matthew 13:9-13

> *He who has ears to hear, let him hear!" ¹⁰ And the disciples came and said to Him, "Why do You speak to them in parables?" ¹¹ He answered and said to them, "Because it has been given to you to know the mysteries of the kingdom of heaven, but to them it has not been given. ¹² For whoever has, to him more will be given, and he will have abundance; but whoever does not have, even what he has will be taken away from him. ¹³ Therefore I speak to them in parables, because seeing they do not see, and hearing they do not hear, nor do they understand*

When God opened my eyes to see Jesus and understand the mysteries of the kingdom, I suddenly realized how blind I had been. Jesus was right in front of me but the devil had blinded me with pride. There are many who still argue about the truth of the gospel of Jesus Christ. I weep in my spirit about the blindness they display. I have been there before so I can empathize with their ignorance. I wish I could somehow penetrate their spirit and land this truth. That would be violating their freewill and God would not allow it. Not even God himself would violate the gift of freewill he has given to us. Everyone would have to open the door to their hearts themselves. When the Holy Spirit comes to live inside you, he opens your eyes to see. Some are given special spiritual gifts to see very deep things in the Spirit. Our Father does not want to hide anything from us. If he has given you his Spirit, then he wants you to see and understand things in the spirit realm. Your eyes are open to perceive things of the Spirit. To see in the spirit is to see the truth. To know the truth is to be set free from deception.

PRAYER

Thank you Lord for opening my eyes to see. I pray that you will open the eyes of all my family and friends to the truth of the Gospel of Jesus Christ.

Further reading: Matthew chapter 13

14th December
YOUR FATHER WILL REWARD YOU

Matthew 6:1-4

"Take heed that you do not do your charitable deeds before men, to be seen by them. Otherwise you have no reward from your Father in heaven. ² Therefore, when you do a charitable deed, do not sound a trumpet before you as the hypocrites do in the synagogues and in the streets, that they may have glory from men. Assuredly, I say to you, they have their reward. ³ But when you do a charitable deed, do not let your left hand know what your right hand is doing, ⁴ that your charitable deed may be in secret; and your Father who sees in secret will Himself reward you openly

Scripture says that it is impossible to please God without faith. It continues to say that all who come to God must believe that he is God and a rewarder of all those who diligently seek him. Our God rewards faith. In the world, people do their charitable deeds to be seen by men. Many rich people blow their own horn about how many charities they support. They want to be hailed by men for their good deeds. Jesus warns against that sort of behaviour. God loves it when we give to those in need. Scripture says that when you give to the poor, you lend to God. Whenever you look for the praise of men, it is an indication that your giving is not from a generous heart. There are strings attached. Jesus tells his listeners that if you seek the praise of men then that is what you would receive. The praise of men does not last. The same people who would shout 'Hosanna' to you will also shout 'crucify him' when it suits them. They did it to Jesus. Remember that God sees everything you do in secret. Jesus promises that though your seed is in secret, your reward shall be open. You cannot hide God's reward. The presence of God with you will be clear to all.

PRAYER
Father, I promise to sow my seed in secret so that you may reward me openly.

Further reading: Matthew chapter 6

15th December
RECEIVE THE GIFT OF THE HOLY SPIRIT

Acts 2:36-38

> "Therefore let all the house of Israel know assuredly that God has made this Jesus, whom you crucified, both Lord and Christ." [37] Now when they heard this, they were cut to the heart, and said to Peter and the rest of the apostles, "Men and brethren, what shall we do?" [38] Then Peter said to them, "Repent, and let every one of you be baptized in the name of Jesus Christ for the remission of sins; and you shall receive the gift of the Holy Spirit.

In the Old Testament, special people were anointed by God to undertake special assignments for God. After Jesus cried out "It is finished" and died on the Cross of Calvary, the veil in the temple tore into two. The veil separated the presence of God from the ordinary people. Only the high priest could go behind the veil once a year to meet with God's presence. When Jesus died, the Holy Spirit was no longer for special people. He was available to 'whosoever'. This is what Peter told those who enquired about what to do. He told them to turn to God, be baptized and they shall receive the gift of the Holy Spirit This meant that they would receive the empowerment of God. The supernatural would become natural. The Holy Spirit brigade talks about healing, deliverance and prosperity as being the natural inheritance of the children of God. It would be cruel on the part of God to have all this power at his disposal and still allow his children to walk in sickness and lack. God is not cruel. He is a loving father who would not allow his children to be deprived. The Holy Spirit is not just to give us the DNA of God. He also empowers us to live like God. The Bible says we have the mind of Christ. This is because the Holy Spirit lives in us. Receive the Holy Spirit.

PRAYER
Holy Spirit, thank you for coming to live in me. Help me never to ignore you or stray from you.

Further reading: Acts chapter 2

16th December
YOU WILL BEAR FRUIT A HUNDREDFOLD

Matthew 13:1-8

> *On the same day Jesus went out of the house and sat by the sea. ² And great multitudes were gathered together to Him, so that He got into a boat and sat; and the whole multitude stood on the shore. ³ Then He spoke many things to them in parables, saying: "Behold, a sower went out to sow. ⁴ And as he sowed, some seed fell by the wayside; and the birds came and devoured them. ⁵ Some fell on stony places, where they did not have much earth; and they immediately sprang up because they had no depth of earth. ⁶ But when the sun was up they were scorched, and because they had no root they withered away. ⁷ And some fell among thorns, and the thorns sprang up and choked them. ⁸ But others fell on good ground and yielded a crop: some a hundredfold, some sixty, some thirty.*

Jesus calls the parable of the sower the first of all parables. This parable talks about the potency of the word of God. God tells us in Isaiah 55:11 that his word will not be wasted. It shall prosper in whatever he sends it to do. Jesus is also telling us in this teaching that unless we are distracted, the word of God in us will bear good fruit. I speak over you today that you would not be distracted and God's word in you would bear fruit a hundredfold. Your first protection against distraction is to make sure that you have received and understood the word. Don't allow any bird to steal the word. The word in you will be tried. Persecution can never overcome you if you don't allow it. Jesus is Lord and he is watching over you. This is the sun that scorches. As attractive as the world may look and money has become the pursuit of many, don't fall for it. These are the thorns that will steal your hundredfold harvest. The word will give you maximum fruit.

PRAYER
Lord Jesus, thank you for the power of your word. Your word will produce a hundredfold harvest in me.

Further reading: Matthew chapter 13

17th December
BE FRUITFUL AND MULTIPLY

Genesis 1:26-28

Then God said, "Let Us make man in Our image, according to Our likeness; let them have dominion over the fish of the sea, over the birds of the air, and over the cattle, over all the earth and over every creeping thing that creeps on the earth." 27 So God created man in His own image; in the image of God He created him; male and female He created them. 28 Then God blessed them, and God said to them, "Be fruitful and multiply; fill the earth and subdue it; have dominion over the fish of the sea, over the birds of the air, and over every living thing that moves on the earth.

God's plan for man has not changed from the beginning. When God made man, he put him on an earth already created. It is impossible to know the origins of man and the earth without knowing God. Every man, including you and I came to meet the earth. It is the height of pride to study the composition of rocks and species of animals and try to speculate on the origin of man. It is sufficient to know our purpose on this earth and fulfil it. Only God has all the answers. God created man to have dominion over the earth he had created. Man was going to achieve this by being fruitful, that is producing after his kind. Fruitfulness will bring multiplication. We would fill the earth, subdue it and rule it. We lost this ability to subdue and dominate by separating ourselves from God. Jesus came to reunite us with God. He has commanded us to do the same as the beginning. That is to make disciples of all nations and to take back the earth from the systems that dominate the earth. The church will be fruitful and multiply to achieve this task. You will be fruitful and multiply. That is the destiny spoken over you. You will increase.

PRAYER
Thank you father for the destiny spoken over me. Nothing can derail it. I am fruitful in every area of my life.

Further reading: Genesis chapter 1

18th December
BRING FORTH ABUNDANTLY

Genesis 9:1-7

So God blessed Noah and his sons, and said to them: "Be fruitful and multiply, and fill the earth. ² And the fear of you and the dread of you shall be on every beast of the earth, on every bird of the air, on all that move on the earth, and on all the fish of the sea. They are given into your hand. ³ Every moving thing that lives shall be food for you. I have given you all things, even as the green herbs. ⁴ But you shall not eat flesh with its life, that is, its blood. ⁵ Surely for your lifeblood I will demand a reckoning; from the hand of every beast I will require it, and from the hand of man. From the hand of every man's brother I will require the life of man. ⁶ "Whoever sheds man's blood, By man his blood shall be shed; For in the image of God He made man. ⁷ And as for you, be fruitful and multiply; Bring forth abundantly in the earth And multiply in it."

God speaks the blessing he spoke over Adam to Noah. It is significant that God adds the word abundantly in verse 7. He tells Noah to bring forth abundantly. God loves abundant fruit. This imagery of abundant fruit is used throughout the bible. If God blesses you, expect abundant increase. You are blessed of God if you are part of the household of God. abundant fruit is your portion. A lot of times, we think in human portions based on our experiences. Let us stop thinking and allow God to invade us with God size portions of blessings. When God wanted to show Abraham, the number of his descendants, he took him out to show him the stars. God promised Abraham innumerable descendants when he didn't have even one son. We have seen this prophecy come to pass as Christians, Jews and Muslims all claim Abraham as father. Bring forth abundantly.

PRAYER

I look forward to bringing forth abundantly to the glory of your name. Help me Holy Spirit.

Further reading: Genesis chapter 9

19th December
YOU SHALL SEE YOUR CHILDREN'S CHILDREN

Psalm 128

Blessed is everyone who fears the Lord, Who walks in His ways. ² When you eat the labour of your hands, You shall be happy, and it shall be well with you. ³ Your wife shall be like a fruitful vine In the very heart of your house, Your children like olive plants All around your table. ⁴ Behold, thus shall the man be blessed Who fears the Lord. ⁵ The Lord bless you out of Zion, And may you see the good of Jerusalem All the days of your life. ⁶ Yes, may you see your children's children. Peace be upon Israel!

One of the blessings of fruitfulness is your fruit shall also bear fruit. The bible always has good promises for those who honour the Lord. The above is a very refreshing psalm for those of us who trust in the Lord and walk in his ways. You shall be happy and it shall be well with you. In other words, don't be afraid of the plagues and economic recessions of this world. Disasters of the world are devil or man-made. Your portion is of the Lord. He will look after you as a mother protects her chicks. It will be well with you in the midst of disaster. His promise is not just to you but also to your household. Your wife shall produce much fruit in the midst of your house. Your wife shall not be a busy body making other people's business her business. You will enjoy the fruit of your wife in the midst of your home. Your husband shall spend time at home. If he is not doing so, stand on this promise and pray him home. Your children will be strong and anointed in your home. They shall not be vagabond. This is God's promise to you. Pray them in if they are straying. Your children will be taught of the Lord. God cannot lie. God's truth is permanent. Every lie is temporary. You shall enjoy your children's children at a good old age.

PRAYER
I praise you my God for these wonderful promises to me and my household.

Meditate slowly on Psalm 128

20th December
YOUR JOY SHALL INCREASE

Isaiah 29:17-20

Is it not yet a very little while Till Lebanon shall be turned into a fruitful field, And the fruitful field be esteemed as a forest? [18] In that day the deaf shall hear the words of the book, And the eyes of the blind shall see out of obscurity and out of darkness. [19] The humble also shall increase their joy in the Lord, And the poor among men shall rejoice In the Holy One of Israel. [20] For the terrible one is brought to nothing, The scornful one is consumed, And all who watch for iniquity are cut off

God has a plan for the world and this plan will not fail but shall surely come to pass. You are part of God's plan. He has saved you for a purpose. He is changing you to be more and more like Jesus. Many are driven by forces in the world unaware of the kingdom of God. As it is getting close to Christmas, many are busily shopping for Christmas. Some are joyfully humming to the Christmas carols played in the shops. Yet many are not interested in the reason for the season. They don't understand this show of love or the joy that seems to fill the air. Christmas comes and goes and they don't care. They have the same attitude towards the gospel. They admit that the Christians are the nicest people on the street; They admire us but will not stop to listen to our message. Friend, don't be discouraged by the lack of interest. God's purpose is working out. It shall not fail. Each day, he is increasing your joy to be more like Jesus Christ. Jesus Christ is the personification of joy. The more you become like him, the more joyful you are. He is the reason for the love and joy that is shared at Christmas. He is the reason for the season. Rejoice. Jesus lives in you.

PRAYER

Thank you father for the joy you have given to the world. I am grateful for the hope of even greater joy.

Further reading: Isaiah chapter 29

21st December
YOUR WILDERNESS SHALL BE A FRUITFUL FIELD

Isaiah 32:15-20

> Woe to those who seek deep to hide their counsel far from the Lord, And their works are in the dark; They say, "Who sees us?" and, "Who knows us?" [16] Surely you have things turned around! Shall the potter be esteemed as the clay; For shall the thing made say of him who made it, "He did not make me"? Or shall the thing formed say of him who formed it, "He has no understanding"? [17] Is it not yet a very little while Till Lebanon shall be turned into a fruitful field, And the fruitful field be esteemed as a forest? [18] In that day the deaf shall hear the words of the book, And the eyes of the blind shall see out of obscurity and out of darkness. [19] The humble also shall increase their joy in the Lord, And the poor among men shall rejoice In the Holy One of Israel. [20] For the terrible one is brought to nothing, The scornful one is consumed, And all who watch for iniquity are cut off

Whilst those who do not put their trust in the Lord expect to be cut off, those who humble themselves must expect their joy to increase. There is nothing that is hidden from the Lord. He sees all things. He knows your thoughts. Godly thoughts are blessed. Wicked thoughts are punished. If you trust in the Lord, your wilderness shall become a fruitful field. In Israel today, you will see a lot of desert reclaimed for farms by modern technology. This is the work of man. God who is able to bring water from a rock does not require machines to change the desert into a fruitful land. He created the heavens and earth by his word. Expect a great change in your life for the better. Where there is lack, expect fruitfulness. I speak over you to be fruitful and multiply in the name of Jesus.

PRAYER

Thank you father for turning my desert into a fruitful land and turning my mourning into dancing,

Further reading: Isaiah chapter 29:15-20

22nd December
THE RIVER OF LIFE

Ezekiel 47:7-10

> When I returned, there, along the bank of the river, were very many trees on one side and the other. *8* Then he said to me: "This water flows toward the eastern region, goes down into the valley, and enters the sea. When it reaches the sea, its waters are healed. *9* And it shall be that every living thing that moves, wherever the rivers go, will live. There will be a very great multitude of fish, because these waters go there; for they will be healed, and everything will live wherever the river goes. *10* It shall be that fishermen will stand by it from En Gedi to En Eglaim; they will be places for spreading their nets. Their fish will be of the same kinds as the fish of the Great Sea, exceedingly many.

Wherever the river of God flows, there is life and there is a harvest. When God speaks, the Spirit of God pushes his Word to go and perform what he has said. This is the river of God. The Holy Spirit follows the word of God. The Holy Spirit is the breath of God. Every word we speak is powered by breath. The breath that follows our word is very important. The breath defines the word. You can say 'thank you' or 'sorry' but the breath with which you say it will determine the real meaning of your word. It is important that our words are powered by the breath of God. A word spoken in love is perceived. By baptizing us in the Holy Spirit, God has poured out his river into us. We as individuals become a source of the river of life. We are able to bring life into dead situations and we are able to produce abundant harvest. Jesus promised that if we would receive his word, rivers of living water will flow out of us. You are a source of life to many. Don't block the flow. Let your river flow.

PRAYER

Thank you for your love dear father. You have blessed me with the ability to distribute life. I will share my gift.

Further reading: Ezekiel chapter 47

23rd December
RIVERS OUT OF YOUR BELLY

John 7:37-39

> *On the last day, that great day of the feast, Jesus stood and cried out, saying, "If anyone thirsts, let him come to Me and drink. ³⁸ He who believes in Me, as the Scripture has said, out of his heart will flow rivers of living water." ³⁹ But this He spoke concerning the Spirit, whom those believing in Him would receive; for the Holy Spirit was not yet given, because Jesus was not yet glorified.*

Water is a very important part of the human life. If our body is starved of water, it will not survive. Water is an essential commodity for the survival of any person. Jesus, however, explains in John chapter 4 that he has water that is infinitely more important than the physical water we all crave. In a conversation with a Samaritan woman at Jacob's well, he assures the woman that there is water which he gives. Water that if you drink, you will never thirst. Instead, it will become a well of water in you which will bring forth life. This water is his word. If we drink his word, a well of life would be built inside of us. When we open our mouths to speak, rivers of living water will flow out of us. God has given us this gift not just for ourselves but for the benefit of the world. It pleases God when we produce abundant fruit. You are indeed the temple of the Holy Spirit. In the old days, Israel would not go to war without the ark of covenant. The ark represented their covenant with God. Why go into a fight without your stronger covenant partner. Moses told God that if he would not go with him then he should not send him. God has promised that he would be with us wherever we go. In fact, if you have opened the door to your heart, he has come to live in you forever. Don't ignore this most honourable guest who is transforming you to be more like God.

PRAYER
Thank you father for making me into a life-giver. May I never stray from this noble responsibility.

Further reading: John chapter 4

24th December
YOUR LIGHT HAS COME

Isaiah 60:1-5

Arise, shine; For your light has come! And the glory of the Lord is risen upon you. ² For behold, the darkness shall cover the earth, And deep darkness the people; But the Lord will arise over you, And His glory will be seen upon you. ³ The Gentiles shall come to your light, And kings to the brightness of your rising. ⁴ "Lift up your eyes all around, and see: They all gather together, they come to you; Your sons shall come from afar, And your daughters shall be nursed at your side. ⁵ Then you shall see and become radiant, And your heart shall swell with joy; Because the abundance of the sea shall be turned to you, The wealth of the Gentiles shall come to you.

Tomorrow is Christmas day. If you are like me, you are so full of joy and excited about the season. Every Christmas reminds me of the light that exploded into the darkness of the world. Where would the world be if Christ had not been born to perform the awesome task of turning a mysterious God into a loving father. I can just imagine the light of the star that appeared to the wise men of the east. I can also imagine the light and the glory of God that appeared to the shepherds watching their flock by night. Think about the activity surrounding the baby Jesus. His parents, Joseph and Mary, entered Bethlehem unknown and unrecognized. They even had to sleep in a stable. Yet, when the light of the world was born they had local and foreign, ordinary and wise people who found it duty-bound to visit them. Even the king of the area was touched by his birth. Today's reading is encouraging you to rise up in your spirit and understand that your glory has come. What was lost is being restored because God himself has intervened. Expect abundance. Your light will shine and bring the world to you.

PRAYER

If the Lord is for me, who can be against me? Thank you for the joy of Christmas. Let me be light that will be seen by all around me.

Further reading: Isaiah chapter 60

25th December
WONDERFUL, COUNSELLOR, MIGHTY GOD

Isaiah 9:6-7

> *For unto us a Child is born, Unto us a Son is given; And the government will be upon His shoulder. And His name will be called Wonderful, Counsellor, Mighty God, Everlasting Father, Prince of Peace. ⁷ Of the increase of His government and peace There will be no end, Upon the throne of David and over His kingdom, To order it and establish it with judgment and justice From that time forward, even forever. The zeal of the Lord of hosts will perform this.*

Have a blessed, peaceful and happy Christmas. When Isaiah prophesied hundreds of years before its fulfilment, the people looked forward to the day of fulfilment. The people of Isaiah's day understood the significance of the coming of the Saviour of the world. Scripture tells us that though the promise was not fulfilled in their day, some believed and walked in faith. Hebrews chapter 11 mentions some of these faithful people. The good news is, you and I are the chosen generation and the fulfilment of this prophecy has happened in our time. The coming of the Wonderful Counsellor, Mighty God, Everlasting Father, Prince of Peace has happened in our time. Jesus has come to pay the price and defeated Satan. The government is upon his shoulders. This season is more than a story or a nativity play in a primary school. This season commemorates a day when the world began to completely change. God through his Son had taken back his world. He has made his son Jesus ruler of all. Jesus wants to share this inheritance with all who would come to him. I trust you are one of those who have said 'yes' to Jesus. You are no longer the same. You are now part of the household of God. Enjoy this Christmas with this understanding. I sing, dance and eat to the glory of God at Christmas. I pray that the love and the joy of the Lord will overflow you this Christmas.

PRAYER

Thank you father for Christmas. I pray that many on this day shall understand that Jesus Christ is the reason for the season.

Further reading: Luke chapter 2

26th December
TO THE PRAISE OF HIS GLORY

Ephesians 1:11-14

In Him also we have obtained an inheritance, being predestined according to the purpose of Him who works all things according to the counsel of His will, ^{12} that we who first trusted in Christ should be to the praise of His glory. ^{13} In Him you also trusted, after you heard the word of truth, the gospel of your salvation; in whom also, having believed, you were sealed with the Holy Spirit of promise, ^{14} who is the guarantee of our inheritance until the redemption of the purchased possession, to the praise of His glory.

Glory to God in the highest, peace on earth, goodwill to all men. We thank God for Jesus. By his sacrifice, we have been brought from far away to be part of the family of God. We are privileged to be part of God's plan. He has called us to be to the praise of his glory. This means that when people see us they will praise God. People will thank God for bringing you into their lives. Many will be happy in their spirits when they see you. They see in you the love, joy and peace of God. Scripture says that the earth groans waiting for the manifestation of the sons of God. Before your arrival, it is groaning. After your arrival, it will be laughter and contentment. You are a messenger of God's glory. If the world sees God's glory, they will praise him. God's glory is everything he is and has. God is love. God is light. God is truth. God is life. The Holy Spirit is God. The Holy Spirit in you is God's glory given fully to you. The hurting world is therefore waiting for you. A lot of Christians are not aware of how qualified they are to bring salvation to the world. Do not be afraid of this awesome responsibility. You will not do it in your own might. The Holy Spirit in you will help you to reap where you have not sown.

PRAYER

Thank you Jesus for making me joint heir with you. Thank you for baptizing me with the Holy Spirit. You are the glory of my life.

Further reading: Ephesians chapter 1

27th December
PRAISE HIM WITH A DANCE

Psalm 150

> *Praise the Lord! Praise God in His sanctuary; Praise Him in His mighty firmament!* ² *Praise Him for His mighty acts; Praise Him according to His excellent greatness!* ³ *Praise Him with the sound of the trumpet; Praise Him with the lute and harp!* ⁴ *Praise Him with the timbrel and dance; Praise Him with stringed instruments and flutes!* ⁵ *Praise Him with loud cymbals; Praise Him with clashing cymbals!* ⁶ *Let everything that has breath praise the Lord. Praise the Lord!*

There are times that I have just felt like sitting down and hanging my instruments up like the people of Israel did by the rivers of Babylon. Everyone goes through the moment when you could feel spiritually, emotionally or physically drained. One of the best ways to revive yourself is to praise the Lord with a dance. When you dance to the Lord, you are ordering your physical body to rise up and fight any negative attack. I have noticed that singing along whilst dancing lifts your emotions. When we lift the Lord up in song, it does good to the soul. When we praise God, he appears on the scene. The presence of God lifts our spirit. Praising God with a dance brings complete deliverance from the spirit of heaviness. I read from the biography of one very effective evangelist that he always started his day with a good dance to the Lord. He recommended it to every Christian. I recommend it to you today. It brings the presence of God. It lifts you up and puts you in a conquering mood. Jesus has all authority in heaven and earth. We need to enforce this authority. The devil is hiding behind systems pretending not to know that he is defeated. Let us be in a spiritual warfare mood. We need to subdue the land and have dominion.

PRAYER

I will sing and dance and rejoice in the Lord my God. I will use everything I have to praise the Lord.

Give the Lord a song and a good vigorous dance today.

28th December
HE HAS TURNED MY MOURNING TO DANCING

Psalm 30:9-12

> "What profit is there in my blood, When I go down to the pit? Will the dust praise You? Will it declare Your truth? ¹⁰ Hear, O Lord, and have mercy on me; Lord, be my helper!" ¹¹ You have turned for me my mourning into dancing; You have put off my sackcloth and clothed me with gladness, ¹² To the end that my glory may sing praise to You and not be silent. O Lord my God, I will give thanks to You forever.

Though the world is obsessed with death, God does not want his people to die. There are martyrs who have lost their lives for the sake of the gospel. God honours this and their deaths are precious in his sight. Yet it is not God's will that any should die. His children are more valuable to him alive here on this earth than dead. I am not afraid to die but I believe God for a long fruitful life here on this earth. If Jesus should tarry, I am looking forward to a mighty harvest of souls. I make myself available to be used by God in this end time harvest. Why don't you do the same. We are blessed to be taken from the darkness we were in into his glorious light. He has turned our mourning into dancing. Our anxiety has been replaced with hope. Think about where you used to be and where salvation has brought you. Some count their success in life by the quantity of worldly goods they possess. Salvation has made you possessor of heaven and earth. A rich young ruler foolishly chose his worldly possessions over being with Jesus. Every time I read that account, I see this man going back into mourning carrying his goods. His wealth has become his God. If he had chosen Jesus, he would have been jumping, leaping and praising God. Don't stop dancing my friend. Jesus has changed your fate.

PRAYER
You have turned my mourning into dancing again. I can't stay silent. I will praise you forever.

Further reading: Psalm 30

29th December
BE UNDIGNIFIED FOR THE LORD

2 Samuel 6:14-16; 20-23

> Then David danced before the Lord with all his might; and David was wearing a linen ephod. ¹⁵ So David and all the house of Israel brought up the ark of the Lord with shouting and with the sound of the trumpet. ¹⁶ Now as the ark of the Lord came into the City of David, Michal, Saul's daughter, looked through a window and saw King David leaping and whirling before the Lord; and she despised him in her heart. Then David returned to bless his household. And Michal the daughter of Saul came out to meet David, and said, "How glorious was the king of Israel today, uncovering himself today in the eyes of the maids of his servants, as one of the base fellows shamelessly uncovers himself!" ²¹ So David said to Michal, "It was before the Lord, who chose me instead of your father and all his house, to appoint me ruler over the people of the Lord, over Israel. Therefore I will play music before the Lord. ²² And I will be even more undignified than this, and will be humble in my own sight. But as for the maidservants of whom you have spoken, by them I will be held in honour." ²³ Therefore Michal the daughter of Saul had no children to the day of her death.

David and his wife Michal had two different priorities. Whilst David was ready to do anything to please God, Michal his wife wanted to be dignified. She was under bondage to the traditions of men. What people thought of her was more important to Michal than God. She wanted to be what the people expected her to be as queen and she expected her husband to behave the same way. There are many Christians today who are stiff before God. Use everything you have to praise God. David ended up as one of the best kings of Israel whilst Michal was made barren for life. Be ready to be undignified for God.

PRAYER

Thank you Jesus for dying naked on the cross for me. I am also ready to be undignified for you. Help me Holy Spirit.

30th December
SING O BARREN

Isaiah 54:1-4

"Sing, O barren, You who have not borne! Break forth into singing, and cry aloud, You who have not laboured with child! For more are the children of the desolate Than the children of the married woman," says the Lord. ²"Enlarge the place of your tent, And let them stretch out the curtains of your dwellings; Do not spare; Lengthen your cords, And strengthen your stakes. ³For you shall expand to the right and to the left, And your descendants will inherit the nations, And make the desolate cities inhabited. ⁴ "Do not fear, for you will not be ashamed; Neither be disgraced, for you will not be put to shame; For you will forget the shame of your youth, And will not remember the reproach of your widowhood anymore.

We are drawing to the close of the year. For many, this is the time to look back at the past year and make new resolutions for the coming year. Some will look back and think what a horrible year it has been. The good news about the prophecy above is the fact that it is a prophecy of hope. Enter into the new year with this instruction: "Sing O barren". To be barren is to be fruitless. Things may have been completely dry in this past year. The challenges may have been overwhelming. The instruction is to sing into the new year. You are singing because your maker is your husband. You are in covenant with the one who makes the desert bear fruit. You are shouting about the hope that lies ahead of you. I am joining the prophet to speak directly into your life today: Enlarge your tent and do not spare. Expect great things. May the Lord expand your faith and capacity to receive. If you trust in the Lord, you will not be put to shame. Your expectation will not disappoint. Yesterday is gone. Tomorrow is going to be great. Prepare yourself for a mighty harvest. Happy New Year.

PRAYER
I will sing unto the Lord as long as I live. Great is thy faithfulness O God my father.

Further reading: Isaiah chapter 54

31st December
DRINK OF THE HOLY SPIRIT

Isaiah 55:1-5

"Ho! Everyone who thirsts, Come to the waters; And you who have no money, Come, buy and eat. Yes, come, buy wine and milk Without money and without price. ² Why do you spend money for what is not bread, And your wages for what does not satisfy? Listen carefully to Me, and eat what is good, And let your soul delight itself in abundance. ³ Incline your ear, and come to Me. Hear, and your soul shall live; And I will make an everlasting covenant with you-- The sure mercies of David. ⁴ Indeed I have given him as a witness to the people, A leader and commander for the people. ⁵ Surely you shall call a nation you do not know, And nations who do not know you shall run to you, Because of the Lord your God, And the Holy One of Israel; For He has glorified you."

Today is the last day of this current year. We give thanks to God for everything he has done for us in this past year. We thank God for life. We are alive on this earth. If today marks the end of one era, then tomorrow begins another. It is only a fool who does not pause and make plans for what lies ahead. Our consolation as believers is the promise of God that he would never leave us nor forsake us. This gives us the assurance that he will be with us this coming year. (Take a praise break. Give him praise for being faithful in this past year). He is good and his mercy endures forever. My counsel to you on this last day of the year is to respond to the invitation above. The father is inviting you to come and drink wine and milk from him. This is an invitation to drink from his Spirit. You need to be equipped with the power of the Holy Spirit for the journey ahead. Don't hesitate, go for it. HAPPY NEW YEAR.

PRAYER

Thank you father for this past year and the coming year. Holy Spirit, I need you. Fill me and walk with me through this coming year.

Further reading: Isaiah chapter 55

www.ingramcontent.com/pod-product-compliance
Lightning Source LLC
Chambersburg PA
CBHW060349080526
44583CB00012B/228